M000169177

HISTORY IN THE MAKING

IRELAND 1868-1966

M E COLLINS

THE EDUCATIONAL COMPANY

First published 1993
The Educational Company of Ireland
Ballymount Road
Walkinstown
Dublin 2

A trading unit of Smurfit Services Ltd

© M E Collins

23456789

Editor: Geraldine Grogan
Design concept: Peanntronic Teo
Disc conversion and layout: Phototype-Set Ltd
Cover Design: identikit

Cover shows *The Liffey Swim* by Jack B. Yeats, courtesy of the National Gallery of Ireland.

Acknowledgements

The publishers wish to thank the following for permission to reproduce illustrations in this book: National Library of Ireland, National Gallery of Ireland, National Museum of Ireland, Municipal Gallery of Modern Art, Bord Fáilte Éireann, Irish Times Ltd, Irish Press Ltd, Independent Newspapers Ltd, Dublin Opinion Ltd, Radio Telefís Éireann, Northern Ireland Government Information Service, Public Record Office of Northern Ireland, Ulster Museum, National Portrait Gallery, London, Imperial War Museum, London, British Film Institute, Dr Emmet Clarke, George Morrison, G. A. Duncan, Fr. Brown SJ Collection.

In a few cases the publishers have failed to trace copyright holders. However, they will be happy to come to a suitable arrangement with them at the earliest opportunity.

CONTENTS

SECTION ONE
1868-1920: POLITICS, SOCIETY & ECONOMY

SECTION TWO
1868-1900: THE LAND QUESTION AND HOME RULE

SECTION THREE
1900-1923: REVOLUTION AND PARTITION

SECTION FOUR
1922-1966: INDEPENDENT IRELAND

SECTION FIVE
1920-1966: NORTHERN IRELAND

SECTION ONE

1868-1920: POLITICS, SOCIETY & ECONOMY

Chapter 1

Parliament, government and society

The United Kingdom of Great Britain and Ireland
From 1801 to 1922 the whole island of Ireland was part of the state called the **United Kingdom of Great Britain and Ireland**. This fact affected every aspect of Irish life.

- Most of the decisions about social and economic issues were made in London. Often they were made by people with little understanding of Irish needs.

- Irish people who wanted to influence the future of their country or to make a career for themselves, had to go to Britain.

- From the 1870s almost the only political question in Ireland was whether or not the Union should be dissolved.

1800: the Act of Union
There had been a separate Kingdom of Ireland until 1800, though it had the same King and government as Britain. However it did have its own parliament in Dublin which made the laws that applied in Ireland.

In 1800 the **Act of Union** united the Kingdom of Ireland with Britain. The King became King of the United Kingdom of Great Britain and Ireland, and the Irish and British parliaments were merged into a single parliament.

The United Kingdom parliament at Westminster
The new United Kingdom parliament consisted of two houses, the **Lords** and the **Commons**. They met in the Palace of Westminster in London.

The House of Lords
A seat in the Lords was hereditary, i.e. it passed from father to son. The monarch, on the advice of the Prime Minister, could give a title to a retired politician, judge or general who had served the state. That title, too, became hereditary and every man who held that title had the right to sit in the House of Lords.

After the Union, Ireland was represented in the Lords by twenty-eight Irish peers (lords) and four Church of Ireland bishops. The peers were elected for life by Irish lords and were known as 'representative peers'. The bishops' role ended when the Church of Ireland was disestablished in 1871.

Most lords were wealthy men, many of them landlords. They saw little reason to change society and as they did not have to answer to the voters, they were not influenced by elections or changes in public opinion. The Conservative party always had a majority in the House of Lords.

The House of Commons

The Commons contained about 650 Members of Parliament (MPs), of whom 105 were Irish. They were elected at general elections which had to take place at least every seven years (this was changed to every five years in 1911). Because of this, the membership of the House of Commons changed from time to time. Up to World War I, it was dominated by two big parties, the **Liberals** and the **Conservatives**. The Irish Home Rule party appeared there after 1870 and the British Labour Party after 1900.

The franchise

In the nineteenth century the **franchise** (the right to vote) was regarded as a privilege to which only property-holding men were entitled.

In 1868 the franchise was restricted to men over twenty-one years of age who owned a house or flat in a town, or a house with a taxable value of £8 a year in the country. About 200,000 men, the most prosperous 3 per cent of the population, qualified to vote. They cast their votes openly on a public platform. That left them open to bribery and intimidation. In 1872, the **Ballot Act** made voting secret.

Through the second half of the nineteenth century belief in democracy developed

The 1874 election was the first one in which working men in the towns could vote by secret ballot.

and the franchise was extended in a series of **Reform Acts**.

- **1884**: All male householders were allowed to vote. This gave the vote to about 700,000 men. But young men living at home still could not vote, nor could any woman.

- **1918**: After a long campaign for women's votes, the franchise was given to all men over the age of twenty-one and to women over the age of thirty. This increased the electorate to 1.5 million.

- **1922**: The **Irish Free State constitution** gave the vote to all citizens over the age of twenty-one. Northern Ireland did the same in **1928**.

Passing an act of parliament

Parliament made the laws for the United Kingdom. When government wanted a law passed, it introduced a **bill** (a proposal) into the Commons or the Lords. When the bill had passed **both** Houses and been signed by the monarch, it became an **act of parliament**, i.e. the law of the land. After the 1911 **Parliament Act** the power of the Lords was curtailed. They could now only delay a bill for two years.

The government of the United Kingdom

Parliament also elected the **government** whose task was to enforce the laws that Parliament passed.

The head of that government was the **Prime Minister**. He was the leader of whichever party won the election. He appointed ministers to take charge of various aspects of the government, e.g. the Chancellor of the Exchequer who controlled taxation and spending or the Foreign Secretary who dealt with foreign affairs. The Prime Minister and his most important ministers formed the **Cabinet** and together they decided on the general policy of the government.

The ministers for Ireland

Two government ministers were responsible for Ireland. They were:

- the **Lord Lieutenant** or **Viceroy,** who was the monarch's representative. He was always a member of the House of Lords. He lived in the **Viceregal Lodge** in Dublin (now Aras an Uachtarain) and carried out the ceremonial tasks of a head of state.

- the **Chief Secretary**, who was a member of the House of Commons where he had to answer questions about the government's Irish policy. Although Viceroys seemed more important, the real power lay with the Chief Secretary. He was always a member of the Cabinet.

The Irish government: Dublin Castle

The Chief Secretary moved constantly between London and Dublin. He had his Irish office in **Dublin Castle** where he was assisted by the head of the Irish civil service, the **Under Secretary**. Most Under Secretaries stayed in Ireland while their Chiefs had to spend a lot of time in Westminster. As a result they knew the country better than their bosses and often had more real power.

The Viceroy was the centre of social life in Dublin. The Castle held receptions and dances at which the landed gentry and business classes launched their daughters on the marriage market. This picture from the 1890s shows the splendour of such occasions.

From **the Castle** these men presided over a government which contained almost fifty Boards, Commissions and Departments. They had been set up at different times and had different powers and roles.

- Some, like the two police forces, the prison service and the magistrates were under the Chief Secretary's direct control.

- Most were independent Boards or Commissions like the Commissioners for National Education or the Congested Districts Board. The Chief Secretary appointed the members but he did not control what they did. Despite that, he had to answer in the Commons for their actions. To make matters worse the money they spent did not come from him but from the **Treasury** in London. The Treasury was always suspicious of Irish requests for money and watched every penny they spent. Chief Secretaries spent a great deal of time begging the Treasury for more money for Irish needs.

- There were some departments that were Irish branches of UK departments, like the Post Office. The Chief Secretary had no control over them at all, though he got blamed for what they did too.

Do not be surprised if this confuses you. It confused everyone at the time. All agreed that the Irish government was a mess and it got worse from the 1880s onwards, as new boards and departments were created to deal with land and social reforms. These often dealt with similar areas (e.g. the Congested Districts Board and the Department of Agriculture were both set up to help farmers) and this added to the confusion.

Everyone condemned the Castle's inefficiency but no one changed it because to do so would have caused even more trouble. A Liberal Chief Secretary in the 1890s called it 'the best machine ever invented for governing a country against its will'. (E. O'Halpin, *The Decline of the Union*, p. 8)

Police

Keeping order was the Castle's main concern. It had two police forces, the unarmed **Dublin Metropolitan Police (DMP)**, responsible for Dublin and the armed **Royal Irish Constabulary (RIC)** which dealt with the rest of the country.

One of the less pleasant aspects of the RIC man's duty was supporting the bailiff at an eviction. This sketch shows them getting ready to set out.

Popularly known as 'Peelers', the rank and file of the DMP and the RIC were ordinary Irishmen, though their leaders were often ex-army officers.

Most of their time was spent dealing with petty criminals and minor breaches of the law, like poteen making and unlicensed dogs. In times of unrest they had to resist riots, protect unpopular landlords and help with evictions.

They were also expected to keep watch on possible trouble-makers. They sent an endless stream of reports to the Castle on the Land League, the IRB, the Gaelic League, Sinn Féin and other nationalist organisations. These reports, which are a valuable source of information for historians, earned the Peelers the reputation of being the eyes and ears of the government and made them unpopular among nationalists.

Magistrates and judges

Justice was administered through a series of courts. At the local level were the

magistrates who dealt with minor offences. They were often local landlords who served as unpaid judges. When no suitable landlord was available, the government appointed paid resident magistrates (RMs), who were usually Englishmen.

Serious offences were tried by the **assize courts** which visited county towns every three months. Above these were the **high courts** in Dublin presided over by the Lord Chancellor who appointed the judges.

Local government

Local government was weak in Ireland, with most decisions being made in the Castle or in London. Counties were ruled by Grand Juries, controlled by the local landlords and big farmers. The cities and larger towns had elected corporations but up to 1898 the right to vote for them was very restricted. The 1898 Local Government Act replaced them with councils elected by all male and female ratepayers. (see page 140)

These bodies set a local rate (tax) which was spent on roads, water supply, sewerage and public buildings. The amount they could collect was limited by the poverty of the population, so they were slow to improve these services. From the 1880s the councils were permitted to build houses for the poorest people in their areas but few did because it might have put up the rates.

The Poor Law Guardians

The other important elected bodies were the **Poor Law Guardians**. They were set up under the 1838 Irish Poor Law which had divided the country into areas called **Unions**. A Union was governed by a **Board of Guardians**, elected by the landlords and big farmers. The Guardians decided on the poor rate, a tax paid by the local property owners and used to help the poor.

Each Union had a **workhouse**. Up to the 1880s people in need only got help if they went into the workhouse. In the depression of the 1880s there was not enough room in the workhouses and rations of food were doled out to people at the gates. By 1900 only the old, the sick and widows and orphans were kept in the workhouse. In 1909 old age pensions were paid to poor people over seventy years of age. They were small amounts, but they made a difference to many old people's lives.

Guardians were also responsible for public health. Unions were divided into **dispensary districts**, each with its own doctor. The doctor provided free treatment for anyone the Guardians decided deserved it. The dispensory system remained the basis of public health provision until the 1950s.

The help given to the poor under the Poor Law system was never generous. The Guardians, elected by the ratepayers, were more concerned with keeping the poor rate low than with treating the poor with dignity. People in need had to undergo a humiliating cross-examination to see if the help was really necessary. They were made to feel that their poverty was due to idleness or wickedness. As a result, going into the workhouse was seen by many as a final horror to be avoided at all cost.

Dispensing doctors prepared and dispensed their own medicines as well as their other medical duties. This picture shows a doctor in Connacht vaccinating babies.

Religion

Religion played a more official role in government in the nineteenth century than it does today. Most states gave a special status to one form of Christianity. In England, Protestantism had become the state religion at the Reformation and this was extended to Ireland. The **Church of Ireland** was recognised as the official **(Established)** Church and this was confirmed in the Act of Union.

The Church of Ireland – the Established Church

In 1868 most landlords and a majority of professional and business people outside Ulster belonged to the Established Church. Over the centuries it had been given large estates and it owned many churches, schools and hospitals. Trinity College, the only university in Ireland until the 1840s, was almost the exclusive preserve of the Church of Ireland. All landholders, whatever their own religion, had to pay a tax (the tithe) to support the Church of Ireland clergy. After protests in the 1830s this was reduced and included in the rent but it still caused resentment.

The Conservatives supported the privileged position of the Established Church but as democratic ideas developed the Liberals became more critical. Their criticism was strengthened when the 1861 census showed that only 11 per cent of the Irish people belonged to the Church of Ireland. In a democratic age, this was difficult to defend and disestablishment followed. (see Table A)

The Presbyterians

The **Presbyterians** were the other large Protestant Church in Ireland. Ruled by their

Religions as shown in the 1861 census			
Roman Catholics	Anglicans (members of the Church of Ireland)	Presbyterians	Others (Methodists, Baptists Jews, etc.)
77.7%	11.8%	9.1%	1.4%

Table A ▲

Distribution of religious denominations (1861 census)				
	Catholics	Anglicans	Presbyterians	Others
Ulster	50.5%	20.4%	26.3%	2.8%
Leinster	85.9%	12.4%	0.9%	0.8%
Munster	93.7%	5.4%	0.3%	0.6%
Connacht	94.9%	4.5%	0.3%	0.3%

Table B ▲

own **General Assembly**, they had the support of 9 per cent of the population and were most numerous among the farmers and business people of east Ulster (see Table B). They sent their ministers to Scotland, where the Presbyterian Church was the Established Church, to be educated, though from the 1840s many went to Queen's College, Belfast.

Like the Catholics, Presbyterians had suffered discrimination at the hands of the Established Church and resented its privileges. But after disestablishment, Presbyterians began to feel they had more in common with their fellow Protestants than with the Catholic majority.

Roman Catholics

With almost 78 per cent of the population, the Roman Catholic Church was by far the most numerous in Ireland. In the eighteenth century Catholics had been persecuted and it was 1829 before they won the right to sit in parliament. This left them in a disadvantaged position compared with their Protestant compatriots. Few of them belonged to the landlord or business classes and the vast majority were poor farmers, workers and small businessmen.

From 1850 the Catholic Church gradually rebuilt itself. Under the leadership of **Cardinal Paul Cullen**, the Archbishop of Dublin, many churches, convents, schools and hospitals were built to cater for the needs of the community. These developments were a sign of the growing prosperity of Catholics. This period was also marked by a big increase in the number of nuns, priests and brothers, up from 5,000 in 1870 to 14,000 in 1900.

Cardinal Cullen was keen to make Irish Catholics into a disciplined body, answerable to the authority of the Pope in Rome. Bishops began to meet regularly in

A modern view of Athlone Cathedral, which was built in the late nineteenth century.

Maynooth and to issue joint statements on the issues of the day. This gave the Church a single voice and made it a unifying force among Catholics. Unfortunately, it also made it appear threatening to people of other religions.

Religion and politics

In 1869 parliament disestablished the Church of Ireland. From then on, the state was officially neutral when it came to dealing with different religions. But this was not always clear to Irish Catholics. The United Kingdom was a sectarian state. The monarch had to be a Protestant and as late as 1902, the King, Edward VII had to make an explicit denunciation of Catholic belief during his coronation.

In addition, most jobs in the government went to Protestants. This was partly because Catholics had little chance to get the necessary education. But it was also true that Conservative governments did not trust Catholics, most of whom were nationalists. This discrimination in jobs made Catholics feel that the United Kingdom was alien to them.

On the other hand, Irish Protestants, watching the growing power and wealth of the Catholics, were uneasily aware that Catholics made up more than three quarters of the population of Ireland. Understandably, they felt that the Protestant United Kingdom was their protector and that outside it they would be at the mercy of the Catholic majority in Ireland. Once Home Rule became the demand of the majority after 1886, religion and politics became inextricably connected. (see page 109)

Education and religion

The connection between religion and politics soured relations between the Churches. Another issue which caused bad feelings between them was the suspicion that each Church wanted to poach members from the others. Children were the most vulnerable members and therefore education became the main battleground between the Churches. Control of their schools and state funding for them was an important issue for all denominations.

Primary education

In 1831 the state began to give funds to primary schools. In theory these 'national' schools were supposed to be non-denominational (not controlled by any particular religion) but in practice each Church set up parish schools controlled by the priest or minister. By the 1860s the government had accepted this situation. In 1900 only 4 per cent of Protestant children and 1 per cent of Catholic children attended a mixed religion school.

There were 770,000 children enrolled in primary schools by 1900 but only 500,000 attended regularly. The Catholic bishops opposed compulsory attendance as an interference with parents' rights. Most children left at ten or eleven when they could sign their names, read a simple newspaper and do easy arithmetic. A small proportion stayed until they were fourteen, learning mathematics, Latin, Irish or other subjects. They went on to become clerks or to compete for the entrance examinations to the civil service.

Up to the 1880s less than half of all primary teachers were trained. The state would not fund Catholic training colleges and the Catholic Church would not employ teachers trained in the state run institutions. This began to improve when Catholic training colleges won state recognition in the 1880s.

Secondary education

Until 1879 there was no state aid for secondary schools. The Established Church, with its greater resources, was better placed to meet the need than the other Churches, but by 1870 Catholics had built seventy secondary schools.

Most of these were boarding schools for boys. They charged a fee which put secondary schooling outside the reach of most families. There were no scholarships and only the Christian Brothers provided a free, or nearly free, education to poor boys. Schools were unevenly distributed throughout the country and educational opportunity varied from place to place. In Connaught only one student in every thousand got to secondary school while in cities like Dublin and Limerick, one in every twenty did so.

In 1878 the government passed the **Intermediate Education Act.** (see page 71) It introduced a system of 'payment by results'. Payments of between £3 and £10 were made to schools for each student who passed the Intermediate examinations. As a result of a campaign by girls' schools, it was decided that girls were to be allowed enter for the examinations.

This opened secondary education to many more students. Girls, whose education might otherwise have been neglected, gained most. They sat the examinations on the same terms as boys, despite protests that study was unladylike and damaging to their health! In the first year 3,000 boys and 700 girls sat the examinations. By 1921 this had risen to 12,000 of whom 36 per cent were girls.

The Intermediate system allowed Irish second level education to expand. But the emphasis on examinations meant that much of the teaching in schools was focussed on passing them. This led to a lot of learning off by heart. In 1912, Patrick Pearse, who set up his own school, described the education that resulted from this system as a 'murder machine' which destroyed students' minds and failed to teach them about Irish history or culture.

University education

Until the 1840s Trinity College was the only university in Ireland. It was closely tied to the Established Church and only members of that Church could teach there. In 1845, the government, trying to win over the Catholic and Presbyterian middle class, set up the Queen's University with colleges in Cork, Galway and Belfast. The colleges opened their doors in 1849.

University College Galway.

In an attempt to avoid religious controversy, the government decided that the Queen's colleges were to be non-denominational.

The Catholic bishops objected and they became known as 'the Godless colleges'. The bishops forbad Catholics to attend them. This limited the success of the colleges in Galway and Cork, which in 1881 had only 600 students between them. Belfast, which was supported by the Presbyterians, was more successful with almost 600 students of its own.

The Catholic bishops wanted a Catholic university where they could control what was taught. In the 1850s they set up their own **Catholic University** in Dublin. But it had no funds, could not give degrees and, apart from its medical school, was not very successful. Through the 1860s and 1870s the Catholic bishops and Irish MPs who represented Catholic constituencies, tried to get the government to provide funds for it. But the British public were suspicious of anything run by Catholic bishops. (see page 62)

In 1879 the government passed the **Royal University Act**. This set up the Royal University as an examining board. Anyone, including students at the Catholic University, could sit for its examinations and it awarded them degrees. It also provided scholarships by which they could pay their fees, and fellowships by which teachers in the Catholic University could be paid.

In fact, anyone could sit for the Royal University examinations. Soon, new private colleges began to appear to prepare students for them. They included colleges for women students. This allowed Irish women to take university degrees before that was permitted in England. In 1901 1,380 men and 399 women passed the examinations set by the Royal University and only a minority of these had studied in a university.

In 1909, this system was finally abandoned. Queen's College, Belfast became a separate **Queen's University,** while Cork, Galway and the Catholic University in Dublin were combined into a new **National University**. Some historians regard this as a kind of 'educational partition'.

The lack of technical education

A great weakness of Irish education was its lack of concern for technical education. This was partly due to lack of demand. The underdevelopment of industry meant that there were few jobs for technical graduates. As a result, the Royal College of Science in Dublin, set up in 1845 and under the control of the Department of Agriculture from 1899, had only about fifty full-time students in 1900, many of whom were from England.

Assessment

By 1920, Ireland had an educational system which met its basic needs. A large majority got a basic education which enabled them to claim to be literate, even if they read little. A small proportion could get a higher education, though access to that depended mainly on a family's ability to pay. Scholarships were introduced by the local councils in 1900 but they remained few in number until the 1960s. In fact, apart from the introduction of compulsory Irish in the 1920s, the new state changed almost nothing about its inherited educational system until the 1960s.

Chapter 2

Rural Ireland

The importance of land

In the nineteenth century, agriculture was the most important industry in Ireland. Out of a population of five million people, three million were directly involved in farming and another one million were involved in servicing the farming community by processing or transporting their produce or supplying the farmers' needs. That made the whole question of land a matter of vital importance to everyone in the country.

Landlords

The ownership of land in Ireland

In 1876 the government carried out a survey to see who owned land in the United Kingdom. It found that in Ireland almost all of the land belonged to 10,000 individuals. These were the landlords. But the survey also showed great differences among landlords. Some had enormous tracts of land; others had just a few hundred acres.

The great landlords

The wealth and status of a landlord depended on the size of his estate. At the top, there were the 750 richest landlords who owned half of the country between them.

One of them was the Marquis of Downshire who had 115,000 acres. Most of it was in Co. Down, but he also had several smaller estates in four other counties. Another was the Duke of Leinster who held 73,000 acres in Kildare and Meath. These two were **resident** landlords, that is, almost all their land was in Ireland and they lived here most of the time.

Other landlords were **absentees** who lived in Britain where they also had large estates. They were immensely rich. They included the Duke of Devonshire, with 60,000 acres in Cork and Waterford and Lord Lansdowne, with 120,000 acres spread over six counties. These men paid agents to manage their Irish estates and only visited them occasionally. In most cases these big estates were well run.

Income and expenditure

A large estate with thousands of tenants, produced an enormous income for its

Castletown House, Celbridge, Co. Kildare, belonging to the Conolly family is typical of the huge homes of great landlords.

owner. The Marquis of Downshire, for example, collected close to £100,000* a year in rents and the Duke of Devonshire got £44,000 from his Irish lands alone.

But great landlords also had heavy expenses. They paid income tax to the government and rates to the local authorities. On a big estate there were workers to pay and buildings to repair. Most landlords had several large houses, staffed with servants, where they were expected to entertain on a lavish scale. They were also expected to help with local charities, contribute to church building, pay for schools and build roads or even railways through their estates to benefit the local community.

Many landlords inherited heavy debts which had to be repaid with interest. For example, in 1858 when the Duke of Devonshire inherited his estates from his father he also inherited debts of £1 million. Often, too, they had to pay pensions to their mothers, lump sums to their younger brothers and dowries to their sisters. All of these expenses ate into an income, however big it was.

Smaller landlords

The majority of landlords did not have huge estates. The average size was between 2,000 and 5,000 acres. The future nationalist leader, Charles Stewart Parnell, was fairly typical of the smaller landlords. In the 1860s he inherited 3,807 acres in County Wicklow which brought him an income of £1,789 a year.

Like their richer counterparts, small landlords had to pay rates and taxes, bear a burden of debt, support their family and live in the style expected of a landed gentleman, with a big house, servants and horses. This left very little money over to invest in the land or to be generous to tenants. The estates of small landlords were often less well run than those of their richer neighbours and the tenants were more harshly treated. In fact, many Irish landlords were always on the edge of bankruptcy.

---

*Multiply all figures by seventy to get a rough estimate of today's value.

Avondale, Co. Wicklow, home of C.S. Parnell, was typical of the houses of smaller landlords.

The economic role of landlords

In the 1870s landlords, large and small, had great economic power in their areas. The 'big house' was often the main source of employment in country districts where jobs were scarce. Local people worked in it as labourers, gardeners, grooms, maids and cooks and its inhabitants were valued customers in the local shops.

Some landlords invested money in improving their estates. They built roads and houses or encouraged industries like forestry, mining, quarrying or fishing.

Parnell, for example, had granite quarries on his land in Wicklow and sold the granite to pave Dublin streets. Lord Dillon, who owned 93,000 acres in Mayo and Roscommon, built schools and roads and brought in a rail link so that his tenants could get their produce to market more easily. By increasing the prosperity of their tenants they hoped to increase their own income.

But 'improving' landlords like these were unusual. Landlords as a whole drew over £10 million in rents from Irish land, which was more than the government got in taxes, but they only re-invested 5 per cent of that in improvements, a smaller proportion than landlords did in Britain.

The political power of landlords

In the 1870s Irish landlords still had great political power in their areas.

- The government relied on them to help it run the country. It appointed them as magistrates to try people for petty crimes, like making poteen, poaching or fighting.

- Landlords were on the Boards of Guardians which ran the local workhouse. (see page 12) The guardians decided how much should be raised in rates to help the poor of the district, and who deserved to be admitted to the workhouse.

- Landlords formed the Grand Juries which ruled all Irish counties until the Local Government Act of 1898 replaced them with elected county councils.

Landlords and parliamentary elections

Landlords also had great influence on the elections for Members of Parliament. Well over half of the 105 MPs elected in 1868 were landlords. There were several reasons for this.

- Until the **Ballot Act** of 1872, voters had to cast their vote in public. Many tenant farmers felt it was wise to vote for the candidate their landlord favoured.

- MPs were not paid until 1911. Landlords were among the few men who could afford to spend six months of the year in London without pay.

- Until Home Rule and the land question became important in the late 1870s many voters were not much interested in political issues. They were willing to leave them to the landlord to look after.

The decline of the landlords' power

Landlords' political power declined from 1880. Secret voting after the Ballot Act and the rise of the Land League encouraged tenants to vote for men who supported their demands rather than those of the landlords. In the 1880 election, fewer than half the MPs elected were landlords and their number continued to fall after that.

From 1880 tenant farmers took over the Boards of Guardians and when the new County and District councils were elected after 1898, few landlords won seats on them. By the twentieth century the political power of landlords had ended everywhere in Ireland except in Ulster.

The decline in landlord power was partly due to the Land Acts (see chapters 4, 8 & 13) which reduced their control over their estates. But it was also caused by the growth of democratic ideas. Voters were becoming better educated and informed. They no longer believed that landlords knew best. They wanted to control their own lives and their own country.

Farmers and Labourers

Tenant farmers

Landlords divided their estates into farms and let them out to tenant farmers for a fixed annual rent. This rent was the source of the landlords' wealth. Rents varied from place to place, but in the 1870s an average rent was about £1.50 per acre per year.

In 1870 there were approximately 600,000 tenant farmers in Ireland. But these farmers were not all the same. As with landlords, the income, status and standard of living of a farming family depended on the size of their farm and, to a lesser extent, on its location.

Large farmers

About 30,000 Irish tenants rented farms with over 100 acres. These men were prosperous and their standard of living was not much below that of the poorer landlords. Their houses usually had two storeys with a slated roof and five or more rooms. They employed labourers to work on the land and their wives had servants to help with the house work.

Sissy O'Brien, writing in the 1930s, recalled her family's farm at Lough Gur in Co. Limerick in the 1870s:

> My father... farmed about 200 acres of land... He gave constant employment to a number of men and women, some of whom lived in the four cottages on the farm... Our farm was like a little colony, self-contained, where everyone worked hard... Besides the fields, the farmhouse and its good out buildings, there was a quarry, a lime-kiln, a sand-pit, a turf bog and the productive eel-weir. Eels were sent to the Limerick market... (Mary Carbery, *The Farm at Lough Gur*, (1937), p. 9-22)

The sons and daughters of these prosperous farmers usually got a secondary school education. Sissy O'Brien was sent to a convent boarding school. After that, the girls got a good dowry to ensure they married well. One son, usually but not always the eldest, would get the farm and the other boys would be sent to train as priests, lawyers or doctors.

A big farmer in Meath

One big farmer about whom we know a good deal was Edward Delaney. He lived in an eight-roomed house in Co. Meath. In the 1850s he rented 300 acres from two separate landlords. He bought and sold cattle and sheep and made enough money to rent a further 200 acres in the 1870s. At that time he was paying £342 a year in rent.

In 1871 Delaney bought one of his farms under the Bright Clause of the 1870 Land Act. (see page 58) He was thus one of the first farmers in the country to use the land purchase arrangements to turn himself from a tenant into an owner of his land.

The leadership role of the big farmers

Although they were few in number, these prosperous tenant farmers between them farmed about half the land in Ireland. When the land war came, they were the leaders of the tenants' campaign. Like Edward Delaney, they took advantage of the land purchase acts the end of the century to turn themselves into landowners. They were the people who gained most from the land wars. (see page 145)

The average farm

The majority of Irish farms were much smaller, on average between 15 and 50 acres. Farms of this size were run by the family, with little outside help except from the neighbours at harvest time. The men worked in the fields, ploughing, sowing and tending the animals. The women cooked, milked the cows, raised poultry and pigs and helped with other work when needed.

These farming families lived in small houses, most of which were thatched, though slated roofs became more common as the growing of corn declined after 1850. Most houses had three or four rooms, the kitchen in the centre with a parlour on one side and a bedroom or two on the other. The amount of furniture in farmhouses increased throughout the nineteenth century, and a well-furnished parlour was a sign of a family's prosperity.

This neat farmhouse was photographed in the 1890s. The windows suggest that it had three rooms and the cart indicates that the farmer owned a horse or a donkey.

The children of the farmers

The children of these families got a primary school education which was often interrupted by the need to help on the farm. Most left school at eleven or twelve years of age.

When they grew up, one son was promised the farm. He would marry when his parents handed it over to him. His marriage was usually arranged through a matchmaker with a the daughter of another farmer. She had to have a suitable dowry, for a girl without a dowry had little chance of marrying. Usually each family had enough saved to provide a dowry for just one daughter.

These sketches of turf-cutting in Roscommon in the 1880s show how much women were involved in the hard work of the farm. Turf provided a cheap fuel in many parts of the country and the right to cut turf on the bog was a vital part of any farming family's economy.

The other children in the family faced a stark choice. Either they remained on the farm as unpaid, unmarried workers or they emigrated. Most emigrated. Between 1870 and 1920 about 50 per cent of emigrants went to the United States, 25 per cent to Britain and almost all the rest to Canada and Australia.

When the emigrants got work in their new homes, they sent back money to pay the passage of brothers and sisters, nieces and nephews. They also sent money (known as **remittances**) to support their parents as they grew older. Altogether, remittances amounted to about £1 million a year. Irish farming families had an average of six children. These large families may be seen as a kind of insurance policy for old age.

Small farmers

In 1870 there were about 100,000 farmers with less than fifteen acres of land. These were the poorest section of the farming community. They were to be found in every part of Ireland but they were most numerous in the western sea-board counties from Donegal to Cork.

They lived in one- or two-roomed cottages, often with little furniture and an earthen floor that was difficult to keep dry. They had a cow or two, a few pigs and chickens and grew mainly oats and potatoes. But because their farms were so small, they could not grow enough both to feed themselves and pay a rent to their landlord.

As a result, many of these farmers depended on other sources of income, apart from farming, to make ends meet. Some worked as fishermen. Others gathered and sold kelp (a type of seaweed) which was used as a fertiliser. An important source of additional income was the remittances sent by relatives who had emigrated.

Migratory labour

Many small farmers earned money by working part-time as labourers for the bigger farmers in the east or in Britain. Sissy O'Brien recalled:

> Extra men called *spalpeens*, usually from Cork or Kerry, were hired for the potato digging in October. My father's head man used to go to Bruff... and he inspected and engaged the required number of *spalpeens* who were waiting in the street to be hired by the highest bidder. (Mary Carberry, *The Farm at Lough Gur*, p. 10)

A group of labourers taking a rest during the hay-making.

One man who worked in this way was Paddy Gallagher. He was born in 1873 in the Rosses in Donegal where his father farmed twenty acres, most of it barren mountain. At the age of ten he left school and walked to a hiring fair in Strabane:

> When we reached Strabane, we all huddled together and were scared at first but the big fellows told us to scatter out so that the farmers could see us. They made us walk up and down to see how we were set up... Anyone who looked tired or faulty in any way was passed over. The strong boys were picked up quickly and I was getting scared I would be left. In the end two men came to me.
>
> 'Well,' said one of them, 'Wee fellow, what wages do you want for six months?'
>
> I said, 'Three pounds, ten.'

◆

He said, 'Get out, you would be dear as your meat. Walk up there to the market clock till I see what you are like.'

I walked up and he followed me... I heard him whispering to the other fellow 'He is wee but the neck is "good",' and he offered me two pounds ten.

The other man caught one of our hands in his, hit our hands a slap and said 'Bought and sold for three pounds.' (Patrick Gallagher, *Paddy the Cope*, (1942), p. 7)

Gallagher worked for his master for six months, then returned with his earnings to his family. Later, like many others, he went to work on the big farms of Scotland, harvesting corn or potatoes. Each year, many thousands of small farmers and their sons did the same. Eventually many of them ceased to be migratory labourers (i.e. returning to Ireland every year) and settled permanently in Britain.

Landless labourers

The poorest section of Irish rural society were the labourers. They had no land of their own but lived on the wages they earned working for landlords or bigger farmers.

This photograph from the 1890s shows a row of labourers' corrages at the edge of Foxford, Co. Mayo. It is called 'the turf-sellers'. The boys would supplement the family income by selling turf to town families who did not have their own piece of bog.

Some labourers had a full-time job. If they were lucky, their employer provided a cottage and looked after them well, though the wages they paid were usually low, seldom more than 50p a week. But many farmers were harsh with their labourers, evicting them when they grew too old to work and forcing them to end their days in the workhouse.

Most labourers did not have regular work. They were 'casuals', taking a day's work whenever they could find it. Spring sowing and harvest were the best times when extra hands were needed and good wages could be earned. But at other times they were unemployed and often had to rely on charity or the Poor Law to get by.

Usually casual labourers lived in country towns, walking out to neighbouring farms looking for work. Their houses were damp, one-roomed thatched cottages which ranged like a rural slum along the roads into most towns. They lacked even the most basic comforts. Labourers suffered from diseases like TB, which were associated with malnutrition and bad housing.

In the 1880s the government offered grants to build 'labourers cottages' around the country. Some of the cost would have to be born by the local ratepayers who were mainly the more prosperous farmers. Since they controlled the Boards of Guardians who had to approve this expenditure, few of the grants were taken up. By 1900, only 15,000 cottages had been built.

Labourers had little chance to better themselves in Ireland so many emigrated with their whole families. The number of landless labourers fell steadily after the famine and by the 1880s they were only a small section of the rural population. As a result, the land movement was able to ignore their needs and they gained nothing at all from the land wars.

The Farming Economy

The agricultural industry

Farming was the main industry in Ireland. The farmers grew the crops and raised the animals which formed the country's chief exports.

In the eastern two thirds of the country farming was mixed but certain regions did specialise in certain types of farming.

- In Munster, dairying predominated with farmers making butter and selling it to Britain through the Cork butter market.

- South Leinster was the grain growing region with barley for brewing as the main crop.

- Beef cattle were raised on the large grassland farms of the midlands.

- In east Ulster flax for the linen industry was a useful cash crop for many small farmers.

Along the west coast from Donegal to Cork, many of the farms were very small and the farmers suffered serious disadvantages. The land was poor, there were few railways and they were a long way from markets. Their main crops of potatoes and oats were mainly for home consumption. They did not earn enough from farming to live and they depended on their earnings from migratory labour or on remittances to pay their rents.

Farming families who lived near a city supplemented their incomes by selling vegetables in the local market. This work was done by the woman. These two were photographed around 1900.

1850-1876: the years of prosperity

The prosperity of farmers depended on British demand for their produce. From the late 1840s to the mid 1870s Britain experienced an industrial boom and well paid British workers bought Irish beef and butter. Beef prices doubled and the price of butter increased by 50 per cent in these years. Wheat, which was being imported from America, was less in demand and prices for it remained static.

Irish farmers responded to these market conditions by switching from wheat growing to cattle raising. This needed less labour and was bad for the small farmers and the labourers, many of whom emigrated. But the average and big farmers did very well. Their standard of living improved, with better houses and food and more education for their children.

The people indirectly dependent on farming

The prosperity of the farmers spread to other groups in the community who serviced the agricultural sector. They included:

- workers in industries like milling, brewing and bacon curing who processed the farmers' produce.

- workers on the railways and ships which carried the farmers' produce to the British market.

- shopkeepers in small country towns who sold clothing, tea, sugar, fertiliser, tools and seeds to farming families, lent them money when times were hard and bought the eggs and chickens raised by the farmers' wives.

- dressmakers, shoemakers, blacksmiths, bank clerks, teachers, priests, lawyers, etc. whose main clients were the farmers and their families.

All of these groups prospered with the farmers and when the farmer's prosperity declined in the mid-1870s, they suffered too.

Landlord gains

The landlords also gained from the farmers' prosperity. Rents were paid regularly and without too much trouble. Some landlords took advantage of the increased prices by raising rents. On average rents rose by about 12 per cent between 1850 and 1875, but this was less than the rise in prices.

The Land Question

The political importance of farmers

Throughout the period of our course (1868-1966) farmers were politically important. There were a number of practical reasons for this.

- Farmers had more votes than any other group in Ireland.

- Farming was the country's biggest industry.

- Many others depended on the farmers for their living.

Therefore any political leader, Irish or British, who wanted to win support in Ireland, had to think about what the farmers wanted. It was for this reason that the 'land question' became the key issue in Irish politics.

What was the 'land question'?

Many things interested farmers – the weather, the prices they got for their produce, the quality and quantity of the land they held. But the central issue that concerned them from the 1850s onwards was **the ownership and control of land**.

The landlords owned the land. The tenant farmers paid them a rent in order to be allowed to use it. The 'land question' was about the relationship between landlords and their tenants. It concerned issues like:

- whether the rents paid by the tenant farmers to a landlord were fair.

- whether it was just that the profits which came from the farmers' hard work had to be shared with the landlords.

- whether or not a landlord had the right to evict tenants from their farms.

The Three Fs (the Ulster Custom)

From the 1850s bigger farmers formed associations to put forward their views on the land question. They drew up a list of demands which were summarised in the slogan **'the Three Fs'** – **fair rent, fixity of tenure** and **free sale**.

By **fair rent**, tenants meant a lower rent which they could easily pay. By **fixity of tenure** they meant that they would not be evicted so long as they paid this rent. By **free sale** they meant that if a tenant decided to leave his farm he could sell the good will of it to the next tenant. Conditions like this existed in some areas, especially in Ulster and for this reason the Three Fs are also called **the Ulster Custom**.

In later chapters we will look more fully at how these issues developed in the 1870s and 1880s. Here we will try to answer the question: what was the relationship between landlords and tenants in Ireland when our course begins?

Good relations when the rent came in

What most landlords wanted was the rent. If it was paid, they left the tenants alone. During the prosperous years from 1850 to the mid-1870s most farmers could pay their rents easily and that led to good relations between tenants and their landlords.

A tenant who failed to pay his rent was evicted from his farm. Everyone took that for granted. But few landlords evicted a tenant immediately. Usually they gave him time to pay and if the tenant was normally reliable, they might make some arrangement with him. In years when harvests were poor, the papers were full of announcements by landlords that they were reducing their rents by 15 or 20 per cent.

Were rents unfairly high?

Tenant leaders complained that rents were too high and demanded 'fair' rent. But were rents really too high at this time? The only answer possible is that the situation varied from estate to estate.

- We know that during the prosperous years between 1850 and 1876 rents in general went up by 12 per cent. That was less than the rise in prices that farmers usually got for their produce. That suggests that the profits of the good years were shared fairly equally between tenant and landlord.

- But a report in 1880 found that 40 per cent of rents had not risen at all since 1850. In those cases, the farmers kept all the profit and the landlord gained little.

- Thus there had to be estates where the rents went up by a lot more than 12 per cent. On those estates, tenants gained nothing from the prosperous years while their landlords creamed off all of the profit.

Were many tenants evicted?

Most tenants were 'yearly tenants'. That means that they held their farms on a verbal agreement with their landlord which was renewed every year. (They were also called 'tenants at will'.) Tenant leaders claimed that this left the farmers insecure and likely to be evicted at the whim of the landlord. Was this true? Were tenants insecure and were evictions common up to the mid-1870s?

During the famine years (1846-52) evictions had been very common and they became common again during the agricultural crisis after 1877. But a very different situation existed in the years between these two crises.

Historians estimate that only about one tenant in a thousand was evicted each year during the prosperous years. Very few of these evictions were due to the malice of the landlord. It made no sense for a landlord to get rid of a good farmer. It took several years for an eviction order to take effect and in that time the landlord got no rent for his farm. We know that some landlords helped competent farmers to weather a bad patch by reducing or postponing the rent.

Most evictions occurred because a tenant was unable to pay his rent. That could be due to a variety of reasons – a death in the family, a number of bad harvests, the death of animals or the tenant's own incompetence or drunkenness. Family quarrels

Evictions were most common among the small farmers for whom any rent was too high. The poverty of this evicted family can be seen by the state of the roof.

could also lead to an eviction in which the landlord was not involved at all.

Overall, up to the late 1870s evictions were rare and were usually caused by the tenant's failure to pay the rent. But for many of the smallest farmers, the rent was always difficult to raise and therefore the threat of eviction always hung over them, even in the prosperous times. This made them feel insecure and they knew that the police and the courts would always favour the landlord rather than the tenant.

A new idea

Some of you may be surprised by the idea that relations between landlords and tenants were good. No doubt you have heard stories about cruel landlords driving poor helpless tenants from their farms and letting them die by the side of the road or in the workhouse.

There is some truth in that idea. Mass evictions did happen during the famine when some landlords did undoubtedly treat their tenants with great cruelty. But mass evictions ended with the famine and from then on harsh landlords were the exception not the rule.

Historians and the land question

However it is only in the past twenty years that historians have discovered the truth of this situation. It is worth looking at how this came about because it tells us how historians use evidence to build up a picture of the past and how finding new evidence can change that picture profoundly.

A propaganda war

Between 1879 and 1882, as we shall see in chapter 8 there was a 'land war' between the tenant farmers, led by the Land League, and the landlords. As in all wars, each side used propaganda to win public sympathy for its cause.

The Land League's case

The Land League was good at the propaganda war. In speeches, in newspapers reports, and before government enquiries, leaders like Michael Davitt put over their case. They claimed:

- that landlords were heartless and indifferent to their tenants' conditions.

- that they were absentees who never came near Ireland but spent the tenants' hard earned rents on high living in other countries.

- that all tenants were poor and helpless and forced to pay very high 'rack rents' to their landlords.

- that tenants who could not pay the rack rents were cruelly evicted from their homes and left to die by the side of the road or to seek a humiliating refuge in the workhouse.

The evidence

The tenants' leaders produced evidence to support their case.

- They highlighted examples of harsh landlords. A favourite was John Adare, owner of the Derryveagh estate in Co. Donegal. In 1861 he threw sixty families out of their homes in the depths of winter because he suspected them of being involved in the murder of his agent. Another example was the Tipperary landlord, William Scully, who evicted many of his tenants in 1868.

- They brought newspaper reporters to witness evictions when poor families were forced out of their homes. They even had some of these evictions photographed to show the world the misery involved. Two of these photographs appear on page 123.

Davitt's memoirs

Towards the end of his life, Michael Davitt, who founded the **Land League**, wrote a book called *The Fall of Feudalism in Ireland*. He was a good writer and an honest man. People were impressed by his moving story of the tenants' struggle for justice. His book, which was published in 1905, carried the Land League side of the land question into the twentieth century.

Victory for the tenants

The tenants' won the land war. Various British governments, hoping to get the farmers to support British rule in Ireland, changed the land laws in the tenants' favour. They gave the tenants lower rents and limited the landlords' power to evict them. Eventually they even lent money to the tenant farmers so that they could buy their farms from the landlords. By the 1930s there were virtually no landlords left in Ireland.

Historians accept the tenants' case

It was not only the British government which was convinced by the propaganda of the Land League. Historians, too, accepted their version of events. When they came to write about the land war they gave only the tenants' side of the story. Until the 1960s no one seriously examined the landlords' case. After all, they had lost.

Looking at new evidence

Since then however, historians have begun to think again. The main reason for this was that they found new evidence to put alongside the Land League propaganda.

The most important new evidence was the papers belonging to the landlords' estates. Most of them are rather dull. They include lists of tenants' names, account books with the rents they paid and the leases they signed. (A lease is a written agreement between a landlord and tenant setting out how long a tenant could have a farm and what rent he must pay.) Some estate papers contained letters from tenants and landlords or diaries in which the landlords or their Irish agents set out their policy for managing their estates.

A more complicated picture

This new evidence gave a quite different picture of the relations between landlords and tenants from the one accepted up to then. It became clear that the old image of harsh rich landlords and poor starving tenants was not true on most estates. As a result, historians went back and looked again at the case the landlords themselves had been making during the land war.

From these new sources came a different picture of the relationship between landlords and tenants. It is the one you read above.

But it is important to stress that the Land League did not lie. There were a small number of harsh and unreasonable landlords and the land system gave them great power over their tenants. This was especially true if the tenants were very poor. The Derryveagh evictions really did take place and William Scully did exist. The Land League did not invent them. It just used them to help the tenants' case by implying that they were typical of all landlords.

What is now clear is that landlords like Adare and Scully were exceptional, not typical. Most landlords did not behave as they did. In fact, other landlords disapproved of them because they gave landlords as a whole a bad name.

At the time most tenants were aware of that. They knew that they got on well with their own landlord and that he was fair to them. But they also heard the stories about the other kind of landlord and they lived with the fear that if their own landlord died or sold up, they too might get a harsh and unjust landlord. This sense of insecurity may explain why many tenants accepted the Land League propaganda and joined in its campaign.

Chapter 3

Industry and towns

Industrial decline

During the nineteenth century Ireland experienced a decline in manufacturing industry. Before the famine, almost a million people were involved in manufacturing. By 1881 this had fallen to 375,000 and by 1907 it was 290,000. Much of the decline can be explained by changes in technology and the failure of Irish industries to adapt to changing circumstances.

Before the famine most of those employed in manufacturing were engaged in domestic industry. They worked at home or in small units of a dozen or so workers, making things mainly by hand. As various industries moved over to mass production in factories, these domestic industries declined.

Small scale industry up to the 1870s

Up to the 1870s small industries still survived in most towns. They included craft workers like blacksmiths, carpenters, nailers, coopers, shoemakers, tailors and so on. They made or mended household goods and farmers' tools. There were also breweries, distilleries, flour mills and textile factories which employed, at most, a few dozen people.

Changing industrial environment

Distance protected them from competition. The cost of transport to an inland town would have made imports too expensive to compete with the local products. This began to change in the 1870s. A number of factors account for this change.

- In the 1860s and 1870s technology developed to allow shoes, furniture, farming tools and so on, which had previously been hand-made, to be mass produced in factories. The quality was often lower but the costs were greatly reduced.

- By 1860 most of Ireland, apart from the western seaboard, was covered by two thousand miles of railways. Few towns were far from a railway station and factory-made goods could be brought in at a much reduced cost.

- The great depression which began in the mid-1870s encouraged greater competition among manufacturers. They cut prices and this gave a further advantage to factory-made goods.

These developments destroyed the craftsmen and small-scale local producers. Some held out into the twentieth century but their standard of living was greatly reduced and no one came forward to follow in their footsteps.

By 1920 few of the traditional craftsmen survived. Inland towns had become commercial centres, where farmers came to shop and to sell their produce. They had shops, pubs, banks, insurance companies and lawyers' offices. But very few of them had any manufacturing industries.

Railways linked the main towns and cities together but most towns were linked by local mail cars like this one which ran from Thurles to Kilkenny. The mail car also carried a few paying passengers.

Cheap imports

With a few minor exceptions, the Irish woollen and cotton industries had collapsed in the 1830s and from then on most cloth used in Ireland came from Britain. A similar development took place with furniture, shoes, leather, pottery and most household goods after the 1870s.

There were still some Irish firms producing these items but they were at the luxury end of the market. Hand-made shoes or Beleek pottery were not within the reach of most Irish consumers who preferred the cheap products from British or continental factories.

Food processing

A similar development occurred in the food processing industries. Irish butter was traditionally made by farming women. It was heavily salted, packed in barrels and sold to the market when the barrel was full. This did not always guarantee a high level of freshness or hygiene. Cork was the main centre of the butter trade and the great butter merchants of Cork sold huge quantities on the London market up to the 1870s.

Then the market changed. Refrigeration and competition from Denmark and Holland led British housewives to expect clean, fresh, unsalted butter. The Irish industry failed to adapt, perhaps due to the vested interest of the butter merchants. British demand for Irish butter fell. Co-operative creameries (see page 136) regained some of the domestic market in the 1890s but were never strong enough to compete in Britain. The British market for Irish butter was lost until the 1960s. Bacon curing suffered a similar fate and even Irish farmers were buying imported bacon by 1914.

Successful industries

Not all Irish industries suffered a decline. When they adapted to changing times, they were often successful. Most were in the ports where they had easy access to raw materials and fuel and where they were well placed to export. Successful industries needed a strong export base because the Irish market, with its declining and often poverty-stricken population, was too small and too poor to sustain a large industry alone.

Brewing

In the 1850s there were 100 breweries around the country but by 1914 this had fallen to twenty-four. These included Beamish and Crawford and Murphy in Cork, and Smithwicks in Kilkenny but by far the biggest was the Guinness brewery in Dublin which made two thirds of all the beer drunk in Ireland. Guinness owed its success to its policy of investing in new technology and to exporting beer to Britain and the British empire. But the technology cut the demand for labour. Although Guinness was the country's biggest export earner, it only employed 2,000 people in Dublin.

Guinness brewery, around the turn of the century.

Distilling

Distilling spirits goes back a long way in Ireland but whiskey became a popular drink when the modern patent-still allowed distillers to produce large quantities of good whiskey cheaply. However, the patent-stills were expensive to install and by

1914 only a few distillers such as Jamesons and Powers in Dublin survived. Most of these were controlled by overseas companies. Up to World War I they competed successfully with Scotch whisky.

Milling

Water-driven flour mills existed in most areas, using stone millstones to grind grain for the local community. From the 1850s on Irish farmers grew less grain and imports from Canada and the United States increased. American grain was hard and coarse when ground in stone mills and customers disliked it.

A breakthrough occurred with the invention of steel mills which ground the American corn into a fine flour. These mills were expensive to install and only a few companies, situated in ports like Limerick and Dublin, were able to afford them. Imports of American grain trebled between 1870 and 1900. By 1914 most milling was confined to the ports and most of the old mills had fallen into disuse.

The industrialised north east

The only area in Ireland to have sustained industrial growth in the nineteenth century was the city of Belfast and the surrounding Lagan valley. Here linen, ship-building, engineering and other industries flourished, creating conditions more like the industrial centres of Britain than the rest of Ireland.

The linen industry

Linen was made throughout the northern half of Ireland in the eighteenth century. With the move to factory production between 1820 and 1850, the trade came to be concentrated around the Belfast area. In the 1860s it experienced a boom when the civil war in the US cut off supplies of cotton. The number of power looms rose from 4,500 in 1860 to 12,000 in 1870.

A typical nineteenth-century Belfast linen mill.

After that, the industry grew slowly. The mill-owners were reluctant to invest in new machinery and by the early twentieth century they were being displaced on the British market by more efficient continental producers. They were also in danger of losing their American markets as the US raised tariffs against Irish linen. The industry revived briefly during World War I when there was a huge demand for textiles. But the decline resumed thereafter.

The linen workers

By 1900 linen employed 70,000 workers, 68 per cent of whom were women and 26 per cent children. This allowed the employers to keep wages down. The average pay was only 60p per week in 1913, the lowest factory wage in the United Kingdom, though the small number of men employed in the industry were better paid.

Working conditions were bad. The factories were damp and steamy, leading to various lung diseases. Most workers were dead by the age of forty-five. Up to 1874 the working day ran from 5.00am to 7.00pm with two forty-five minute breaks. When an act in that year limited work to ten hours on weekdays with a halfday on Saturdays, there were loud protests from the employers. The act also made ten the minimum age for children to do factory work and this was raised to twelve by 1901.

Shipbuilding

Ships were built in many ports around the coast and up to the 1850s Cork was the country's main shipbuilding centre. A small shipyard, making coastal steamers, survived in Arklow and many small shipyards supplied the needs of the fishing industry.

The development of a major shipbuilding industry in Belfast owed more to foreign investment than to native enterprise. In the 1850s an English engineer, Edward

The *Titanic*

Harland, opened a shipyard and established contacts with the Liverpool-based White Star shipping line. It had no space to build ships in the crowded port of Liverpool and saw the advantages of Belfast's fine and under-used harbour.

Harland's revolutionary designs for flat-bottomed cargo ships doubled their carrying capacity without doubling the cost of building them. The demand for his products grew. In 1870 the Harland and Wolff shipyard built the 4,000 ton *Oceanic*, the first transatlantic passenger ship. It was fast, comfortable and reliable, crossing the Atlantic in a mere two weeks. The company went on to become famous for its luxury liners. The best known is the ill-fated *Titanic*. Launched in 1912, it was the biggest ship ever built (46,000 tons) and boasted a gymnasium, squash courts and electric lifts.

The success of the Belfast shipbuilders depended on their innovative designs. The other big yard, Workman and Clarke, pioneered refrigerated ships. They provided mass employment. In 1860 the yards employed 500 workers. By 1915 the number had risen to 15,000. The yards also generated other industries such as engineering, rope-making, and carpentry to fit out the ships. Most of these provided skilled and relatively well-paid jobs for men. The average wage in the industry was £1.50 per week.

Irish towns

Between 1871 and 1914 Ireland, like most European countries, became more urbanised. In 1871 22 per cent of the population lived in towns and by 1911 this had grown to 33 per cent. But this increase was slower than in other countries. Much of it is due to the decline in rural population, as labourers and small farmers left the land, and to the growth of Belfast and, to a lesser extent, Dublin. As Table A shows, the population in other cities actually declined in size.

Population of Irish cities 1871-1911		
	1871	**1911**
Dublin	280,000	390,000
Belfast	174,000	480,000
Cork	78,600	76,600
Limerick	39,300	38,500
Galway	15,500	13,000

Table A ▲

Belfast

All accounts of Belfast at this time compare its energy and vigour with the depressed appearance of other Irish cities. Between 1870 and 1914 it grew more rapidly than any city in the United Kingdom and it outstripped Dublin as the largest city in Ireland.

Housing conditions for the working class were reasonable. Because of Belfast's rapid growth, most houses were newly built. Since in most families both father and

Belfast housing about 1900.

mother worked, they could afford to rent a four-roomed terraced house with a cold tap and a small back-yard containing a privy (toilet). Belfast Corporation set minimum standards for these houses. But with big families, they were very crowded, and diseases like TB and typhoid were common. Belfast's death rate was higher than the UK average, and second only to Dublin's.

Middleclass families tended to move out to the suburbs, encouraged by improving transport. Trams, at first horse-drawn and then electric, allowed the men to commute to work. The women stayed at home where they were usually helped by a resident domestic servant.

Sectarian divisions in the workforce

The distinctive characteristic of Belfast was its sectarianism. From the 1850s religious riots between Protestants and Catholics became a regular feature of life. The worst were in 1886 at the time of the first Home Rule bill when fifty people were killed.

After this, religion became increasingly connected with politics, and sectarian divisions in the workforce got worse. Encouraged by preachers like the Rev. Hugh Hanna and by the Orange Order, Protestant workers steadily eased Catholics out of the better paid jobs in shipbuilding and engineering. They were mainly confined to lower paid work on the docks and to working as general labourers. Partly as a result, the Catholic proportion of the population fell from 34 per cent in 1861 to 24 per cent in 1901.

Dublin and other cities

Unlike Belfast, other Irish cities stagnated between 1870 and 1914. (see Table A, page 41) As industry declined, most cities lost population. Only Dublin showed any growth and this was due to expansion in government and commerce rather than to manufacturing.

The stagnation affected employment opportunities and wages. Most workers were unskilled 'casuals' who did a day's work whenever someone hired them. A great deal of casual work was on the docks, in transport and in the building trade. It was badly paid, with the average worker seldom making more than £1 a week at a time when £1.10 was considered the minimum needed to keep a family of four.

Housing

Poorly paid workers could not afford decent houses. As the middle class moved out to the suburbs, the poor moved into their abandoned houses in the town centres. A report in 1885 found 9,836 tenement houses in Dublin. Usually one family occupied each room. One nine-roomed house had nine families, with sixty-three individuals, living there. Houses like this usually had one tap in the yard to serve all the inhabitants, with a single privy nearby. In fact 40 per cent of Dublin families lived like this, compared with 1 per cent in Belfast.

The dreadful slums attracted attention and various efforts were made to improve housing. Most were by philanthropic individuals or groups. The Dublin Artisans' Dwellings Company, for example, built terraces of four-roomed houses in various locations and the Iveagh Trust, set up by the Guinness family, built flats. Even the Corporation made some attempt to clear the worst slums.

Artisan dwellings in Dublin built at the turn of the century.

But they all shared the belief that they must charge a realistic rent of between 15p and 25p a week. This was outside the reach of all but a minority of skilled workers. It was only in the 1930s, when the idea of subsidised housing became acceptable, that any progress was made in improving housing conditions.

Bad housing and low wages bred disease. Working families, paid by the day, could only buy food in small and expensive quantities and could not easily store or cook what they bought. As a result, most lived on bread, potatoes and tea. Drunkenness was common and it added to the problems of malnutrition. Dublin had one of the highest death rates in Europe from TB, measles, typhoid and other diseases associated with bad housing and malnutrition, and other Irish towns and cities were little better off.

Population

Ireland was the only European country whose population declined between 1871 and 1914.

Population from 1861 to 1911	
1861	5,800,000
1871	5,400,000
1881	5,175,000
1891	4,700,000
1901	4,459,000
1911	4,390,000

Table B ▲

Marriage patterns

One important reason for this was the pattern of marriages. More Irish people married late or not at all than other Europeans. In 1861 the average age of marriage for women was twenty-three which was close to the European average. But as the economic depression set in in the 1870s, the average age for marriage rose, so that by the 1920s it was twenty-nine for women and thirty-three for men. Even then, 25 per cent of people never married. Late marriages cut the number of children a couple could have, though the average Irish family still contained six children.

Attitudes to marriage, especially in the farming community, help explain this development. Most marriages were arranged between the matchmaker and the parents, who regarded the whole thing as a business. Their main concern was that the bride had a dowry and the groom a farm.

Few landless men and few women without a dowry could expect to marry. The dowry took time to gather and many families could only raise enough for one daughter. The others could stay single or emigrate. The groom, too, had to wait until his parents were ready to give him the family farm before he could look for a bride and he might have to wait a long time.

Emigration

The other factor which explains the decline in population is emigration. In farming families most landless sons and dowryless daughters left the farm. Since there were

In the 1850s whole families emigrated but after that it was mainly young people. Conditions on the emigrant ships improved when steam ships became common in the 1870s, partly because the journey was much shorter.

few industries outside Belfast to absorb them, most emigrated. Labourers and small farmers also left to find a better life than they could make in Ireland.

Between 1870 and 1914 half of all the children born in Ireland emigrated, over two million people in all. The majority went to the United States but many others went to Britain, Canada, Australia and other parts of the British empire.

People usually emigrated young and, unlike the situation in other European countries, girls were as likely to go as boys. They often went to uncles or aunts who sent the money to pay their fares. They in their turn sent money home to pay for younger brothers and sisters, as well as money to help with the family's expenses. A few came home to buy a farm or a pub and end their days among their families but the vast majority never returned.

Emigration was affected by economic factors. It was low in the 1870s when conditions were good in Ireland but rose steeply in the 1880s when they deteriorated. It declined after that and almost stopped completely during World War I. Emigration was mainly from the eastern counties up to the 1870s but after that the west caught up. In the west, many people worked as migratory labourers in Britain (see pages 26 & 27) before finally settling there.

The impact of emigration

The impact of emigration is difficult to assess. Historians have suggested that it damaged Ireland by draining away many of those whose youth and energy might have solved the country's problems. The ease with which the discontented could leave also meant that many problems could be ignored and left to fester.

Emigration also had an economic effect. The departure of so many young people left an unbalanced society in which a small working population supported a larger than average number of elderly people and children. On the other hand, as the population fell and the country's wealth increased after the famine, the standard of living of those who remained rose steadily. The national cake was not very large but emigration ensured that the number who had to share it was kept small.

Questions

ORDINARY LEVEL – A

Answer the following briefly. One or two sentences will be enough.

1. Explain the role of **each** of the following:
   (a) the Lord Lieutenant (Viceroy).
   (b) the Chief Secretary.
   (c) the Under Secretary.

2. Which **Church** was disestablished in 1870?

3. Why was the **university question** a problem in the 1870s?

4. What was the **Ballot Act** and why was it important?

5. Who were the **Boards of Guardians** and what did they do?

6. What were **remittances**?

7. What were the **Three Fs** and why did farmers want them?

8. Who would you meet at a **hiring fair**?

9. What is a **lease**?

10. What was a **tenant at will**?

11. Give **two** reasons why the north east of Ulster was more industrialised than the rest of Ireland.

12. Give **two** reasons why a person might emigrate from Ireland in the 1880s.

13. Give **two** reasons why a shipbuilding industry developed in Belfast after 1850.

14. What were the **Royal Irish Constabulary** (RIC) and the **Dublin Metropolitan Police** (DMP)?

15. What were the **three** main religious denominations in Ireland in the nineteenth century?

Questions

ORDINARY LEVEL – B

Write a short paragraph on each of the following.

1. The Dublin Castle government.
2. The Act of Union.
3. The Catholic Church at the end of the nineteenth century.
4. The university question.
5. Life in Belfast, 1868-1914.
6. A landlord's power.
7. The shipbuilding industry.
8. The Three Fs.
9. The linen industry.
10. Emigration, 1868 to 1914.

ORDINARY LEVEL – C

Write a short essay on each of the following.

1. The government of Ireland up to 1920 under the headings:
   (a) Irish representation in the Lords and the Commons.
   (b) The Lord Lieutenant and the Chief Secretary.
   (c) Dublin Castle.

2. Irish agriculture in 1868 under the following headings:
   (a) Ownership of land.
   (b) Agricultural production.
   (c) Prices and markets.

3. Irish industry from 1868 to 1914 under the headings:
   (a) The general state of industry in Ireland.
   (b) Industrial development in the north east.
   (c) The successful industries elsewhere.

Questions

HIGHER LEVEL

Write an essay on each of the following:

1 Discuss the government of Ireland at the end of the nineteenth century under the headings: Ministers for Ireland, Dublin Castle administration, Irish representatives in Westminister, the franchise, parties. (80)

2 Treat of the fortunes of Irish landlords in the period 1868-1920. (80)

3 Treat of the changes (other than changes in land ownership) which took place in the lives of people living in rural Ireland in the period 1868-1918. (80)

4 Treat of the economic conditions of Irish farming in the period 1879 to 1914. Your answer should refer to such matters as farm size, tenure arrangements, farming methods, markets, etc. (80)

5 Treat of relations between landlords and tenants in Ireland in the 1870s. (80)

6 Discuss the fortunes of the major Churches in Ireland during the period 1868 to 1918. (80)

7 Discuss developments in university education in the period 1868 to 1914. (80)

8 Treat of the main developments in primary, secondary and university education in Ireland up to 1914. (80)

9 Treat of living conditions in Irish towns and cities during the period 1868 to 1920. (80)

10 Discuss the main developments in manufacturing industry in Ireland in the period 1868 to 1920. (80)

11 Discuss the factors which contributed to the decline in the population of Ireland in the period 1868 to 1918. (80)

SECTION TWO

1868-1900: THE LAND QUESTION AND HOME RULE

Chapter 4

1867-70: The Fenians and Gladstone's Irish mission

Nationalists and unionists

The Act of Union of 1800 had ended the Irish parliament. From that time on Irish MPs went to the Westminster parliament and the laws for Ireland were made there. From the beginning, Irish people were divided about the Union.

- Some disliked it and wanted to return to having an Irish parliament making laws for Ireland. They were called **nationalists**.

- Others liked the Union and wanted to keep it. They were called **unionists**.

A sense of identity

There were several reasons why people chose one side or the other. One was a sense of identity.

People who opposed the Union felt that they were Irish. They did not feel comfortable as part of a British state. They wanted the Irish nation to have its own parliament and government.

People who supported the Union also felt Irish, but they felt British, too. Many of them were descended from English or Scottish settlers who had come to Ireland in the sixteenth and seventeenth centuries. They were content to be part of the British system of government under a British monarch, to whom they felt a strong sense of loyalty. These people were sometimes called '**loyalists**' because of their loyalty to the monarchy.

Protestants, Catholics and the Union

Religion was another important reason why people chose to be nationalist or unionist. In Ireland, 75 per cent of the population were Roman Catholic, but in the United Kingdom as a whole, the majority of people were Protestant and Protestantism was the official religion (e.g. the monarch had to be a Protestant).

Irish Protestants supported the Union because it made them part of the majority in the United Kingdom. This made them feel secure. If Ireland had its own elected parliament, they would always be in a minority. They feared that the Catholic majority would discriminate against them in education, jobs and so on. For that reason, most (though not all) Protestants wanted the Union to continue.

Irish Catholics felt that they were at a disadvantage in the United Kingdom. They believed that they suffered discrimination in jobs, education and other areas. But if there was an Irish parliament, Catholics would be in a majority and control the country. For this reason, most (though not all) Catholics were nationalists who wanted to end the Union.

Opposing the Union by peaceful means

In the 1830s nationalists attempted to have the Act of Union repealed. They were led by **Daniel O'Connell**. He wanted an independent Irish parliament but he was quite happy to have Queen Victoria remain as Queen of Ireland.

O'Connell's **Repeal party** got MPs elected to parliament and tried to persuade the British to agree to repeal the Union. They failed, and the Repeal movement disappeared after O'Connell's death in 1847.

After that there was no Irish party in Parliament and Irish voters, like voters in other parts of the United Kingdom, chose between Conservatives and Liberals.

Opposing the Union by force

In the 1840s a different kind of nationalist group appeared. This group was known as the **Young Irelanders**. Some of them believed that Ireland would be better off if it **cut all links** with Britain and set up a **completely separate** Irish state.

They knew that the British would never agree to this, so they planned to win independence by force. During the famine in 1848 they tried to stage a revolution but were defeated.

The Irish Republican Brotherhood (the Fenians)

In 1858 a former Young Irelander called **James Stephens** set up a new revolutionary movement. He called it the **Irish Republican Brotherhood (IRB)** but it was also

James Stephens, the founder of the I.R.B. Stephens, who ran the I.R.B. like a dictator, failed to give the order to rise in 1865 when the Fenians were at their strongest. This allowed the British to arrest many leaders and destroyed any chance of an extensive rebellion.

known as the **Fenian Brotherhood**, which was the name of the American branch that was set up about the same time.

Like the Young Irelanders, the Fenians were **separatists**. They wanted Ireland to be completely separate from and independent of Britain. And they were prepared to use **violence** to achieve their aims.

The IRB was a **secret, oathbound** society. When a member joined he took a solemn oath in which he swore:

- to fight for the complete independence of Ireland.

- to keep the secrets of the IRB.

- to obey the orders of his superiors in the IRB.

The Fenians and the Catholic Church

The Catholic Church disapproved of secret oathbound societies and of the use of force to solve political problems. It forbad Catholics to join the IRB. Despite this, many did and by 1865 it felt strong enough to organise a rebellion against British rule.

1867: the Fenian rebellion

Stephens failed to give the order in time and this allowed the British, who had spies in the IRB, to arrest many of the leaders. When the order to rise finally came in 1867,

Fenian attack on a prison van in Manchester. The Fenian leader Thomas Kelly was rescued but a policeman was shot. Three men, Allan, Larkin and O'Brien, known as the 'Manchester Martyrs' were executed for the crime.

the IRB's ablest men were in prison and the rising in Ireland was a total failure.

In Britain, the Fenians were involved in two major incidents. In Manchester a policeman was shot during an attempt to rescue a prisoner. Three men were arrested, found guilty of murder and executed. In Clerkenwell near London some people were killed in a bungled escape attempt.

The effect of the Fenian rising in Britain

These two events had an unforeseen result. They made British political leaders pay attention to Ireland. During the years of prosperity that followed the famine, many of them had assumed, since there was no nationalist party in parliament, that all the Irish had come to accept the Union. The Fenian rising shattered this illusion.

The Liberal party and Gladstone

At this time, the Liberal party was the biggest party in Ireland. It drew its support mainly from Catholic and Presbyterian voters and over sixty of the 105 Irish MPs belonged to it. Moreover in the south Liberals had the backing of the Catholic Church led by Cardinal Paul Cullen.

In 1867 the Liberals got a new leader, **William E. Gladstone**. He was keen to reform the government of the United Kingdom and Ireland seemed a good place to start. He also believed that if he could remove Irish grievances, he would undermine support for the Fenians. When a general election was called in 1868, Gladstone included 'Justice for Ireland' among the proposals the Liberals put before the voters.

W.E. Gladstone, who became leader of the Liberal Party in 1867 was alerted to Irish grievances by widespread support for the Fenians.

The Liberals won the election and Gladstone became Prime Minister. When the news of his victory reached him, he declared, 'My mission is to pacify Ireland'.

Irish demands

Sixty-five Irish Liberal MPs were elected in 1868. Gladstone consulted them and they told him what they wanted. The list included:

- the disestablishment of the Church of Ireland.
- the reform of the land laws to give tenant farmers the Three Fs.
- government grants to Catholic secondary schools and the Catholic university.

Disestablishment

Gladstone at once began his Irish reforms. It suited him to do so because although the Liberal party was bitterly divided on many issues, they would unite behind him in dealing with Ireland. The reform they were most eager to tackle was the disestablishment of the Church of Ireland.

The position of the Church of Ireland

As you read in chapter 1 the Church of Ireland had been the official State Church (i.e. the **Established Church**) in Ireland since the Reformation. All the bishops and other leaders of the Church were appointed by the government in London. All official ceremonies were carried out in its cathedrals and it received a tax (the tithe) which was paid by all landholders, whatever their religion.

But only 11 per cent of Irish people belonged to the Church of Ireland. Most of the rest were either Roman Catholics or Presbyterians. As belief in equality and democracy grew in the nineteenth century, the privileged position of the Church of Ireland became harder to defend. By 1868 even some of its own members were willing to disestablish their Church and place it on equal terms with the other Churches in the country.

The disestablishment of the Church of Ireland was also popular among Gladstone's British followers. Many English and Welsh Liberals belonged to the Methodist and Baptist Churches. They resented the privileges which the Established Churches in their countries enjoyed. They hoped that by disestablishing the Church of Ireland they would set an example they could later follow at home.

1869: the Disestablishment Act

Parliament passed the Disestablishment Act in 1869. Under the Act:

- The Church of Ireland became self-governing. It was given its own parliament, the **Representative Church Body**, composed of bishops and of elected representatives of the clergy and the laity. It was to make all the laws of the Church of Ireland.
- All the Church's property, worth about £16 million, was taken over by a body

called the **Commissioners of Church Temporalities**. Ten million pounds were returned to the Church, in the form of churches, parsonages, schools and salaries and pensions for the clergy. The remainder, the **Church Surplus Fund**, was set aside to be used for education, the relief of poverty and the encouragement of agriculture and fisheries.

- The estates belonging to the Church were sold to the tenant farmers who lived on them. The government lent them most of the purchase price, which they had to repay in annual instalments. Under this scheme 6,000 tenants became the owners of their farms. This worked so well that it became the model for the land purchase schemes which later helped all tenant farmers to buy their farms from their landlords.

- Up to this time, the Roman Catholic and Presbyterian Churches had got annual grants from the government. When the Church of Ireland was disestablished, these grants were also stopped. The other Churches each received a lump sum in compensation. From now on, all Churches in Ireland had to depend on the voluntary contributions of their members.

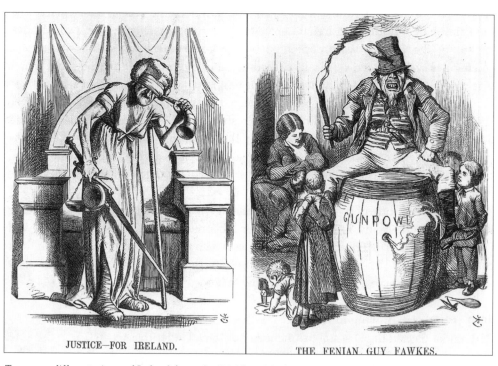

JUSTICE—FOR IRELAND.

THE FENIAN GUY FAWKES.

Two very different views of Ireland from the British satirical magazine, *Punch*. The first dates from 1866 and shows a sympathetic awareness that Ireland had received scant justice from Britain up to then. The second was published in 1867 after the Clerkenwell explosion. *Punch* is often accused of being anti-Irish but in fact it alternated between believing that Britain must help Ireland and presenting the Irish as sub-human brutes.

1 January 1871: independence for the Church of Ireland

Disestablishment took effect on 1 January 1871. Since then the Church of Ireland has been completely independent, able to make its own rules and elect its own leaders. At first many members resented what Gladstone had done to them. They regarded it as a betrayal. But gradually their freedom and independence came to be valued as a source of strength.

Land reform

For many people in Ireland reform of the land laws was more important than disestablishment. But this was much harder for Gladstone to achieve. To understand why, we must look at the issues involved.

Tenant right and the Ulster Custom

Ever since the 1850s Irish tenant farmers had been demanding '**tenant right**' (see page 31), which was summed up in the slogan '**the Three Fs**' – fair rent, fixity of tenure and free sale. Something like it existed in parts of Ulster and for that reason, tenant right was sometimes called '**the Ulster Custom**'. People believed that farmers in Ulster were more prosperous than tenants elsewhere in Ireland and attributed that to the greater security they had under the Ulster Custom.

In 1869 tenant farmers formed a **Tenant League** to renew the demand for tenant right. Its president was **Isaac Butt**, a Protestant lawyer who had defended the Fenians at their trials following the rising in 1867.

The Liberals and tenant right

Most British Liberal MPs opposed tenant right. They did not think that Parliament should tell landlords how to manage their estates or what rent to charge. One MP said: 'Tenant right is landlord wrong'.

Gladstone, however, was determined to do something for Irish tenant farmers who made up about 70 per cent of the population. He believed that satisfying them would undermine support for the Fenians.

He knew he could not get his party to agree to give all the Three Fs, so he set up a committee to look into the Ulster Custom. They discovered that similar customs existed in many places. Gladstone knew his followers would agree to legalise a custom that already existed, even if they would not accept full tenant right.

1870: Gladstone's first Land Act

In 1870, parliament passed Gladstone's first Land Act. It divided the country into two parts.

- Where the Ulster Custom or similar customs existed, they were made law.

- Where no custom existed, a tenant who was unfairly evicted was to be paid 'compensation for disturbance'. The maximum compensation was £240. But a tenant who was evicted because he had not paid his rent got no compensation.

- The Act also contained the **Bright Clause**. It was suggested by **John Bright**, a leading Liberal who believed that government-aided land purchase (like that in the Disestablishment Act) was the real answer to Irish land problems. Under the Bright Clause the government lent two thirds of the purchase price to any tenant who wished to buy his farm. The farmer repaid the loan in annual instalments over thirty-five years. Under the Bright Clause, 800 tenants bought their farms.

An assessment of Gladstone's first Land Act

From the tenants' point of view, Gladstone's first Land Act had many faults.

- It did not spell out what the Ulster Custom was. A tenant who claimed it applied to him had to go to court to prove his case. This involved high legal costs and judges were more sympathetic to landlords than to tenants.

- A tenant who was unjustly evicted was compensated. But tenants did not want to be compensated after they had been evicted. They wanted a rent they could afford and security from eviction.

- A tenant who was evicted for not paying his rent got no compensation. But as we saw (page 32) not paying rent was almost the only reason for evictions in the 1850s and 1860s.

Gladstone's Act was useful for tenants in one way only.

- For the first time, Liberal MPs voted for an Act which favoured the tenants rather than the landlords. The Act set the pattern by which British governments tried to overcome Irish discontent by doing something for Irish tenant farmers.

Not that Gladstone saw the defects in his Act. From his point of view it was a generous concession to Irish tenants. Because the Act was followed by a period of prosperity which lasted up to 1876, the country remained quiet and peaceful. This hid the Act's weaknesses and for some years Gladstone could feel that he had satisfied the demands of Irish tenant farmers.

Chapter 5

1870-74: Isaac Butt and the start of Home Rule

The Fenians in prison

While Gladstone was dealing with disestablishment and the land question, another problem had come to the fore in Ireland. It concerned the treatment of Fenians who had been imprisoned after their unsuccessful rebellion in 1867.

Newspaper reports appeared saying that some of them were being ill-treated. One Fenian, O'Donovan Rossa, refused to wear prison clothes. As a punishment, he spent thirty-five days in solitary confinement with his hands handcuffed behind him.

1868: the Amnesty Association

A campaign began to free the Fenians. It was led by the **Amnesty Association**. It organised marches and petitions and raised money to help the prisoners' dependants. Some members of the Amnesty Association were Fenians but many were people who just disapproved of the treatment the Fenian prisoners were receiving. The most important of them was **Isaac Butt** who was also the leader of the Tenant League.

Isaac Butt: 1813-1879

Butt was the son of a Church of Ireland clergyman. He trained as a barrister and became one of the best lawyers of his time. At first he supported the Act of Union but the famine of the 1840s had convinced him that Ireland needed its own parliament to look after Irish affairs.

Butt spent most of the 1850s and the early 1860s in England, but returned to Ireland in 1865 to practice at the Irish bar. He had lived extravagantly in England and was deeply in debt. Despite this, he gave up the chance to earn higher fees in order to defend the Fenians in court. This earned him the trust of the Fenians and he became leader of the Amnesty Association.

Early in 1869 a petition for amnesty, signed by 250,000 people, was presented to parliament. Gladstone released forty-nine of the eighty-one Fenian prisoners but this did not satisfy the Association and the agitation continued.

Dissatisfaction with Gladstone's reforms

In May 1870 Butt spoke at a meeting in Dublin. The audience contained many people who were dissatisfied with Gladstone's reforms.

Isaac Butt

- There were members of the Church of Ireland who were unhappy at disestablishment. They felt that the United Kingdom parliament had betrayed them.

- There were landlords who were angry about Gladstone's Land Act. They feared that the London-based parliament might go even further the next time. Some of them wondered if they might not be better off with an Irish parliament which, because voters had to declare their vote publicly, they could control. After all, most voters were their tenants who seldom dared to vote against their landlords' wishes. (see page 8)

- There were tenant farmers who were disappointed with Gladstone's Land Act and wondered if this was the best they could get from a Liberal government. Perhaps an Irish parliament, where tenants would have the main voice, would respond better to their needs?

- There were even a few Fenians who wondered if they could make use of Butt.

May 1870: the Home Government Association formed

All these people listened when Butt argued that what Ireland needed was a local parliament. It would make laws about internal Irish affairs like education, land and the police. Foreign policy issues such as international trade, war and peace and treaties with other countries would still be dealt with by the United Kingdom parliament in Westminster.

The meeting founded the **Home Government Association** with Butt as leader. It was a very mixed body. Among its sixty members were Protestants and Catholics, landlords and tenants, Conservatives, Liberals and Fenians.

The revival of the IRB

After the Fenian prisoners were freed in 1870, the IRB began to re-emerge under new leaders.

Up to 1865 James Stephens had run it as a one man show and many Fenians blamed the failure of the rising on that fact. They were determined to prevent any one leader gaining that kind of power again.

In 1873 they adopted a new constitution. Under it, the IRB was to be led by an elected **Supreme Council**, containing representatives of the members in Ireland and Britain. The Supreme Council, in turn, was to elect a President, Secretary and Treasurer, who were to run the organisation. The first IRB President elected under this constitution was the novelist **Charles J. Kickham**.

Charles J. Kickham

Kickham's ideas

Almost blind and deaf as a result of an accident, Kickham was a committed separatist. He believed that the IRB must concentrate on winning complete independence for Ireland. If it became involved with any other issue, such as land reform, Kickham thought it would become corrupted and forget its real purpose.

For extreme nationalists like Kickham, an Irish republic could only be won by a rebellion led by the IRB. The time to rebel was when Britain was involved in a major war. This view was summed up in the phrase, 'England's difficulty is Ireland's opportunity'. Unfortunately for Kickham there was no war in the 1870s, but he was content to wait.

1870-77: the Fenians and Home Rule

Most Fenians had less patience. They wanted to do something straight away. They had worked with Butt in the Amnesty Association and had come to respect him, so when he started the Home Government Association, they backed it too. Although they did not think that his 'home government' plan would give Ireland enough independence, they saw it as a useful first step to full separation from Britain.

1870-73: success of the Home Government Association

The demand for Home Government (or Home Rule as it soon came to be called) proved popular. The Association won several by-elections. In 1872 Gladstone brought in the Ballot Act. It allowed voters to mark on paper the name of the candidate they preferred. This reduced the power of the landlords over the voters. As a result, many of them left the Association. By 1873, a majority of the Association's supporters were Catholics and tenant farmers.

1873: Gladstone's failure on education

Cardinal Cullen and most Catholic bishops opposed the Home Government Association at first. They were worried by the number of Protestants and Fenians in it. They continued to support Gladstone and the Liberals because they hoped for grants for Catholic education.

However, Gladstone found it impossible to satisfy them. There was a deep anti-Catholic feeling in Britain at that time which made it hard for any government to give money directly to the Catholic clergy. In addition, many British Liberals wanted the state to run its own schools. They did not want to give money to the Churches to run theirs.

Cardinal Cullen

Early in 1873 Gladstone introduced his proposals for education. They fell far short of Catholic hopes. The Catholic bishops denounced the proposals and thirty-nine Irish Liberal MPs voted against them in parliament. The plan was defeated and Gladstone's government fell.

November 1873: the foundation of the Home Rule League

This quarrel between Gladstone and the Irish Liberals increased the popularity of Butt's Association. In November 1873 he turned it into a proper political party, called the **Irish Home Rule League**.

The new party planned to get MPs elected to Westminster. There they would try to persuade the British politicians to give Ireland its own parliament to look after internal Irish affairs.

The 1874 Election

A few weeks later, Gladstone called a general election. The League was unprepared and had little time to get suitable candidates. They were not easy to find. Since MPs were not paid, a candidate had to be a wealthy man who could afford to keep himself in London while he attended parliament.

In desperation, the Home Rulers in many constituencies chose former Liberal MPs who had quarrelled with Gladstone over education. These men were glad to adopt the Home Rule label because it improved their chances of being elected, but their hearts were not really in the Home Rule cause.

The election was a triumph for the new party. Fifty-nine Home Rule MPs were elected. But the success was not as great as it appeared on the surface. Only about twenty-five were fully committed to working for an Irish parliament. They included Butt himself and **Joseph Biggar**, a wealthy shopowner from Belfast who was a member of the IRB Supreme Council. The other MPs were Home Rulers in name only. It remained to be seen if Butt could hold his party together in the House of Commons.

Chapter 6

1874-80: The early years of the Home Rule party

1874: the tactics of the Home Rule party

After the 1874 general election in which fifty-nine Home Rule MPs were elected, the party met and resolved:

> to form a separate and distinct party in the House of Commons, united on the principle of obtaining self-government for Ireland. (D. Thornley, *Isaac Butt and Home Rule*, p. 213)

This resolution committed the Home Rulers to a policy of **independent opposition**. They would remain independent of the two British parties, the Liberals and the Conservatives, but they would offer their votes to whichever party was willing to grant their aims: reform of the land system, grants for Catholic education and above all, a Home Rule parliament for Ireland.

Disraeli as Prime Minister

Butt's Home Rule party was not in a strong bargaining position in 1874. Gladstone had lost the election and the new Prime Minister was leader of the Conservative Party, Benjamin Disraeli.

Disraeli was an imperialist, more interested in the British Empire and in European issues than in Ireland. He believed that Irish grievances had had enough attention under Gladstone and he ignored Irish demands for reform.

Butt's leadership

Between 1874 and 1880 the Conservatives had an overall majority in the Commons and did not need Irish votes. This made it hard for the new Home Rule party to make much of an impact. A strong leader might have made a difference but Isaac Butt was not a strong leader.

Butt was heavily in debt. In 1871 he owed £10,000 (over £500,000 today). He had to work constantly as a barrister to pay off his creditors. As a result, he was often absent from the Commons, even when important issues were being debated. Naturally, many of the less enthusiastic Home Rule MPs followed him in this, if in little else. And because of his debts and his frequent absences, he did not have the moral authority to order them to attend.

Apart from his personal failings, Butt was not an effective political leader. He saw

Benjamin Disraeli (1804-81) was Prime Minister from 1874-80.

the Home Rule movement as a pressure group rather than a political party. Therefore he made no attempt to organise branches around the country. This meant he lacked widespread public support in Ireland.

In the Commons too, Butt's tactics were at fault. He believed his role was to persuade the British MPs to remedy Irish grievances. He brought in bills to give tenant right and state aid for Catholic education. He moved resolutions in favour of Home Rule and amnesty for the remaining Fenian prisoners. He spoke earnestly and well in favour of each cause. Each time, British MPs listened politely and then defeated his proposals by huge majorities. On some occasions even members of his own party voted against him.

The Fenians' involvement in Home Rule

Butt's tactics satisfied most Home Rule MPs but one small section of the party soon lost patience with them. They included the Fenians. Two members of the Supreme Council, **Joseph Biggar** and **John O'Connor Power**, were Home Rule MPs. In England another Supreme Council member, **John Barry**, dominated the **Home Rule Confederation of Great Britain**. Its aim was to organise Irish emigrants living in British cities to vote for candidates sympathetic to Home Rule.

At first the IRB Supreme Council was divided on the attitude it should take towards the Fenians who joined the Home Rule movement. Kickham opposed them but others preferred to wait and see what the outcome would be. In 1877 it finally decided to forbid Fenian involvement in the Home Rule movement. Biggar and O'Connor Power refused to obey, so they were expelled.

This decision had little effect on the ordinary Fenians, many of whom continued to work for Home Rule. In areas such as Connaught and Munster, where the IRB had many members, they provided the main organisers of the Home Rule party and later of the Land League.

1875: obstruction

The Fenians were soon disillusioned by Butt's parliamentary tactics. In 1875 Biggar and a handful of other MPs began a more aggressive policy. They started to **obstruct** the work of the House of Commons.

Joseph Biggar obstructing the Commons. Biggar was a poor speaker with a strong Belfast accent that most British MPs could not understand. His speeches mainly consisted of reading long extracts from government reports, a pile of which are on the bench beside him. His effect on other members is also clearly visible.

They made boring speeches that went on for hours, read out long passages from government reports and demanded votes on every possible occasion. This forced the House of Commons to sit far into the night and delayed bills which the British considered important.

Obstruction was not new. British and Irish politicians had often obstructed bills they disliked. What was new was that Biggar and a handful of Irish MPs were obstructing all sorts of bills, even ones in which they had no interest. They argued that since British MPs blocked Irish reforms, they were entitled to do the same with laws the British wanted.

Butt disapproves of obstruction

Butt and most Home Rule MPs strongly disapproved of the obstruction campaign. They feared that it would anger British MPs on whose goodwill all Irish reforms depended. But in 1875 the obstructionists gained a valuable new recruit when **Charles Stewart Parnell** was elected MP for Meath.

PIGHEADED OBSTRUCTION.

Punch's view of obstruction in 1877. The man is a British MP who joined in the fun. The pigs are labelled with their constituency. Can you find Parnell?

Charles Stewart Parnell (1846-1891)

Parnell was a Protestant landlord with a small estate in County Wicklow. His mother was an American. She may have given him a dislike of the English which his experiences at school and university probably strengthened.

When Parnell entered Parliament in 1875, he was twenty-nine years old. Handsome, charming and a little aloof, he was a natural leader who drew people to him. At first, he was a poor speaker and during his first year in the Commons he said little but quietly watched the way events were moving.

1876: Parnell and the obstructionists

In the Commons, Parnell had to choose between supporting Butt and the majority of Home Rule MPs, or joining the obstructionists. In 1876 he came down on the side of the obstructionists and soon emerged as their leader. In July 1877 he and five others kept the House of Commons sitting for forty-five hours. Butt disowned their actions but the obstructionists' tactics earned them a great deal of popularity in Ireland.

This may be why Parnell joined them. Another reason may have been that the obstructionists had Fenian support. The Fenian network in Ireland, Britain and the

---

ASSESSING PARNELL

Historians have great difficulty in assessing Parnell's motives. Ever since his death they have argued over these points:

- did Parnell work with the Fenians because he shared their dream of complete independence, or because they could help him to become the leader the Home Rule movement?

- did he see Home Rule as enough independence for Ireland, or as a first step on the way to complete separation from Britain?

- was Parnell an unselfish patriot destroyed by small-minded people who were jealous of his greatness, or a ruthless, power-hungry man who used any means to forward his own career?

The reason for the uncertainty is that Parnell left few records. He seldom wrote letters (except to Katharine O'Shea, and they were mainly love letters with few political comments). He did not keep a diary or write his memoirs. Therefore we know very little of his intimate thoughts.

Of course there are the things he said in public. He made many speeches but these are often contradictory. It seems probable that these speeches were intended to please his audience, whether it was Irish tenants, American Fenians or British MPs, rather than reveal the real Parnell.

In the end, we can only judge him by his actions. As you read through the next few chapters you will get an account of decisions Parnell made throughout his political career. Try to make up your own mind about the motives and ambitions of this most enigmatic man.

US could be very useful to a young MP who wanted to take over the leadership of his party.

1876-79: Parnell and the Fenians

Parnell certainly seems to have deliberately courted Fenian support. One of his earliest remarks in parliament was a defence of the Manchester martyrs (three men executed in Manchester in 1867 for killing a policeman during a Fenian escape attempt). He also worked hard to get an amnesty for the remaining Fenian prisoners, among them **Michael Davitt** who had been imprisoned for gun-running in 1870.

In 1877 Parnell reaped his reward. The Fenian-controlled Home Rule Confederation of Great Britain deposed Butt as their president and elected Parnell in his place.

In 1877 and 1878 Parnell had several meetings with leading Fenians. One of them was Davitt who had just been released on parole as a result of Parnell's amnesty

Parnell being suspended from the Commons during a bout of obstruction. His calm disregard for the jeers of British MPs won widespread admiration in Ireland and was one of the things that helped him win the leadership of the Home Rule party.

campaign. He was impressed by the young MP. Soon after, Davitt went to the US where he reported on Parnell to the leading Irish American Fenian **John Devoy.**

John Devoy (1842-1928)

Kildare-born Devoy had been a leading Fenian in the 1860s. He had recruited many Irish soldiers who were serving in the British army into the movement. He was arrested and sentenced to fifteen years in jail. He was freed as a result of Butt's amnesty campaign but on condition that he stayed out of Ireland for the remainder of his sentence. Devoy went to the United States where millions of Irish emigrants had settled since the famine.

Clan na Gael

Most emigrants were too busy earning a living to have time for plotting revolution back in Ireland. However, they were always willing to contribute generously with their money, if not their time, to any Irish cause. There were some Irish Americans, however, who wanted to to win for Ireland the republican freedom they now enjoyed in the United States. They had formed organisations to help the cause of Irish independence.

Devoy joined and later took over one of these organisations, **Clan na Gael**. Under his leadership it became the main Irish-American republican organisation. It had close ties with the IRB in Ireland and channelled money into a variety of Irish causes over the next fifty years. Devoy had taken an interest in the Home Rule movement and he soon began to think that some sort of a link should be formed between the Fenians and the obstructionists.

John Devoy

Parnell's relations with the Fenians

Devoy sent William Carroll to check out Parnell. Carroll was impressed but reports of these meetings all agree that Parnell carefully avoided making any definite commitment to the Fenian cause.

We can only guess at what Parnell was up to. It seems likely that he was playing a delicate balancing game. He was trying to use the Fenians in his campaign to become leader of the Home Rule Party. But he had to be careful how he did this. If his association with them became public, it might frighten off other, more conservative groups, whose support he also needed if he was to win the leadership.

1878-79: Parnell and the Catholic Church

The most important of these groups was the Catholic clergy. Many of them were suspicious of Parnell, because he was a Protestant. They were also unhappy about his connection with the obstructionists and the Fenians. Parnell for his part did his best to win their backing by supporting their demand for state aid for Catholic schools and for the Catholic university.

State support for education

In 1878 and 1879, Disraeli's government at last made some concessions to Catholic education demands. Butt claimed the credit, but in fact the government acted partly to counter the obstructionists' growing popularity.

1878: the Intermediate Education Act

Anti-Catholic prejudice in Britain made it hard for any government to give state funds directly to Catholic schools. Disraeli's government solved this problem by giving the funds indirectly through a system known as 'payment by results'. Under the 1878 **Intermediate Education Act** students who sat for the state-run examinations received grants. (see page 16)

1879: the Royal University Act

The Conservative government applied a similar solution to the demand for state aid for the Catholic-run university.(see page 18) They set up the **Royal University**. It was not a real university where students were taught, merely an examination-setting body. Students who passed its examinations got degrees and scholarships out of which they could pay fees to the place where they had studied.

Parnell attacked the the Intermediate Education Act and the Royal University Act on the grounds that they did not give enough funds to Catholic education. But most of the Home Rule MPs, including the leader, Isaac Butt, supported these reforms.

1878-79: divisions in the Home Rule Party

The division over education was only a symptom of the split that had developed in the Home Rule party by 1879. The main debate, however, was over the leadership.

About twenty MPs, now called '**Parnellites**', were dissatisfied with Butt. They wanted Parnell as leader and a more active policy in parliament. The remaining MPs, called the '**Whigs**', supported Butt and his gentlemanly approach to British politics. They were mainly ex-Liberal landowners, who regarded the Parnellites as dangerous revolutionaries.

In a number of by-elections, 'Parnellite' and 'Whig' Home Rulers fought for the same seat. The Parnellites were popular but in some places the Whigs won with the backing of the Catholic clergy.

May 1879: the death of Isaac Butt: Shaw elected leader

In May 1879 Isaac Butt died suddenly. In the vote for the leadership which followed, the Whig majority elected a banker called **William Shaw** to be the new leader. It must have been clear to Parnell that if he was to win the leadership he had to get the backing of public opinion in Ireland. Although he did not yet realise it, the opportunity to do so was about to present itself to him.

Chapter 7

1878-80: Davitt, Parnell and the Land League

Michael Davitt (1846-1906)

The man who gave Parnell his chance to win widespread popularity was the Fenian, **Michael Davitt**. Davitt had been born in Mayo in 1846, the son of a small tenant farmer. Evicted, the family moved to England in 1852, where the young Michael soon went to work in a cotton-mill. When he was eleven, he lost his right arm in an accident. With the compensation he got, he was able to return to school and finish his education.

Michael Davitt

Davitt became a journalist and joined the IRB. In 1870 he was arrested and given a fifteen-year sentence for gun-running. In 1877 Parnell helped him to get out of jail on a ticket-of-leave (as probation was called at that time). Davitt had not changed his republican views and once free, rejoined the IRB and became a member of the Supreme Council.

1878-9: the New Departure

Soon after his release, Davitt met Parnell and was greatly impressed by him. He thought Parnell might agree to co-operate with the Fenians to win a greater measure of Irish independence than Butt had asked for. He carried this view to America in 1878 where he met John Devoy who was also interested in Parnell.

Together, the two men worked out a plan for a **'New Departure'** in Fenian policy. Up to this the Fenians had refused to take part in constitutional (i.e. legal electoral) politics. Davitt and Devoy now proposed that the Fenians should co-operate with the more extreme Home Rulers around Parnell. Together they would work, both in Westminster and Ireland, for independence and for land reform.

1879: IRB Supreme Council rejects the New Departure

Early in 1879 Davitt and Devoy came to Europe. In Paris they put their plan for a new departure to the Supreme Council of the IRB. Kickham, always suspicious of any move away from simple republicanism, opposed their proposal and it was defeated. As a result, this aspect of the 'New Departure' never got off the ground.

On the other hand, the Supreme Council decided to leave individual Fenians free to take part in constitutional politics if they wished. This permission was later withdrawn, but by then it was too late to change the situation.

1879: Parnell and the New Departure

Davitt and Devoy also held a number of discussions with Parnell to get his response to their proposals. Although accounts of these meetings differ, it seems clear that Parnell listened carefully but said nothing. Devoy, however, got the impression that Parnell was seriously considering the proposal. As a result, he returned to the US to organise financial support for the Parnellites.

March 1879: Michael Davitt returns to Mayo

While these meeting were going on, Davitt went to visit relatives in Mayo. To his surprise he found the county in the grip of an economic crisis.

The long depression

After the famine of the 1840s, Irish farmers had enjoyed a period of prosperity (see page 29) which lasted, with some gaps, for a quarter of a century. It was mainly due to the steady demand for Irish produce on the booming British market. But this boom ceased in the mid-1870s. The world economy entered a period of decline, usually called the 'long depression' which lasted up to the late 1890s.

Industrial decline

The long depression damaged the Irish economy. Outside the Belfast area and a few big ports, Irish industry suffered badly. Small companies, often using old-fashioned production methods, could not compete with British or Irish companies which had the most up-to-date technology.

The cotton industries at Drogheda and Portlaw collapsed. Paper-making, ship-building, rope-making and tanning almost disappeared. Small local breweries could not produce beer as good or as cheap as Guinness' in Dublin or Murphy's in Cork, so they closed down. Flour milling ceased in most inland towns when faced with competition from the big mills, which developed in Dublin and Limerick and which used more modern machinery.

Small craftsmen suffered too. As mentioned in chapter 3, the newly built railways, which by the mid-1870s covered most of the country, brought mass produced factory goods quickly and cheaply to the remotest village. Local craftsmen were unable to compete with them. Irish towns which up to this had supplied most of their own needs, came to depend on goods made elsewhere. As a result, unemployment, poverty and emigration all increased.

The agricultural depression

Farmers, too, were badly hit by the depression. Up to 1876 harvests had been good and prices remained high. Then, as unemployment grew in Britain, the demand for Irish beef and butter fell, leading to a fall in prices.

Prices were also affected by competition from abroad. Aided by faster and bigger ships and by refrigeration, food products began to flow into Britain from Europe, the United States, South America and Australia. They competed with Irish products which up to then had had a virtual monopoly on the British market.

Competition kept food prices low in Britain even after the depression ended. It was not until the outbreak of World War I that Irish farmers (and British farmers too) regained the level of prosperity they had enjoyed before 1876. It is no accident that the years of severe agricultural depression (1877-1895) are also the years of the 'land wars' in Ireland.

The big farmers suffer from falling prices

When Davitt went to Mayo in March 1879, these developments were just beginning. Prices were down and to make matters worse, the weather was terrible. 1879 was the wettest and coldest year of the nineteenth century. Crops failed to ripen and hay to feed the animals could not be saved.

As a result even the usually prosperous large farmers were in trouble. They could no longer pay rents which had seemed reasonable in good times. Unless they could persuade their landlords to lower their rents they faced eviction.

The small farmers face famine

But the condition of the small farmers whom Davitt met in Mayo was even worse. They had tiny farms – no more than a few acres of land – on which they grew potatoes for food and fattened a calf or two to sell. (see page 25) Finding money for the rent was always a struggle. Usually they paid it and bought clothes and other necessities with money they earned by working for British farmers at harvest time, by fishing, or by gathering and selling seaweed for manure.

When a farmer failed to pay his rent, his cattle could be taken and sold. Here is a sale in Sligo, heavily guarded by the RIC.

In 1879 all these sources of earnings had dried up. British farmers, their own prices falling, had no work for Irish labourers. It is estimated that the small farmers of the west lost £250,000 in wages as a result. In addition, cheap imported fertilisers cut the demand for seaweed, and the fishing industry had collapsed.

Small farmers could no longer pay their rents or the debts they owed the local shopkeepers. Nor had they any hope of earning money in the future. And the cold, wet summer of 1879 destroyed about three quarters of the potato crop, thus robbing them of their basic food. Davitt found them facing not only eviction, but starvation as well.

March-May 1879: organising the farmers in Mayo

In Mayo, the Fenians had an extensive network. In 1874 they had secured the election of the Fenian, John O'Connor Power, as a Home Rule MP, in spite of considerable opposition from the Catholic clergy.

Davitt found them organising the farmers to resist eviction and joined their campaign. At **Irishtown**, they mounted a mass demonstration against a local landlord and got him to reduce his rents. Further demonstrations followed throughout Mayo.

This drawing is called 'summoning the people to resist evictions'. It is probably romanticised but does reflect some reality.

June 1879: the Westport meeting

Davitt became convinced that the land question was the way to win the farmers' backing for Irish independence. He invited Parnell to join him in helping the tenants. Although Parnell had always supported the demand for the Three Fs, he was at first reluctant to get involved. However, after the success of the Irishtown meeting, he agreed to speak at another rally at Westport.

Parnell took a risk in agreeing to go to Westport because the Catholic Archbishop had condemned the rally. He may have reckoned that the risk was worthwhile if it meant he got the support of the farmers in his drive to replace Shaw as the Home Rule leader.

At Westport Parnell gave a forceful speech, telling his audience to demand a 'fair rent' which he defined as 'a rent a tenant can reasonably pay according to the times'.

This rather stylised view of Parnell and other prominent Land League leaders addressing a meeting was printed in America. It was probably intended for propaganda purposes. Joseph Biggar is on the left and Tim Healy on the right.

Parnell ended with a rallying cry to tenants which became famous and which clearly identified him as being on their side:

> You must show the landlords that you intend to keep a firm grip on your home-steads and lands. You must not allow yourselves to be dispossessed as you were dispossessed in 1847. (F.S.L. Lyons, *Charles Stewart Parnell*, p. 92)

October 1879: the Land League founded

After the Westport meeting, Davitt founded the Land League of Mayo. Throughout the wet summer of 1879, similar organisations appeared in other counties. By the autumn, Davitt was ready to unite them into a nation-wide movement and he invited Parnell to be its leader.

At a conference in Dublin in October 1879, the **Irish National Land League** was founded. It aimed:

- in the short-term to reduce rents and stop evictions.

- in the long term to abolish the landlord system altogether and to make the tenants the owners of their farms through state-aided land purchase.

It hoped to achieve these aims by a combination of peaceful agitation in Ireland and parliamentary pressure at Westminster.

Parnell was elected President of the League but he did not control it. It was in the hands of the Fenians, as can be seen from the fact that four of the six officers elected along with him were active in the IRB. The question was whether, in the end, the Fenians would control Parnell too?

1879-80: Parnell in America

Soon after the League was formed, Parnell went to the United States to get money and support for the League's aims. He stayed there for several months and got an enthusiastic welcome. He collected about £80,000. Much of it was given to prevent the famine which, in the winter of 1879/80, seemed to threaten the western counties of Ireland with a repeat of the suffering of the 1840s.

Averting famine

There was hunger in many homes that winter, but no famine. This was partly because almost £2 million was distributed by the government, the Land League and various charities to feed the people. Famine was also less likely to occur in the 1870s than in had been in the 1840s. By then the railways had spread across the country and a network of small shops had developed. They distributed imported food so that even when the potato was gone, food supplies were available.

March 1880: Gladstone wins the general election

Early in 1880 the Conservative Prime Minister, Disraeli, called a general election. Parnell hurried back from America to take part. In Britain, Disraeli and the Conservatives were defeated and Gladstone returned as Prime Minister. He was sympathetic to the Irish case but he was elected to deal with urgent questions of imperial and foreign policy, not with Ireland. As one historian put it:

> Irish distress, Irish discontent, Irish grievances had become pressing questions. Gladstone, his mind on Bulgaria, Afghanistan, the Zulus and the Boers, gave them little of his attention. (J. L. Hammond, *Gladstone and the Irish Nation*, p. 165)

Victory of the 'Parnellite' Home Rulers

In Ireland, the election showed up the splits within the Home Rule party. In many constituencies, 'Parnellite' Home Rulers fought 'Whig' Home Rulers for the same seat. The party won sixty-one seats, with Parnell holding three of them. The MPs were divided into three groups.

- Twenty-four were committed Parnellites. They included **John Dillon**, **Tim Healy** and **Timothy Harrington**, all of whom were to play important roles in the Home Rule Party.

- Only twenty-one were 'Whigs', one of whom was **William Shaw**, the party leader.

- There were fourteen MPs who hesitated between the two camps but who backed Parnell when he looked like winning. One of them was **Captain William O'Shea** whose wife, **Katharine**, met Parnell later that year.

These results can be seen as Parnell's reward for siding with the tenant farmers who made up the bulk of the voters.

1880: Parnell elected leader of the Home Rule party

Soon after the election, the Home Rulers met to pick their leader. Parnell easily defeated Shaw. A few months later, Shaw and eleven of his supporters, left the Home Rule Party and joined the Liberals.

Parnell was now the leader but he faced the formidable task of leading a divided party and a country on the brink of chaos.

Chapter 8

1880-82: The land war

1880: Parnell's problems as leader

After the 1880 election, Parnell led a large but unstable coalition of Irish interests, all with different aims.

- There were the Home Rule MPs divided between enthusiastic supporters of the tenants, like John Dillon, and cautious landlords who were interested in Home Rule but nervous of the Land League.

- There were the tenant farmers and their supporters in Ireland, banded together in the still growing Land League. They backed Home Rule but in the short-term were much more interested in land reform.

- Behind the League were the Fenians both in the United States and in Ireland. They saw the land agitation chiefly as a way to stir up a revolution and win complete separation between Ireland and Britain.

It remained to be seen whether Parnell could maintain a balance between these conflicting groups and their conflicting aims.

Continuing economic problems

The election had solved none of the economic problems which faced the farmers. The summer of 1880 was fine. The harvest was good and that eased the threat of famine. But prices stayed low and everywhere tenants were unable to pay their rents. The number of evictions rose from 1,238 in 1879 to 2,110 in 1880.

Traditionally, when evictions took place tenants resorted to violence. They formed secret societies and went out at night with blackened faces to deliver threatening letters, burn barns or maim cattle. Occasionally they shot at a landlord, his agent or a tenant who had taken over a farm from which another family had been evicted.

1880: the spread of the Land League

In 1880 the Land League tried to take the place of the secret societies. That summer, it spread all over the country, though it was least successful in Ulster. It included every class: big and small farmers, agricultural labourers, townspeople, shopkeepers and priests.

The League's success was due to the way the depression hit all parts of the community. Farmers, whether they had big farms or small, faced eviction; labourers could not find jobs either on the farms or in the towns; shopkeepers were owed money that they might never recover unless the farmers were saved from eviction.

For all of them the League's slogan, 'the land of Ireland for the people of Ireland', had a strong appeal. It seemed a way of solving all their problems. Farmers hoped to gain ownership of the land and so be secure from eviction. Small farmers and labourers hoped to get a share of the land held by the big farmers. Shopkeepers hoped that farmers would pay their debts if they did not have to pay rents. Of course, some of these hopes were incompatible but not many people saw that in 1880.

Autumn 1880: the Land League campaign

After the election, Parnell demanded that the new Liberal government do something to help the farmers. Gladstone introduced a bill to increase compensation to evicted tenants. It was rejected by the Lords and nothing further was offered.

Parnell then returned to Ireland to put pressure on Gladstone by stepping up the agitation. 'Depend upon it,' he told a meeting in September, 'the measure of the land bill next session will be the measure of your activity and energy this winter.'

The pace of agitation increased. League meetings were held all over the country attended by thousands of people, carrying banners and led by bands. In speech after speech, the League leaders told them to resist evictions and hold onto their farms. They said that the land rightfully belonged to the tenants because they were the descendants of the Gaelic owners whose land had been confiscated in the plantations of the sixteenth and seventeenth centuries.

These demonstrations had two aims. They showed the government the extent of popular support for the League and its demands. But they also channelled the anger of the tenants into peaceful agitation and away from their traditional violence which brought bad publicity and damaged their cause in Britain.

Moral force

The same aims lay behind the League's most famous weapon, moral force. At a League meeting in Ennis, Parnell asked the crowd, 'What do you do with a tenant who bids for a farm from which his neighbour has been evicted?' Voices yelled back, 'Kill him!', 'Shoot him!'. But Parnell replied:

I wish to point out to you a much better way... When a man takes a farm from which another has been evicted, you must show him on the roadside when you meet him, you must show him in the streets of the town, you must show him at the shop counter, you must show him in the fair and in the market-place, and even in the house of worship, by leaving him severely alone, by putting him into a moral Coventry, by isolating him from his kind as if he were a leper of old – you must show him your detestation of the crime he has committed. (F.S.L. Lyons, *Charles Stewart Parnell*, p. 134)

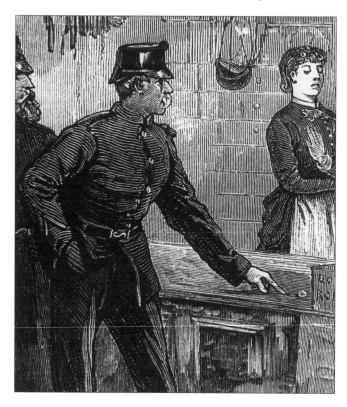

This was the practical result of Parnell's call to 'show him at the shop counter . . . your detestation of the crime he has committed'.

October-November 1880: Captain Boycott

In Mayo in October 1880 this 'moral force' policy was used against a land agent, Captain Boycott. Servants would not work in his house, postmen would not deliver his letters, shopkeepers refused to serve him, his labourers left his crops to rot in the fields.

Boycott wrote to the London *Times*, describing his plight. Landlords took up his cause and the Orange Order sent fifty labourers from Ulster to save his harvest. Protected by several hundred police and soldiers the Orangemen achieved their purpose but it cost several times what the crops were worth. Soon after, Boycott left Ireland.

The whole affair attracted enormous publicity. Newsmen from all over the world went to Mayo to report on what was going on. Within months, Boycott's name had entered the English language to describe the League's favourite weapon.

Publicity

The Boycott affair won useful publicity for the League. Many reporters were appalled at the poverty they saw in Mayo. They heard from the League about the heartless behaviour of some landlords and they publicised these stories too. Their reports stirred the consciences of Liberal voters in Britain who pressed Gladstone to act.

Captain Boycott and his family collecting their harvest under armed guard. Later labourers from the North, organised by the Orange Order, went to help them.

November 1880: Gladstone takes on the League

By the end of 1880 Gladstone could no longer ignore the power of the League which by now seemed to be acting as if it were the real government of Ireland. Some members of his government, especially the Irish Chief Secretary, **W. E. Forster**, were horrified by the spread of violence, of demonstrations and of boycotting. They wanted special powers which would enable them to imprison trouble-makers without trial.

Gladstone opposed this. He believed that they should first try to deal with the situation using the ordinary law. In November 1880 Parnell, Davitt and others were arrested and charged with conspiring to prevent the payment of rent. The jury at their trial failed to agree and they were freed.

Coercion and reform

Gladstone now realised that no Irish jury would find the League leaders guilty. He would have to give the government special powers through a **coercion act** if the League was to be controlled. But he also knew that he must combine coercion with a generous land act if he was to win Irish tenants away from the League.

At the end of 1880 the Bessborough Commission, which had been investigating the working of the 1870 Land Act, came out in favour of giving tenants the Three Fs.

This was Gladstone's own view but he knew it would be rejected by the House of Lords and even by some members of his own party, unless it was preceded by a severe coercion act.

Unfortunately for Gladstone's good intentions, this programme of coercion first and reform second was only likely to increase Irish bitterness. Thus the scene was set for a serious collision between the Liberal leader and Parnell.

January-February 1881: Confrontation in Westminster

Early in 1881 the government introduced the **Protection of Person and Property Bill** into the House of Commons. It gave them power to imprison without trial anyone they *suspected* of encouraging unlawful activities.

Parnell and twenty of his MPs at once began to obstruct the bill. Forty-one hours later they were still at it and looked like going on forever. At that point the Speaker stopped the debate and the next day the rules of the House of Commons were changed to prevent that sort of obstruction ever happening again.

Then word came that Davitt's ticket-of-leave (parole) had been cancelled and that he had been re-arrested. John Dillon stood up in the Commons to protest but he was suspended and ejected from the House. Parnell did the same, followed, one after another, by thirty-four Home Rule MPs. They met outside, where Dillon and a few others urged Parnell to return to Ireland and continue the struggle there. He refused. Instead he returned to the Commons to wait for Gladstone's promised land bill.

Parnell: a constitutional politician?

For many historians this episode is important. They claim that it shows that Parnell was fundamentally a constitutional politician, however much he mixed with Fenians. On the other hand it could be argued that he had little choice but to return to the Commons, as it is doubtful if more than six out of the thirty-six MPs could have followed him to Ireland.

The arrest of the 'suspects'

By March 1881 the Coercion Act was passed. Soon 'suspects' (i.e. leading members of the League) were being arrested. Contrary to Forster's expectations, however, the violence did not end. On the contrary, the number of agrarian crimes rose as the League's ability to control its followers was reduced as more and more of the leaders were put in prison.

April 1881: introduction of Gladstone's second land bill

On 7 April 1881, Gladstone introduced his second land bill. It gave tenant-farmers the Three Fs they had so long demanded. The main terms of the bill can be summarized briefly.

- A **Land Court** was to be set up to which landlords and tenants could go to get a fair rent fixed.

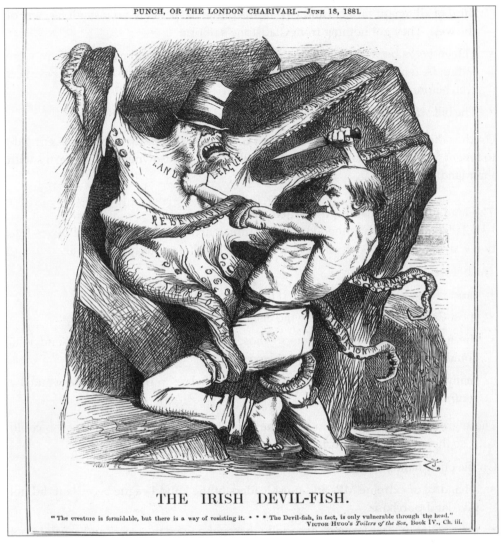

THE IRISH DEVIL-FISH.

" The creature is formidable, but there is a way of resisting it. ⁎ ⁎ ⁎ The Devil-fish, in fact, is only vulnerable through the head."
VICTOR HUGO's *Toilers of the Sea*, Book IV., Ch. iii.

An English view of the reasons for the Coercion Act.

- This 'judicial rent' was to last for **fifteen years** and the tenant who paid it could not be evicted.
- After fifteen years a tenant could return to the Court to get a new rent fixed.
- There was also a land purchase clause.

The bill was had many weaknesses.

- Tenants who had leases and tenants who were in arrears (behind with their rents) were not allowed to go to the Land Court. Between them, these groups made up a third of all tenant farmers and two-thirds of the desperately poor small farmers of the west. They got nothing from Gladstone's reform.

- Fifteen years between rent adjustments was too long at a time when prices were falling. A tenant who had a fair rent fixed in 1882 might have difficulty paying it well before the fifteen years were up.
- The bill was very complicated and this caused thousands of law cases.

On the other hand the bill was the biggest concession that parliament had ever made to tenant farmers. It's main effect was to make them **joint-owners** of their farms with their landlords.

The land bill threatens to split Parnell's followers
As Gladstone probably intended, the bill threatened to split Parnell's followers into two warring factions. Some of them welcomed it. Others bitterly opposed it.

The bill was supported by:

- most Home Rule MPs who wanted the land question settled peacefully.
- most Catholic clergy, especially the bishops, who took the same view.
- the more prosperous big farmers whose rents were paid up to date and who could go to the Land Court to get them reduced.
- many shopkeepers and the prosperous middle class in the towns who wanted a return to peace and order.

These groups had most to gain from the bill. They were also the people who could vote, so they were very important to Parnell and his party.

On the other hand, the bill was rejected by:

- a handful of extreme MPs and most leaders of the Land League because it did not give land purchase.
- the smaller, poorer farmers, especially those who were in arrears and so could not go to the Land Court. They gained nothing from the bill as it stood.
- the Fenians who had hoped to use the tenants' discontent to stir up a revolution. A bill which satisfied the tenants and ended the agitation would also end that hope.

If Parnell supported the bill, the small farmers would split off from the League and he would lose the backing of the Fenians. But he still needed their organisation around the country and also the American money which their support ensured.

April-October, 1881: Parnell and the land bill
Parnell thus faced a dilemma. If he supported the bill he lost one group, if he rejected it he lost the other. How was he to balance these opposing interests without splitting apart the fragile but powerful coalition he had built up?

His solution was to avoid taking sides. After the bill was introduced he got his followers to abstain from voting for or against it. On the one hand they criticised its failings and tried to improve it; on the other they stood by, ready to support it if it ever seem in danger of defeat.

Shortly before the final vote on the bill, Parnell made a protest in the Commons which led to his being suspended. As a result he was not there to vote, leaving the question of his real opinion of the bill still a mystery.

The Land League falls apart

After the Land Act was passed in September, Parnell's balancing act became more difficult. He called a League Convention to decide what to do. The members agreed neither to approve the Act nor to reject it, but to 'test' it. They asked tenants not to go to the the Land Court but to wait while the League brought a few typical farms to the Court to see if the rents it set were really 'fair'.

13 October 1881: the arrest of Parnell

Meanwhile, Parnell made a number of violent speeches attacking Gladstone. At this point Gladstone's patience gave out. He was convinced that his Act was good for Irish tenants and that Parnell was preventing them from taking advantage of it. On 13 October 1881, he ordered Parnell's arrest.

14 October 1881: the No Rent Manifesto

Along with several hundred other 'suspects', Parnell was lodged in Kilmainham jail. From there, the League leaders issued a **No Rent Manifesto** calling on tenants not to pay rent and to boycott the Land Court until the 'suspects' had been released. Gladstone responded at once by declaring the Land League illegal.

Why did Parnell agree to the No Rent Manifesto?

The more extreme leaders of the League had been urging Parnell for months to issue a No Rent Manifesto and he had always refused. Why had he changed his mind?

It may be that in the enclosed confines of Kilmainham he allowed himself to be convinced by arguments he rejected outside. But it is also possible that Parnell realised that the League was finished. Already the big farmers were flocking to the Land Court while the small farmers were resuming their traditional violence. The morning he was taken to Kilmainham, he wrote to Katharine O'Shea:

> Politically it is a fortunate thing for me that I have been arrested, as the movement is breaking up fast. (F.S.L. Lyons, *Parnell*, p. 175)

He probably guessed that Gladstone would ban the League if the Manifesto were issued. Then the blame for its collapse would fall on the Prime Minister and not on Parnell. Meanwhile he was acquiring the crown of martyrdom by suffering imprisonment for the cause.

(a)

THE RESOURCES OF CIVILISATION.

(b)

TWO FORCES.

Speaking in Leeds in October 1881, Gladstone warned Parnell and the League, 'If there is still to be a final conflict in Ireland . . . then I say without hesitation that the resources of civilization are not yet exhausted'. A few days later he ordered the arrest of Parnell.

Here are two cartoons which appeared after these events. That on the top (a) was Irish, that on the bottom, British (b). Look at them closely and then say a) How the Irish interpreted these events and b) How the British interpreted them.

The Ladies Land League

After the Land League was banned, its work was continued by the **Ladies Land League**. This had been founded in January 1881 by **Anna Parnell**, Charles's sister. Davitt had encouraged them, believing they could take over if the men were arrested. Parnell was much more doubtful. He feared a women's league would bring ridicule on the movement.

A meeting of the Ladies Land League being raided by the police.

When he was arrested, the Ladies Land League had over 300 branches around the country. They organised resistance to evictions and financial help for evicted tenants and the relatives of imprisoned 'suspects'. The Catholic Archbishop of Dublin, Cardinal McCabe, condemned the Ladies Land League for taking women out of their proper place in the home. Several of the women were arrested and sent to jail where, unlike the men, they were treated like ordinary criminals.

Growing chaos

The Ladies League kept the Land League ideals alive in difficult circumstances but they could not restore the old unity. The more prosperous farmers went to the Land Court in large numbers. On average their rents were reduced by 20 per cent. The 100,000 tenants who were unable to go to the Land Court turned to violence.

Land Commissioners visited farms around the country assessing the value of the land and deciding on a fair rent. Here we see them at work on what is clearly a very poor farm near Limerick. On average they reduced rents by 20% but it is unlikely that this reduction helped this farmer much.

Parnell had predicted that if he were arrested 'Captain Moonlight (the old secret societies) would ride again'. He was proved correct. In the six months before he was arrested there were forty-six attacks on individuals; in the six months that he was in Kilmainham (October 1881 to April 1882) the number of attacks rose to seventy-five. Lesser crimes like burning, cattle maiming and sending threatening letters increased even more.

Towards a compromise

By the start of 1882 it was clear to both Gladstone and Parnell that it was time to compromise. The government was not in control of the country and needed Parnell's help to restore order. Parnell, though well treated in prison, needed to get out. Lack of fresh air and exercise affected his health and as long as he was away it was possible that some other MP might take over the leadership of the Home Rule Party.

He also had a very private reason for wanting his freedom. Katharine O'Shea, with whom he had been having an affair since the end of 1880, had had his child while he was in prison. The baby had died and Parnell wanted to be with its grief-stricken mother.

FEBRUARY 18, 1882.]   PUNCH, OR THE LONDON CHARIVARI.   75

ESSENCE OF PARLIAMENT.
EXTRACTED FROM
THE DIARY OF TOBY, M.P.

Governess Gladdy Blarneystone (to Master Paddy, who is still crying for the Moon). "COME AND TELL ITS GLADDY QUIETLY THEN! AND, IF HE CAN'T HAVE IT ALL, HIS GLADDY WILL SEE IF SHE CAN GIVE HIM A LITTLE BIT OF IT!"

TUESDAY, February 7.—This is our opening day, and the way in which the merry, merry men uprose-ye-then was quite surprising. Crowd outside, crowd inside, crowd everywhere. Rush for seats and standing-room. Everyone striving to be first. Genial surprise to RANDOLPH and *his* merry men when, having got up very early in the morning, and swallowed a hasty breakfast, they discovered that Someone had been there before them.

"Sure to be a Scotchman," RANDOLPH growled. "Probably sitting for an Irish Constituency," DRUMMOND remarked, gloomily adjusting his spectacles. So it was. The MACFARLANE, having provided himself with an oat-meal cake and a noggin' o' whiskey, borrowed the daily papers from a friend, and making them into a sort of blanket, covered himself up therewith, and camped out all night in Palace-Yard. As soon as

An English comment on Gladstone's negotiations with the Irish party which led to the Kilmainham Treaty. Read the caption. What does it tell us about the English view of Home Rule in 1882?

2 May 1882: the 'Kilmainham Treaty'

Early in 1882 he entered into indirect negotiations with the government. Katharine's husband, William O'Shea, acted for Parnell, and Joseph Chamberlain, leader of the Radical wing of the Liberal Party, acted for Gladstone.

An agreement was reached. Under the co-called **Kilmainham Treaty** Gladstone promised:

- to amend the Land Act so as to allow lease-holders into the Land Court.

- to help tenants in arrears to pay their rents so they too could go to the Land Court.

- to drop coercion and release the 'suspects'.

In return Parnell promised:

- to try to pacify the country.

- 'to co-operate cordially with the Liberal Party in forwarding liberal principles and measures of general reform'. (Conor Cruise O'Brien, *Parnell and his Party*, p. 77)

On 2 May 1882 Parnell and the 'suspects' were freed from Kilmainham jail. A few days later Davitt was also released.

Chapter 9

1882-85: Building a strong Home Rule party

6 May, 1882: death in the Phoenix Park

The Kilmainham Treaty aroused much opposition. The Fenians disliked it and so did Davitt and the more active MPs like John Dillon.

Some of Gladstone's Liberal followers also opposed any compromise with Parnell and the Land League. One of them was them was the Chief Secretary, W. E. Forster. When the agreement was announced, he resigned in protest. Gladstone replaced him with Lord Frederick Cavendish.

Cavendish arrived in Dublin on 6 May. That evening he and T. H. Burke, the Under Secretary, went for a walk in Phoenix Park where they were set upon and murdered with butchers' knives. The assassins were members of a small secret society, the **Invincibles**. They had broken away from the IRB and had been trying for months to assassinate Forster and Burke. Cavendish had not been their intended target.

The decline of Fenian influence

The murders in the Phoenix Park sent a wave of shock and dismay through Britain

Lord Frederick Cavendish

T.H. Burke

PUNCH, OR THE LONDON CHARIVARI.—May 20, 1882.

THE IRISH FRANKENSTEIN.

"The baneful and blood-stained Monster * * * yet was it not my Master to the very extent that it was my Creature ? * * * Had I not breathed into it my own spirit?" * * * (*Extract from the Works of* C. S. P-RN-LL, M.P.

A famous British comment on the Phoenix Park murders. Several things are worth noting about it: a) Parnell is presented as Dr. Frankenstein who fell victim to a monster of his own creation. What does this tell us about the British view of Parnell and the Land League? b) Look at the way the Irish assassin's face is presented. What does this tell us about British attitudes to the Irish?

and Ireland. Parnell was sure it had ruined everything he had achieved so far. For a time he considered retiring from public life. As things developed, however, the murders actually strengthened him.

The Fenians were discredited by the attack. No one wanted to be associated with people responsible for such a terrible crime. Davitt and other prominent members left and rank and file Fenians drifted into the Home Rule movement. For the next twenty years the IRB ceased to be an important force in Irish politics. Parnell and the Home Rule party were left as the undisputed leaders of the nationalist community in Ireland.

More coercion

The British response to the murders also helped Parnell. Faced with outraged British public opinion, Gladstone had to break his promise to drop coercion. Instead, he introduced a new and harsher act. The Irish united in condemning it and this helped to keep them together.

Parnell's new tactics

Historians argue that the Kilmainham Treaty and the Phoenix Park murders mark a change in Parnell's tactics. From then until the last year of his life he concentrated on constitutional politics and had little contact with revolutionary groups. He was also less interested in the land question. Instead he devoted himself to winning Home Rule by negotiations with the British parties in Westminster. Two decisions Parnell took later in 1882 support this view.

Ending the Ladies Land League

The first was his refusal to back the Ladies Land League which wanted to continue the land war. By cutting off their funds, Parnell forced them to close down. His sister, Anna, was bitterly angry at this decision and never spoke to him again.

October 1882: Parnell sets up the Irish National League

The second was Parnell's rejection of Davitt's advice to revive the Land League. In October 1882 he replaced it with a new movement called the **Irish National League**. Its aims were:

- the establishment of Home Rule.

- the introduction of land purchase.

- reform of local government.

- the introduction of a wider franchise (i.e. giving more people the vote).

- the encouragement of Irish industry.

The order in which these aims were set out shows the change in Parnell's approach. Home Rule rather than land reform was now his first priority.

Unlike the Land League which was a mass movement with revolutionary overtones, the National League was a political party. It had local branches and a central council. Its main purpose was to get MPs elected to parliament where they would work for Home Rule.

The foundation of the National League shows Parnell's victory over the Fenians. They had founded and dominated the Land League, but they were excluded from the National League which was controlled by Parnell. As Davitt said, its foundation was 'the overthrow of a movement and the enthronement of a man'. (Michael Davitt, *The Fall of Feudalism in Ireland*, p. 377-8)

Davitt's plan for land nationalisation

The one man who might have lead an opposition to Parnell was Michael Davitt. But his influence was weakened by the new policy towards the land question which he began to advocate in 1882.

In prison, Davitt had time to read and think. He came to the conclusion that land purchase, which would allow each tenant to buy his farm, was unfair to small farmers and labourers who had little or no land to buy. Instead he argued that the state should take over the landlords' estates and lease the land to all farmers.

Parnell knew that Davitt's proposal for **land nationalisation** would not appeal to Irish farmers. They wanted to own their own farms, not to have the state as their new landlord. He carefully disassociated himself from Davitt's proposal.

Davitt's later career

Davitt disapproved of Parnell's move away from the land agitation but he valued unity highly and in public he remained loyal to Parnell. Although he was on the central council of the National League, he withdrew from active politics. He made his living as a journalist and lecturer. He advocated closer links between factory workers in Britain and small farmers of Ireland, both of whom suffered at the hands of the British ruling class.

Davitt became involved in the Plan of Campaign (see chapter 11) and when the O'Shea divorce case came to court, he was one of the first to speak out against Parnell. He believed that Parnell had lost the moral right to lead and called on him to retire, at least temporarily. In 1892 Davitt was elected as an anti-Parnellite MP and remained in the House of Commons until 1900. He did not like the Commons but did good work on prison reform there.

In his later years he used his journalism to highlight various injustices around the world. These included the case of the Boers in South Africa who were resisting British imperialism and that of the Russian Jews who were suffering pograms at the hands of the Tsarist government. He died in 1906.

1882-85: Parnell withdraws from Ireland

Between 1882 and 1885 Parnell, his health damaged by the months in Kilmainham, played a less active role in politics. His secret affair with Katharine O'Shea, who bore him two more children, and his work in Westminster as leader of the Irish Parliamentary party kept him away from Ireland. He left developments there to his trusted lieutenants on the central committee of the National League.

Parnell's lieutenants build up the National League

The most important of these lieutenants were **Timothy Harrington**, Secretary of the League, **William O'Brien**, editor of Parnell's newspaper *United Ireland* and **Timothy Healy**. Between 1882 and 1885, while Parnell remained in England these men built the National League into a powerful, tightly disciplined political party. It was the first such party in Ireland and one of the first in the world.

1882-86: the spread of the National League

The strength of the National League lay in its network of local branches. Many were taken over from the Land League. By 1886 there were 1,200 League branches spread across the country, though they were least numerous in Ulster.

The Catholic clergy played a prominent role in the local branches. This ensured that the League had the backing of the Catholic Church but it alarmed Protestants. They saw Catholic Church involvement as evidence of the political power which Catholic priests might wield under a Home Rule parliament.

The function of the League branches

League branches had a number of tasks to perform.

- They **collected money**. The National League had £30,000 left over from the land war but the flow of funds from America dried up after the Kilmainham Treaty. League branches organised collections and between 1882 and 1885 they raised over £60,000 in Ireland. This money was used to pay election expenses, reckoned at about £300 per candidate. The League also gave grants to help poor but valuable MPs meet the cost of attending parliament in London.

- Branches **organised the elections** in their areas. They saw to it that voters were registered. They organised meetings and printed election literature. On polling day, they made sure the voters came out to cast their votes for Home Rule candidates.

- Shortly before an election, the branches in each constituency organised a **convention** to pick the Home Rule candidate. Catholic priests were usually prominent at these conventions, often acting as chairmen.

The conventions appeared democratic but in fact they were tightly controlled by the central committee. It had usually picked the candidate in advance and then passed his name on to the local convention. In 1886 Parnell forced a very reluctant Galway convention to nominate Captain O'Shea as their candidate, even though he had refused to take the pledge to work with the party.

Once nominated, a candidate had to take the **party pledge**. It stated:

> I .... pledge myself that, in the event of my election to parliament, I will sit, act and vote with the Irish Parliamentary party, and if, at a meeting of

the party convened upon due notice specially to consider the question, it be decided by a resolution supported by a majority of the entire parliamentary party that I have not fulfilled the above pledge, I hereby undertake to resign my seat. (Conor Cruise O'Brien, *Parnell and his Party*, p. 143)

The party pledge was the greatest innovation of Parnell's Home Rule party. It guaranteed that MPs obeyed him and that he had a **tightly disciplined** and united party behind him in Westminster when he came to negotiate for Home Rule.

1882-1890: the 'uncrowned king'
The spread of the National League is the clearest sign that Parnell had outwitted the Fenians and moved the nationalist movement from a revolutionary to a constitutional path. Its success meant that there was no one left to oppose him. From 1882 till 1890 he was the undisputed leader of the nationalist community in Ireland. MPs like Tim Healy or John Dillon grumbled in secret about his dictatorial ways but until the O'Shea scandal was revealed none of them dared openly to challenge 'the uncrowned king of Ireland'.

1883: the Parnell Testimonial
In 1883, Parnell's popularity was shown in a remarkable way.

When he had inherited his Wicklow estate, he had also inherited heavy debts. His political career, at a time when MPs were not paid, cost him a lot of money. By 1883 he owed £18,000 and he put his estate up for sale to clear his debts.

When word of the sale came out, the National League organised the **Parnell Testimonial** to show the country's appreciation of his work. The Catholic Archbishop of Cashel, Thomas Croke, gave his support, as did many other priests.

This annoyed some of Parnell's opponents, especially the Catholic Archbishop of Dublin, Cardinal McCabe. They persuaded the Pope to condemn the testimonial in May 1883. The reaction was predictable. Money poured in and in the end a cheque for £40,000 was handed over to Parnell.

1882-85: the Liberals and the Home Rulers
After 1882 relations between Gladstone's Liberal government and the Home Rule party were bad. In the Kilmainham Treaty, Parnell had agreed to co-operate with the Liberals if Gladstone dropped coercion, but after the Phoenix Park murders, Gladstone had increased it. The Home Rulers considered this was a breach of faith, so they felt no need to keep their part of the bargain. They continuously attacked his government's policies in Ireland.

1882-84: more Liberal reforms
Despite this, Gladstone brought in a number of important Irish reforms.

- The 1882 **Arrears Act** helped 100,000 of the poorest tenants to pay off their arrears of rent. As a result, they could go to the Land Court to get their rents reduced.

Unfortunately, most of them had such small farms that they found it almost impossible to pay even a reduced rent.

- In 1883 the **Labourers' Dwellings Act** gave grants to local authorities to build cottages for landless labourers who were the poorest section of the community. The local authorities, which were dominated by big farmers, were reluctant to take on the cost involved and few cottages were built.

- The 1883 **Tramways Act** began the building of narrow-gauge railways in western districts. This was aimed at opening up these areas to industry and tourism.

PUNCH, OR THE LONDON CHARIVARI.—June 3, 1882.

" ARREARS."

Pat. " IS IT A *GIFT*, YER HONOUR? SURE, WE WANT IT BADLY, SORR !! "

The British view of the Arrears Act. Read the caption and say what message it gave to British readers. Do you think that was a fair interpretation of the Act?

1884: the Reform Act

The most important of Gladstone's reforms at this time applied to the whole United Kingdom and not just to Ireland. It was the 1884 **Reform Act** which gave the vote to all male householders (i.e. men who owned or rented even a single room).

In Ireland this increased the number of voters from 220,000 to over 700,000. Many of the new voters were poor farmers who supported Parnell. It has been calculated that this reform gained the Home Rule party an extra ten seats in the 1885 general election.

Parnell's tactics

Parnell welcomed these reforms, but for him the only reform that really mattered was Home Rule. Like Butt before him, he hoped to win it by the tactic known as 'independent opposition'. That meant that the Irish MPs would stay independent of the two British parties but would offer to vote for whichever one would agree to give Ireland its own parliament.

This tactic would only work if:

- the Conservatives and Liberals were almost equal in size so that the Irish held the balance of power between them .

- the Irish party was strong and well-disciplined.

Between 1880 and 1885 the Liberals had a clear majority in the Commons and did not need the Irish votes. In any case, Parnell had less than fifty MPs in his party and this left him in a weak bargaining position.

1885: considering Home Rule

Up to 1885 neither the Liberals nor the Conservatives would even contemplate Home Rule for Ireland. But this began to change in 1885. By then British politicians expected that Parnell's party would gain many more seats in the next general election, thanks to the work of the National League and the extra voters created by the 1884 Reform Act. Even before the election, some men in both parties began to make overtures to Parnell in the hope of gaining his backing afterwards, should they need it.

Liberal quarrels

By 1885 the Liberal party was deeply divided. Quarrels flared up over imperial policy, over the succession to Gladstone who was now seventy-five years old and over the best way to deal with Ireland.

The right wing of the party, led by **Lord Hartington,** (the brother of Lord Frederick Cavendish) wanted to keep the Coercion Act. On the other hand, the Radicals disliked coercion. If Parnell won a majority of Irish seats in the next general election, they asked, would it be right for Britain to go on holding down the Irish in that way?

1884-85: Joseph Chamberlain and the Central Board plan

The leading Radical was **Joseph Chamberlain**. He hoped to work out some way, short of Home Rule, of letting the Irish run their own affairs. Late in 1884, he drew up a plan for elected county councils, with a **Central Board** chosen by these councils, to deal with some Irish issues. He gave his plan to Captain O'Shea and asked him to show it to Parnell.

Parnell told O'Shea that he was prepared to consider Chamberlain's Central Board idea as a step towards Home Rule but not, he emphasised, instead of it. Unfortunately, O'Shea did not make this clear to Chamberlain who thought that Parnell had accepted his plan. When Parnell made it clear that he had not, Chamberlain felt let down and became less sympathetic to Ireland.

9 June 1885: Gladstone' government falls

Although Parnell turned down Chamberlain's plan, it pleased him because it showed that some Liberal MPs were willing to consider self-government for Ireland. At the same time, Conservatives were also seeking the support of the Irish. In the Commons, Conservative and Irish MPs joined together to attack the Liberal government. On 9 June 1885 they defeated Gladstone and he resigned.

June 1885-January 1886: Salisbury's minority government

Normally when a government falls there is a general election but this was not possible in June 1885. The 1884 Reform Act led to the re-drawing of constituency boundaries all over the United Kingdom and this was still going on. Therefore, an agreement was reached to allow the Conservative leader, **Lord Salisbury**, to become a caretaker Prime Minister until the election could be held in November.

Conservative concessions to Parnell

To form his government, Salisbury needed Parnell's votes. He secured them by making a number of concessions to the Irish.

- **Lord Carnarvon**, a Conservative who was well known for supporting Home Rule for Ireland, was made Lord Lieutenant.

- The Coercion Act was allowed to lapse.

- A Conservative minister, **Lord Ashbourne**, brought in the first full **Land Purchase Act**. Under it, the government lent £5 million to Irish tenants to enable them to buy their farms. Unlike earlier purchase arrangements, the Ashbourne Act lent tenants the full purchase price and the period of repayment was forty-nine years. The Ashbourne Act was very popular, especially with farmers in Ulster. Under it 25,000 tenant farmers became owners of their farms.

June – November 1885: Parnell's negotiations

These concessions were useful but the only one that really mattered was Home Rule. Could Parnell persuade one of the British parties to agree to it?

He seemed in a strong bargaining position. Both Liberals and Conservatives needed his votes in the Commons. They also needed the votes of the Irish living in Britain who would support whichever party Parnell recommended. During the months before the general election was held, he tried to negotiate with them.

The Conservatives seemed the more promising. The Prime Minister, Lord Salisbury, refused to meet Parnell, but Lord Carnarvon did and he sounded encouraging. Another leading Conservative, **Lord Randolph Churchill**, hinted in secret talks that he was sympathetic to Home Rule. The problem for Parnell was: did these men represent the whole of the Conservative party or were they just speaking for themselves? It was impossible to say.

PUNCH, OR THE LONDON CHARIVARI.—JANUARY 30, 1886.

THE LIVE SHELL.

(WHICH OF 'EM WILL THROW IT OVERBOARD?)

The two British leaders, Gladstone and Salisbury wondering what to do about the Irish question.

102

The Liberals were equally mysterious. Chamberlain continued to talk about his Central Board plan but Parnell dismissed him rudely. He was more concerned with Gladstone, but the Liberal leader refused to discuss Home Rule until after the election. He claimed later that he had decided in favour of Home Rule but was waiting to see what the Conservatives would do. Parnell, however, did not know that.

21 November 1885: Parnell's choice

At last Parnell had to make his choice. He came down in favour of the Conservatives. He may have been influenced by Carnarvon and Churchill but he may also have remembered that that party controlled the House of Lords. If the Conservatives backed Home Rule it would pass through the Lords; if they did not, it would fail.

On 21 November 1885 Parnell called on the Irish in Britain to vote for Conservative candidates. It is impossible to know how many of them did but it has been estimated that this won about twenty-five extra seats for the Conservatives.

November 1885: the general election

In Ireland the election was a triumph for Parnell and the National League. The Home Rule party won eighty-five of the Irish seats and one in Liverpool. Apart from Trinity College which elected two Unionists, Home Rulers won every seat in Leinster,

Parnell surrounded by his 85 M.P.s after their triumph in the 1885 election.

Munster and Connaught. Only in east Ulster, where sixteen Unionist MPs were elected, was there a solid block of opposition to them.

In Britain the election results were disappointing for Parnell. The Liberals won **335 seats** and the Conservatives **249 seats**. The gap between the two was eighty-six, exactly the same number as the Home Rule party. This weakened Parnell's bargaining position. By combining his votes with the Liberals, he could make Gladstone Prime Minister, but he could not do the same for Salisbury. He was no longer of any use to the Conservatives.

16 December, 1885: the Hawarden Kite

After the election, events moved quickly. On 16 December Gladstone's son, speaking at the family's home in Hawarden, told the press that his father was impressed by the large majority in Ireland in favour of Home Rule and intended to bring in a Home Rule bill.

27 January 1886: fall of Salisbury. Gladstone returns as Prime Minister

Following this, Salisbury let it be known that he intended to re-introduce coercion when parliament met again. This broke up the alliance between Parnell and the Conservatives. When Parliament met in January 1886 Parnell supported Gladstone, who became Prime Minister once more. Home Rule, it seemed, was on the way.

Different reactions in Ireland

News of these developments produced great rejoicing in the nationalist community in Ireland. Here at last was the goal towards which they had been working for so long.

But there was another community for whom Home Rule would spell disaster. They were the unionists. How they reacted to these developments we will see in the next chapter.

Chapter 10

1885-86: The emergence of the Unionist party and the defeat of Home Rule

Unionist security

As we mentioned earlier, (page 51), there were always people in Ireland who supported the Union. Most of them were Protestants. They preferred to belong to the United Kingdom, with its Protestant majority, than to an independent Ireland where Catholics would predominate.

Until the early 1880s most of these people felt secure. Both British parties, the Liberals and the Conservatives, were determined to uphold the Union and Home Rule could never come without their approval. For that reason, Irish unionists supported either Liberals or Conservatives and did not bother to form a party of their own. However, this situation changed suddenly in 1885-86, and it was the unionists in the south who were the first to react.

The southern unionists

In the three southern provinces (Leinster, Munster and Connaught) Protestants were not very numerous (see Table A). But they made up for their small numbers by being economically powerful. Most landlords, some of the biggest tenant farmers and many business and professional people were Protestant and unionist. Some of them were members of the House of Lords, such as the Earl of Mayo, who was a landlord, or Lord Iveagh, who was head of the Guinness company.

In the 1850s and 1860s, when only well off people could vote, these wealthy and powerful men dominated elections and backed either the Liberal or the Conservative party.

Distribution of religion in 1871				
	Catholic	Church of Ireland	Presbyterian	Other
Leinster	85%	12%	0.9%	1%
Munster	93%	5%	0.3%	0.8%
Connaught	95%	4%	0.4%	0.4%
Ulster	49%	22%	26%	3%

Table A ▲

The Irish Loyal and Patriotic Union

As long the two British parties supported the Union, the southern unionists felt safe. But after 1885 Parnell's party grew in strength and to their alarm some Liberals and Conservatives began to talk about giving Ireland Home Rule. (see page 100)

To fight this development, southern unionists formed **the Irish Loyal and Patriotic Union** in 1885. In the November general election, they put up fifty-two candidates but only won 31,700 votes compared with the 231,400 cast for Home Rule. Apart from the two MPs representing Trinity College, a unionist stronghold, not a single unionist MP was elected in the south. The southern unionists had to fall back on their position in the House of Lords and on their friends in the two British parties to block Home Rule.

The Ulster unionists

In Ulster, unionists were in a much stronger position. In that province, just over 50 per cent of the population was Protestant. They belonged to all classes – farmers, landlords and labourers, factory owners and factory workers, shopkeepers and professionals. They were most numerous in the eastern half of the province, least numerous in the west.

Up to the 1880s the Protestant community in Ulster was divided by religion and

A great Unionist demonstration in Belfast. Only in Ulster could the unionists have produced such a large body of support. Elsewhere they were in a small minority.

by class but these divisions began to disappear as various reforms took effect. This made it easier for them to join together to fight Home Rule.

Religious divisions: Anglicans and Presbyterians

About half of Ulster Protestants were **Anglicans** who belonged to the Church of Ireland. This Church had enjoyed a privileged position until it was disestablished by Gladstone in 1869. Most Anglicans supported the Conservative party.

The other big group in the Protestant community were the **Presbyterians**. Like the Catholics, they resented the privileges which the Anglicans enjoyed. Both Catholics and Presbyterians in Ulster voted for the Liberal Party which had disestablished the Church of Ireland in 1869. This ended the privileged position of the Anglicans and removed one of the divisions within the Protestant community.

Class divisions: landlords and tenants

In country areas in Ulster, as in the rest of Ireland, the land belonged to landlords and was rented by tenant farmers who were both Catholic and Protestant. Almost all landlords were Protestant but that did not mean they always got on well with their Protestant tenants.

In the 1850s and 1860s Ulster tenant farmers were just as keen on the Three Fs as farmers elsewhere in Ireland and in the depression of the late 1870s they found it just as hard to pay their rents. The Land League spread to Ulster and, though few Protestant tenants joined it, they supported its aims and welcomed Gladstone's 1881 Land Act.

But once that Act was passed, the situation changed. With the Three Fs won, Protestant tenants had the security they wanted. Now they felt they had more in common with their Protestant landlords than with fellow tenants who were Catholics.

Ulster Protestants' growing fear of Home Rule

After 1882 Parnell, as we saw, turned his attention from land reform to Home Rule. As his National League grew in strength, spreading even into Ulster, Protestants, whether Anglican or Presbyterian, landlord or tenant, watched with dismay.

- They saw that Catholic priests played a key role in the party branches. They asked if priests would have the same amount of power in a Catholic-dominated, Home Rule parliament?

- Would Home Rule, they wondered, be Rome Rule, with Catholic bishops telling Catholic MPs how to vote?

- Might Irish Protestants not lose their civil and religious liberty if Home Rule was granted?

Faced with the growing power of the Home Rule party and the growing threat of Catholic domination, Protestants throughout Ulster sank their differences and joined together in support of the Union.

The economic reasons for unionism

There was another reason, apart from religion, why Ulster Protestants supported the Union. It had to do with the development of industry. (see pages 39 & 40)

By 1880 the area around Belfast had became a major industrial region, the only one in Ireland. Unlike the rest of the country, jobs were plentiful. People worked in the linen mills, in shipbuilding and engineering, in building and transport.

The economy and the Union

The growth and prosperity of Belfast depended on its links with Britain.

- Much of the capital for its industry came from Britain.

- The raw materials like coal and iron came from Britain.

- The linen and ships that Belfast produced were sold mainly in Britain or the British Empire.

Anything that broke the link with Britain would endanger Belfast's prosperity. Many people in Ulster feared that a Home Rule parliament would interfere with that link.

They had reason to worry. Parnell said that an Irish parliament must protect Irish industry. He was thinking about the south where industry was in decline and may have needed protection. But Belfast's industry did not need to be protected. It only needed the free access to Britain which the Union guaranteed. This fact ensured that both Protestant businessmen and their Protestant workers became committed unionists.

The Orange Order

Protestant alarm at the growth of the Home Rule movement led to the revival of the **Orange Order**. This sectarian organisation was founded in the 1790s but had been in decline for many years. It began to revive around 1880, first to oppose the Land League, then Home Rule. Its aim was to uphold the Protestant constitution of the United Kingdom with its Protestant monarch.

The Order was spread through Ulster, with some branches in the south as well. In each town and village, the Orange hall provided a place where unionist men of all classes could meet to oppose the common enemy.

The Order organised demonstrations, the most famous being the annual marches associated with Protestant victories over Catholics, like the seventeenth-century siege of Derry or the Battle of the Boyne. These demonstrations, which became increasingly political, gave the Protestant community a sense of unity and strength in the face of what they saw as the Catholic nationalist threat.

January 1886: the foundation of the Irish Unionist party

When the general election was held in November 1885, Ulster Protestants were still divided between Conservatives and Liberals. Together they won only sixteen of the thirty-three seats in Ulster, while the Home Rule party won seventeen.

But the shock of the 'Hawarden Kite' in December, when Gladstone's son announced his father's conversion to Home Rule, drove all Ulster Protestants into one camp. In January 1886 Ulster unionists combined to form the **Ulster Loyalist Anti-Repeal Union**.

It grew rapidly and some of its members began to talk of opposing Home Rule by force if necessary. Meanwhile, urged on by the Orange Order, Irish Conservative and Liberal MPs met in Dublin and agreed to form a **Unionist party** in parliament. They chose as their leader a wealthy landlord from Co. Cavan, **E.J. Saunderson**.

April 1886: Gladstone's first Home Rule Bill

Gladstone finally laid his Home Rule bill before parliament in April 1886. Under it:

- Ireland was to have its own parliament in Dublin consisting of two houses.

- this parliament was to elect the Irish government.

- it would deal with all Irish affairs *except* the Crown, defence, war and peace, trade and navigation, coinage, the post office and colonial relations. These would still be under the control of the Westminster parliament.

- there would be no Irish MPs in Westminster.

- Ireland would pay one-fifteenth of the Imperial budget.

By modern standards the bill gave Ireland only a very limited amount of control over its own affairs. But it aroused enormous hostility it Britain.

Colonel Edward Saunderson (1837-1906) was the first leader of the Irish Unionist party. Elected a Liberal MP in 1865, he left the party over the Disestablishment of the Church of Ireland and became a Conservative. In 1882 he joined the Orange Order to fight against Home Rule and in 1885 was elected MP for North Armagh. He led the Unionists until his death in 1906.

THE GLADSTONE NEW YEAR CARD TRICK; OR, ONE UP HIS SLEEVE!

A cynical view of Gladstone's 'conversion' to Home Rule as displayed by the Hawarden Kite. Do you think the cynicism is justified? Was Gladstone simply hungry for power and in need of Parnell's votes, or did he genuinely believe in Home Rule? What do you think? Give reasons for your answer.

British Unionism

There were many reasons why British people opposed Home Rule for Ireland.

- Defence

Many British people saw Home Rule as a first step towards full Irish independence. They feared that an independent Ireland would join with Britain's enemies in a war and provide a back-door through which they might invade Britain.

People who felt this way pointed to a speech Parnell made in Cork in January 1885 in which he said: 'No man has the right to set bounds to the march of a nation. No man can say to his country "thus far shalt thou go and no further".' They asked if this meant that he wanted full separation from Britain.

During the debate on the Home Rule bill, Parnell assured the Commons that he wanted no more than Home Rule. But many in Britain refused to believe him. They also pointed out that even if Parnell was sincere, he could not speak for future leaders of the nationalist community who might go on to separate Ireland from Britain. The best way to prevent this from happening, they believed, was to keep Ireland in the Union.

- Economy

Ireland was an important customer for British exports. If Ireland was cut off from Britain this valuable market might be lost.

- Imperialism

In the 1880s the British empire was expanding and many British people were enthusiastic imperialists. They feared that Irish independence might undermine the unity and strength of the empire.

- Concern for Irish unionists

Many British people felt a sense of identity with Irish unionists. They did not want to leave them to the mercy of a Catholic-dominated Irish parliament.

- Anti-Irish attitudes

Some British people considered that Irish Catholics were backward and unfit to rule themselves. This racist view of the Irish was strengthened by recent episodes such as violence during the land war and the Phoenix Park murders.

The Conservatives and the 'Orange Card'

The Conservatives led the opposition to Home Rule. They were deeply divided on many issues and this was something on which they could unite.

Lord Randolph Churchill, who only months before had hinted to Parnell that he might favour Home Rule, now came out as a leading unionist. He realised that the best way to block Home Rule was to join with the Irish unionists. 'The Orange Card,'

A British view of what a Dublin parliament would be like. Anti-Irish prejudice, such as that shown here played a part in defeating Home Rule.

he declared when he heard of Gladstone's decision to bring in a Home Rule bill, 'is the one to play.'

Churchill went to Belfast and in a speech to a unionist rally told them that 'Ulster will fight and Ulster will be right'. He promised them the backing of the Conservative party in any action they took to oppose Home Rule. The newly formed Irish Unionist party became a part of the Conservative party which changed its name to the 'Conservative and Unionist party'.

The Liberal unionists

Some leading members of Gladstone's own party were also opposed to Home Rule. They became known as the **Liberal Unionists**.

Joseph Chamberlain was one of their leaders. He was a reformer who wanted to make Ireland more democratic and more efficiently run, but he was also an imperialist. He believed that the British Empire was a civilising force in the world and he feared that Irish independence would undermine it.

Chamberlain was also annoyed by the way Parnell had rejected his proposal to set up Irish councils and by Gladstone's failure to consult him on his plans for Home Rule. These personal resentments contributed to his opposition to Home Rule.

Anti-Home Rule riots in Belfast in the summer of 1886 caused fifty deaths.

8 June 1886: the defeat of Home Rule

When the House of Commons came to vote on the Home Rule bill, ninety-three members of Gladstone's party voted against him. The bill was defeated. At once Gladstone called a new general election. There was only one issue before the voters in Britain and Ireland: did they or did they not agree to Home Rule for Ireland?

In Ireland the election changed nothing. The Home Rule party again won eighty-five seats and the Unionist party won eighteen.

In Britain however the result was very different. The Conservatives and the Liberal unionists between them won a clear majority. Gladstone resigned and Lord Salisbury again became Prime Minister. He and his Conservative party were now committed to maintaining the Union and to opposing the demand for Home Rule.

The results of 1885-86

The months between June 1885 and June 1886 are among the most important in Irish history.

- For the first time one of the British parties had accepted the idea of ending the Union and giving Ireland its own parliament.

- When the Liberals agreed to Home Rule, Parnell and the Home Rule party lost

Supplement Gratis with **THE UNION.** *December 24th, 1887.*

THE UNION TRIUMPH, 1887.

LORD SALISBURY

SURROUNDED BY THE HEROES OF THE DAY—

J. CHAMBERLAIN
COLONEL SAUNDERSON
JOHN BRIGHT
LORD HARTINGTON

W. H. SMITH.
A. J. BALFOUR.
G. J. GOSCHEN.
LORD R. CHURCHILL.

THE UNION FOR EVER.

An illustration of the triumph of unionism, with Lord Salisbury leading them and the heroes of unionism clustered round him.

their independence. No longer could they go from Liberal to Conservative, offering their votes to whichever party would grant Home Rule. Even though they liked to pretend otherwise, the tactic of **independent opposition** was dead. It was replaced by the **Liberal alliance** which was now the only way to get Home Rule. How this limited the freedom of the Home Rule party became very clear at the time of the O'Shea divorce case when Gladstone was able to force the Irish party to choose between its leader and Home Rule.

- 1885-6 also saw the emergence of the Unionist party to replace the Liberals and Conservatives in Ireland. From 1886 onwards, the Unionist party was the voice of the Irish Protestant community as the Home Rule party was the voice of the Irish Catholics.

- In the 1885 election, Ireland was divided into two distinct areas, one represented by Home Rulers, the other by unionists. (see map) With only minor variations, this remained the pattern of elections in Ireland until the country was partitioned in 1920. In many ways, this year could be seen as the moment when the partition of Ireland began.

- In Britain too this was an important year. The Liberal party which had dominated British politics since the 1860s had split on the question of Home Rule. This weakened it and for the next twenty years, the Conservatives were the dominant party. And as long as this was the case, Home Rule was impossible.

Results of the 1885 election.

115

Chapter 11

1886-90: The Plan of Campaign

Conservative rule
After Gladstone's defeat in 1886, the Conservatives under **Lord Salisbury** formed the government, but they had no Irish policy apart from opposing Home Rule and re-introducing coercion. For several months they did nothing. Soon, however, a new agricultural crisis forced them to rethink their negative approach.

The long depression in Britain
The economic depression which had begun in the mid-1870s grew deeper in the late 1880s. In Britain it left 22 per cent of the population unemployed and reduced the wages of those who had work. As a result, British demand for Irish agricultural produce was low and prices continued to fall.

A new agricultural crisis in Ireland
By 1885 Irish farmers were as badly off as they had been before the 1881 Land Act. The Land Court, set up under this Act, had cut rents by 20 per cent, but as prices fell these new judicial rents (i.e. set by the Land Court) became too high for many small farmers to pay. In 1885 over 3,000 families were served with eviction notices.

1885-86: land agitation recurs
In the winter of 1885-6 some farmers resisted eviction by sending threatening letters, maiming cattle, burning crops and attacking landlords and their agents. Parnell and the National League feared such violence might damage the delicate negotiations for Home Rule and they managed to restrain it.

But once the Home Rule bill was defeated the need for restraint was gone. In parliament Parnell introduced a bill to reduce judicial rents. It was defeated. **John Dillon**, the tenants' most outspoken champion among the Home Rule MPs, stormed out of the Commons declaring:

> I go to tell the tenant that if he wishes to live he must trust to his own exertions.
> (F. S. L. Lyons, *John Dillon*, p. 81)

Dillon returned to Ireland where he organised a new land campaign with **Timothy Harrington** and **William O'Brien**, both leading members of the National League. Parnell himself played little part in it. After the exertions of the last year, his health had worsened and he retired to live quietly with Katharine O'Shea.

This drawing was used to illustrate a newspaper report of a violent incident in Cork when a tenant who co-operated with his landlord was beaten up and his dog killed. Incidents like this became common when economic conditions led to an increase in evictions.

October 1886: proposal for a 'Plan of Campaign'

On 23 October 1886 the League's paper *United Ireland* published an article by Harrington, entitled '**A Plan of Campaign**'. It set out the tactics which the tenants should follow in order to force landlords to reduce their rents.

- All the tenants on an estate should agree among themselves how much rent they could afford to pay (e.g. 15 or 20 per cent less than the judicial rent).

- They should go together to the landlord and offer him that rent.

- If he refused to take it, they should pay him nothing but should lodge what they had offered in an estate fund.

- If the landlord evicted any tenants, this fund should be used to support the families. Meanwhile, their farms were to be left empty and anyone who rented them should be boycotted. Without his income, the landlord would have to give in and reduce his rents.

- Harrington promised that the National League would help evicted tenants when the estate fund ran out.

The Plan was first tried at Woodford, Co. Galway on the estate of the miserly Earl of Clanricarde, whose rents were very high. Four hundred tenants, led by bands and banners, marched into Portumna to hear O'Brien and Dillon explain the Plan. They then went to the agent's office and demanded that rents be cut by 40 per cent. When this was refused, they withdrew and paid their money to Dillon and O'Brien.

Parnell stops the Plan

The Plan spread quickly and by December it was in operation on 116 estates. At this point, Parnell intervened. He feared that a new land war would alarm English Liberals whose support he needed to get Home Rule.

He ordered O'Brien to stop the Plan. When O'Brien protested that the tenants depended on them, he changed his mind. The Plan could continue wherever it was already in operation, but it must spread no further. O'Brien and Dillon were resentful of Parnell's intervention but they obeyed him.

1887: Arthur Balfour becomes Chief Secretary

At first the Conservative government was unsure what to do about this new agitation but early in 1887 Lord Salisbury appointed a new Chief Secretary to deal with it. The man he chose was his nephew, **Arthur Balfour**. A young man at the start of his political career, Balfour had very definite ideas of how to deal with the Plan. He declared:

> I shall be as relentless as Cromwell in enforcing obedience to the law, but, at the same time, I shall be as radical as any reformer in redressing grievances and especially in removing every cause of complaint in regard to the land. (L. P. Curtis, *Coercion and Conciliation in Ireland*, p. 179)

Tenants refusing to pay the rent.

The Conservative government had difficulty deciding what to do about Ireland as this cartoon from September 1886 shows. The little man on the table is Randolph Churchill. The big man watching him gloomily is the Prime Minister, Lord Salisbury.

Like Gladstone with the Land League, Balfour used a two-pronged approach to the Plan:

- win over tenants by removing the grievances which led them to support it.
- at the same time destroy it by removing its leaders.

But he was much more ruthless than Gladstone had ever been.

Arthur Balfour when he became Chief Secretary.

1887: amending the 1881 Land Act

One of Balfour's first actions was to amend Gladstone's 1881 Land Act. Under that Act, a tenant could go to the Land Court to have a judicial rent set every fifteen years. Balfour reduced this interval to three years. As a result, rents were again reduced, this time by an average of 15 per cent. Balfour also allowed the 100,000 lease-holders to go to the Land Court for the first time.

1887: Balfour's Perpetual Crimes Act

Balfour's tough policy began with the **Perpetual Crimes Act**. It allowed the Lord Lieutenant:

- to declare that certain organisations were illegal.

- to 'proclaim' districts where disturbances were taking place.

- In a 'proclaimed' district, people accused of offences like boycotting or encouraging tenants to resist an eviction, were tried by a magistrate sitting without a jury. If he found them guilty, the magistrate had to impose a jail sentence.

Under the Crimes Act, many Plan agitators, including twenty-four MPs, were imprisoned. Unlike Gladstone's suspects who were allowed wear their own clothes and have their own food in prison, these men were treated like ordinary criminals. Some, like William O'Brien, refused to co-operate by wearing prison clothes and were roughly treated. One man, John Mandeville, died soon after his release.

Under the Crimes Act a politician could be arrested for inciting a crowd to boycott someone. Here, at a Plan meeting, a government agent surrounded by police makes notes of the speech so that a prosecution could later be brought.

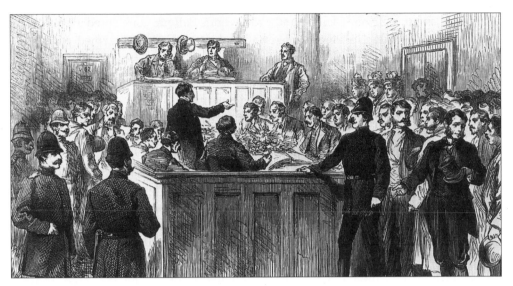

William O'Brien on trial in Mitchelstown before three Resident Magistrates. He got six months in jail.

April 1888: the Pope's intervention

Balfour did not rely on acts of parliament alone. He knew that some Catholic bishops disapproved of the Plan and he encouraged them to ask the Pope to condemn it. The British government also sent representatives to Rome to let the Pope know of its wishes. In April 1888 Pope Leo XIII, anxious to please a great power, issued a **Papal Rescript**, condemning boycotting and the Plan of Campaign and ordering priests not to take part.

Nationalists were outraged. The Catholic members of the Home Rule party met and resolved that:

> We, as guardians, in common with our brother representatives of other creeds, of those civil liberties which our Catholic forefathers have resolutely defended, feel bound solemnly to reassert that Irish Catholics can recognise no right in the Holy See to interfere with the Irish people in the management of their political affairs. (Conor Cruise O'Brien, *Parnell and his Party*, p. 222)

The Pope's Rescript had no effect on the Plan.

Balfour and evictions

Balfour also decided to fight the Plan, using its own weapons. For this he needed the co-operation of Irish landlords but he found them a disappointing lot. On eighty-four of the 116 estates on which the Plan had been implemented, the landlord gave in to the tenants. Others who stood up to the Plan, like the Earl of Clanrickard, were bad landlords who had treated their tenants harshly. Balfour had no wish to be allied to such men and he put pressure on them to make a deal with their tenants.

But on about a dozen estates landlords whom Balfour considered decent men were still holding out. He concentrated on helping them. He sent armed police and even soldiers to assist at evictions.

1887-8: eviction scenes win sympathy for the tenants

Tenants, urged on by the Plan leaders, often resisted eviction by barricading themselves in their houses. The police had to force their way in, sometimes after a siege lasting several days.

These scenes attracted journalists and news photographers, whose cameras were only recently able to take action pictures. Their photographs of British police and soldiers battering down the doors of little mud cabins were printed around the world. (The two pictures on page 123 are examples of this.) The journalists wrote vivid accounts of the evictions. Some British Liberal MPs attended evictions and a few were arrested and sent to prison under the Crimes Act.

The pictures and the reports aroused sympathy in Britain for the plight of Irish tenants. They also embarrassed the government. Balfour realised that this part of his policy was not helping his case and and he had to ease it off.

The landlords fight back

A more successful strategy was to encourage the landlords to fight the Plan with its own weapons – money and unity. In Youghal, Co. Cork a landlord called **Charles Ponsonby** had resisted the Plan, but he was about to give in because of lack of funds. Balfour decided to help him. He secretly encouraged several wealthy landlords to contribute £10,000 each to a landlord syndicate, headed by the Tipperary landlord, **Arthur Smith-Barry**.

The syndicate bought the Ponsonby estate and evicted most of the tenants. Because it had money, it could leave farms empty and pay labourers to come and work the land. The estate fund which the tenants had collected soon ran out and the burden of supporting them fell on the National League.

'New Tipperary'

The Plan's leaders soon heard about Smith-Barry's role in the syndicate. They encouraged the tenants on his Tipperary estate to stop paying their rents as a protest. They too were evicted, along with most of the population of the market town of Tipperary. William O'Brien then organised the building of a village called 'New Tipperary' to house the evicted families.

1890: the Plan runs into difficulties

New Tipperary alone cost the League £50,000 and by 1889 they were spending £3,600 a month to support about 1,000 evicted families. These activities bled the League's funds dry and by 1889 it was deeply in debt.

These two photographs were among the many that conveyed the stark reality of evictions. In one an RIC man supervises the operation of a battering ram. In the other an evicted family sits beside their pathetically few possessions in front of their boarded up house.

The leaders appealed to Parnell. He received them coldly, pointing out that the Plan had not been his idea. In the end, however, he agreed to back an appeal for funds. Within months it collected £61,000. This money, together with contributions from America and Australia, helped the fight to continue in some estates for the next few years.

But more was needed. In 1890 Harrington, Dillon and O'Brien decided on a fund-raising trip to the United States. To gain publicity they made some inflammatory speeches, were arrested under the Crimes Act and then jumped bail. They were in the US when the Parnell scandal broke.

The results of the Plan

The split over the O'Shea divorce case (see chapter 12) diverted attention away from the Plan and from the plight of the evicted tenants. This makes it difficult to assess the results of the Plan. However, it was possible for both sides to claim some degree of success.

Balfour's gains

- Balfour could claim that his tough policy had quietened the country. In 1886 there were 1,056 violent crimes reported; in 1889 there were only 535. In January 1887 4,900 persons were boycotted; in January 1891 not one person was.

- Balfour's policies cost the National League at least £200,000 which might otherwise have been spent campaigning for Home Rule.

Gains for the Home Rulers

- On the other hand, the National League could claim that the Conservative's tough policy made tenant farmers in the south more determined than ever to demand Home Rule.

- Despite Parnell's fears, the agitation resulting from the Plan of Campaign strengthened the links between British Liberals and the Home Rule party. The news reports, the pictures, the speeches of MPs who witnessed evictions, all won sympathy for the Irish cause. By 1890 it seemed likely that the next election would produce a Liberal victory and with it a Home Rule bill.

- During the Plan of Campaign Irish MPs pointed out that all Irish tenant farmers wanted were the same rights which British trade unionists enjoyed – the right to bargain collectively for better conditions. This helped to win support for Home Rule from the growing labour movement in Britain.

The plight of the tenant farmers

Whoever won the Plan of Campaign one thing is certain: the evicted tenants lost. Many of them had to depend on the funds supplied by the National League. When the Parnellite split occurred, these funds got caught up in the in-fighting between the two sides and little money reached the tenants. The politicians lost interest in them and it was not until 1907 that the last of the tenants evicted under the Plan were restored to their farms.

Chapter 12

1886-91: Parnell's years of triumph and disaster

1886-90: Parnell in England

After 1886 Parnell seldom visited Ireland. He left affairs here to Dillon, O'Brien and Harrington. This development, along with his opposition to the Plan of Campaign, caused resentment among some party members but he remained as popular as ever with nationalist voters.

Between 1886 and 1890 he stayed in England where he concentrated on leading the Home Rule party in parliament. He worked to improve relations with the Liberals. Any hope of achieving Home Rule depended on his alliance with them.

1887: 'Parnellism and Crime'

In 1887 the Liberal alliance appeared in danger when the London *Times* published a series of articles under the title **'Parnellism and Crime'**. The articles claimed that Parnell had known and approved of the Phoenix Park murders and backed this up with letters which, they said, he had written at the time.

1887-89: the Times Commission

Parnell scornfully denied the accusation but the Conservative government, anxious to discredit him, set up a Commission to look into links between the Fenians and the Home Rule and land movements. It sat for months. Many witnesses, including Davitt and Parnell, were called before it and questioned about their involvement in the Land League. Parnell himself was remarkably evasive and forgetful about his meetings with John Devoy and other Fenians ten years before.

1889: Parnell vindicated

For most people the climax of the Commission came during the evidence of a Dublin journalist, **Richard Pigott**. Under skilful cross-examination, he was shown to have forged the letters which implicated Parnell. Pigott confessed, then fled and killed himself in Madrid.

It was a triumph for Parnell. When he returned to the Commons, Gladstone led a standing ovation in which the whole Liberal party joined. He invited Parnell to his home at Hawarden, where in December 1889 the two leaders discussed the contents of the next Home Rule bill. Parnell had never been so popular in Britain and the Liberal alliance looked stronger than ever.

24 December 1889: William O'Shea sues for divorce

Parnell left Hawarden on 19 December. Five days later William O'Shea filed for divorce from his wife, Katharine, and named Parnell as co-respondent.

1880-91 Parnell and Katharine O'Shea

Parnell's love affair with Katharine O'Shea had lasted since 1880 and they had three children. It is most unlikely that O'Shea had not known what was going on. Gladstone, many leading British MPs and some of the Home Rule MPs were certainly aware of it, though, as long as it remained private, they raised no objection. Why, then, did O'Shea wait until 1889 before suing for divorce?

Many of Parnell's supporters at the time believed that Chamberlain and Parnell's other enemies, defeated in the *Times* Commission, had put him up to it. This is possible but no evidence to prove it conclusively has ever come to light.

The Woods' inheritance

Katharine O'Shea's explanation – given in an interview years later (in H. Harrison, *Parnell Vindicated*) – was that O'Shea hoped to get part of a legacy she expected from her wealthy aunt, Mrs Woods. Katharine was a great favourite with her aunt who had been keeping her and the good-for-nothing William for years.

But when Mrs Woods died in 1889, her money was left in trust. This made it impossible for Katharine to use it to buy William off. When some cousins decided to contest Mrs Woods' will, O'Shea agreed to co-operate with them. After the divorce, they won their case and Katharine lost her inheritance.

Katharine O'Shea in 1880 when she met Parnell for the first time.

First reaction to the case

In Ireland public opinion at first supported Parnell. Many believed it was another plot to discredit him. He assured members of the party that he would escape without a stain on his character and such was their trust in him that they accepted this assurance. It is not quite clear what he meant. Perhaps, since he considered himself morally married to Katharine already, he thought the divorce irrelevant.

1890: the case in court

The case finally came to court late in 1890. To everyone's surprise, Parnell did not contest it. He wanted to marry Katharine and if the divorce had been contested, she would have stayed married to O'Shea. Unfortunately this meant that only O'Shea's side of the case was presented in court. He was able to portray Parnell as the heartless adulterer who had broken up a marriage and betrayed his loyal follower. The divorce was granted on 17 November.

November 1890: Irish and British reaction

Even then, very few people in Ireland questioned Parnell's position. Several party meetings endorsed his leadership. The only prominent person to demand his resignation was Davitt and even he suggested no more than a temporary retirement to allow the scandal to quieten down.

In Britain, however, the reaction was different. Liberal party branches all over the country urged Gladstone to cut his links with 'the adulterer'. Preachers in Protestant chapels, and newspapers usually sympathetic to the Liberals, all joined in the attack. It was clear to the Liberals that they would lose votes if they remained in alliance with an Irish party led by Parnell.

25 November: the party re-elects Parnell

On 25 November the Home Rule party was due to hold its annual leadership election. As had been the case each year since 1880, Parnell was the only candidate. Before the meeting Gladstone called in Justin MacCarthy, the Vice-Chairman of the party, and warned him that he could no longer guarantee Home Rule if Parnell remained as leader. He also set out this opinion in a letter.

At the meeting, MacCarthy gave Gladstone's message to Parnell but did not tell the other MPs. They re-elected Parnell as their leader but it seems that many of them did so as a gesture of loyalty, hoping he would respond by resigning voluntarily. He did not. Instead he made a speech calling for unity and loyalty.

25-30 November: re-opening the leadership issue

When Gladstone heard of Parnell's re-election, he published his letter. This placed Irish MPs in a very difficult situation. They faced two unpalatable options.

- Should they abandon their leader, the man who achieved so much for them, on the orders of an English politician?

- Should they remain loyal to Parnell and risk destroying the Liberal alliance without which Home Rule was impossible?

A majority of MPs demanded that the leadership question be re-opened. Reluctantly, Parnell agreed to hold another meeting on 1 December.

29 November: Parnell's diversionary tactic

Before the second meeting, Parnell tried to divert attention away from the divorce question. On 29 November he issued a manifesto entitled **To the People of Ireland**. In it he attacked Gladstone for trying to dictate to the Irish party and said that the terms for Home Rule which Gladstone had offered him at their Hawarden meeting were too limited.

By this tactic, Parnell hoped to turn Irish attention away from the divorce and on to other issues including the following.

- Was it wise for the Irish party to get too close to English politicians through the Liberal alliance?

- Was the Home Rule offered by the Liberals good enough?

The problem was that Parnell himself had never raised these questions before and

Parnell's publication of the Home Rule terms he had discussed with Gladstone created a breach between the two men.

that shortly after the Hawarden meeting he had praised Gladstone's Home Rule proposals.

This tactic possibly won Parnell some support in Ireland, especially among extreme nationalists for whom Home Rule had never been enough. But it destroyed his alliance with the Liberals. Gladstone regarded it as a breach of confidence which made any future co-operation with Parnell impossible.

1-6 December: the party splits in Committee Room 15

On 1 December seventy-three Irish MPs met in **Committee Room 15** of the House of Commons. (Six others were in the US on a fund-raising tour, five were ill, one was in prison in connection with the Plan of Campaign and the MP for Kilkenny had recently died.)

At first Parnell's opponents asked him to resign temporarily until the scandal had blown over. He would not discuss it. Each time someone called for a vote on the leadership, he used his position as chairman to turn the debate on to the Liberal plans for Home Rule and whether Gladstone should be allowed to dictate to them about their leader.

For six days they argued. As each weary day passed, the tone if the discussion got more bitter and more personal. **Timothy Healy** was the most outspoken in his attacks on his former leader of whom he had long been jealous.

Parnell controlled the debate. Although the majority was against him, he avoided a vote on the leadership. At last, on 6 December, forty-five exasperated MPs, led by MacCarthy, walked out, leaving a defiant Parnell still occupying the chair and surrounded by twenty-seven faithful followers. He ended the meeting with the words:

> Gentlemen, we have won today. Although our ranks are reduced in numbers, I hold this chair still... [Our opponents] stand today in the most contemptible of all positions – the positions of men who, having taken a pledge to be true to their

The motion that was debated in Committee Room 15. Parnell managed to avoid allowing a vote on it. What does it say?

party, to be true to their leaders, to be true to their country, have been false to all these pledges. (F. S. L. Lyons, *Charles Stewart Parnell*, p. 529)

3 December: the Catholic bishops condemn Parnell

After the split, both sides returned to Ireland to organise their supporters. The anti-Parnellites elected MacCarthy as their leader. They had the powerful backing of the Catholic Church. On 3 December, while the meeting in Committee Room 15 was still in progress, the bishops had issued a strongly worded condemnation of Parnell.

Parnell's supporters

The Parnellites, meanwhile, gained the support of the Fenians and other extreme nationalist groups. They approved of Parnell's defiance of Gladstone and his criticism of the limitations of Home Rule. Support for Parnell was greatest in Dublin and in some of the poorer areas of the west but elsewhere it was patchy.

20 December: the Kilkenny by-election

The by-election in Kilkenny was an opportunity to test Irish opinion. The campaign was a bitter one. The anti-Parnellites, especially Healy and Davitt, made personal attacks on Parnell and on Katharine O'Shea. Parnell, in his speeches, appealed for support to the old Fenian tradition which he had last courted during the Land League campaign. There were demonstrations, and both Parnell and Davitt were physically attacked. In the end the anti-Parnellites won by two to one.

January 1891: mediation at Boulogne

Meanwhile, attempts were being made behind the scenes to heal the split. When the scandal broke, William O'Brien and John Dillon had been in the US on a fund-raising tour. Although they opposed Parnell, they tried to remain neutral so that they could act as mediators. Because they had jumped bail in Ireland, they could not land in the United Kingdom without being arrested, so they met Parnell in Boulogne in January 1891.

Dillon and O'Brien urged him to resign as party chairman. They promised he would still have influence behind the scenes if he did so. Parnell seemed to consider this offer, but insisted that the Liberals must change their Home Rule proposals first. When the Liberals refused even to talk about it, he walked out. The last hope of a peaceful reconciliation was gone.

January – October 1891: growing bitterness

From then on, the split got worse. There were two more by-elections in 1891, one in north Sligo, one in Carlow. Catholic bishops came out strongly against Parnell, though there is evidence that, in north Sligo at least, not all priests took the same line. The anti-Parnellite press, especially that controlled by Healy, was unsparing in its personal attacks on the deposed leader and his wife. (Parnell and Katharine O'Shea were finally married on 25 June 1891.)

The Parnellites replied by accusing their rivals of an unpatriotic submission to Gladstone. Parnell worked untiringly. Travelling constantly between Britain and Ireland, he made speech after speech appealing for support, especially from the Fenians. They rallied to him and helped to counter the influence of the clergy. But it was not enough to win the by-elections.

6 October 1891: the death of Parnell

During the last year of his life, Parnell's health was bad. Many who met him commented on how ill he looked. In September 1891 he caught cold while speaking at a meeting and on 6 October he died in Brighton in Katharine's arms. His funeral in Dublin was attended by 200,000 people, many of them members of the newly founded Gaelic Athletic Association. (see page 171) It was a demonstration of his continuing popularity in Dublin.

The Parnell legend

During his last months, Parnell convinced the Fenians that he now backed their belief in an Ireland completely separate from Britain and their willingness to use force to achieve it. Because of this, Parnell, after his death, came to be counted as part of the

Parnell's funeral.

republican tradition in Irish history. Many of the next generation of political leaders like **Arthur Griffith** and **Patrick Pearse** who moved away from constitutional politics, regarded him as an inspiration.

Parnell also became a hero to a young generation who were attracted by the romance of his life and the tragedy of his fall. Writers like **W. B. Yeats** and **James Joyce** saw his life and death as the stuff of epic drama. They despised the politicians who had abandoned him in his hour of need.

But were these views justified?

Historians, like F. S. L. Lyons in his biography *Charles Stewart Parnell*, have carefully analysed the speeches Parnell made during his last campaign. They point out that he never, in so many words, supported the use of force or backed the complete separation of Ireland from Britain. His speeches were always ambiguous. They sounded extreme but on closer analysis, they never quite committed him to an extreme position.

This was not new. During the Land League period and the years that followed (though less often after 1886) Parnell had made speeches which seemed to hint at an extreme nationalism. But he also made others that took a different, much more moderate, line. This raises the question: what was Parnell's real attitude to Irish independence and the use of force to achieve it?

The most likely answer is that Parnell did not have a fixed position. He was a practical politician who had to please several different audiences if he was to achieve anything.

- He needed the backing of the Fenians and they would never have supported land reform or Home Rule unless they could be convinced that these movements would lead on to full independence. Their support was most important to him during his early years (1875-82) and again during the last months of his life. These are the periods when his speeches are most extreme.

- He needed the backing of moderate nationalists and the Catholic clergy who would have been satisfied with a limited independence and who were opposed to the use of force to achieve more. Their backing was most important after the formation of the National League in 1882.

- From 1886 he needed the votes of British Liberal MPs without whom no Home Rule bill would pass. They would never have backed it if they thought it would lead to Irish independence.

As a result, Parnell tailored his speeches to his audience. Since he wrote so little, we do not have any way of knowing what his real attitude was or even if he had one. As Lyons points out, even in his last desperate campaigns he never committed himself completely to the Fenians. Perhaps as a practical politician he always remembered that if he won, he would need the support of the moderates and have to negotiate with British politicians once more.

The Parnellites from 1891-1900

After Parnell's death, the Parnellites elected **John Redmond** as their leader and continued their fight. In the general election of 1892 they did badly, only winning nine seats. But almost one third of the voters supported them in the face of massive intimidation by the Catholic clergy. Throughout the next eight years the Parnellites kept a strong body of popular support.

The anti-Parnellites after 1891

Although the anti-Parnellites had far more MPs (seventy-two after the 1892 election), they were unable to make much of an impact. Led by the weak **Justin McCarthy**, they were committed to an alliance with the Liberals, so they were in no position to bargain when Gladstone, at the age of eighty-three, was returned to power in 1892.

1893: the second Home Rule bill

In 1893 Gladstone brought in a second Home Rule bill which differed only slightly from the 1886 bill. This time it passed the House of Commons but was defeated in the Conservative-dominated Lords. Gladstone proposed a campaign to reduce the Lords' power, but his party was not as enthusiastic about Home Rule as he was. They forced him to retire in 1894.

His successors were less committed to Home Rule. In the 1895 general election the Liberals played it down. Even so, they lost the election and the Conservatives returned to power. They remained in office until 1905 and during these years Home Rule was out of the question.

The anti-Parnellites from 1895 to 1900

Because of their commitment to the Liberal alliance, the anti-Parnellites were unable to influence these developments. They were also weakened by quarrels about the leadership. MacCarthy was just a stop-gap and the real choice lay between the two strong men of the party, **Timothy Healy** and **John Dillon**.

- Healy had support among the Catholic clergy. He wished to give local branches, where priests were influential, a greater say in policy-making.

- Dillon believed that the party needed a single strong leader, like Parnell had been. He also disapproved of the part the clergy played in Parnell's downfall and wanted to limit their influence in the party.

These divisions led to a number of undignified rows which reached a climax when, in 1895, a Healyite and a Dillonite fought a by-election in south Kerry. Healy's candidate lost and soon afterwards, Dillon was elected to the leadership of the party. He restored discipline and Healy and his followers were gradually pushed out.

Thus by 1897 there were three quarrelling parties in place of the single disciplined and effective party which Parnell had built. Demands for unity began to be heard.

Chapter 13

1890-1905: The years of Conservative reform

Balfour's new approach

While the Home Rule party tore itself apart over the divorce issue, the Conservatives remained in power. By 1890 the Chief Secretary, Balfour, had defeated the Plan of Campaign and he wanted to try a more conciliatory policy towards Ireland.

Chamberlain's *Unionist Policy for Ireland*

Balfour was influenced by Joseph Chamberlain who wrote a pamphlet called *A Unionist Policy for Ireland*. In it, Chamberlain argued that most people in Ireland did not want Home Rule. Their real concerns, according to Chamberlain, were:

- land ownership.

- poverty.

- the lack of democracy in local government.

It was because the Westminster parliament had not dealt with these problems that Irish people listened to agitators like Parnell and Davitt. If Westminster solved their problems, Chamberlain said, the Irish would realise that they benefited from the Union and would stop looking for independence.

Horace Plunkett: 1854-1932

Another man who influenced Balfour was **Horace Plunkett**. The son of an Irish landlord, Plunkett had become a rancher in the American west when he was young, but returned to Ireland in 1888. He noted that Irish farmers had lost their share of the British markets in the 1880s and blamed this on their inefficient methods of pre-paring and distributing their produce and on their failure to work together.

Each Irish farm was a single economic unit. The farmer bought seed, tools and fertiliser in small quantities from the local shop where he paid the highest prices. He sold his butter or grain or calves to the local dealers and got only a low price. Much of what he produced was of poor quality but there was no one to show him how to make it better.

Sir Horace Plunkett

Co-operatives in Denmark

Plunkett pointed to Denmark where farmers had faced similar problems in the 1880s. They had then formed co-operatives, setting up shops to buy seed, etc. in bulk and to sell them cheaply to the members. They processed their own produce, set high standards of quality and sold their products at the best prices. As a result of co-operation, Danish farmers had not only become prosperous but had displaced the Irish as the main suppliers of butter and bacon on the British market.

1889: the foundation of the co-operative movement

Plunkett suggested that Irish farmers imitate the Danes. In 1889 he founded his first co-operative society in Doneraile. The movement spread, mostly in the dairy-farming areas. In 1894 he formed the **Irish Agricultural Organisation Society (IAOS)** to co-ordinate the work of the local societies and in the following year he started a paper, *The Irish Homestead*, to spread his message.

Opposition to the co-ops

Plunkett's movement was opposed by various groups. Some Home Rulers opposed it because he was a unionist, though he always insisted that the co-operative movement was outside politics. Some Catholics disliked him because he was a Protestant, though his closest associate was a Jesuit priest, Thomas Finlay.

The main opposition came from shopkeepers (usually both Catholic and nationalist) who feared that they would lose business if the co-operatives took off. Their attitudes are neatly summed up in this statement recorded by Plunkett's biographer, Margaret Digby:

Rathkeale is a Nationalist town – Nationalist to the backbone – and every pound of butter made in this creamery must be made upon Nationalist principles or it won't be made at all. (Margaret Digby, *Horace Plunkett*, p. 55)

The spread of co-operation

Plunkett's movement spread despite opposition. By 1914 the IAOS had over 1,000 affiliated societies with an annual turnover of over £3.5 million.

It was most successful in dairy-farming areas. Small co-operative creameries provided work for local people and an income for the members. The creamery butter they produced was better than farm butter and soon captured the Irish market. But the co-ops were too small and uncoordinated to recover the export market in Britain. Co-operation had little impact on other aspects of farming.

Balfour's constructive unionism

Balfour decided to make the Union more popular in Ireland by tackling some of the problems identified by Chamberlain and Plunkett. With the Home Rule party split into quarrelling factions after 1890 he had little opposition.

The main part of his programme of **constructive unionism** was **land purchase** by which the government made mortgages available to farmers to allow them to buy their farms. The Conservatives had already passed the **Ashbourne Land Purchase Act** of 1885, so they knew it could be successful.

1891: Balfour's Land Act

In 1891 Balfour brought in a major land act. It contained two parts:

- the biggest land purchase provision so far introduced.

- an attempt to help the poorer farmers of the west and south, through a new organisation called the **Congested Districts' Board**.

Land purchase in Balfour's Act

The Act set £33 million aside to enable tenants to buy their farms. Tenants were to repay the loans in annual instalments (**annuities**), spread over forty-nine years.

The British Treasury was reluctant to give out large sums of tax-payers' money. It insisted that landlords be paid in government stock rather than cash and that tenants fulfil complicated legal conditions before they could buy their farms. These provisions made the land purchase parts of Balfour's Act unpopular with both landlords and tenants.

- In the 1890s the London Stock Market was low, so that land stock could not be sold for its full value. Many landlords decided to wait for better times before selling up.

- When buying his farm, a tenant had to pay high solicitors' fees. He also found his annuities were higher than his old rents. As a result, only 47,000 tenants bought their farms under this Act.

It was altered in 1896 by Gerald Balfour, to ease some of these conditions, but it was never very successful.

Helping the poorest farmers through the Congested Districts' Board

The second part of the Act was more successful. It was the first systematic attempt to help the poorest tenants. They lived mainly along the west coast. Their poverty was caused by:

- the tiny size of their farms.
- the poor quality of the land.
- difficulties with transport and markets.
- the lack of alternative employment.

Buying their farms would not solve these problems.

The Congested Districts' Board

Under Balfour's Act 3,500,000 acres in Cork, Kerry, Galway, Mayo, Roscommon, Leitrim and Donegal were identified as 'congested' (i.e. too many people were trying to make a living out of too little arable land). **The Congested Districts' Board** was set up to help the people in these areas. It was given an annual income of £41,000.

The purpose of the CDB was:

- to increase the size of farms by buying up and redistributing unused land, and by

Small farmers in the west gained little from most land acts. These were from Mayo and their farm clearly had more rocks than arable land (i.e. land where crops could grow). The size of their fields makes clear what a congested district really was.

resettling people from congested districts in areas where land was available.

- to improve the quality of farming by education.
- to promote local industries so as to provide alternative employment for the farmers and their families.

Later another 3 million acres were added to the Board's area and by 1910 it was spending £500,000 a year.

The work of the Congested Districts' Board

Between 1891 and 1923, when the CDB was dissolved, it bought up 2,000,000 acres. This land was distributed among small farmers to try to increase the size of their farms. The Board also spent £2 million improving the land through drainage and farm building and it paid instructors to teach the farmers better farming methods.

The Board encouraged cottage industries such as lace-making, tweed manufacture and knitting. Donegal tweed and Foxford blankets were two results of its work. It helped the fishing industry by giving loans for boats and equipment and by building piers. It also built bridges and roads to open up the west to tourism. All of these provided off-farm jobs for the people in the congested districts. The Board also built 3,000 houses for small farmers and helped to renovate 6,000 more.

1895-1905: Balfour's continuing involvement in Ireland

The Conservatives lost the 1892 election but they were returned to power in 1895. Balfour was now a senior member of the government and in 1902 he succeeded his uncle as Prime Minister, a post he held till 1905. In 1895 his brother, Gerald, became Irish Chief Secretary and later his cousin **George Wyndham** held the post. Through them, he kept in contact with the programme of Irish reforms which is often referred to by the phrase 'killing Home Rule with kindness'.

1895: Horace Plunkett and the 'Recess Committee'

In 1892 Horace Plunkett had become a Unionist MP. He proposed that MPs from all parties should get together to draw up a programme of reform and give it to the government. His suggestion was welcomed by some unionists and by the Parnellites though not by the anti-Parnellites. They joined together to form the **Recess Committee** in 1895.

1899: the Department of Agriculture

One reform they proposed was a **Department of Agriculture** to improve the quality of Irish farming. It was set up in 1899, with Plunkett as its first head. It was responsible for agricultural and technical instruction.

By 1914 the Department had 138 instructors travelling the country, telling farmers about new methods in agriculture, horticulture and poultry-keeping. Its aims were:

- to improve the quality of crops and livestock.

- to deal with animal and plant disease.

- to encourage fishing and afforestation.

- to collect statistics on many aspects of Irish life.

It had some success, but it was a slow and laborious task to persuade farmers to change their old, familiar methods of farming.

1898: the Local Government Act

One of the Irish problems which Chamberlain identified was the lack of a democratic system of local government. Such a system had been set up in Britain in 1888. In 1898 it was extended to Ireland.

The **Local Government Act** set up county, district and urban councils. They were elected by both men and women ratepayers (the first time that Irish women had the vote). The councils were responsible for maintaining roads and public buildings, and for water, lighting and sewerage services. They could raise local rates and also received government grants to pay for these services.

This cartoon, entitled 'Riding the pig' suggests that the Conservative policy of controlling the Irish party with reforms was being successful. But have you spotted how Balfour kept the Crimes Act in reserve?

Local councils in action

The new councils were very political. In the south they were dominated by the Home Rulers and in the north east by the unionists. In fact most were one-party bodies and this led to corruption. Work, such as road-building, was always given to loyal party supporters, and bribery and corruption were common. Some councils were disbanded as a result and when the Free State was set up the Cosgrave government took powers to improve the situation.

But the councils did give some political experience to future Labour and Sinn Féin members, and to a few women, who because of the laws at the time could not be elected to parliament. Several prominent people from the post-independence period, like W. T. Cosgrave, Sean T. O'Kelly and Jennie Wyse-Power, started in politics as local councillors.

The slow pace of reform

By 1900 the Conservatives had brought in several useful reforms. But for most people they made little difference. Even the work of the Congested Districts' Board and the Department of Agriculture were slow to show results. As far as many small farmers in the west were concerned, their living conditions were as bad as ever. It was this fact that lay behind a new land movement that developed at the very end of the 1890s.

Small farms in Connaught

The man who led this movement was Parnell's former lieutenant, **William O'Brien**. In 1895, fed up with the constant bickering among Home Rulers, he had retired to Co. Mayo. He soon grew bored and began to look for a new political crusade. He found it in the uneven distribution of land in Connaught where the 6,000 largest farmers held the same amount of land as the 70,000 smallest.

Outside his windows he saw huge sheep-farms, many of them created by the cruel clearances that followed the famine, when thousands of poor families were driven off their land. Alongside them were tiny plots of stony ground on which whole families depended for their living. To make matters worse, many of the sheep-farms were unused, since competition from Australia had cut British demand for Irish wool.

1898: the United Irish League

O'Brien wanted the Congested Districts Board to buy the big farms and redistribute the land among the small holders. Early in 1898 he founded a new movement to work for this. In honour of the centenary of the 1798 United Irish rebellion, he called it the **United Irish League**. The League soon spread beyond Mayo and added two new demands to its list: the reunification of the Home Rule party and a new land purchase bill.

1900: re-uniting the Home Rule movement

The United Irish League attracted members from both factions of the Home Rule movement. John Redmond, the Parnellite leader, and John Dillon, who led the anti-

William O'Brien, the former Home Rule MP who started the United Irish League in 1898 and encouraged the re-unification of the Home Rule party.

Parnellites, realised that the voters were weary of the quarrel. With Davitt and O'Brien acting as mediators, they opened negotiations.

Early in 1900 the Home Rule party was re-united. Dillon agreed to let Redmond become the leader. O'Brien's United Irish League took over as the party's organisation in the country, replacing Parnell's Irish National League.

Even Tim Healy joined the new party, but that did not last. Within two years he and a few followers broke away and formed a separate party which remained in existence until 1918. It drew most of its support from Healy's native Cork.

A new land agitation

Meanwhile the United Irish League continued to grow. By 1901 it had over 100,000 members. The government feared a new land war and districts where the League was strong were proclaimed under the Crimes Act.

1902: the Land Conference

However, **George Wyndham,** who became Chief Secretary in 1900, preferred conciliation to coercion. In 1902 he backed a proposal from a Galway landlord, John Shawe-Taylor, for a conference of landlords and tenants to work out an arrangement that would suit both sides.

The **Land Conference** met in December 1902 under the chairmanship of a southern unionist, Lord Dunraven. The tenants were represented by O'Brien, Redmond and Harrington. It quickly drew up proposals for an extensive scheme of land purchase. Wyndham presented them to parliament and they were passed in 1903.

1903: the Wyndham Land Act

The **Wyndham Land Act** was the biggest land purchase scheme of all and it is usually seen as solving the question of land ownership in Ireland. The Act contained a number of important points.

- The government was to set aside £100 million for land purchase.

- Landlords were to get between eighteen and twenty-seven times the annual rent for a farm. This was a higher price than they could hope to get by selling their estates on the open market.

- Tenants were to get loans to buy their farms which they had to repay in annual instalments spread over sixty-eight years. This long repayment period made the annuities lower than the old rent. This encouraged tenants to buy their farms.

- Previous purchase acts let one farmer at a time buy his farm. That pushed up legal costs for both landlord and tenant. This Act encouraged a landlord to sell his whole estate in one go by giving him a bonus of 12 per cent if he did so. This saved a lot in legal costs and made many landlords willing to sell.

- Where the landlord agreed to sell and three-quarters of the tenants agreed to buy, the Land Commission could take over the estate and oversee any tenant who refused to buy his farm.

The success of the Wyndham Act

John Dillon and Michael Davitt objected that the Wyndham Act was too generous to the landlords but the tenants ignored them. The Act was a tremendous success. Under it and an amendment passed in 1909 which slightly altered its terms, the peaceful revolution in land ownership, which had begun in 1870, was completed. As these figures show, by 1920 390,000 farming families had acquired possession of their land and the power of the landlords was gone forever.

	Land Purchase	
Acts	**No. of farms purchased**	**Area of land affected**
1870	877	52,000 acres
1881	731	30,000 acres
1885 & '87	25,367	942,625 acres
1891 & '96	46,834	1,482,749 acres
1903 & '09	270,396	9,037,392 acres (completed by 1921)
	46,621	1,492,522 acres (pending in 1921)
Total	390,826	13,037,318 acres

LAND PURCHASE ASSESSED

Why land purchase?

Land purchase was the cornerstone of the Conservative policy towards Ireland between 1885 and 1905. At first glance it seems strange that the Conservatives, the party of the landlords, should adopt a policy which ended the power of Irish landlords. But there were sound practical reasons for this.

Helping the landlords

The years of the 'long depression' (*c.* 1875-1895) were bad for everyone who was involved in agriculture in the United Kingdom, whether landlord or tenant. Competition was intense and prices for agricultural produce stayed low.

Irish landlords had their own additional problems. Gladstone's Land Courts had reduced most rents by about 20 per cent and Balfour's 1887 amendment reduced them by a further 15 per cent. And collecting even this reduced rent was often difficult and unpleasant.

As a result, by 1890 many landlords wanted to sell their estates but no one wanted to buy except the tenants. By helping them to do so, the Conservatives were also helping their friends, the landlords.

Killing the demand for Home Rule

The Conservatives also hoped that land purchase would make Irish farmers, who were a majority of the population, less inclined to support Home Rule. They thought that once they owned their land, farmers would become cautious and be unwilling to change the familiar United Kingdom for a new, untried Home Rule.

As things developed, the opposite happened. Once they owned their lands, nationalist farmers were even more in favour of an Irish parliament which they controlled through their votes, than of a Westminster parliament where they were in a minority.

Giving landlords a leadership role

Conservatives believed that once the farmers had become owners of their lands, their relationship with their former landlords would improve. Then the landlords (most of whom were unionists) would take their place as the leaders of the countryside.

This happened in Ulster where by 1910 landlords had emerged as the leaders of the Unionist party, a position they continued to hold until the 1960s. But it did not happen in nationalist areas, probably because the religious and cultural divisions between landlords and the farmers were too great and the wounds inflicted by the land war too deep.

Did land purchase make farmers better off?

Many Home Rulers supported land purchase because they thought that it would improve the farmers' living standards. Were they right?

Living conditions did improve for farming families between 1890 and 1914 but land purchase was only partly responsible for this.

The farmers' repayments under the Wyndham Act were lower than their old rents. This left them with more money to spend on houses, food and clothes. At the same time, the price of these items and other things a farmer needed like fertiliser, tools and seed fell between 1870 and 1914. This was due to improved technology, communications and more competition. This contributed even more than land purchase to the rise in farmers' living standards.

Did land purchase make farmers more efficient?

One of the arguments used against the landlord system was that tenants were afraid to spend money to improve their land in case they were evicted and the investment went to the landlord. It was argued that if tenant farmers bought their farms, they would also invest in the land because it belonged to them. Did this turn out to be correct?

It is not easy to say what every farmer did, but on average, ownership does not seem to have made any difference. In fact in a few cases, farmers seem to have invested less because they were afraid of what would happen if they could not pay their annuities to a government far away in London, which they could not influence in the way they had been able to influence their landlords.

The main reason for the inefficiency of Irish farming was the large number of small farms. Small farmers lacked the capital to invest in new processes or new technology. For example, in 1918 there were only seventy tractors and 300 hay bailers in the country. Land purchase did not change this situation and it remained a problem for Irish governments long after the landlord system was swept away.

How did land purchase affect small farmers and labourers?

The most important element in a farming family's prosperity was not their landlord but the amount of land they had. A big farmer was well off; a small farmer was poor; a landless labourer was almost destitute.

Land purchase changed none of this. A tenant with a big farm bought the big farm; a tenant with a few acres of bog and rock got just that; a labourer with no land got nothing at all.

This caused great resentment among the small farmers and labourers who had believed that the Land League slogan 'the land of Ireland for the people of Ireland' meant that they would get a fair share of the land. This did not happen and it left a deep bitterness which emerged again during the Sinn Féin period and in the 1930s.

O'Brien leaves the party

The success of the Land Conference in solving the land purchase issue convinced William O'Brien that other issues, such as education, could be solved by similar round table conferences. But this proposal was criticised by John Dillon.

He had opposed the Wyndham Act because he feared that removing the farmers' grievances would indeed kill Home Rule. Now he argued that all other problems must wait till Ireland had its own parliament. Redmond, who had backed O'Brien over the Wyndham Act, now came down on Dillon's side. An angry O'Brien left the party and joined forces with Tim Healy.

Timothy Healy

1904: the Irish Reform Association and Sir Antony MacDonnell

A similar development occurred on the unionist side. A group of southern unionist landlords led by Lord Dunraven who had been involved in the Land Conference, also thought they could solve other issues by negotiation. In 1904 they set up the **Irish Reform Association** to organise conferences. Dunraven went for advice to the Under Secretary, **Sir Antony MacDonnell**.

Mayo-born MacDonnell had had a distinguished career in the British civil service in India when Wyndham appointed him Under Secretary (head of the Irish civil service) in 1902. He was the first Catholic to hold that post. In response to Dunraven's approach he drew up a plan to run Ireland through elected councils which would have some tax-raising powers.

This plan fell far short of Home Rule but it provoked an outcry from the unionists, especially in Ulster. They were already deeply suspicious of the many concessions the Conservatives had made to the nationalists and this plan, coming from a Catholic Under Secretary, was the last straw.

1904: Wyndham's departure and the end of constructive unionism

They forced Wyndham to repudiate the plan. The outcry so damaged his health that he had to resign. In Ulster, the various unionist groupings formed the **Ulster Unionist Council** to co-ordinate their actions. This Council was later useful in orchestrating the unionist resistance to the third Home Rule bill.

This episode marked the end of constructive unionism. It showed that while the Conservatives could tackle other issues such as the land problem, there was no room to manoeuvre on the core issue of Home Rule versus the Union.

1905: the Liberal landslide

Late in 1905 Balfour's government was defeated. The general election was held early in 1906. It produced a landslide victory for the Liberal party. At first there was great rejoicing among Irish nationalists but it soon became clear that the Liberals were in no hurry to re-introduce Home Rule, and with their huge majority there was little Redmond could do to push them along. It was to be several frustrating years before Home Rule finally became an issue once again.

Questions

ORDINARY LEVEL – A

Answer the following briefly. One or two sentences will be enough.

1 What was the **Disestablishment Act** and who introduced it?

2 Give **two** points from Gladstone's **first Land Act** (1870).

3 Give **two** reasons for the early success of Butt's Home Government Association.

4 What was **obstruction** and who started using it?

5 Give **two** reasons for the economic crisis that hit Irish farmers in the late 1870s.

6 What was the **New Departure**? Name the two men who proposed it.

7 How did **boycotting** begin?

8 Why did Anna Parnell set up the **Ladies Land League**?

9 Name the men who made the **Kilmainham Treaty** and mention **two** things they agreed on.

10 Why was the **Reform Act of 1884** important for Parnell?

11 Give **two** reasons why Gladstone decided to bring in a **Home Rule bill** in 1886.

12 Give **two** reasons why **the Ulster unionists** opposed Home Rule in 1886 and **two** other reasons why **British unionists** were against it.

13 What was the **Plan of Campaign**?

14 What were the '**Piggot forgeries**'? How did they affect Parnell's career?

15 Why was '**New Tipperary**' built in 1890?

16 By whom was the **Congested Districts Board** set up? Give **two** things it aimed to achieve.

17 What happened in **Committee Room 15**?

18 Give **four** of the clauses in the **Wyndham Land Act** (1903).

19 How did the **land purchase acts** affect (i) rich farmers and (ii) landless labourers?

20 Set out **two** reasons for the Conservative policy of 'killing Home Rule with kindness'.

Questions

ORDINARY LEVEL – B

Write a short paragraph on each of the following.

1 Isaac Butt.

2 Michael Davitt.

3 Parnell and obstruction.

4 The Ladies Land League.

5 Gladstone and Home Rule.

6 The fall of Parnell.

7 The Congested Districts Board.

8 The Wyndham Land Act.

9 Sir Horace Plunkett and the Co-operative movement.

ORDINARY LEVEL – C

Write a short essay on each of the following:

1 Parnell's career as an Irish leader under the headings:
   (i)   Gaining the leadership of the party.
   (ii)   Leading the land war.
   (iii) Strengthening the party.
   (iv)   Negotiating for Home Rule.
   (v)   Fall.

2 The Land War (1879-82) under the headings:
   (i)   Why tenant farmers were in difficulties at the end of the 1870s.
   (ii)   How the Land League was set up.
   (iii) Boycotting and agitation.
   (iv)   Gladstone's Land Act.
   (v)   The Kilmainham Treaty.

3 Conservative policy towards Ireland under the headings:
   (i)   Why they opposed Home Rule.
   (ii)   Balfour's policies as Chief Secretary.
   (iii) Land purchase.
   (iv)   Local government reform.
   (v)   Assess the success or failure of the policies.

Questions

HIGHER LEVEL

Write an essay on each of the following:

1 Discuss the development of Gladstone's policies towards Ireland. (80)

2 Compare and contrast the careers of Butt and Parnell as political leaders. (80)

3 The Kilmainham Treaty (1882) was a turning point in the career of Charles Stewart Parnell and in the history of his party. Discuss. (80)

4 Parnell's attitude to violence and his involvement with the men of violence are difficult to assess.
Discuss the career of C.S. Parnell in the light of this statement. (80)

5 (i) Treat of Michael Davitt's involvement in Irish affairs. (60)
(ii) Discuss the view that Davitt saw none of his ideals achieved. (20)

6 (i) Trace the events leading to the introduction of the first Home Rule Bill in 1886. (50)
(ii) How do you account for unionist opposition to these proposals? (30)

7 Parnell was partially responsible for his untimely downfall.
Discuss, with general reference to Parnell's leadership of the Home Rule party after 1880 and to the events of 1890-91.

8 Treat of Conservative policies towards Ireland in the period 1886 to 1906.

9 'The Conservatives did more than the Liberals to solve the Irish land question in the period 1870 to 1903.'
Discuss. (80)

10 (i) Outline the progress of land purchase from 1870 to 1903. (60)
(ii) Discuss critically the view that land purchase failed to tackle the real problems of rural Ireland. (20)

11 Why was it that, at the end of the nineteenth century, the land agitation had been successful while the Home Rule campaign had failed? (80)

SECTION THREE

1900-1923: REVOLUTION AND PARTITION

Chapter 14

Socialism and Feminism

Ireland at the start of the new century

Around the start of the twentieth century, Ireland appeared quiet. The Home Rule movement was weakened by the divisions that followed the O'Shea divorce scandal. The land question was being answered by land purchase. Unionists were lulled into security by the dominance of the Conservatives and the power of the House of Lords.

On the surface at least, the country seemed more reconciled to membership of the United Kingdom than at any time since the 1860s. Yet behind this apparent peace, new movements were gathering force, as they were elsewhere in Europe.

Groups like industrial workers and women, who had been neglected by the spread of liberal democracy, began to demand their rights. A more extreme nationalism, linked to a cultural revival, emerged and provoked a reaction from unionists which deepened the divisions between the two communities. These developments, combined with the indirect impact on Ireland of world events, were to lead to war and partition within two decades.

Excluded groups

Between 1891 and 1910 while hope of Home Rule was suspended, new political movements emerged to fill the vacuum. Two of these, the socialist and feminist movements, brought to the fore groups that had been ignored by the leaders of both the unionist and nationalist movements.

The Labour Movement

Problems of the Irish labour movement

The labour movement was slow to organise in Ireland and was never very successful. This was due to several factors:

- Farmers who made up the majority of the population, were not interested in supporting industrial workers' demands for better wages and working conditions. They also viewed with suspicion labour calls for old age pensions, unemployment benefit and state aid for decent housing. Farmers would gain little from these developments and might have to pay for them through higher taxes.

- The decline of industry in many parts of the country reduced the number of skilled industrial workers. Most of those left were unskilled casual workers. It was difficult to organise them into trade unions and they were not well placed to bargain with employers.

- In the north east, the one area where there was extensive industrialisation, workers were divided along sectarian lines. This weakened their ability to form a common front against their employers. In 1905 the British Labour Party failed to win a parliamentary seat in Belfast when many Protestant workers refused to support the Labour candidate (who was a Protestant) because they thought Labour favoured Home Rule.

- The question of Home Rule versus the Union dominated all political discussions. Although nationalist and unionist leaders were middle or upper class, they claimed to speak for all the people in their communities. They discouraged labour politics, saying they would only distract attention from the main issue, the Union.

The craft unions

In the nineteenth century, the only trade unions in Ireland were the craft unions. They were alliances of skilled tradesmen, e.g. printers, bricklayers, carpenters or coopers. These skilled workers were relatively well-off.

Some craft unions were Irish based but many were Irish branches of British unions. All of them belonged to the British-based **Trades Union Congress** which was formed in 1868. By the 1890s Irish trade unionists felt that their interests were being neglected. In 1894 they founded their own **Irish Trades Union Congress (ITUC)** which, by 1900, represented about 60,000 workers, half of them in Belfast.

The emergence of socialism

In the 1880s in Europe, socialism, especially as expressed in the writings of Karl Marx, began to make an impact. This brought workers into contact with ideas about the class struggle and the rights of labour. In Britain, at the same time, a number of social studies brought to light the appalling conditions in which many workers lived and the effect on their health of bad housing, poor nutrition and widespread disease.

All this helped a more militant labour movement to emerge. In Britain, unskilled workers began to form trade unions to fight for better conditions and to use their votes to influence elections. In the 1890s Keir Hardy was elected as the first working class MP and in 1900 the British Labour Party came into existence.

These developments affected Ireland. Early in the twentieth century socialism emerged, new unions were formed, trade union activity increased and the Irish Labour party was set up. Many people were involved in these developments but two are particularly associated with them, **James Connolly** and **James Larkin**.

James Connolly

Connolly was born in Edinburgh of Irish parents in 1868. He grew up in poverty, worked as an unskilled labourer and was for a time in the British army. In 1889 he married and settled down in Edinburgh, working as a corporation carter.

Slums in Dublin, *c.* 1900.

In his spare time, Connolly read economics, history and socialist theory and wrote a number of articles. He became involved in politics and stood as a socialist candidate for Edinburgh corporation. He lost the election and was sacked. He was thinking of emigrating to America when an offer came from some Dublin socialists to act as organiser of the Dublin Socialist Society. They promised to pay him £1 a week and he came to Ireland with his wife and young children in 1896.

Connolly in Ireland

Connolly stayed for seven years. In 1896 he founded the **Irish Socialist Republican Party**, which aimed at 'the establishment of an Irish Socialist Republic based upon the public ownership by the Irish people of the land and instruments of production, distribution and exchange'. In 1898 he published a paper, *The Workers' Republic*, which appeared at irregular intervals over the next few years.

Connolly's ideas

In the *Workers' Republic*, Connolly developed his ideas about socialism and Irish nationalism.

- Marx had said that workers should have nothing to do with nationalism, but for Connolly the Irish struggle for independence and the workers' struggle for social justice went together.

155

James Connolly

- The British empire, Connolly argued, was the enemy of both the Irish and British working classes. It must be overthrown before they could be free and Ireland was a good place to begin the struggle.

- But he warned that Irish independence by itself was useless. It had to be accompanied by a social revolution, which would bring all the means of production into the hands of the workers.

Connolly won few recruits to his party, though he got an international reputation as a socialist thinker. This led to an invitation to work in America. It was becoming difficult to support his family in Ireland, so Connolly accepted and went to the United States in 1903. He remained there until 1910.

Industrial unrest

In the early years of the twentieth century the living conditions of workers around Europe got steadily worse. Inflation cut the purchasing power of their wages. In Ireland between 1895 and 1912, food prices rose by 29 per cent but wages did not go up at the same rate. By 1912 unskilled Irish workers were spending 59 per cent of their wages on food alone, with little left to spend on clothes or housing.

The growth of militant trade unionism in Ireland from 1907 to 1913 can be traced back to these conditions. Workers became so desperate that they joined trade unions and went on strike. The wave of strikes between 1906 and 1914 were the result. They are part of a pattern of industrial unrest that affected the whole of Europe from Ireland to Russia during these years.

James Larkin (1876-1947)

The man who led Irish workers in this struggle was **James Larkin**. A hot-headed and emotional man, he was a brilliant mob-orator who could inspire a crowd, a man who evoked great love as well as great hatred.

Larkin was born in Liverpool of Irish parents. Working as a docker, he became involved in trade union activity. In 1907 he came to Belfast as an organiser for the British-based National Union of Dock Labourers. He got the dockers and transport workers, all unskilled men, to join the Dockers' Union.

1907: the Belfast strike

In May 1907 the Belfast dockers went on strike. When the employers brought in strike-breakers from Liverpool, other workers came out in sympathy. Even the RIC went on strike because they were not getting paid overtime. The city came almost to a standstill. The transport men got a pay rise but the dockers had to go back to work without one.

Dublin's casual workers

Larkin then moved to Dublin, where workers' conditions were even worse than in Belfast (see page 43). Dublin was a trading rather than an industrial city, so a majority of workers were unskilled. In 1900, out of an estimated 40,000 male workers, only 10,000 were skilled. Of the rest, 7,000 were classed as 'carriers' (i.e. dockers and carters) and 23,000 were casual labourers.

A casual worker never knew from one day to the next if he would have a job. Each morning a queue of eager men gathered outside the docks or some other likely place.

James Larkin

157

The employers selected from among them the men they wanted for that day. The rest left without work or wages.

Employers seldom picked a 'troublesome' man, that is one who tried to organise the others to look for better wages. If a man was blacklisted, it could mean starvation for himself and his family. Even if a union were started, the employers had no trouble finding men among the desperate workers to help them break a strike by doing blackleg labour. Such conditions existed not merely in Dublin but in all other Irish towns and made it very hard to form a union.

Social conditions
While a skilled man could earn a living wage, women and casual male workers could not. On average, the wages of a casual worker in Dublin were between 75p and £1 a week. At that time the minimum considered necessary to keep a family of four was £1.10. The rise in prices made things even worse.

Low wages led to bad housing, bad food and bad health. In 1910, 20,000 Dublin families lived in single-roomed tenements in decaying Georgian houses, without light, heat, running water or sanitation. Disease and malnutrition were rampant. Out of every thousand babies born each year in Dublin, 142 died before they were a year old, compared with ninety-five per thousand in the rest of Ireland.

Drunkenness was widespread as people tried to forget their miseries, and prostitution was forced on many women by sheer economic necessity. Soon after he came to Dublin, Larkin asked:

> If Dublinmen are so proud of their city, why did they not look after the little children who were running about their streets, hungry and dirty and badly clothed; why did they not put a stop to the disgraceful scenes in O'Connell Street, when fellows from the slums of London in red uniform were coming along with Irish girls on their arms whom they would ruin in body and soul. (Emmet Larkin, *James Larkin*, p. 41).

Founding the Irish Transport and General Workers' Union
Larkin wanted to bring unity, strength and self-respect to these people. Within a year he had enrolled 2,500 men in the Dockers Union and in 1908 led them in three successful strikes. This displeased the leaders of his British-based union, especially when he demanded that they support the Irish strikers financially. Instead they suspended him.

Larkin then formed a new union, the **Irish Transport and General Workers' Union (ITGWU)**. It spread quickly, not just in Dublin, but in Cork, Limerick, Belfast and other ports.

The growth of the ITGWU
Larkin's new union was involved in a number of unsuccessful strikes in 1909 and 1910. After one in Cork, Larkin was imprisoned. The tide turned in 1911 as the ITGWU gained a dominant position in the Irish Trade Union Congress. This was

mainly due to the organising ability of a young tailor, **William O'Brien** (1881-1968), and of James Connolly.

1910: William O'Brien and the return of Connolly
O'Brien, from Clonakilty, County Cork, was a friend of Connolly. In 1904 he had formed the **Socialist Party of Ireland** out of Connolly's old party and other socialist groups. In 1910 he got Connolly to return to Ireland.

Syndicalism
Connolly settled in Belfast and became the local organiser of the ITGWU. He and Larkin were different in temperament and tended to irritate one another. Connolly was deeply concerned about the theories of socialism. Larkin, while he knew the theories, was mainly involved with the practical issues of trade union organisation.

Both Connolly and Larkin were influenced by the European and American idea of **syndicalism**. This was a socialist theory which said that the best way to overthrow the capitalist system was to organise the workers into big unions and call a general strike. Then capitalism would collapse and workers would gain control of the means of production.

1912: the founding of the Irish Labour party
Meanwhile both men were also willing to work politically. In 1912 when Home Rule seemed certain, Connolly got the ITUC to form the **Irish Labour Party**. This would guarantee that workers would have a voice in the expected Home Rule parliament.

1911-13: successful action
Trade conditions deteriorated in 1911 and Larkin led carters, dockers and railway-men in a series of strikes. He used the policy of the sympathetic strike (i.e. other unions agreed not to handle goods belonging to firms on strike) to intimidate employers. The ITGWU won better wages and the recognition by employers of the workers' right to form unions.

In 1912 and early 1913, Larkin succeeded in organising Dublin port and securing a contract with the employers. He also organised the farm labourers of Co. Dublin, and gained a wage increase for them. As a result of all this, the membership of the ITGWU grew from 4,000 in 1911 to 10,000 by 1913.

The employers fight back
Larkin's success alarmed the employers and roused them to action. They were led by **William Martin Murphy**. Murphy was a Cork-born businessman who made a fortune building railways throughout the British empire. Elected as a Home Rule MP in 1885, he used his money to build up a chain of newspapers including the **Irish Independent**.

Murphy owned several businesses in Dublin, among them the **Dublin United**

Tramway Company. In 1911 he formed an **Employers' Federation** to oppose the spread of trade unions.

The Dublin lock-out

During 1913 the Tramway Company began sacking ITGWU members and replacing them with non-union men. In August it declared that it would not recognise the ITGWU.

Larkin fought back. During Horse Show week, one of the busiest of the year, he called his men out on strike. But only 700 of the 1,700 men employed by the Tramway Company followed him. Larkin also hit Murphy by stopping the circulation of the **Independent**, and by preventing goods destined for Murphy and his allies from entering Dublin port.

Murphy's response was to get 400 employers to lock out all members of the ITGWU. By September over 25,000 men in and around Dublin were out of work.

The strike

Tension mounted in the city. Larkin, Connolly and other leaders were arrested, and two men were killed in riots with the police. To enable the workers to protect themselves, the **Irish Citizen Army** was set up in November. The British Trade Union movement sent £100,000 in food and supplies to help the strikers. Support, both verbal and financial, came from a wide range of Irish opinion. People like **Countess Markievicz** set up soup kitchens to feed the strikers' families.

This sketch by the artist William Orpen conveys the mood rather than the reality of hunger and despair felt during the strike.

Opposing the strike

There was also a lot of opposition to the strike.

- Although individual priests and bishops, including Archbishop Walsh of Dublin, sympathised with the poverty of the workers, the Catholic Church as a whole, feared socialism and denounced Larkin.

  Relations between the Church and the union broke down when some English sympathizers offered to take Dublin children into their homes while the dispute lasted. Archbishop Walsh objected to sending children 'to be cared for in a strange land without security of any kind that those to whom the poor children are handed over are Catholics, or indeed persons of any faith at all'. (D. W. Miller, *Church, State and Nation in Ireland*, p. 272) The scheme was dropped and thousands of children remained in Dublin to share their parents' privations.

- The Irish Parliamentary party, whose members were mostly middle-class and drew their support from the farming community, was hostile to the strikers. Even those who felt some sympathy for their plight, feared that it would distract attention from what, to them, was the much more serious struggle with Carson's Ulster unionists. (see chapter 18)

  John Dillon, Redmond's second-in-command, and the party leader in closest touch with Ireland, expressed the party's exasperation with the Dublin situation when he wrote:

  > Murphy is a desperate character, Larkin is as bad. It would be a blessing for Ireland if they exterminated each other. (F. S. L. Lyons, *John Dillon*, p. 335)

- Most extreme nationalists supported the strikers. Griffith was the main exception. He wanted to develop a native Irish capitalism and this led him to oppose Larkin's socialism.

The failure of the strike

At first it seemed the strike might succeed. In October a government inquiry suggested a compromise, but this was rejected by the employers.

Larkin then called on British trade unions to support the strike by staging sympathetic strikes in Britain. They refused. This provoked Larkin, always hot-tempered, into furious personal attacks on British labour leaders who withdrew their financial support. Without it, Larkin could not help his followers throughout the freezing winter of 1913-14.

By January men began to drift back to work. They had to accept the employers' insistence that they leave the ITGWU. Bitterly, Connolly wrote in February:

> And so we Irish workers must go down to hell, bow our backs to the lash of the slave-driver, let our hearts be seared by the iron of his hatred, and instead of the sacramental wafer of brotherhood and common sacrifice, eat the dust of defeat and betrayal. (S. Levenson, *James Connolly*, p. 247)

In the short-term the employers had achieved a victory. Larkin, soured by his experience, grew restless and in the autumn of 1914 left for America. Connolly replaced him and he and O'Brien began to put the pieces of the ITGWU together again.

After 1913, revolutionary socialism virtually disappeared in Ireland. Larkin went into voluntary exile and Connolly formed an alliance with extreme nationalism which led to his death in 1916. O'Brien, who then took over the leadership of the ITGWU, was more interested in the bread and butter issues of better pay and conditions than in socialism. After 1916 he rebuilt the ITGWU and by 1918 it had 100,000 members. Its members played an important role in the struggle for independence which followed.

The Struggle for Women's Rights

Women emerging
Throughout Europe women, like workers, began to emerge onto the political stage in the early years of the twentieth century. Better education and job opportunities gave them confidence while the growth of democratic ideas led them to demand equal citizenship with men.

Women's status
Up to the 1860s, a woman in the United Kingdom had very few rights. She could not vote in parliamentary elections or hold public office. A single woman could own property, but once she married anything she owned passed to her husband. Even her wages were his and he alone had control over their children. A husband could divorce his wife more easily than a wife could divorce her husband.

Women's work
The public view was that a woman's only role was as a wife and mother but this was not true. Until they married, many working class women had jobs as domestic servants or in factories. Middle class women were not expected to work before marriage but if they remained single, they had to support themselves in badly paid jobs as governesses or seamstresses. After marriage, many women worked alongside their husbands running the family's farm, shop or business which probably could not have survived without their labour.

But as industrialisation spread, women's economic role declined in wealthy middle class families. The family home moved into the suburbs, well away from the business area. There, the wife spent the day as housekeeper and mother, while the husband 'went to work' in the city, earning the family's income. Because this class set the standards in society, it became fashionable to see paid work as the only activity that could be called 'work'. And since women who worked within the family were not paid, they were not considered to be workers.

Re-classifying women

The changing attitude to women's work can be seen in the way the Irish census dealt with women between 1861 and 1881.

In 1861 women working in the family business were classified as doing the same work as their husbands. In 1871 the English-based Census Commissioners ordered a change. These women were to be re-classified as 'domestic' workers. In 1881 the record was changed again. Now all women at home were classified under the heading 'indefinite and non-productive'. Thus the work of women disappeared from official record at the stroke of a bureaucrat's pen.

Passive resistance

Not all women accepted society's view that their only role was as wives and mothers.

- Many Irish women escaped through emigration. In other countries, emigration was more common among men than women, but men and women left Ireland in equal numbers.

- Others found an outlet for their energies in doing voluntary work. They set up orphanages, visited prisons and opened refuges for prostitutes. Among Protestants this kind of work was done by middle class married women, but among Catholics it gradually came to be done mainly by nuns.

- The number of nuns grew rapidly from 1850. It is possible that some able women saw the life of a nun as chance to build an independent existence for themselves. Many of them ran schools and hospitals in a way which would have been impossible had they been lay women.

Early women's movements

In the 1860s, a few women began to demand their rights. Most of the pioneers of the women's movement were middle class Protestants, probably because they were better off and had contacts with similar movements in Britain.

Isabella Tod (1836-96) in Belfast and **Anna Haslam** (1829-1922) in Dublin led the Irish wing of a campaign to change the law on women's property rights. As a result Parliament passed acts in 1870, 1874 and 1882 which gradually gave married women control over their property, including their wages, after they married.

The campaign involved women in political activity and made them aware of the importance of voting. In 1876 Haslam and her husband Thomas, founded a move-ment which was later called the **Irish Women's Suffrage and Local Government Association** (IWSLGA) to demand votes for women. Mainly Protestant and middle class, it organised meetings and petitions. Up to the 1890s it was involved in the campaign for property rights and made little headway on the suffrage issue.

The campaign for education

About the same time a campaign to get a better education for women began. Up to the 1880s girls were taught little more than reading and writing. While middle class boys studied Greek, Latin and mathematics, their sisters learnt needlework, painting, music and a smattering of French.

These subjects showed what parents expected for their children. A boy would go into the professions while a girl had to catch a husband, not to earn her living. But not every girl married and those who remained single were not qualified for anything. The campaign to improve girls' schooling arose from this problem as well as from a desire by some women to develop themselves more fully.

One of the leaders of the movement was **Anne Jellico**. She was born in Laois in 1823. Like Haslam and other early campaigners for women's rights, she was a Quaker. In 1861 she set up a Dublin branch of the British-based **Society for Promoting the Employment of Women** to help working class women train for jobs.

The Society soon found there was a demand from middle class women needing an education to earn a living. In response Jellico set up Alexandra College in 1866 to train governesses and Alexandra School in 1873 to give girls a decent secondary education.

In 1878 the government's Intermediate Education Bill (see pages 16 & 17) proposed giving money to secondary schools whose pupils passed examinations. Women campaigned successfully to have the examinations opened to girls as well as boys.

Schools like Alexandra as well as Catholic convents entered their girls for the examinations. Since the syllabus was the same for all, girls had to study Latin, Maths and so on. To the surprise of many, they did just as well as the boys, and in many cases, even better. The examination system funded secondary education for girls.

University admission

The 1879 Royal University Act set up a similar examination board to award university degrees. So long as one passed the examination, it was not necessary to attend a university. Girls colleges were set up to give women a university-level education and from the early 1880s women graduated from the Royal University. In 1904 Trinity admitted women to its degrees and in 1908, when the National University and Queen's University were set up, women were entered on equal terms with men.

The result of these changes in education can be seen in Table A. They were mainly of benefit to prosperous middle class women since no one without money could take advantage of them.

Growing confidence

Better education gave women the confidence to become involved in politics. The **Ladies Land League** (see page 89) was an early example of this trend, though individual women had certainly helped in political activity before that. Parnell and

Education in 1871 and 1911			
	Primary	Secondary	University
1871			
Boys	316,300	12,000	2,900
Girls	299,400	9,200	none
1911			
Boys	325,500	27,500	3,100
Girls	335,700	13,600	280

Table A ▲

many Home Rulers disapproved, but later nationalist organisations like the Gaelic League (1893) and Sinn Féin (1905) admitted women as equal members.

Votes for women

After 1900 women concentrated on demanding the right to vote. The Haslams' IWSLGA had been quietly working for years, writing letters and organising petitions. In the 1890s they urged women to get involved in local government.

Women had always been able to vote for Poor Law Guardians but few had bothered. In 1896 they got the right to be elected as Guardians and in 1898 when local government was reformed, they got the right to vote for local councils and to sit on district councils, though still not on the more important county councils.

Fanny Parnell, one of the founders of the Ladies Land League.

The IWSLGA urged women to use these rights. In 1899 eighty five women were elected as Poor Law Guardians and thirty five to district councils. These victories aroused women's political awareness. A number of vocal women's groups, some nationalist, some unionist, emerged all demanding greater participation by women in public life.

Inghinidhe na hÉireann

In 1900, when the aged Queen Victoria paid her final visit to Ireland, a group of women, led by the wealthy nationalist Maud Gonne and the Dublin business woman, Jennie Wyse-Power, organised a counter-demonstration. They followed this up by forming **Inghinidhe na hÉireann**, a nationalist organisation for women.

They ran 'buy Irish' campaigns, held free classes for children in Irish, history and music, organised céilí and put on small plays. Yeats said he got the idea for *Kathleen ní Houlihan* from one of their plays and several of the actresses who later won fame in the Abbey got their first acting experience with the Inghinidhe.

The Inghinidhe were republican in outlook. They were involved in many of the nationalist activities of the time and were one of the groups that formed Sinn Féin in 1905. Wyse Power was on the executive of the new party from the beginning. She had a long career in nationalist movements, starting with the Ladies Land League and ending in the Free State Senate in the 1930s.

The Irish Women's Franchise League

Early in the new century educated women became very conscious of their lack of citizenship rights. Hanna Sheehy Skeffington wrote:

Maud Gonne

I was then an undergraduate and was amazed and disgusted to learn that I was classed among criminals, infants and lunatics – in fact that my status as a woman was worse than any of these. (R.C. Owens, *Smashing Times* p. 39)

In 1903 she married Frank Skeffington, a convinced feminist and they adopted the joint name of Sheehy Skeffington. At first they supported the IWSLGA but grew impatient at its moderation. In 1908 Hanna Sheehy Skeffington helped to found the the **Irish Women's Franchise League** to lead a more militant campaign for the franchise.

Votes for women

The issue of votes for women came to the fore in 1910-12. Several bills to give the vote to women were introduced at Westminster but all were defeated because of disagreement within the political parties.

Although many Home Rule MPs wanted to back these bills, Redmond and Dillon were opposed. Dillon told a women's deputation:

Women's suffrage will, I believe, be the ruin of our western civilisation. It will destroy the home, challenging the headship of man, laid down by God. (R.C. Owens, *Smashing Times*, p. 48)

In 1911 they forced Home Rule MPs to vote against a franchise bill in case it might bring down the Liberal government on whom they depended for Home Rule.

Women and Home Rule

When the third Home Rule bill was introduced in 1912, Redmond refused to consider giving women a vote in an Irish Home Rule parliament. Suffragists organised demonstrations in protest and heckled Redmond and other Home Rulers at public meetings.

Some resorted to violence and between 1912 and 1914, thirty five women, including Hanna Sheehy Skeffington were convicted of suffrage offences. Some went on hunger strike. When the Liberal Prime Minister, Herbert Asquith, visited Dublin in 1912, two English suffragists threw a hatchet at him.

Unionist women

The all-pervading division between nationalist and unionist divided women too. Although the IWFL tried to avoid the issue, women from a unionist background thought it was too nationalist.

Some like Anna Haslam considered that the cause of women's rights transcended all political differences and supported the IWFL, even when they disapproved of some of its policies. Others preferred to ignore the suffrage issue altogether and concentrate on supporting the unionist cause, though Carson was no more sympathetic to women's rights than Redmond.

The Ulster Women's Unionist Council

In 1911 the Ulster Women's Unionist Council was founded. By 1912 it had a membership of about 45,000 women and declared 'we will stand by our husbands, our brothers and our sons in whatever stand they may be forced to take in defending our liberties against the tyranny of Home Rule'. They organised signatures for the Ulster Covenant, acted as back-up to the Ulster Volunteers and did propaganda work for the unionist cause.

Women and the labour movement

Work on women's right drew many middle class women towards the labour movement. Working women whose wages were far lower than men's were the most under-privileged section of society. Attempts to get them involved in trade unions had begun in Belfast in the 1880s but had only limited success.

In 1911 the **Irish Women Workers' Union** was set up. Delia Larkin was secretary and it had the backing of Constance Markievicz, Hanna Sheehy Skeffington and others. It was supported by James Connolly who was an enthusiastic feminist.

During the 1913 strike, members of the IWFL organised soup kitchens to feed the strikers. In spite of this, however, the suffrage movement drew mainly on middle class women. Only a few working class women ever became involved.

The war

After war broke out in 1914 the women's movement began to fragment. Like the

Unionist women signing the Ulster Covenant.

Constance Markievicz.

men, women were divided between those unionists and nationalists who supported the war effort and the extreme nationalists and the socialists who rejected any part in it.

The IWFL opposed Irish involvement as did Cumann na mBan which was set up as a women's auxiliary to the Irish volunteers in 1914. (see page 206) Extreme nationalists welcomed the women's support. In 1916, probably because of Connolly, the Proclamation of the Republic was addressed equally to 'Irishmen and Irishwomen'.

Votes at last

In 1918, the United Kingdom government at last agreed to give the vote to women over thirty. In the election of that year the ninety-year-old campaigner, Anna Haslam, was one of those who cast their votes for the first time. Two women contested seats and one, Constance Markievicz, was elected as an MP.

Women played a leading role in the struggle for Irish independence which followed. The 1922 Constitution of the Free State acknowledged their contribution by giving the vote equally to women and men. Only in 1928 did the United Kingdom parliament concede this right to women in Northern Ireland.

Chapter 15

Cultural nationalism

Introduction
Nationalist Ireland was quiet during the two decades that followed the fall of Parnell. Until the beginning of the Home Rule crisis in 1910 there was little of the political excitement that had marked the 1880s.

But behind the scenes, changes were taking place. New movements which would shape our country in the twentieth century were beginning, and the men and women who were to lead it were emerging to take their places on the stage of history.

Cultural nationalism
The land and Home Rule movements had been concerned with economic and political issues but the new movements were different. They stressed the importance of Irish identity, Irish race and Irish culture. They tried to answer the questions like:

- what makes a person Irish?
- what makes the Irish different from the English?
- what entitles the Irish to demand their own government?

Questions like these had first been put in the 1840s by the Young Irelanders. Afterwards they were laid aside while people concentrated on practical issues like Home Rule and land ownership. But they were always there in the background. In the 1890s and even more in the early 1900s they came to the fore in the development we call **cultural nationalism**.

The decline of native traditions
The most obvious difference between the English and the Irish was the existence of the Irish language and the customs, stories, music and traditions associated with it. These were the distinguishing marks of Irishness. But by the end of the nineteenth century these marks were disappearing fast. Ireland was developing an English culture which was indistinguishable from that in Britain.

The decline in Irish traditions had begun with the plantations of the seventeenth century. By 1800 the upper- and middle-classes, and most townspeople were English in speech and customs. In the nineteenth century this process speeded up. Widespread education, growing literacy, the mass production of newspapers and books, and the comparative ease of travel made English culture more accessible.

The Gaelic Athletic Association

The start of organised games

One area where the arrival of English traditions was easy to see was sport. Up to the nineteenth century sport was not organised. All over Europe country people played games which involved kicking a ball, carrying it over a line or hitting it with a stick. Each locality had its own rules, the number of players varied from a handful to hundreds and fighting was common. Games like these were more fun for the players than for the spectators.

With the industrial revolution, more people went to live in cities where unregulated sport was impossible. In Britain, the first country to be urbanised, organised spectator sport began to be developed. Groups like the Football Association and the Rugby Union created the games we know today. They drew up rules, bought pitches and organised tournaments.

These games provided entertainment for spectators as much as for players. As other countries became urbanised, they adopted the British rules for soccer, rugby, cricket and tennis.

From the 1860s onwards these sports spread to Ireland. This dismayed nationalists who saw them undermining Irish traditions. This view was expressed by the Catholic Archbishop of Cashel, Thomas Croke, when he lamented:

> Ball-playing, hurling, foot-ball kicking according to Irish rules, leaping in various ways, wrestling, hand-grips, top-pegging, leap-frog, rounders, tip-in-the-hat and all such favourite exercises and amusements amongst men and boys may now be said to be not only dead and buried, but in several localities to be entirely forgotten and unknown. And what have we got in their stead? We have got such foreign and fantastical field sports as lawn tennis, polo, croquet, cricket and the like ... (*Sixty Glorious Years: a history of the GAA*, p. 11)

Michael Cusack

The man who helped to develop distinctively Irish games was **Michael Cusack**. Born in Clare in 1847, Cusack was a big, bearded man given to extravagant gestures and eccentric behaviour. He was a teacher and a keen sportsman who played rugby and cricket with enthusiasm. He was also a nationalist, involved with the Fenians and with an early movement to revive the Irish language.

In 1882, perhaps influenced by nationalism but also disliking the snobbery which kept farmers and working men out of cricket and rugby clubs, he called for 'Irish' games. He set up the Dublin 'Hurling Club' in opposition to the Trinity College 'Hurley Club' which had been in existence for years. His club played a much more vigorous game than the hockey-like 'hurley' favoured by the Trinity men.

Michael Cusack

1 November, 1884: the foundation of the GAA

Cusack then began to campaign for a movement to sponsor Irish games. He won the backing of some Fenians and of **Maurice Davin**, a Tipperary man who was then Ireland's most famous athlete. They called a meeting in Thurles on 1 November 1884, at which the **Gaelic Athletic Association (GAA)** was set up. Davin was elected President, with Cusack as secretary. Parnell, Davitt and Archbishop Croke became patrons of the new Association.

Archbishop Croke

The GAA and Irish nationalism

The choice of patrons showed that the GAA was a nationalist organisation from the start. Its rules, first drawn up in 1885, contained two items which reinforced the division between unionist and nationalist.

- Games were played on Sunday. This was necessary to achieve Cusack's aim of allowing working men, with no other free time, to be involved, but it was offensive to many Protestants who saw it as desecrating the sabbath.

- Members of the GAA were 'banned' from playing other games. This was necessary if the GAA was to survive the competition of stronger, British-based sports but it was also divisive.

The IRB's role in the GAA

From the start, IRB men were prominent in the Association and by 1886 they controlled it. Cusack, who was an inefficient secretary, was expelled in 1885 and Davin, who opposed the dominance of the IRB, was expelled in 1887. However, Catholic priests who also became involved in the Association, resented the role of the IRB. When the Parnellite split occurred, the GAA divided in two. The clerical wing opposed Parnell and the republican wing supported him. The split ended when the Home Rule party reunited in 1900.

Although later leaders of the GAA remained strongly nationalist and even republican, they had learnt their lesson. From then on they kept sport and politics apart. The GAA remained neutral during divisions in nationalist politics such as the split in the Irish Volunteers in 1914, the Treaty and the Civil War. It provided a central ground on which nationalists of all views could meet.

The spread of the GAA

The GAA drew up its first set of rules in 1885 though they were constantly adjusted thereafter. It got off to a good start in the 1880s, with hundreds of clubs being set up. It organised the first All-Ireland in 1887.

Weakened by the Parnellite split, the GAA declined in the 1890s, but after 1900 it expanded rapidly. It spread through the countryside, with a club in every parish, usually named after some nationalist hero or event. But it was less successful in the cities. County, provincial and All-Ireland competitions were organised and drew large attendances on Sundays. Keen followers thought nothing of cycling fifty miles to see their team play and then cycling home to face a day's work on Monday.

The GAA and cultural nationalism

After 1900 the GAA linked itself to the cultural nationalist movement by insisting on using the Irish language and on giving Irish-made prizes. The ban on 'foreign games' (such as rugby and soccer) was vigorously enforced and it was extended to stop members of the RIC and the British army from joining the Association.

The 1907 *Gaelic Athletic Annual* described the GAA's ideal member:

> a matchless athlete, sober, pure in mind, speech and deed, self-possessed and self reliant, self-respecting, loving his religion and his country with a deep resistless love, earnest in thought and effective in action.

It aimed at developing a strong sense of local and national pride, helped its members to develop organisational skills and, at club level, provided a training in democracy.

Some members also saw the sports field as the place where the soldiers of a future Irish struggle would get their training. The IRB avoided public involvement after 1900, but it seems to have used the GAA as a recruiting and training ground for members. It has been said that the GAA trained the footsoldiers of the independence struggle that developed after 1916.

The Gaelic League

The decline of the Irish language
The Irish language declined steadily throughout the nineteenth century. In 1851 23 per cent of the population spoke Irish; by 1901 only 14 per cent did so. Most of them lived in the more inaccessible areas around the west and south coasts. Elsewhere English was the only language most people knew.

English replaced Irish for a number of reasons.

- English was the language of power, used by landlords and their agents, by courts and police, by the government and even by Irish politicians. Davitt was one of the few Irish leaders able to address an audience of Mayo farmers in their own language.

- Irish was associated with poverty and ignorance. Those who spoke it were the poorest people in the country. As a result many despised it and wanted to forget that they knew it.

- There were few books and no newspapers in Irish, so people who wanted to learn to read and write it could not easily do so. When J. M. Synge visited Aran in 1904 he found that children who spoke Irish could hardly read it but they could read English.

- Many parents knew their children might have to emigrate and that English would be more useful than Irish wherever they went. So they encouraged the schools to teach English. Some parents who spoke Irish between themselves, never used it when speaking to their children.

Rediscovering Gaelic culture
Of course, Irish had a long and rich history but only scholars were aware of it. From

the 1870s that began to change. European scholars began to study the origin of languages. Irish, which has one of the oldest written literatures in Europe, attracted their attention. They came to Ireland to read ancient Irish manuscripts and their interest aroused a response among Irish people.

In 1879 **Standish O'Grady** published a book called the *Bardic Literature of Ireland*. It contained an English version of many of the old myths about Finn and the Fianna and Cuchulainn and the Red Branch Knights. People read them for the first time and were amazed to find that Ireland had a history much older than England's and stories as good as those of Greece and Rome.

At the same time other people began collecting the folktales that the country people told in their cottages at night and the songs they sang. **Douglas Hyde** (1860-1949) was one of those involved. He was born in Roscommon, the son of a Church of Ireland rector. As a boy he learnt Irish from the local people and later studied it in Trinity. In the 1890s he went to the west to collect stories and poems and published the material he collected in three books: *Leabhar Sgéalaigheachta* in 1889, *Cois na Teine* in 1890 and *Abhráin Grádh Cúige Connacht* in 1893.

These books opened up a new world to many Irish people. **Lady Gregory** has described their impact on her:

> It was an upsetting of the table of values, an astonishing excitement... I was becoming conscious of a world close to me and that I had been ignorant of. It was not now in the corners of the newspapers that I looked for poetic emotion, nor even to the singers in the streets. It was among the farmers and the potato diggers and the old men in the workhouses and the beggars at my own door that I found what was beyond these in the expression of love and grief and the pain of parting that are the disclosure of the individual soul. (E. Coxhead, *Lady Gregory*, p. 42)

Douglas Hyde

Saving Irish

These discoveries made people aware that it would be a tragedy if Irish were allowed to die. In 1877 the **Society for the Preservation of the Irish Language**, was set up with the backing of some Fenians and Home Rulers.

It was a pressure group rather than a mass movement. It got Irish included among the subjects in the Intermediate Examination in 1878. It tried to encourage schools to teach Irish but with only a limited success. It published the *Gaelic Journal* and a *First Irish Book* with simple lessons. Many of the later leaders of the Gaelic League became involved in the language movement through the Society. However from 1880 onwards it was weakened by a number of quarrels among its members.

The National Literary Society

In 1892 an old Fenian, **John O'Leary** and a number of young men, including Hyde and the poet **W.B. Yeats** founded the **National Literary Society**. Its aim was to publicise the literature, folklore and legends of Ireland.

1892: Douglas Hyde's challenge

In 1892 Douglas Hyde gave a lecture to the Society. He called it 'The Necessity of De-Anglicising the Irish People'. He recalled that an Italian nationalist said that the Irish were not really a nation because they had lost the 'notes of nationalism', that is, their language and culture. Hyde challenged the people to prove him wrong.

The lecture caused a sensation and people took up his challenge. Among them was **Eoin MacNeill** (1867-1945). Born in an Irish-speaking community in Co. Antrim, MacNeill was a student of early Irish history and later professor in UCD.

4 August 1893: the foundation of the Gaelic League

In August 1893 Hyde and MacNeill founded the Gaelic League. They planned to halt the anglicisation of Ireland in several ways:

- they wanted to encourage Irish people to take pride in their language and culture.

- they wanted to stop the decline of Irish and restore it as a spoken language.

- they wanted to create a new Irish literature and to publish books and newspapers in modern Irish.

The progress of the League

The League spread slowly at first. By 1897 it had only forty-three clubs. Its aim of reviving spoken Irish was helped when a textbook, *Simple Lessons in Irish* appeared. It was written by **Eugene O'Growney**, the professor of Irish in Maynooth. *Simple Lessons* made Irish easier to teach and to learn.

After 1900 the League began to expand rapidly. This owed much to the enthusiasm of teachers who often cycled miles from village to village, teaching Irish classes in their spare time. By 1904 there were 600 League clubs throughout the country.

An Claidheamh Soluis

In 1899 the Gaelic League started a newspaper, *An Claidheamh Soluis*, which was edited by **Patrick Pearse** from 1903 to 1909. It published articles, poems and stories in Irish and encouraged new writers in Irish like **Padraic Ó Conaire**, an t**Athair Peadar Ó Laoghaire** and Pearse himself. It also published books by these and other writers.

The League organised dancing and singing classes, *feiseanna* and *ceilidhe*. From 1898 it organised an annual festival of culture, *an tOireachtas*. Summer courses in Gaeltacht areas were another of the League's popular activities.

This social aspect of the League's work may have been its biggest attraction for young people, especially women. Stern parents could be persuaded to allow them to go out for the serious and worthy business of learning Irish. Marriages could be made through the League, like that of **Eamon de Valera** and **Sinéad Flannagan** in 1910. Although many thousands of people joined the League, it is likely that only a tiny fraction of them became good Irish speakers. Most probably learnt no more than a *cupla focal* but they had a lot of fun in the process.

The League was also involved in a number of popular agitations. It campaigned successfully to have Irish made compulsory for admission to the new National University in 1909. It got the Post Office to accept letters addressed in Irish and changed the law to allow shopkeepers to put their names in Irish over their shops.

The League and the national movement

By 1906 the League had about 75,000 members. They were not confined to nationalist areas. There was a branch in Belfast and several others throughout Ulster, which attracted people of a unionist background. This pleased Hyde who had hoped that love of the Irish language would be a bridge between Catholic and Protestant, unionist and nationalist.

But this hope became harder to maintain as time passed. Hyde's ideal was attacked by both sides.

• Many unionists believed that the League undermined the Union because it stressed the things that made Ireland different from Britain. They felt that no one could belong to the League and be a good unionist.

• On the other hand, nationalist members came to believe that only an Irish government could protect the Irish language and culture. This belief led them to favour a more complete form of independence than Home Rule offered. Many joined the IRB and in 1915 they forced a change in the League's constitution, committing it to support a separate Irish republic. Hyde, his dream of a neutral organisation in tatters, resigned as president.

In 1915 a new ideal for League members was put into words by Patrick Pearse in a famous speech. He wanted, he said, an 'Ireland, not free merely but Gaelic as well; not Gaelic merely but free as well'. This phrase expressed what many members of the League had by then come to see as their purpose. They hoped to lead Ireland to a full independence, where the Irish language could be preserved. **Pearse**, **MacDonagh**, **O'Rahilly**, **Brugha**, **Collins** and **de Valera**, to name but a few, drew the inspiration for their republican separatism from the League.

The Irish Literary Revival

The literary revival
Not all of those who were excited by the discovery of ancient Irish literature and legends wanted to revive the Irish language. Some wanted to create a new and clearly Irish literature, using the English language. We call this the **Irish literary revival**.

W. B. Yeats (1865-1939)
At the centre of the movement was the poet, **W. B. Yeats**. Born in Dublin, the son of a portrait painter, Yeats wanted to be a poet and left Dublin for London. In the late 1880s he met O'Leary and Standish O'Grady and became interested in Irish legends. In them he found a new and distinctive source for poetry and drama. As he wrote later:

> I made my song a coat
> Covered with embroideries
> Out of old mythologies
> From heel to throat.

Lady Augusta Gregory

From then on, many of his poems used legends, folktales and the placenames of Ireland, especially of Sligo, where he spent many childhood holidays.

In 1889 Yeats met the beautiful **Maud Gonne** and fell hopelessly in love with her. Under her influence he became involved with the IRB. He returned to Ireland, met other writers and in 1892 helped to found the **National Literary Society**.

The Irish Literary Theatre

Among the writers Yeats met were **Edward Martyn** and **Lady Augusta Gregory**. They were both landlords from Galway who were interested in collecting Irish folktales and in using these as a basis for novels, poems and plays.

In 1898 at Lady Gregory's home in Coole Park, Co. Galway, they set up the **Irish Literary Theatre**, to put on plays by Irish writers using Irish subjects. Their first play was Yeat's own *The Countess Cathleen* which was put on in 1899. In 1902 he wrote *Cathleen Ní Houlihán* in which Maud Gonne played the lead. This play was about Ireland and the willingness of young men to die for her. Years later Yeats questioned the influence this play may have had:

> Did that play of mine send out
> Certain men the English shot?

The Abbey

The Literary Theatre had two problems:

* it lacked good actors.

W. B. Yeats and Sarah Allgood

- it lacked a permanent theatre.

They solved the first problem by linking up with a group of talented amateur actors led by two brothers, **Frank and William Fay**. They developed a distinctive style of acting and encouraged gifted actors like **Sarah Allgood**. The actors worked during the day and gave their services free to the Literary Theatre at night.

In 1904 a wealthy Englishwoman, **Annie Horniman**, who admired Yeats, solved their second problem. She bought a hall in Abbey Street and had it refurbished to make a 500 seat theatre. This theatre, renamed the **Abbey** and supported until 1911 by a subsidy from Miss Horniman, became the permanent home of the Irish Literary Theatre.

J. M. Synge and the Abbey

The Abbey put on plays by Lady Gregory, Hyde and others but the most brilliant dramatist of the early years was **John M. Synge**.

Synge (1871-1909) was born in Dublin and as a young man went to Paris to write. He heard about the literary revival and returned in 1899. He went to live on the Aran islands, learning Irish and listening to the stories and songs of the people there.

From these stories he wrote two plays, *The Shadow of the Glen* in 1903 and *Riders to the Sea* in 1904. The *Shadow of the Glen* was about a young woman who leaves a loveless arranged marriage with an older man, to run off with a tramp. Nationalists objected that this was a libel on Irishwomen who were always chaste and pure. In the row that followed, Hyde resigned from the Abbey.

There was an even bigger row in 1907 when the Abbey staged Synge's most

John Millington Synge

famous play, *The Playboy of the Western World*. It is about a man who thinks he has killed his father. Written in the language of country people in the west, it sounded strange to Dublin ears.

Many nationalists felt it mocked Irish people and showed them in a bad light. On the first night, there were riots. In *An Claidheamh Soluis*, Pearse attacked the play on the grounds that it 'showed bitter contempt for all that is fine and worthy'. He later regretted this attack and apologised for it.

The Revival Goes Sour

The literary revival and nationalism

The rows about Synge's plays showed that there were two ways of seeing the literary revival.

- For some, its main purpose was to make propaganda for the nationalist cause. It did not matter if the poems, plays and novels produced were bad, so long as they presented the Irish people in a good light and encouraged their pride and self-reliance.

- For others, the main aim was to produce good books that would make Ireland an important part of the mainstream of European literature. Yeats put this clearly when he wrote in 1903:

I had a very vivid dream one night and I made Cathleen Ní Houlihán out of this dream. But if some external necessity had forced me to write nothing but drama with an obvious patriotic intention, instead of letting my work shape itself to the casual impulses of dreams and daily thoughts, I would have lost in a short time the power to write movingly upon any theme. (Una Ellis-Fermor, *The Irish Dramatic Movement*, p. 17)

The tension between these two points of view was complicated by the difficulty of deciding who exactly 'the Irish people' were. Many believed, with Arthur Griffith and Douglas Hyde, that anyone living in or working for Ireland, regardless of religion or race, was Irish. But others had a narrower definition of Irishness. To some, only Irish-speaking peasants in the west were truly 'Irish'. Others would limit Irishness to Irish Catholics.

D. P. Moran and the *Leader*

The most outspoken advocate of the latter position was **D. P. Moran**. Born in Waterford in 1871, Moran was a journalist. He worked in London and returned to Dublin in 1898. He joined the Gaelic League and set up a newspaper, the *Leader* in 1900. In it he put forward his view of Irishness and in 1905 set it out in his book, *The philosophy of Irish Ireland*.

Moran believed that the Irish and the English were at war in what he called 'the battle of two civilisations'. The Irish language and Catholicism were the Irish weapons in this war, and he saw Protestants as representing England.

Moran rejected anything that linked Ireland to Britain. He condemned the Irish Parliamentary party which he thought was corrupted by its activities in London. He also attacked the literary revival and even the co-operative movement because some of their leaders were Protestant. His weapon was mockery. He invented terms like 'West Briton' and 'Seonín' to mock those who admired and tried to copy English ways or indeed, anyone who took a different line from Moran's own.

The growth of sectarianism

Moran's ideas appealed to the Catholic middle-class, many of whom felt that they did not get their fair share of jobs in the government or in industries which were mainly controlled by unionists.

He also had the support of a number of Catholic movements which emerged about this time. These included the **Temperance Crusade** which campaigned against excessive drinking and the **Literature Crusade** which attacked British newspapers on the grounds that they were corrupting Irish morals.

Naturally, Moran's intolerant views alarmed Protestants. They help to explain why many of them began to withdraw from the cultural revival after about 1908.

Ne Temere

Another blow to good community relations was the *Ne Temere* decree which Pope

Pius X issued in 1908. This forbad mixed marriages between Catholics and Protestants, unless the Catholic guaranteed to bring up any children of the marriage as Catholics. Up to this, boys had followed their father's faith and girls had gone with their mother's.

Ne Temere aroused fears among Protestants who were always uncomfortably aware that they were only a small minority in Ireland. If it was enforced, Irish Protestants could disappear. It had a very damaging effect on the relations between the two communities.

Decline of cultural nationalism

After about 1908 cultural nationalism lost much of its energy. There were a number of reasons for this.

- The sectarianism and racism advocated by Moran and his like, while never widely accepted, made it more difficult for Protestants such as Hyde, Yeats, Lady Gregory or Horace Plunkett to feel completely comfortable in the movements they had helped to create.

- The Gaelic League quarrelled with the Catholic bishops over its policy of getting Irish into schools and the new National University. This led many priests to withdraw their support. The number of branches fell from 964 in 1906 to 388 by 1913.

- The revival of interest in Home Rule after 1910 drew attention away from the whole area of cultural nationalism.

Many of those involved in the exciting early days of the revival were bitterly disillusioned. Yeats summed the feeling up when he wrote in 1913:

> Romantic Ireland's dead and gone,
> Its with O'Leary in the grave.

Chapter 16

The new nationalism

Introduction

Cultural nationalism contributed to the emergence of two nationalist movements after 1900. Both despised the constitutional nationalism of the Home Rule party and were more extreme both in their aims for Irish independence and in the means they proposed to use to achieve it. One of them, **Sinn Féin**, was a completely new movement; the other, the **IRB,** was a revitalised and more effective version of an old organisation.

Sinn Féin

Arthur Griffith 1871-1922

Arthur Griffith was the founder of Sinn Féin. Born in Dublin in 1871, he trained as a printer and became involved in the Gaelic League and the literary movement. He was also sworn into the IRB. In 1897 unemployment and ill-health forced him to emigrate to South Africa.

In 1898 he returned and founded a weekly newspaper, *The United Irishman*. For the next twenty years he made a precarious living producing, and often writing, little newspapers under various titles. Through them, he exercised a great influence on the development of a more extreme kind of nationalism.

Griffith encouraged cultural nationalism. Early contributors to his paper included Yeats, Hyde and Edward Martyn. He was close to Maud Gonne who contributed £1.25 each week towards the costs of *The United Irishman*.

In 1900 Griffith founded an organisation, **Cumann na nGaedheal** to co-ordinate the activities of various nationalist groups. Its programme included the teaching of Irish history, literature, language and music, the encouragement of Irish industries and the cultivating of a fraternal spirit among Irishmen.

Griffith's ideas

Griffith's main concern was with political issues. He himself was a republican, but he knew that the violence necessary to win complete independence was not acceptable to most Irish people. At the same time he was contemptuous of Home Rule. He believed that it would leave Ireland too much under British control and that the Home Rule leaders had been corrupted by the years they spent in Westminster trying to persuade the British to concede it.

Arthur Griffith

1904: the Resurrection of Hungary

Griffith looked for an alternative to these two policies. He found it in the experience of the Hungarians in their struggle for independence within the Austrian Empire. He developed his ideas in *The United Irishman* and in 1904 published them in a book called *The Resurrection of Hungary*.

In this book Griffith described how in 1866 the Hungarians had withdrawn their representatives from the Austrian parliament and refused to recognise the Austrian government. This led to Hungary being given equal status with Austria in the Empire, while the Emperor of Austria became King of Hungary.

Griffith argued that Ireland should do the same. These were his proposals.

- Irish MPs would leave Westminster. In Dublin, they would join with representatives from local councils to form a **council of three hundred**. It would become the government of Ireland, set up an Irish civil service and Irish departments of government and peacefully displace the British administration.

- Griffith hoped to win over unionists by keeping the King of England as King of Ireland. This idea, known as **Dual Monarchy**, was similar to the Hungarian solution. In fact, this was also the system that existed in Ireland before the Union in 1800.

- Griffith wanted economic as well as political independence. He borrowed the ideas of the German economist, **Friedrich List**. List said that the right to protect its own industries by tariff barriers was as necessary for a nation's independence as its own language and literature. His ideas had influenced the economic policy of the German Empire which by 1900 had surpassed Britain in industrial output.

Griffith argued that an independent Ireland, too, must build up its own industries behind tariff walls. He ignored the fact that successful Irish industries, such as shipbuilding, linen and brewing, already existed. They depended for their success on British markets and would be more harmed than helped by such a policy. In his economic policy, Griffith showed the usual nationalist ignorance of the economic basis of the unionist opposition to Irish self-government.

Setting up Sinn Féin

In 1905 Griffith formed a movement to put these ideas into effect. It was called **Sinn Féin** (*ourselves*). The use of an Irish name showed the impact of the Gaelic revival and the meaning echoed the sense of self-reliance and self-confidence which marked this period. This may explain why the name Sinn Féin survived long after Griffith's party ceased to exist.

Sinn Féin aimed:

- to re-establish the independence of Ireland by withdrawing from the Westminster parliament and setting up a government in Dublin.

- to develop Irish industry by setting up a national bank to encourage the investment of Irish capital in Irish industries, by establishing an Irish merchant navy and stock exchange, and by fostering a 'buy Irish' campaign.

- to reform the poor laws and the education system.

Other clubs and societies joined Sinn Féin. In 1908 it became a political party with over 100 branches throughout the country. It was the first Irish political party to admit women as full members.

Griffith's tactics

Sinn Féin won some seats on the new local councils and on the Boards of Guardians. In 1908 an opportunity came to contest a parliamentary election. The Liberals, who had returned to power in 1905, offered the Irish party a council scheme which the party rejected. (see page 193) One MP, **Charles Dolan**, resigned his seat in North Leitrim in disgust. He joined Sinn Féin and then fought for his old seat as a Sinn Féin candidate. He was defeated, but he did win a third of the votes.

The decline of the first Sinn Féin*

Griffith was overjoyed. He believed that there was widespread support for his ideas and he decided to encourage it by turning his weekly newspaper, now called *Sinn Féin*, into a daily publication.

---

*Griffith's Sinn Féin, which lasted from 1905-1910, is usually called the 'first' Sinn Féin to distinguish it from the very different 'second' Sinn Féin which was formed in 1917 after the 1916 rising.

The venture failed. Quarrels developed in the movement and people left it. Then in 1910 the constitutional crisis in Britain made it seem as though Home Rule would soon be a reality. The Home Rule party revived and Sinn Féin declined. Finally, the revival of the IRB made some of Griffith's young followers impatient with his pacifism. They set up their own paper, *Irish Freedom* which took many of Griffith's readers.

All this left Griffith on the verge of bankruptcy. Sinn Féin almost disappeared, but Griffith did not give up. Over the next few years he continued to preach his ideas to an apparently indifferent world. His persistence paid off. The party might be dead but the name Sinn Féin lived on, associated in people's minds with the cause of extreme nationalism.

The Revival of the IRB

The decline of the Fenian tradition

After the Phoenix Park murders and the growth of the Home Rule movement, the IRB and its American ally, Clan na Gael, declined in power and influence. In Ireland, only a few devoted republicans resisted the lure of Parnell's success and most Irish-Americans preferred to contribute their dollars to him.

Those who remained in the republican movement began to demand action. In response, a 'skirmishing fund' was set up and, in 1884, a number of buildings in England were blown up with dynamite. This futile policy led only to the death of some republicans and the imprisonment of others, one of whom was **Tom Clarke**.

After the failure of the bombing campaign, republicans concentrated on influencing other movements. They were active in the GAA, the Gaelic League and Sinn Féin. During the Parnellite split, they enjoyed a brief revival but it did not last. By the turn of the century the IRB was no more than a few old men meeting in public houses and waiting, as their constitution provided, for the Irish people to call them to war against England.

McCullough, Hobson and the revival of the IRB

The IRB experienced a revival in the early years of the century. Behind the revival were a number of young men, mostly from Ulster and mostly influenced by the cultural revival.

Two of them were **Denis McCullough** and **Bulmer Hobson**, both born in Belfast in 1883. McCullough's father was a Fenian and when Denis was eighteen he, too, was sworn into the IRB. He was bitterly disappointed to find it so inactive, but he soon set about reforming it. He expelled those, including his own father, who did not meet his standards of sobriety and discipline.

About this time he met Hobson, the son of a Quaker businessman. As a boy, Hobson had joined the Gaelic League and become a dedicated nationalist. He

187

founded the **Protestant National Association** to draw Ulster Protestants into the national movement. From this grew the **Ulster Literary Theatre**, a movement as successful in its day as the Abbey.

In 1904 McCullough swore Hobson into the IRB. They decided to found an open movement to spread republican ideas. In 1905 they began the **Dungannon Clubs**, which held discussions on national topics and campaigned against Irishmen joining the British army. Two valuable recruits to the clubs were the Leitrim man, **Seán MacDermott**, and the Tyrone man, **Patrick MacCartan**. Both soon joined the IRB.

In 1907 the Dungannon clubs merged with Sinn Féin, and Hobson and MacDermott moved to Dublin. Hobson made his living as a journalist and MacDermott became national organiser for Sinn Féin. He cycled about the country setting up branches and secretly swearing promising recruits into the IRB. In 1909 Hobson and **Countess Markievicz** founded **Na Fianna**, a nationalist boyscout-type movement which also became a recruiting ground for the IRB.

Seán MacDermott

The young men take over

The young men were revitalising the Brotherhood but the leadership was still in the hands of older men, who were sceptical of their policies. The reformers therefore plotted to gain control of the Supreme Council.

They were helped by **Tom Clarke** who had served fifteen years in jail for his part in the bombing campaign of the 1880s. Released in 1898 he went to America where he made contact with Devoy and Clan na Gael. In 1907 he returned to Dublin as Devoy's representative. His age, suffering and American contacts made him a much respected figure in the movement.

Countess Markievicz

Countess Markievicz with Na Fianna.

Tom Clarke

Clarke sided with the younger men and helped them to victory. In 1910, in the teeth of opposition from the old guard, Hobson began publishing a republican newspaper, *Irish Freedom*. One of the older men resigned in protest. Another was expelled for the alleged misuse of funds and a third resigned. By 1912 the change in personnel was complete. Hobson, MacDermott and the others could now turn the IRB in a more active direction.

The new IRB

The original IRB had been a mass movement with many members. This made it hard to keep secrets and easy for the police to penetrate the organisation. The new IRB now taking shape was different.

It was smaller, with only about 2,000 to 3,000 members. They were handpicked for their dedication, their discipline and their sobriety. They were too few in number to bring about a revolution on their own, but they systematically infiltrated other organisations to use them for republican purposes. As we shall see in chapter 18, this policy achieved its greatest success in 1913 with the **Irish Volunteers**.

Chapter 17

1900-10: John Redmond and the Home Rule party

John Redmond: 1856-1918 and John Dillon: 1851-1927

From its re-union in 1900 (see page 142) to 1918 the Home Rule party was led by **John Redmond**. He had first been elected to Parliament in 1881 and remained loyal to Parnell when the party split over the O'Shea divorce. After Parnell's death, he took over the leadership of the Parnellite faction.

When the party re-united in 1900, **John Dillon**, leader of the anti-Parnellites, stepped aside in favour of Redmond. After a short period of mutual suspicion, Dillon and Redmond began to work well together. Each man had different interests and talents and they formed a successful team.

Redmond, who was a fine speaker, liked the House of Commons and spent much of his time in London. He was a skilful negotiator and developed a good relationship with leading British politicians.

Dillon, a Mayo man who had been an ardent Land Leaguer, disliked London. He distrusted the British system which he felt could corrupt Irish leaders. He mostly stayed in Ireland and kept Redmond in touch with Irish feelings.

John Redmond

John Dillon

Joseph Devlin: 1879-1934

Another prominent member of the party at this time was Joseph Devlin. A native of Belfast, Devlin entered parliament in 1902. He represented Ulster Catholics and was the leader of the Ancient Order of Hibernians, the Catholics' answer to the sectarian Orange Order. This gave him considerable influence. From 1906 he also controlled the party branches in the constituencies.

Joseph Devlin

Further disunity

Between them, these men gave effective leadership to the Home Rule movement until it was undermined by the change of Irish public opinion during World War 1. But their party was never as strong or united as Parnell's had been.

This was mainly due to quarrels with **T.M. Healy** and later with **William O'Brien**. (see page 146) They broke with Redmond and formed their own party, which was based mainly in the Cork area. However, the quarrels were more about personalities than issues. The 'Healyites' supported Home Rule, so this split made little difference to the general development of Irish affairs.

1900-1909: the years of frustration

The years after 1900 were frustrating for Home Rulers. Up to 1905 the Conservatives were in power and Home Rule was impossible.

In 1906 Redmond's allies, the Liberals, won a general election and hope of Home Rule revived. It was quickly dashed. The Liberals still promised Home Rule but none of them was as committed to it as Gladstone had been. They made it clear to Redmond that they were in no hurry to bring in a Home Rule bill.

There was a simple reason for this. The Liberals did not control the House of Lords, so any Home Rule bill was sure to be defeated there. Thus it was a waste of time to bring one in in the first place. Liberals felt it would be more sensible to concentrate on social reforms like old age pensions and unemployment and sickness benefits.

Unfortunately for Redmond, he could do nothing to make the Liberals change their minds. They had a huge overall majority in the Commons and did not need the Irish votes.

1906-7: the Irish Council proposal

Instead of Home Rule, the Liberals offered Redmond an Irish Council. This was much the same as the devolution scheme that Sir Anthony MacDonnell had proposed some years before. (see page 146) The Council would be partly elected and partly appointed and would control certain government departments, such as agriculture and education.

At first Redmond considered accepting the Council but when it became clear that it was unpopular with his followers, he turned it down. One Home Rule MP, C. J. Dolan became so frustrated with failure of the Liberal alliance to deliver Home Rule that he left the party in 1907 and joined Sinn Féin.

1906-9: Liberal reforms

Instead of Home Rule, the Liberals introduced social reforms. Several of these affected Ireland.

- Under a Land Act brought in by the Chief Secretary, **Augustine Birrell**, in 1909 more money was made available to continue the Wyndham land purchase programme.

- 3000 tenants who were still homeless after being evicted during the Plan of Campaign were restored to their farms.

- Money was provided to build houses for labourers. By 1920 50,000 labourers' cottages had been built under this and other Acts.

- Old age pensions were introduced. Although very small (25p a week for a single person, 37.5p for a married couple) they were very welcome to many poor people in Ireland.

- In 1908 Birrell gave the Catholic bishops the university they had long demanded when he set up the **National University**. In theory the National University was non-denominational but in practice it was Catholic-controlled.

1909-11: the clash with the Lords

Between 1906 and 1909 several other reforms the Liberals had planned were thrown out by the Conservative-controlled House of Lords. Leading Liberals became very angry at this. They had won the election by promising the voters to deal with poverty and social injustice but the Conservatives were using the unelected Lords to defeat the voters' wishes. They came to feel that the Lords' veto (their power to block any bill) must be removed.

The issue came to a head over the 1909 budget. The Chancellor of the Exchequer

Augustine Birrell speaking to the House of Commons. He was Chief Secretary from 1907 to 1916, one of the largest terms of office in history. This sketch of the Commons' empty benches shows how little interest Irish affairs aroused in Westminster.

(i.e. finance minister), **David Lloyd George**, needed £16 million to pay for reforms like the old age pension and to build ships in the naval race with Germany. To get the money, he proposed to increase income tax and death duties, to impose an extra tax on incomes above £5,000 a year and to raise the taxes on tobacco and alcohol.

This taxation hit the rich who were well-represented in the Lords. They threw out the budget. This was almost a revolution. For two hundred years the Lords had always accepted any taxation bills passed by the Commons where the elected representatives of the tax-payers sat. Now they had broken that tradition.

The Liberal Prime Minister, **Herbert Asquith**, called a general election. He wanted the voters to decide whether the powers of the Lords should be reduced.

1910: Redmond wins the balance of power

Redmond recognised the importance of these developments. If the Liberals won and limited the power of the Lords, the way to Home Rule would be open. Therefore, although the new taxes on alcohol were unpopular in Ireland, he threw his support behind Asquith in the election which took place in January 1910.

The results were everything Redmond had hoped for, as Table A shows.

Results of the January 1910 election	
Liberals	272 MPs
Conservatives	252 MPs
Labour	42 MPs
Irish Unionists	19 MPs
Redmondites	73 MPs
Healy and O'Brien	11 MPs

Table A ▲

He now held the balance of power in the Commons more clearly than Parnell had in 1886. The Liberals needed his votes to stay in power and he could demand Home Rule in return.

1911: the Parliament Act ends the Lord's veto

First the Lords' veto had to be removed. This was achieved by the **Parliament Act** which was finally passed in 1911.

The Act reduced the veto to a delaying power. Any bill which passed the Commons in three successive years would become law, even if the Lords continued to reject it. The Act also brought in payment for MPs and reduced the interval between elections from seven to five years.

1912: Redmond's reward – the third Home Rule bill

Throughout the passage of the Parliament Act, Redmond loyally supported Asquith

Home Rulers outside the Palace of Westminster. Devlin, known as 'Wee Joe' has his back to us, Redmond is beside him and Dillon is the tall man facing them. Behind are two dissident Home Rulers, O'Brien with the beard and Healy in the top hat.

and the Liberal government. Then he claimed his reward: a third Home Rule bill. This time, with the Lord's veto gone, it should at last become law and give Ireland its own Home Rule parliament.

An unfriendly comment on the power that Redmond wielded after the 1910 elections.

Chapter 18

1910-14: The Home Rule crisis

Different reactions to these developments

The destruction of the Lords' veto was greeted with enthusiasm in the nationalist community in Ireland. But what was a triumph for Irish nationalists was a catastrophe for Irish unionists.

Unionists had not changed their opposition to Home Rule since Gladstone's first bill in 1886. (see page 109) The long period of Conservative rule that followed had given them a sense of security. Even the Liberal victory of 1906 had not seemed a threat while the Lords retained their veto. Now the Parliament Act had removed that safeguard. What they had feared for a quarter of a century seemed about to happen.

Edward Carson (1854-1935)

Since 1886 the Unionist party in parliament retained its separate identity while co-operating closely with the Conservatives. From 1906 to 1910 it was led by an Englishman, Walter Long, but when he retired, the party chose Sir Edward Carson as their leader.

Carson was born in Dublin. He studied law and as a young barrister was employed by Balfour in his struggle against the Plan of Campaign. In the 1890s he moved to

Edward Carson

London where he built up a very successful legal practice. From 1892 to 1918 he was MP for Dublin University (Trinity) and from 1900 to 1905 had been a minister in the Conservative government.

Carson's tactics

Carson was a committed supporter of the Union. Like most southern unionists, he believed that Home Rule would be a disaster for the country and that Ireland as a whole was better off in the United Kingdom. He did not want to partition Ireland and leave Ulster within the Union while the rest of the country got Home Rule. To do so would have left his fellow southern unionists as a tiny minority in a nationalist state.

But Carson was willing to use the threat of partition to wreck Home Rule. He hoped that rather than lose Ulster, nationalists would give up the idea of self-government. Like most unionists, he believed that Ireland could not survive economically without the industries of Belfast. The partition of Ireland in 1920 was as much a defeat for Carson as it was for Redmond.

Sir James Craig (1871-1940)

These views were not fully shared by the Ulster unionists, whose leader was **James Craig**. Craig was a wealthy Belfast businessman. In 1906 he was elected MP for East Down and soon emerged as a prominent member of the Unionist party.

Throughout the campaign against the third Home Rule bill Craig acted as Carson's second-in-command, organising the meetings and demonstrations at which Carson spoke. He was also responsible for the formation of the **Ulster Volunteer Force** which threatened to fight against any Home Rule government.

James Craig

Like Carson, Craig hoped to stop Home Rule completely. But if that proved impossible, he was quite willing to accept partition. That would allow Ulster to remain within the Union while the rest of the country got Home Rule. Partition for him was an acceptable outcome to the struggle and he went on to become the first Prime Minister of Northern Ireland.

1911: the campaign against Home Rule begins

As soon as the Parliament Act passed, the unionists went into action. On 23 September 1911 Carson spoke to a rally of 50,000 unionists at Craigavon outside Belfast. He told them they must be prepared:

> the morning Home Rule passes, (ourselves) to become responsible for the government of the Protestant province of Ulster. (A. T. Q. Stewart, *The Ulster Crisis*, p. 47)

Two days later the first steps were taken to set up a provisional government which would take over the government of Ulster if Home Rule passed.

The Conservatives and the Home Rule bill

Thus even before the third Home Rule bill was introduced, the unionists showed that they intended to resist it by force. This was illegal but that did not prevent the British Conservatives from giving them their full support. There were two reasons for this.

- In 1911 the Conservative party was in disarray. It had lost three general elections and its stronghold, the House of Lords, had been destroyed. Many members felt

Carson speaking at an anti-Home Rule meeting. Note the prominent place of the Union Jack and the presence of a Protestant clergyman on the platform (right). The Protestant clergy were as emphatic in their support for the Union as Catholic priests were in backing Home Rule.

◆

bitter and were quarrelling among themselves. One of the few issues on which they could unite was the defence of Irish unionists.

- The Conservative leader, **Andrew Bonar Law,** had a strong personal commitment to Irish unionists. A Canadian by birth, his family originally came from Ulster and he had a romantic attachment to the province. In 1912 at a rally of British unionists he proclaimed 'I can imagine no length of resistance to which Ulster can go in which I would not be prepared to support them'. (R Blake, *The Unknown Prime Minister*, p. 130)

1911-12: preparing the Third Home Rule bill

After the Parliament Act passed, the Prime Minister, Asquith, the Chief Secretary, **Augustine Birrell**, and other Liberals began to prepare a Home Rule bill. They modelled it on Gladstone's bill of 1893 and spent a lot of time trying to decide how much power an Irish parliament should have over taxation. But they paid no attention to the protests of the unionists.

April 1912: the Third Home Rule bill in parliament

The Third Home Rule bill was introduced into the Commons in April 1912. Like its predecessors in 1886 and 1893, it proposed to set up an Irish parliament to deal with internal Irish affairs but excluding most taxation and the police. The Westminster parliament, to which Ireland would elect forty MPs, was to remain responsible for foreign and imperial policy (peace and war, trade, the Crown, etc).

The bill gave Ireland only a very limited independence but it was enthusiastically welcomed by nationalists. It was debated in the Commons but the debate was unreal. Everyone knew that with the support of the Liberal, Labour and Irish parties, it would pass. Then, after two years delay by the Lords, it would become law in 1914.

There was nothing the unionists could do in parliament to prevent this. If they wanted to stop Home Rule they had to organise their resistance outside the parliamentary arena.

The southern unionists

Unionist resistance varied according to the area in which they operated. Southern unionists were a small but wealthy minority in the three southern provinces of Ireland. (see page 105) There was little they could do in Ireland but they had powerful friends in Britain.

- Many senior army generals, including the Kerry-born field marshal, Lord Kitchener and the Longford born Sir Henry Wilson, were southern unionists.

- Eighty-six noblemen with estates in the south sat in the House of Lords and two of them, the Marquis of Lansdowne and the Earl of Midleton, were leading members of the Conservative Party.

- Eighteen southern unionists had been elected as Conservative MPs in British constituencies.

These men were well placed to influence British opinion. They concentrated their efforts on anti-Home Rule propaganda in Britain. They issued pamphlets and organised speeches and demonstrations to put the unionists' case before British voters.

The Ulster unionists

In Ulster the unionists, who made up half the population (see page 106), were in a much stronger position. They too relied on propaganda and pressure but they were also strong enough to engage in direct action.

1912: the Ulster Covenant

Throughout 1912 Carson held demonstrations all over Ulster, stirring up unionist support. The most famous of them occurred in September. Before it, unionist leaders drew up a document, setting out their views. In this document they stated that they opposed Home Rule because it would be:

> disastrous to the material well-being of Ulster as well as of the whole of Ireland, subversive of our civil and religious freedom, destructive of our citizenship and perilous to the unity of the Empire.

And they pledged themselves to:

> stand by one another in defending... our cherished position of equal citizenship in the United Kingdom and in using all means which may be found necessary to defeat the present conspiracy to set up a Home Rule Parliament in Ireland. And in the event of such a Parliament being forced upon us we further solemnly... pledge ourselves to refuse to recognise its authority.

They gave this document the title **'Ulster's Solemn League and Covenant'**, deliberately calling up biblical echoes of God's covenant (i.e. contract) with the Jewish people in the Old Testament. On 28 September 1912 at simultaneous rallies throughout Ulster, about 400,000 men signed it. Some even signed it in their own blood. About 250,000 women signed a separate Covenant at the same time.

1911-13: the Ulster Volunteer Force

The Covenant contained the words 'using *all means* that may become necessary to defeat the present conspiracy'. What that meant was made clear by the presence of well-drilled and armed men at unionist demonstrations. They were the **Ulster Volunteers**.

In 1911 some Orangemen in Tyrone had begun to drill and arm. Soon after that, an old law was revived. It allowed Justices of the Peace to permit men to arm and drill 'for the purpose of maintaining the constitution of the United Kingdom as now established'. Since many Justices were unionists, they were happy to give permission. Groups of Volunteers began to appear all over Ulster.

For Carson and Craig this development was a mixed blessing. The Volunteers could be used to put pressure on the government but there was a danger that some of them might engage in violence and damage the cause. To bring them under control, the Ulster Unionist Council decided early in 1913 to organise the separate groups into one body, to be known as **the Ulster Volunteer Force**.

Arming the Ulster Volunteers

The UVF appointed a retired general, Sir George Richardson, as their commander.

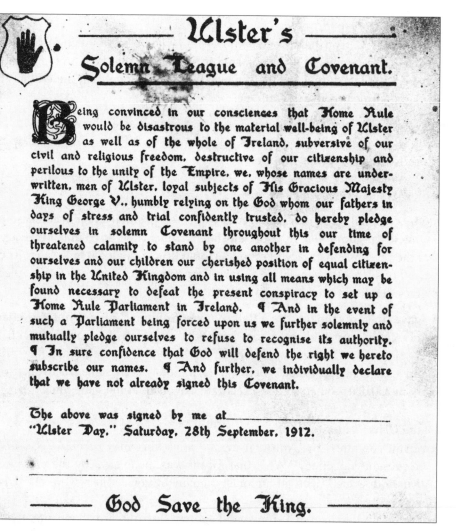

The Ulster Covenant

Many former soldiers joined the UVF and it began to acquire a military discipline. But it still lacked arms.

A few Volunteers smuggled in guns, but more were needed. A fund was set up and soon reached £1 million. Plans were laid to import a large consignment of arms from Germany. It was kept a closely guarded secret and in the meantime the UVF drilled with dummy wooden rifles.

This led many many Liberals and nationalists, to underestimate their seriousness. As late as November 1913 Redmond was able to write to Asquith 'I do not think that anything like a widespread rebellious movement can ever take place'. (R. Jenkins, *Asquith*, p. 328)

1912: proposals for compromise

Some British politicians, however, were less sure. As early as 1912 two Liberal ministers, David Lloyd George and Winston Churchill, had proposed that each county in Ulster be allowed to vote on whether to accept Home Rule or stay in the Union. This idea was called 'county option'.

1912-14: drifting towards disaster

Asquith and Birrell turned this proposal down, and throughout 1912 and 1913 did nothing to deal with the growing resistance in Ulster. There were various reasons for this:

- Like Parnell and most nationalists, Redmond knew very little about the Ulster unionists and he made no attempt to understand their fears.

- In Ireland as a whole the unionists were a small minority. In December 1910 they had won only nineteen seats compared with the eighty-four won by the Home Rulers. To the Liberals and their nationalist allies it seemed undemocratic that such a small minority could block the will of the majority.

- Traditionally, unionists had always been law abiding. Liberals and nationalists could not believe that they intended to use force. They thought Carson and Craig were bluffing and would accept Home Rule once parliament passed it. For this reason Redmond advised Birrell not to use force against the unionists.

- The police were more used to watching nationalists than unionists, so they had few informers in the unionist community. Thus they were unable to give the government much information about the strength of the UVF. As a result no one in London realised how strong they were.

- Asquith always preferred to put off dealing with a problem, hoping that it would go away. The Chief Secretary, Birrell, was coping with his wife's fatal illness and lacked the energy to deal with the crisis. Thus the two men mainly responsible for Ireland let the situation drift until it was too late.

1913-14: defining partition

Nevertheless, by late 1913 even they realised that some sort of compromise was essential if civil war was to be avoided. The only thing likely to work was to partition (divide) Ireland and give Ulster some kind of special treatment. But that raised some questions.

- What was meant by 'Ulster'?
- What kind of special treatment should it have?
- For how long should the 'special treatment' last?

The next few months were taken up in desperate attempts to answer these questions.

What was 'Ulster'?

This was the most difficult issue and the one on which all talks broke down. There were nine counties in Ulster, but not all of them had the same political point of view.

- Four counties – Antrim, Down, Armagh and Derry – had clear Protestant, unionist majorities but parts of them (i.e. Derry city, south Armagh and south Down) had local nationalist majorities.
- Three counties – Donegal, Cavan and Monaghan – had Catholic, nationalist majorities.
- Two counties – Tyrone and Fermanagh – were almost equally divided between the two sides.

So if 'Ulster' was to be excluded from Home Rule, which territories did that mean? Nine counties? Six counties? Four counties? Or some other division?

By 1914, Redmond had more or less accepted that areas with a unionist majority should be left out but he was determined that Tyrone, Fermanagh and other nationalist areas must be under a Dublin government. By then Carson too had given up hope of keeping the three Catholic counties but was determined to have the remaining six. By mid-1914 no agreement on this point was in sight.

What arrangement should be made for the excluded area?

Redmond offered Carson 'Home Rule within Home Rule' (i.e. a separate Belfast parliament under the overall control of the Dublin parliament). The unionists turned that down. They wanted to remain under the direct rule of the Westminster parliament. By 1914, this seemed the most likely solution.

How long was the exclusion to last?

Redmond offered a transition period of six years but Carson rejected this. He wanted a permanent exclusion. By 1914, the solution everyone seemed to accept was that there would not be any time limit on the exclusion. This suited both leaders. Redmond could claim that it was a temporary arrangement while Carson could claim that it was permanent.

1913: nationalist reaction

Among Irish nationalists the excitement that followed the introduction of the Home Rule bill soon faded. Many were disappointed at the limited amount of independence the bill offered. Then it seemed that unionist opposition might block even that. When rumours began to circulate that Redmond was negotiating for the partition of the country, there was outrage.

This played into the hands of the IRB. Since its revival (see page 187), its new leaders had been looking for a way to advance the republican cause. Disillusionment about Home Rule gave them the opening they had hoped for.

1913: Eoin MacNeill's 'The North Began'

In November 1913 an article appeared in the Gaelic League Journal, *An Claidheamh Soluis*. Called 'The North Began', it was written by **Eoin MacNeill**, the respected Professor of Irish at UCD and one of the founders of the Gaelic League. In it, MacNeill suggested that nationalists form their own Volunteers to put pressure on the British to keep their promise of Home Rule.

MacNeill's article was just what the IRB had been waiting for. They knew that a body of armed nationalist volunteers would provide them with the means of staging a rebellion against British rule. **Bulmer Hobson**, a member of the Supreme Council, approached MacNeill and suggested he call a meeting to discuss his idea.

25 November 1913: the Irish Volunteers

The meeting was held in the Rotunda in Dublin on 25 November 1913. Thousands attended and the **Irish National Volunteers** were set up at once. On that first night 3,000 men enrolled. They elected MacNeill as their commander and picked a Provisional Committee to run the movement.

Always voted Unionist

Always voted Nationalist

Evenly divided between Unionist and Nationalist

Donegal · Derry · Antrim · Tyrone · Down · Fermanagh · Armagh · Monaghan · Cavan

Political points of view in Ulster.

A comment on Redmond's dilemma.

Unknown to MacNeill twelve members of the Committee were in the IRB and three others were soon to join. Thus from the start, the Volunteers were dominated by a secret society which had different aims from its leader, MacNeill, and from the majority of the members.

The Volunteers grew rapidly. By May 1914 about 75,000 men had joined. As with the UVF, the problem of arms soon arose. A few English Liberal sympathisers collected £1,500, and laid plans with Hobson, MacNeill and **Roger Casement**, a member of the Provisional Committee, to buy guns in Germany.

April 1914: Cumann na mBan

A number of women had attended the Rotunda meeting but they were not allowed to join the Volunteers. The issue of votes for women was a divisive one at the time, with many women demanding that the new Home Rule parliament should give Irishwomen the right to vote. Redmond rejected their demands and Home Rulers were divided on the issue. The founders of the Volunteers did not want to be involved in such divisions, so they kept the women out.

In April 1914 some women, many the wives or sisters of prominent Volunteers, founded **Cumann na mBan** as an auxiliary to the Volunteers. They saw their role as fund-raisers, nurses and messengers. This limited view was not acceptable to all members and as time passed their role was gradually expanded.

These two cartoons appeared in Punch in the summer of 1914. Look at them closely and say a) What point is the artist making with the picture on the left? b) What point is he making with the picture on the right? c) Which point of view, unionist or nationalist, does he support? Give reasons for your answer.

1914: the crisis reaches a climax

By 1914 Ireland was in crisis. Two large and growing private armies, both busy acquiring arms, faced each other. At last even Asquith grew alarmed. Early in March, he forced a reluctant Redmond to agree that individual Ulster counties might be allowed to opt out of Home Rule for a six year period. Carson scornfully rejected this as 'sentence of death with a stay of execution for six years'.

March: the Curragh Mutiny

A big problem for Asquith was the doubtful loyalty of the British army in Ireland. Many officers sympathised with the unionists. Would they obey the government if it ordered them to move against the UVF?

An unwelcome answer to this question came in March. The government decided to send some soldiers north to guard ammunition depots. Fearing that they were being sent to disarm the unionists, fifty-eight officers at the Curragh offered to resign. The government quickly assured them that no such order had been issued but in doing so it lost its freedom to use force to stop a unionist rebellion against Home Rule.

24/25 April: the Larne gun-running

The weakness of the government was shown even more clearly on the night of 24/25

The effect of the army resignations on the Home Rule hopes.

April. The UVF landed thousands of German rifles at Larne, Bangor and Donaghadee and distributed them quickly and efficiently throughout Ulster.

The police were either taken by surprise, or, as nationalists believed, showed their unionist sympathies by not interfering in the operation. Influenced by Redmond who wanted no unionist martyrs, Asquith made no attempt to punish the gun-runners.

9 June: Redmond's take-over of the Irish Volunteers

Meanwhile the growth of the Irish Volunteers began to worry Redmond. As leader of the nationalist community, he could not afford to allow a big rival organisation to emerge. He had to establish control over it.

In May he demanded that MacNeill include twenty-five Home Ruler nominees on the Provisional Committee. MacNeill tried to avoid giving an answer. If he accepted, the IRB members might leave, but if he refused then Redmond would set up a rival Volunteer movement and most Volunteers would join him. Exasperated by the delaying tactics, Redmond published his demands on 9 June.

The Provisional Committee held an angry debate about what to do. MacNeill and Hobson argued that it was better to agree to Redmond's demands than to split the movement. Most other IRB men on the Committee disagreed. They lost the debate, and Redmond's demands were accepted.

From then on the leadership of the IRB, especially Tom Clarke and Seán MacDermott, distrusted Hobson. He was forced to resign from the Supreme Council and when they came to plan the Easter Rising in 1915 they did not let him in on the secret.

26 July: the Howth gun-running

By July there were about 180,000 Volunteers. On 26 July they landed some German arms at Howth from **Erskine Childers'** yacht, the *Asgard*. The police and troops tried to intervene. On the way back from Howth, a crowd jeered at soldiers who opened fire, killing three people. The contrast with the unionist experience at Larne was not lost on nationalists.

Failure to find a compromise

Meanwhile, the desperate search for a compromise continued. Asquith forced Redmond to agree to the exclusion, for an unspecified period, of any Ulster county whose people voted against inclusion under a Home Rule parliament. This meant that Redmond had agreed to the more-or-less permanent loss of the four north-eastern counties.

But the unionists wanted to keep Tyrone and Fermanagh. As a result, they rejected Redmond's concession. A civil war seemed more than ever likely as the final deadline – the passage of the Home Rule bill in September 1914 – grew closer.

Molly Childers and Mary Spring Rice on board the *Asgard*.

21-24 July: the Buckingham Palace Conference

A worried King George V proposed an all-party conference to seek a last minute compromise. Doubtfully, Asquith and Redmond agreed. It met on 21 July 1914.

Asquith, Lloyd George, Redmond and Dillon faced Bonar Law, Lord Lansdowne, Carson and Craig across a table at Buckingham Palace. The Speaker of the Commons presided. By the second day Asquith knew that no solution was going to emerge. He wrote to a friend:

> We sat again this morning for an hour and a half, discussing maps and figures, and always getting back to that most damnable creation of the perverted ingenuity of man – the County of Tyrone.
>
> The extraordinary feature of the discussion was the complete agreement (in principle) of Redmond and Carson. Each said 'I must have the whole of Tyrone or die; but I quite understand why you say the same!' The Speaker, who incarnates bluff English sense, of course cut in. 'When each of two people say they must have the whole, why not cut it in half?' They wd. neither of them look at such a suggestion.
>
> L. G. and I worked hard to get rid of the county areas altogether and to proceed on Poor Law Unions wh. afford a good basis of give and take. But again both Irish lots would have none of it. Nothing could have been more amicable in tone or more fruitless in result....
>
> I have rarely felt more hopeless in any practical affair; an impasse with unspeakable consequences, upon a matter which to English eyes seems inconceivably small and to Irish eyes immeasurably big. Isn't it a real tragedy? (R. Jenkins, *Asquith*, pp. 358-9)

War!

The Buckingham Palace Conference ended in failure on 24 July. On that same day Austria-Hungary delivered its ultimatum to Serbia. Out of a clear sky, war struck Europe and by 3 August Britain was involved.

Chapter 19

1914-16: Ireland and the war

18 September 1914: Home Rule at last
The start of the European war in August 1914 brought a sudden end to the Home Rule crisis. As soon as Britain declared war in defence of Belgian neutrality, Redmond and Carson pledged their support to the war effort.

The unionists agreed reluctantly to allow the Home Rule bill to pass provided it did not come into force until the war was over and provided there was a guarantee that parliament would then reconsider the Ulster question. On 18 September 1914 the bill received the royal assent. At last, after forty years of campaigning, Home Rule was won.

Among nationalists in Ireland this was seen as a victory. At this stage everyone expected the war to be over by Christmas, so they believed the suspension of Home Rule was only for a few months. In 1914 no one dreamed that the war would go on for four weary, blood-soaked years, nor that before it ended, all would have changed utterly.

Redmond's Woodenbridge speech
A few days after the passing of the Home Rule Act, Redmond made a speech at Woodenbridge in Co. Wicklow. He called on members of the Irish Volunteers to join the British army and resist German aggression in Europe. Redmond did this for a number of reasons.

- Like most Irish people at that time, he genuinely believed that Germany was a threat to liberty and peace everywhere and had to be stopped.

- He wanted to prove to sceptical British unionists that an Irish leader would give whole-hearted support to Britain in its time of danger.

- He was a practical politician who expected to be back negotiating with Carson in a few months. Carson had already called on the Ulster Volunteers to join the British army and that won him support in Britain. Redmond knew that if he did not do the same, British politicians would be very unsympathetic to him when the talks resumed.

The Volunteers split
Redmond's Woodenbridge speech caused a split in the Volunteers. MacNeill and about 11,000 of the more extreme nationalists refused to follow him. They set up a

Propaganda and some facts about behaviour of the Germans when they invaded Belgium were used to influence the public attitude to the war. These recruiting posters play on the fears aroused.

separate organisation which kept the name Irish Volunteers, though they were often inaccurately, called the 'Sinn Féin Volunteers'.

The vast majority of Volunteers, about 170,000, followed Redmond. They called themselves the **National Volunteers**. They retained their military organisation under the command of Colonel Maurice Moore. About 25,000 of them took Redmond's advice and joined the British army.

Ireland and the war effort

At first the war was popular in Ireland. Thousands of young men, both unionists and nationalists, joined the army. Officially they went to fight for the 'freedom of small nations', but many had other motives, like love of adventure or the need for a job. They joined the large number of Irish who were in the army before the war began and the many thousands of Irish emigrants in Britain who also joined.

Altogether about 200,000 Irishmen fought in World War I, of whom 60,000 lost their lives. The biggest casualties occurred in the Gallipoli landings in 1915 and the battle of the Somme in 1916.

But enthusiasm for the war was never as great in Ireland as in Britain. Only about 10 per cent of Irishmen of a military age went to fight, compared with about 25 per cent in

Britain. And enthusiasm cooled in 1915 as the war dragged on and reports of the slaughter in the trenches reached men back home. As the recruitment figures in Table A show, even before the the Easter Rising, support for the war had begun to decline.

August – December 1914	43,000 men enlisted
January – August 1915	37,000 men enlisted
September 1915 – March 1916	12,000 men enlisted

Table A ▲

The Irish economy and the war

The war brought prosperity to Irish farmers. As the German U-boat blockade cut Britain off from other food sources, the demand for Irish beef, butter, eggs, etc. rose. This pushed up the prices farmers received. Some exploited their good fortune by selling poor quality produce at the highest prices and their profiteering damaged the reputation of Irish produce after the war.

Recruiters also played on Irish pride. The message in the poster on the left is that Ireland's flag flies alongside those of the other allies in the war. Of course this was untrue. Recruiters also made great use of individual Irishmen who had been decorated for bravery.

◆

Landless labourers and small farmers did less well in the war. The big farmers who employed the labourers were unwilling to raise their wages in line with rising prices. And farmers with small holdings lacked the capital to take advantage of rising demand.

This, and the halting of land purchase for the duration of the war, caused discontent, especially in the west where a number of agrarian incidents occurred. Farm labourers joined the Irish Transport and General Workers' Union (ITGWU) which expanded rapidly in the last years of the war.

In the towns and cities the situation varied. With a huge demand for shipping and for linen to make uniforms, tents, etc. Belfast flourished. In other towns there was some increase in employment and the departure of men to fight opened up jobs to women. Among the poorest people, separation allowances paid to soldiers' wives and pensions to their widows provided a small but steady income.

1914-16: Redmond loses out

In September 1914 Redmond was at the peak of his career. He had achieved what had eluded Parnell, a Home Rule Act on the Statute Book. But his triumph was short lived. From that moment on, his power and influence and that of the Home Rule Party went into decline. There were several reasons for this.

- With Home Rule passed, the party was left without a purpose. Home Rule had been won, and yet not won. There was no parliament in Dublin. Redmond was not Prime Minister of Ireland and could not reward his followers. Nationalists came to see the passage of the Home Rule Act as a hollow victory.

- There was still the question of Ulster. Many nationalists, especially those who lived in the north, were appalled by the prospect of partition, yet Redmond seemed to have accepted it.

- Redmond also lost his influence in London. The unionist-dominated War Office turned down his request that all Irish soldiers be formed into an Irish brigade, even though they allowed the Ulster Volunteers to have an Ulster division with its own badges and emblems. They were also reluctant to let Irish Volunteers become officers. Even when fighting for the Empire, it seemed, some Irishmen were more equal than others.

- The greatest blow to Redmond's power came in June 1915. Victory in the war seemed as far away as ever, so the various British parties formed a coalition government. Both Carson and Redmond were invited to join.

Carson accepted and became Attorney General. Redmond, loyal to his party's tradition of independent opposition (never joining a government), refused. His decision was popular in Ireland but it meant that he was on the outside while his unionist opponent sat at the Cabinet table where important decisions were made. Although Redmond was able to persuade the British not to include Ireland when

TO THE YOUNG WOMEN OF IRELAND.

Is your "Best Boy" wearing Khaki? If not don't **you think** he should be?

If he does not think that you and your country are worth fighting for do you think he is **worthy** of you?

Don't pity the girl who is alone her young man is probably a soldier fighting for her and her country and for **you.**

If your young man neglects his duty to Ireland, the time may come when he will **neglect you.**

Think it over then ask your young man to

Join an Irish Regiment TO-DAY.

IRELAND WILL APPRECIATE YOUR HELP.

INCREASED SEPARATION ALLOWANCES

For Soldiers' Wives and Children.

FROM MARCH 1st the Separation Allowances paid by the Government to the wives and children of soldiers have been increased, so that the total weekly payment to the family, if the soldier makes the usual allotment from his pay, is as follows:—

		Corporal or Private.	Sergeant.
Wife	per week	12/6	15/-
Wife and 1 Child	per week	17/6	20/-
Wife and 2 Children	per week	21/-	23/6
Wife and 3 Children	per week	23/-	26/6

and so on with an addition of 2 - for each additional child.

Each Motherless Child ⋅ 5/-

From February 1st, 1915, Separation Allowance is payable for all children up to the age of 16 years.

ALLOWANCES FOR OTHER DEPENDENTS.

If an unmarried soldier has supported a dependent or dependents for a reasonable period, and wishes to continue the support he gave, the Government will help, during the war, by making a grant of Separation Allowance, provided he will contribute part of his pay.

The maximum rate of allowance to a dependent will, as a rule, be the same as for a wife; but in cases where the soldier supported more than one dependent the maximum allowance will be at a wife's rate for one dependent and at children's rate for the others, as shown in the following examples

If a soldier supported his mother only, the weekly maximum allowance will be 12/6
" " his father and mother " 17/6
" " his mother and 3 brothers or sisters " 22/6

Further particulars can be obtained at any Post Office or Recruiting Office.

JOIN AN IRISH REGIMENT TO-DAY

and your dependents will be well provided for.

The government tried to reach men of military age via their women folk. These two posters appeal to very different instincts. Which do you think would have more effect? Explain your answer.

it introduced conscription in Britain in 1915, his power to influence events was lessened.

Until 1916 the growing weakness of Redmond and his once great Home Rule party was hidden from view. As late as April 1916 the police reported unprecedent quiet and prosperity all over the country. It took the unforeseen blow of the Easter Rising to hasten the party's disintegration.

Chapter 20

1914-17: The origins and results of the Easter Rising

Opposing Redmond

Between 1914 and 1916 two groups actively opposed Redmond's support for the war. They were James Connolly's Irish Citizen Army (see page 160) and Eoin MacNeill's Irish Volunteers who had rejected Redmond's call to enlist in the British army. They continued to drill, to parade armed and in uniform, and to oppose recruitment to the British army.

1914: the re-organisation of the Irish Volunteers

In the winter of 1914 the Irish Volunteers were re-organised along more military lines.

A new **Headquarters Staff** was formed and MacNeill was elected Chief of Staff. **Bulmer Hobson** was Quartermaster General and **The O'Rahilly** was Director of Arms. In addition, **Patrick Pearse** was Director of Organisation, **Joseph Plunkett** was Director of Military Operations, **Thomas MacDonagh** was Director of Training, and (after 1915) **Eamonn Ceannt** was Director of Communications. All except MacNeill and O'Rahilly were in the IRB.

Around the country the Volunteers were organised into Companies and Battalions. Here, too, many officers were in the IRB. All of them would take their orders from the IRB leaders rather than from MacNeill.

MacNeill's view of the purpose of the Volunteers

For MacNeill the purpose of the Volunteers was to defend Home Rule. By being ready to fight, he argued, the Volunteers would guarantee that the British did not go back on their promise to give Home Rule when the war ended.

But he did not think the Volunteers should start a rebellion. Only two things would justify that:

• if the government tried to disarm them or

• if it decided to extend conscription to Ireland.

To rebel for any other reason would be wrong, said MacNeill. The Irish people clearly did not want a rebellion and it would cause unnecessary suffering to innocent civilians without any hope of success.

MacNeill's views were probably shared by a majority of the Volunteers, including O'Rahilly and Hobson. Others at Headquarters had different ideas. So had two key men in the IRB, **Thomas Clarke**, the Treasurer to the Supreme Council and **Seán MacDermott**, the Secretary.

The IRB seeks German aid

From the beginning, Clarke and MacDermott saw the war as an opportunity to stage a rebellion. They hoped to enlist the aid of Britain's enemies in their plans. Through their American ally, John Devoy, they contacted the German Ambassador to the United States to ask for armed support. They then sent **Roger Casement** to Germany as their agent.

Casement's mission to Germany

Sir Roger Casement, famous for his humanitarian work in Africa and South America, had resigned from the British diplomatic service in 1912. He later joined the IRB and was in the US when the war began. His mission was:

- to raise an Irish Brigade from among Irish prisoners of war.
- to secure German recognition for an Irish republic.
- to arranged for arms and men to be sent to Ireland.

In Germany, Casement achieved little success. Only a handful of Irish prisoners of war joined his brigade. The Germans did not believe the IRB could stage an extensive rising in Ireland. They gave him recognition, which cost them nothing, but were

Roger Casement

◆

unwilling to send troops or large quantities of guns. In the end they agreed to send a shipload of arms, far less than Casement and the IRB had hoped for.

1915: a rising is planned

Meanwhile Clarke and MacDermott were making their plans. They were convinced that the failure of earlier rebellions was due to the ease with which police spies had infiltrated the secret societies and learned their plans. They were determined to prevent this happening again, so they took as few people as possible into their confidence. Since most of those were executed in 1916, it is difficult for historians to discover exactly what they were up to.

The Military Council

It seems that the planning began in earnest in the summer of 1915. The Supreme Council of the IRB set up a committee (later called the Military Council) to draw up plans for a rising. On it were **Pearse, Plunkett, Ceannt, MacDonagh, Clarke** and **MacDermott**. In theory they were to report back to the Supreme Council but they did not do so.

Picking a date

The first plan seems to have been to rebel in the autumn of 1915. In May 1915, Joseph Plunkett went to Germany to arrange for a consignment of arms. This plan was cancelled, probably because German help was not forthcoming. Early in 1916, they decided the rising would take place on **Easter Sunday, 23 April 1916**.

Laying plans

The plan the Military Council drew up was straightforward. The arrival of German arms in Tralee bay was to be the signal to begin. Volunteer battalions from the south-west would meet the ship and distribute the arms. Elsewhere Volunteers would seize and hold strongpoints. The plan did not say which strongpoints were to be seized or of what to do with them afterwards.

The men who drew up the plan were Dublin based and the only precise orders they gave were for Dublin Volunteers. They were to seize a ring of key buildings around the city centre and to defend them from attack.

The plan put great stress on holding strongpoints and standing to fight the enemy. This appealed to the conspirators' romantic and unrealistic ideas of soldiering. But from a military point of view it was useless. It would rob them of the flexibility which a small, ill-equipped force needed against a much more powerful and well-equipped enemy. Only by using hit and run guerrilla tactics (such as developed in 1919-21) would they have had any hope of success.

THE IDEA OF A BLOOD SACRIFICE

Was there a 'blood sacrifice' idea?

Did the men who planned the Easter rising want a successful rebellion? Or was it more important for them to make a gesture to keep alive Ireland's claim to independent nationhood?

The answer must be that many of the rank and file and some of the leaders, such as MacDermott, certainly hoped for success. But there were others who were more concerned with gestures. The most famous of them was **Patrick Pearse**.

Patrick Pearse (1879-1916)

Throughout 1914 and 1915 Pearse emerged as the spokesman for the conspirators. The son of an English stonemason, he had joined the Gaelic League as a young man and for several years edited its paper *An Claidheamh Soluis*.

Though he trained as a barrister, Pearse was more interested in education. He founded a school, St. Enda's, where he tried to break away from the 'murder machine', as he called the examination-dominated Irish education system. (see page 16) He fostered in his pupils a love of Ireland and of Irish culture. Lessons and games were in Irish and Pearse set before his students, as an ideal, the boy-hero of ancient Ireland, Cuchulainn, who had died in the single-handed defence of his land.

As late as 1912 Pearse had not been very interested in politics and had supported Home Rule. The formation of the Ulster Volunteers changed that. He became convinced that a peaceful solution to Irish demands was impossible. Although St. Enda's was now in deep financial trouble, Pearse threw himself into the Irish Volunteers and a military solution to the Irish problem. In 1913 he wrote: 'A thing which stands demonstrable is that nationhood is not achieved otherwise than in arms'. (F. X. Martin, *The Irish Volunteers 1913-16*, p. 65)

A shy man with a slight stammer, Pearse forced himself to become an effective speaker. His speeches and writings set out the case for full independence, achieved through force. This led the IRB to overlook his former support for Home Rule, and to swear him into the movement late in 1913. When the Military Council was set up, he was one of its first members.

Pearse and the idea of blood sacrifice

Like many people in Europe at this time, Pearse gloried in militarism and saw bloodshed as a reviving and restoring force. In 1915, he wrote of the European war: 'It is good for the world that such things should be done. The old heart of the earth needed to be warmed by the red wine of the battlefields'. (P. H. Pearse, *Political Writings*, p. 215)

He extended this idea to Ireland arguing that the spirit of Ireland could only be restored by the blood of patriots. In 1915, over the grave of the old Fenian, O'Donovan Rossa, he expressed this clearly, saying: 'Life springs from death, and from the graves of patriot men and women spring living nations'.

In his poems, especially in *The Mother, The Fool* and *Renunciation,* Pearse showed clearly that he was prepared to sacrifice his own life in pursuit of this ideal. The choice of Easter Sunday for the rising almost certainly reflects this view. Ireland would rise again when her sons died for her, as Christ rose on that day after he had died to redeem mankind.

Connolly and the idea of a Rising

This idea of a blood sacrifice for the redemption of Ireland was shared by Joseph Plunkett and Thomas MacDonagh. But after Pearse, the man who gave it clearest expression was James Connolly. He had taken control of the ITGWU and of the Citizen Army when James Larkin went to America in 1914. (see page 162) By 1916 the Citizen Army had about two hundred members.

As a Marxist, Connolly had believed that workers would not fight one another on the order of capitalist governments. This belief was disproved when war broke out in 1914 and workers throughout Europe rallied to the defence of their own countries.

A disillusioned Connolly then came to hope that a rebellion in Ireland would provide the spark to set off a worldwide socialist revolution. For him, the British Empire and capitalism were closely linked. The overthrow of one would lead to the overthrow of the other.

He lamented the fact that Irishmen were serving the Empire in the war and he believed:

> that no agency less powerful than the red tide of war on Irish soil will ever enable the Irish race to recover its self-respect or to establish its national dignity in the face of a world horrified and scandalised by what must seem to them our national apostasy... Without the slightest trace of irreverence, but with all due humility and awe, we recognise that of us, as of mankind before Calvary, it may truly be said: 'without the shedding of blood there is no redemption'. (C. D. Greaves: *The Life and Times of James Connolly,* 2nd ed., p. 396)

Connolly and the IRB

Connolly hoped that the IRB was planning a rebellion in which the Citizen Army could join. But as 1915 passed without action he grew impatient. He threatened to lead his tiny army out to fight alone. This would have alerted the authorities and endangered the IRB's plans, so in January 1916 they took Connolly into their confidence and co-opted him onto the Military Council.

P. H. Pearse

The German arms on the *Aud*

By February 1916 the Military Council's plan was complete. Through Devoy, they sent word to the Germans that their arms ship was to rendezvous with the Volunteers off the Kerry coast between Friday 21 and Sunday 23 April.

A German ship, the *Aud*, loaded with 20,000 rifles and ten machine-guns, left Lübeck on 9 April. After its departure, the conspirators changed their minds and sent an urgent message that the ship should arrive only on Sunday. The *Aud* had no radio so it never got this message, but the Military Council assumed that the change of plan was accepted.

When the *Aud* reached Tralee bay on Friday 21 April, there was no one there to meet it. It cruised around for some hours until it was captured by the British navy. As it entered Cork harbour, the captain ordered his men off the ship and sank it and its cargo of arms.

The need to deceive MacNeill

This, however, was still in the future. Meanwhile the Military Council had another problem to overcome. How were they to get the Volunteers to come out and fight on Easter Sunday?

While volunteers who were in the IRB would take their orders from the conspirators, most Volunteers would only fight if their Chief of Staff, Eoin MacNeill, told them to. And MacNeill had made it clear that he was opposed to a rebellion unless the British tried to disarm them.

Eoin MacNeill

Government tolerance

In 1916 that seemed unlikely to happen. Since 1914, the Chief Secretary, Augustine Birrell, and the Under Secretary, Sir Matthew Nathan, had acted on the advice of Redmond and tolerated MacNeill's Volunteers. They were allowed to parade, armed and in uniform, to take part in mock battles and to campaign against recruitment to the British army.

A few very out-spoken newspapers, like Griffith's *Sinn Féin* were suppressed but they quickly reappeared under new names. A few wild speeches were punished by short jail sentences. Otherwise the Volunteers were left alone. This tolerance infuriated unionists who put pressure on Birrell to take a harder line.

March and April 1916: rumours of a rising

Throughout March and early April 1916 rumours of an intended rising began to reach Dublin Castle. But so tight was the Military Council's secrecy, that the rumours were often contradictory and the authorities had no definite proof that anything was planned.

Ironically British Intelligence, which early in the war had managed to break the German radio code, learned the date of the rising and the planned arms shipment from radio signals between Berlin and the German Embassy in Washington. Whether this information ever reached Dublin Castle is not known.

If it did, it was not taken seriously. On 10 April Nathan wrote: 'Though the Irish Volunteer element has been very active of late, I do not believe that its leaders mean insurrection, or that the Volunteers have sufficient arms if their leaders do mean it'. (L. O Broin, *Dublin Castle and the 1916 Rising*, pp. 72-3)

Wednesday, 19 April: the 'Castle Document'

The government's tolerance forced the Military Council to manufacture its own excuse for fighting.

On Wednesday 19 April a strange document appeared in the newspapers. Written on Dublin Castle notepaper, it contained a list of people, including leading Volunteers, who were to be rounded up by the authorities. This 'Castle Document' was almost certainly forged by MacDermott and Plunkett, but MacNeill thought it was genuine. At once he gave orders that the Volunteers were to resist.

Thursday, 20 April: the conspiracy unravels

On Thursday evening, Hobson, who shared MacNeill's opposition to an unprovoked rising, learned that some Volunteers had been told on the previous Sunday that there was to be a rising at Easter. He told MacNeill and together they went to St Enda's to confront Pearse. He admitted that the IRB had planned a rising.

Friday, 21 April

An angry MacNeill began to cancel his previous orders, but on Friday morning Pearse, MacDermott and MacDonagh came to see him. They told him that a German arms ship was due to arrive on Sunday. MacNeill accepted that this made fighting inevitable and wrote a circular to Volunteers repeating his orders of Wednesday.

IRISH CITIZEN ARMY.

SPECIAL MOBILISATION.

All ranks will parade at *Liberty Hall*

with full equipment, on *Sunday* at *3.30*

James Connolly

COMMANDANT.

The first mobilisation order issued to the Irish Citizen Army for Easter Sunday 1916.

What no one in Dublin yet knew, of course, was that the *Aud* had just been captured off the Kerry coast. About the same time, Roger Casement landed from a submarine near Tralee. He had come home to try to stop a rising because he believed the Germans had sent too few arms for it to be successful.

Almost at once, the police arrested him. He was rushed to Dublin and then to London. The authorities, unaware of what was really going on, believed they had captured the leader of the rising.

Saturday 22 April

On Saturday word of these developments reached Dublin. By evening MacNeill knew that the arms were lost and that a rising no longer had any hope of success. He issued orders cancelling the 'manoeuvres' planned for Sunday. Messengers were sent around the country and, as an added precaution, a cancellation notice was published in the *Sunday Independent*.

Sunday 23 April

On Sunday several meetings were held in Dublin. Under-Secretary Nathan and the Lord Lieutenant met with the military and police chiefs to consider what to do, now that the Volunteers were proved to be in contact with Germany.

The Lord Lieutenant wanted to round up leading Volunteers immediately. Nathan agreed but insisted that they wait till Birrell, who was in England, had been informed. He pointed out that there was no hurry. The German arms were gone, the leader, Casement, was under arrest, and there was MacNeill's cancellation notice in the paper. Reluctantly the others agreed to wait until Tuesday.

In Liberty Hall, meanwhile, the conspirators met to consider the ruins of their plan. Rather than lose everything, they decided to rally as many men as possible and go out to fight on Monday. They knew they had little hope of success but they wanted to make a gesture.

Monday 24 April: the rising begins

Easter Monday was fine and sunny. Dublin was in a relaxed mood as people strolled about enjoying the Bank holiday. Many had gone to the races at Fairyhouse. Few paid any attention as hundreds of Volunteers and Citizen Army men assembled at Liberty Hall and then marched away to various points about the city. They were used to seeing Volunteers on route marches and in mock battles and had no reason to expect that this morning would be different.

But this time the Volunteers were in earnest. About noon they seized a series of strongpoints around the city centre and began to fortify them against attack. In O'Connell Street, Volunteers and the Citizen Army occupied the General Post Office (GPO). Pearse, pale and tense, came to the steps and read, to a puzzled and indifferent crowd, the proclamation of the Republic.

POBLACHT NA H EIREANN.

THE PROVISIONAL GOVERNMENT
OF THE
IRISH REPUBLIC
TO THE PEOPLE OF IRELAND.

IRISHMEN AND IRISHWOMEN: In the name of God and of the dead generations from which she receives her old tradition of nationhood, Ireland, through us, summons her children to her flag and strikes for her freedom.

Having organised and trained her manhood through her secret revolutionary organisation, the Irish Republican Brotherhood, and through her open military organisations, the Irish Volunteers and the Irish Citizen Army, having patiently perfected her discipline, having resolutely waited for the right moment to reveal itself, she now seizes that moment, and, supported by her exiled children in America and by gallant allies in Europe, but relying in the first on her own strength, she strikes in full confidence of victory.

We declare the right of the people of Ireland to the ownership of Ireland, and to the unfettered control of Irish destinies, to be sovereign and indefeasible. The long usurpation of that right by a foreign people and government has not extinguished the right, nor can it ever be extinguished except by the destruction of the Irish people. In every generation the Irish people have asserted their right to national freedom and sovereignty; six times during the past three hundred years they have asserted it in arms. Standing on that fundamental right and again asserting it in arms in the face of the world, we hereby proclaim the Irish Republic as a Sovereign Independent State, and we pledge our lives and the lives of our comrades-in-arms to the cause of its freedom, of its welfare, and of its exaltation among the nations.

The Irish Republic is entitled to, and hereby claims, the allegiance of every Irishman and Irishwoman. The Republic guarantees religious and civil liberty, equal rights and equal opportunities to all its citizens, and declares its resolve to pursue the happiness and prosperity of the whole nation and of all its parts, cherishing all the children of the nation equally, and oblivious of the differences carefully fostered by an alien government, which have divided a minority from the majority in the past.

Until our arms have brought the opportune moment for the establishment of a permanent National Government, representative of the whole people of Ireland and elected by the suffrages of all her men and women, the Provisional Government, hereby constituted, will administer the civil and military affairs of the Republic in trust for the people.

We place the cause of the Irish Republic under the protection of the Most High God, Whose blessing we invoke upon our arms, and we pray that no one who serves that cause will dishonour it by cowardice, inhumanity, or rapine. In this supreme hour the Irish nation must, by its valour and discipline and by the readiness of its children to sacrifice themselves for the common good, prove itself worthy of the august destiny to which it is called.

Signed on Behalf of the Provisional Government,

THOMAS J. CLARKE,

SEAN Mac DIARMADA,   THOMAS MacDONAGH,
P. H. PEARSE,   EAMONN CEANNT,
JAMES CONNOLLY.   JOSEPH PLUNKETT.

The extent of the rising

The confusion of the previous days reduced the impact of the rising. In Wexford and in Galway some Volunteers mobilized but were not involved in fighting. In Ashbourne, Co. Meath, Thomas Ashe and Richard Mulcahy seized arms and ammunition when they captured four police barracks in the most effective military action of the rising. Their tactics foreshadowed the guerrilla tactics which became common in 1919.

Elsewhere Volunteers, confused by a series of contradictory orders and unable to find out what was happening, waited for instructions that never came.

Rebel positions in Dublin

In Dublin about 1,600 Volunteers responded to the call to fight. In the confusion, Cumann na mBan had not been given any instructions but about ninety women offered their services to the various garrisons. Only de Valera, stationed in Bolands Mills, refused to admit them. Mostly they acted as nurses, secretaries and couriers who carried messages from one post to another. But in the Citizen Army women had a fuller role and Countess Markievicz took command of their post in Stephens Green.

The Volunteers seized six strong points around the city centre. (see map) Two of these

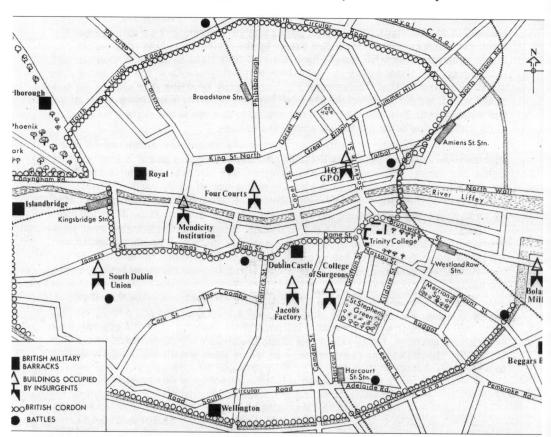

Dublin in Easter Week, 1916

226

– the GPO and the Four Courts – were on the north of the Liffey, and four – Boland's Mills, Stephen's Green, Jacobs Factory and the South Dublin Union – were on the south.

An attempt to take Dublin Castle failed when a policeman opened fire on the attackers. Not realising that only a handful of men were inside, the Volunteers retreated and the chance of a morale boosting success was lost. By Monday evening reinforcements had reached the Castle and this enemy stronghold in the city centre weakened the Volunteers' position.

The British response

With about 2,500 British soldiers and about 1,500 armed police against them at the start, the Volunteers were always outnumbered. The British quickly rushed in reinforcements from Belfast, Athlone, the Curragh and Britain. By Wednesday the odds against the Volunteers had risen to twenty to one. On Tuesday martial law was imposed, and on Thursday **General Sir John Maxwell** had arrived to take supreme command and to deal with the situation.

24-28 April: the fighting in Dublin

The British threw a cordon about the city. Holding Trinity College and Dublin Castle, they were able to cut the links between the Volunteer garrisons on the southside of the city and those on the northside. They then concentrated most of their attack on the Volunteers' headquarters in the GPO. Except for isolated incidents, none of the other strongpoints came under attack. A gun-boat, the *Helga*, was brought into Dublin bay, and field-guns were mounted on Trinity College. These poured a stream of shells into O'Connell Street.

Elizabeth O'Farrell

In order to prevent the further slaughter of Dublin
citizens, and in the hope of saving the lives of our
followers now surrounded and hopelessly outnumbered, the
members of the Provisional Government present at Head-
Quarters have agreed to an unconditional surrender, and the
Commandants of the various districts in the City and Country
will order their commands to lay down arms.

P. H. Pearse

29th April 1916
3.45 p. m.

*I agree to these conditions for the men only
under my own Command in the Moore
Street District and for the men in
the Stephen's Green Command.*

James Connolly

April 29/16

*On consultation with Commandant Ceannt
and other officers I have decided to
agree to unconditional surrender also.*

Thomas MacDonagh.

The surrender signed by Pearse, Connolly and MacDonagh. What reasons does Pearse give for his surrender?

Friday 28 April: surrender

By Friday half of O'Connell Street was reduced to ruins and the GPO was a mass of flames. The rebel garrison withdrew to Moore Street. Pearse, horrified by the slaughter of civilians, sent Elizabeth O'Farrell to seek terms.

The British insisted on unconditional surrender to which Pearse agreed. O'Farrell carried the order to surrender to the other posts, some of which had seen no fighting. The surrender of the rebels was followed by a countrywide sweep of those suspected of involvement.

Sunday 30 April

By Sunday the city was quiet. Four hundred and fifty persons, almost three hundred of them civilians, were dead and 2,614 were wounded. Damage estimated at £2 million had been done to property and the centre of the city was a smoking ruin.

Reaction to the rising

At first Irish people were bewildered by the rising. They had little information about what had happened. Only one Dublin newspaper, *The Irish Times*, was published

The GPO in ruins after the Rising.

during the week and military censorship prevented it from saying very much.

With no certain news, rumours were everywhere. People heard that:

- it was a German invasion!
- it was a socialist revolution led by Larkin!

But no one knew for certain. Even when the fighting ended, hard information remained scarce. It was a week or more before any facts were known. Then the response varied.

- Unionists, of course, saw the rising as a treacherous attack on the empire in its hour of danger.
- Among nationalists, feelings were mixed. Some were angry at the death and destruction. As Volunteer prisoners were being marched through Dublin, some people threw mud on them.
- Others were more ambivalent. They disliked the violence but were proud that the rebels had held out for a week against such overwhelming odds. They might have been wrong and foolish but they had also been brave.

Redmond and Dillon on the rising

The rising was a bitter blow to Redmond. It seemed to undo everything he had worked for. At Westminster on the Tuesday of Easter week, he denounced it as a German plot.

But John Dillon who was in Dublin during the rising, was more in touch with nationalist feeling. On Sunday, as the last of the rebels surrendered, he wrote to Redmond to warn him:

> You should urge strongly on the government the extreme unwisdom of a wholesale shooting of prisoners. The wisest course is to execute no one for the present... So far the feeling of the population of Dublin is against the Sinn Féiners. But a reaction might very easily be created... (F. S. L. Lyons, *John Dillon*, p. 373)

Maxwell deals with the rebels

Redmond gave this message to Asquith, but it was not well received. Deeply involved in a dangerous war, the British saw the rising as a 'stab in the back'. They were in no mood to consider Irish feelings. General Maxwell was given a free hand to do what he felt was necessary.

Rounding up the suspects

Immediately after the rising the military rounded up over 3,500 suspects. Many were in the Gaelic League, Sinn Féin or the GAA and had no connection with the rising. Their arrest angered friends and relatives, especially as no one knew for several weeks what had happened to them.

After questioning, about 2,000 were eventually let go. One hundred and seventy-one were identified as ring leaders and secret courts martial (courts where army officers act as judges) were set up to try them. The rest (about 1,800) were sent to prison camps in England.

Executions

The courts martial found 170 guilty and ninety were sentenced to death. They included the seven men who had signed the proclamation of the republic and the commanders of the various garrisons like Eamon de Valera and Countess Markievicz.

These might reasonably have expected to die. But there were others who were just rank and file volunteers. One was William Pearse, who seems to have been included only because of his famous brother.

The executions began at once. On 3 May Pearse, Clarke and MacDonagh were shot. Over the next few days others were shot in batches of two or three. The first anyone heard of their fate was the notice of their death on the gates of Kilmainham jail.

The effect of the executions

As news of the executions emerged, tension rose. No one knew how many more were to die or who would be next. Since the trials were in secret, no one could judge whether the executed men were guilty or not. As one execution followed another, public opinion swung round to support the rebels.

Stopping the executions

John Dillon realised what was happening. He rushed to London. On 11 May he shocked the House of Commons by praising the bravery of the rebels. He called on the government to stop the killing, warning: 'You are washing our whole life work in a sea of blood'. (F. S. L. Lyons, *John Dillon*, p. 381) He also argued that the only way to save the cause of moderate nationalism was to bring in Home Rule at once.

This time, Asquith listened. He went to Dublin and stopped the executions. Connolly and MacDermott, who were shot on 12 May, were the last men to die. The remainder had their sentences commuted to life in prison.

New Home Rule negotiations

Asquith also renewed the search for a compromise between unionists and nationalists which had been abandoned when the war began. He sent his most able minister, David Lloyd George, to try to work out something between the two sides.

Lloyd George's deal

Lloyd George kept the Redmond and Carson apart and went from one to the other, seeking a deal. After two months of talking, he seemed to have achieved success.

- He got Redmond to accept Home Rule for twenty-six counties and to leave six counties (including the disputed Tyrone and Fermanagh) to the unionists. Redmond understood that the exclusion of these six counties from Home Rule was to be **temporary**.

- He got Carson to agree to the unionists having only six counties instead of nine. But Carson got a written promise from Lloyd George that the exclusion of these counties from Home Rule was to be **permanent**.

The issue of partition

Clearly there was a deception here. When Redmond realised he had been tricked, he renounced the deal. But the whole episode was a bad blow for the Home Rule party. For the first time, Redmond had agreed to give up areas in Ulster like Tyrone and Fermanagh where there was a nationalist majority.

Nationalists, especially those who lived in the six affected counties, were shocked. Some of them left the Home Rule Party and formed the **Irish Nation League** to campaign against partition.

The Home Rule party in decline

Thus by the end of 1916, the Home Rule Party was declining in popularity and power. This was because:

- Home Rule, although passed in 1914, had not come into force.

- sympathy was growing among nationalist voters for the more extreme nationalism associated with the Easter rising.

- Redmond seemed to have accepted partition.

The party still managed to win a by-election in November but that was because there was no alternative party to appeal to dissatisfied nationalists. That changed in 1917.

Chapter 21

1917-18: Defeat for Home Rule – victory for Sinn Féin

1916: opposing Redmond – the Irish Nation League

In the second half of 1916 a number of groups opposed to Redmond's party began to emerge. One of these was the **Irish Nation League**. It was formed by nationalists in Ulster after the Lloyd George negotiations in which Redmond had agreed to partition. It wanted Ireland to have **'Dominion Home Rule'** (that is as much independence as the Dominions of the British Empire like Canada or Australia and more than was offered in the 1914 Act), but it opposed the partition of the country.

Irish National Aid Society

More extreme nationalists also opposed Redmond but the executions and imprisonments after the rising had robbed them of leaders. Towards the end of 1916 this began to change.

Soon after the rising, **Kathleen Clarke**, widow of the executed IRB Treasurer, Tom Clarke, formed the **Irish National Aid Society** to help the relatives of people who had been executed or imprisoned. This organisation:

* collected money.

* held commemorations in which the executed men of 1916 were treated as martyrs for the cause of Ireland.

* provided a cover behind which people who had escaped arrest could begin to rebuild the Volunteers and the IRB.

December 1916: Lloyd George becomes Prime Minister

Events in Britain also helped the cause of extreme nationalism. In December 1916 there was a political crisis there. Asquith was overthrown and **David Lloyd George** became Prime Minister. He was chosen because he seemed the best man to lead Britain to victory in the war. He was to remain in office until 1922 and he had a profound effect on developments in Ireland.

The prisoners are freed

Like Gladstone and Balfour before him, Lloyd George ruled Ireland through a mixture of coercion and conciliation. He began with a conciliatory gesture. As soon as he took office he freed most of the 1,800 prisoners who had not been tried. Lloyd George desperately needed America to enter the war on the British side and his actions with regard to Ireland were intended to win over Americans who disapproved of Britain's policy here.

Another reason for his decision was his desire to conciliate the Irish here, but that back-fired. The freed men had spent nine months in prison camps where extreme nationalism was rampant. They went home as convinced republicans. From their ranks came the new generation who led the struggle for independence in the years that followed.

The new men: Cathal Brugha

Among the Volunteers **Cathal Brugha** now emerged as a leader. He had been badly wounded during the rising so his family hid him and nursed him back to health.

Brugha was a dedicated revolutionary. He believed that there had to be a separate Irish republic and that it must be won by force. But after the Rising he refused to rejoin the IRB. The Easter rising had failed, he believed, because of confusion about who was in charge, the IRB or the leaders of the Volunteers. To prevent this happening again, he wanted no more secret societies. Their time, he felt, was past. From now on there should be only one movement, an open, military one. When his health got better, he began to build up the Volunteers again.

Cathal Brugha

Michael Collins and the IRB

Another man to emerge at this time was **Michael Collins**. He had fought in the GPO

Michael Collins

during the rising and was an admirer of Seán MacDermott. Unlike Brugha, Collins believed that the IRB still had a role to play.

After his release from the Frongach prison camp, Collins became secretary to the Irish National Aid Society. He travelled around the country, dealing with its business. At the same time he was secretly rebuilding the IRB.

In 1917, after the death of Thomas Ashe on hunger strike, Collins became head of the IRB. Through it he developed the network of contacts that were to be so useful to him later in his intelligence work. The IRB remained the main source of his influence.

Arthur Griffith and the new Sinn Féin

Griffith too was freed in December 1916. His Sinn Féin party (see pages 186 and 187) had been almost dead by 1916, but its name had been used (wrongly) to describe MacNeill's Volunteers. In Easter Week everyone, from the government down, referred to the rising as the 'Sinn Féin rebellion'.

In fact Griffith had known nothing about it. On Easter Monday, he had gone to the GPO to offer his services but Pearse had turned him down. The British arrested him but did not think he was important enough to be court martialled.

The Sinn Féin programme

After he was freed, Griffith started to rebuild the Sinn Féin party. He put forward his old programme of:

* dual monarchy.

◆

- withdrawal from Westminster.
- economic development.

When the US entered the war in 1917, he added a new item. One of the American war aims was 'self-determination for small nations'. Griffith proposed:

- that Ireland should appeal to the post-war peace conference to recognise its right to self-determination.

February 1917: the North Roscommon by-election

Early in 1917 the disillusionment with Redmond's Home Rule party became clear in a number of by-elections. The first, in February, was in North Roscommon.

A local group selected **Count Plunkett**, father of Joseph Plunkett, one of the signatories of the 1916 Proclamation, to stand against the Home Rule candidate. Plunkett got support from a variety of groups, including Sinn Féin, the Volunteers, the IRB and the Irish Nation League. All they had in common was opposition to Redmond's party.

Plunkett won easily. After his election he promised not to take his seat at Westminster. This was Sinn Féin policy, but Plunkett refused to join Sinn Féin. Instead he added to the confusion by starting his own party which he called the **Liberty League**.

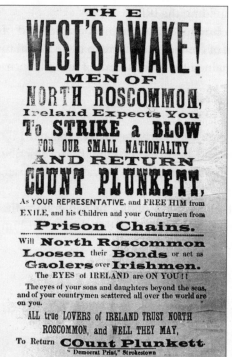

Election poster for Count Plunkett's campaign in North Roscommon. Although he was nominated by people from the Volunteers and the IRB, Plunkett did not belong to these organisations or to Sinn Féin. Nevertheless a vote for him was intended to show support for the Easter Rising.

Disunity

The North Roscommon result showed that many people were dissatisfied with Redmond. But they could only defeat him if they were united. Attempts to achieve unity made little progress because the various groups were divided on aims, methods and leadership.

Aims:

- Members of the Irish Nation League were Home Rulers who would settle for limited independence though without partition.

- Followers of Griffith wanted more independence but were willing to remain linked to Britain by having the same king.

- Members of the IRB and some Volunteers, like Brugha, wanted a republic completely separate from Britain.

Methods:

- The dedicated republicans were prepared to use force to achieve their aims.

- The rest preferred peaceful methods but differed about the strategies they should adopt.

- Some wanted to go to Westminster to negotiate with the British as Parnell and Redmond had done.

- Others backed Griffith's plan of withdrawing from Westminster and setting up an Irish government which would offer passive resistance to British rule.

Count Plunkett.

Leaders:

- Brugha, Plunkett, and Griffith all had a good claim to be the leader of any united movement.

Two more by-elections

North Roscommon was followed by two more by-election victories over the Home Rule party, one in South Longford, the other in East Clare. In East Clare another possible leader emerged. His name was **Eamon de Valera**.

Eamon de Valera (1882-1975)

De Valera was born in America but reared in Co. Limerick. As a young teacher, he joined the Gaelic League. Later, he became involved in the Volunteers and the IRB. In Easter week, he commanded the garrison at Bolands Mills. He was sentenced to death, but his sentence was changed to life imprisonment. In prison he tried to reconcile the various factions among the Irish prisoners and won a reputation as a peace-maker.

In June 1917 Lloyd George made a further attempt to please American opinion, and set the 'life-prisoners' free. De Valera returned to Ireland in time to contest the East Clare election.

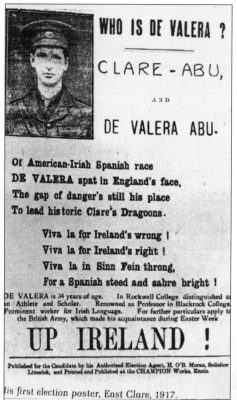

is first election poster, East Clare, 1917.

The most decisive Sinn Féin victory was that in East Clare. Eamon de Valera's election poster shows the parts of his career that Sinn Féin felt it was essential to stress.

During the campaign he made it clear that he wanted a republic, but he showed he was a willing to compromise by adding: 'But if the Irish people wanted to have another form of government, so long as it was an Irish government, I would not put in a word against it'. (Dorothy MacArdle, *The Irish Republic*, p. 224)

October 1917: the second Sinn Féin party is set up

After he won in East Clare, de Valera began talks to unite the various anti-Home Rule groups. By October they had reached an agreement. At the annual Sinn Féin Ard Fheis, Griffith and Plunkett stood down and de Valera was elected unopposed as president of Sinn Féin.

Sinn Féin's aims

He then suggested a form of words to cover the differences in aims between republicans and moderate nationalists:

> Sinn Féin aims at securing the international recognition of Ireland as an independent Irish Republic. Having achieved that status, the Irish people may, by referendum, freely choose their own form of government. (Brian Farrell, *The founding of Dáil Éireann*, p. 20)

The Ard Fheis also adopted Griffith's policies of abstention from Westminster, passive resistance to British rule and an appeal to the post-war peace conference as the means of achieving the republic. It did not discuss whether force should be used if these methods failed.

The second Sinn Féin party (1917-1922)

Historians usually call the party that de Valera now led the 'second' Sinn Féin party. This is to distinguish it from the first, unsuccessful, Sinn Féin party founded by Griffith in 1908.

The second Sinn Féin party was a coalition of different organisations with different aims and different methods. For the time being, Home Rulers, dual monarchists and republicans were willing to blur the differences between them and work together, under de Valera, against a common enemy. But when that enemy was defeated, the differences among the members would certainly re-emerge.

October 1917: the Volunteers line up with Sinn Féin

On the day after the Sinn Féin Ard Fheis the Volunteers held their annual Convention. They elected de Valera as President and picked a twenty-member Executive Committee to run the Volunteers. Cathal Brugha was the chairman and six of its members, including Collins and Richard Mulcahy, were also members of the Sinn Féin executive. This shared leadership united the military movement (the Volunteers) with the political party (Sinn Féin) into a common front against Redmond's Home Rule Party.

July 1917-April 1918: the Irish Convention

Meanwhile Lloyd George, still wooing American opinion, continued his conciliatory approach. He set up an **Irish Convention**, under the chairmanship of **Sir Horace Plunkett**. He invited all Irish groups to attend and asked them to work out a solution to the issue of Home Rule versus the Union. He promised to get parliament to pass any agreement they reached.

The Convention was doomed from the start. Sinn Féin and the trade unions refused to attend. The Ulster Unionists were present but Carson refused to discuss anything less than the permanent exclusion of six Ulster counties that he was offered in 1916.

Redmond's last compromise

Redmond, whose health was failing, tried desperately to find a solution. He held talks with the Southern unionist leader, Lord Midleton. Southern unionists did not want partition because it would leave them as a small and vulnerable minority in a Catholic state.

Midleton and Redmond made a deal to reduce still further the powers that a Home Rule parliament would have. They hoped that this would prevent the Ulster unionists from demanding partition. However, this compromise had no hope of success because:

- Ulster unionists would not agree to Home Rule under any circumstances.

- by 1918 most nationalists wanted an Irish parliament to have more power, not less.

Redmond died in March 1918 before he could put these proposals to his party. His successor, **John Dillon**, quickly dropped them and in April the Convention broke up in failure.

March 1918: Dillon replaces Redmond

Dillon was now leader of the Home Rule party. He had become impatient with Redmond's search for a deal with the unionists. He thought Sinn Féin was a greater threat to his party. To defeat it, the Home Rulers must take a stronger line on national independence.

Sinn Féin loses popularity

In the winter of 1917-18 it looked as if Dillon might be right. Sinn Féin seemed to be losing popularity. Its leaders, having set it up, were not sure what to do next, but some of their followers took matters into their own hands. In the west some small farmers, acting in the name of Sinn Féin, seized big grazing farms and divided them up. And some Volunteers raided private houses and stole arms.

To many Catholic property owners, this was uncomfortably like what Lenin was doing in Russia at that very moment. They swung their support back to the Home Rule party which won three by-elections in a row. It looked as though Dillon might be able to save his party. However the British decision to impose conscription on Ireland put an end to that.

1918: the conscription crisis

Conscription was introduced to Britain in 1915. Redmond had insisted that only an Irish parliament could make such a serious decision for Ireland, so it was not extended to this country. This special treatment for Irishmen was never popular in Britain, especially after the Easter Rising.

Early in 1918, after the defeat of Russia, the German army began to advance along the Western Front. More troops were desperately needed to halt them. The Cabinet decided to increase conscription in Britain but they could not do this unless they also applied it to Ireland. Lloyd George hoped to bring in Home Rule at the same time but the failure of the Convention made this impossible.

Combined resistance

Conscription aroused a storm of resentment in Ireland. Despite Dillon's objections, the conscription bill was passed by the Commons. In protest, he led his party out of the House and home to Ireland.

Nationalists united against conscription.

- Home Rulers and Sinn Féiners formed a committee to resist conscription.
- The Catholic bishops, meeting in Maynooth, issued a strong condemnation.

Two long-standing Home Rule MPs, William O'Brien and Joe Devlin charge against conscription. This cartoon from Punch implies that their charge will be futile and so it proved. But their failure only strengthened the Sinn Féin claim that attendance at Westminster was a waste of time.

- Trade unions organised a one day general strike in protest.

- The Volunteers announced that they would resist the introduction of conscription by force and thousands flocked to join their ranks. By the autumn of 1918, they had about 100,000 members.

May 1918: the 'German plot'

In the middle of the crisis, the government suddenly announced that it had discovered a 'German plot' to import arms and stage another rising. It used this excuse to arrest about a thousand leading Sinn Féiners, including de Valera, Griffith, Kathleen Clarke and Countess Markievicz. It also declared Sinn Féin, the Gaelic League and a number of other nationalist organisations illegal.

No one in Ireland believed in the 'German plot'. Instead, many took it as proof that the government was afraid of Sinn Féin and was trying to destroy it.

Kathleen Clarke

The emergence of more extreme men

The arrests did not stop Sinn Féin. They just drove it underground. Control fell into the hands of younger and, from the government's point of view, more dangerous men.

The most important of these were **Cathal Brugha, Richard Mulcahy**, who became Chief-of-Staff of the Volunteers, **Michael Collins**, who became Director of Organisation, **Rory O'Connor** and **Harry Boland**. They worked feverishly to build up the Volunteers to fight conscription.

The effect of the conscription crisis

In the end conscription was never imposed. In June the German offensive collapsed so extra soldiers were not needed. And Lloyd George realised how impossible it would be to impose conscription on a hostile population.

But the conscription crisis had a profound effect on Ireland.

- The Home Rule party was now discredited. Its leaders had argued that by going to Westminster, they were able to look after Ireland's interests. Yet on this vital matter, the British government would not listen to them. All Dillon could do was leave and return to Dublin, the very tactic that Sinn Féin advocated.

- Sinn Féin emerged as the victor. It had always argued that going to Westminster was a waste of time. The conscription crisis seemed to prove it right. And many people believed that the government only dropped conscription because of the Volunteers' threat to resist it by force.

11 November 1918: end of the war

On 11 November 1918 World War I came to an end. At once Lloyd George called a general election. Because the parties had agreed not to have an election during the war, it was the first time the people had voted in a general election since 1910.

The split in the Liberals

In Britain the election was about the war. Lloyd George, who was the leader of the Liberal party, decided to continue the war-time coalition with the Conservatives. They hoped to win because they had led Britain to victory.

His decision split the Liberals. Some of them, led by Asquith, refused to support the coalition. The split destroyed the great Liberal Party. From this time on, it declined in importance and Labour became the second major party in Britain.

December 1918: the election results in Britain

Lloyd George and his coalition won a massive victory. Together they had 474 seats (Conservatives: 338, Lloyd George Liberals: 136). The Asquith Liberals won only eighteen seats and the Labour Party won fifty-nine.

The number of Conservatives caused problems for Lloyd George. They had enough votes to rule without him. If he went against their wishes they could easily remove him as Prime Minister. This affected his policies, especially towards Ireland, between 1918 and his fall from power at the end of 1922.

December 1918: the election in Ireland

The election in Ireland was very different from the election in Britain.

In part, it was just another episode in the struggle between the unionists, still led by Carson, and the nationalists. But that was mainly confined to Ulster. In order not to split the nationalist vote and let more Unionists win, Sinn Féin and the Home Rulers agreed to divide eight Ulster seats between them.

In the rest of the country this election was about something new. For the first time, nationalist voters were offered a choice.

- Did they want Irish MPs to go to back again to Westminster and try again to persuade the British to give them an Irish parliament with limited power?

  If so, they must vote for Dillon's Home Rule party.

- Did they want Irish MPs to withdraw from Westminster, set up an Irish republic in defiance of the British and appeal for recognition to the Peace Conference which would open in Paris in January 1919?

  If so, they must vote for de Valera's Sinn Féin.

There was another political party in Ireland, the Irish Labour party, which James Connolly had founded in 1912. In 1918 its members decided not to fight the election so that voters could have a clear choice between Sinn Féin and Home Rule.

The two parties
Sinn Féin went into the election with a lot of advantages.

- Its leaders were young and enthusiastic and they had the backing of other organisations like the Volunteers, Cumann na mBan and the Gaelic League.

- It had 1,354 branches and 112,000 members around the country.

- It was credited with defeating conscription and had won a string of by-elections.

- It was able to avail of a 'sympathy vote' because many of its candidates were in English jails and the government had censored their election literature.

By contrast, the old Home Rule Party was in poor shape.

- Although Dillon was a more vigorous leader than Redmond, he was almost seventy years of age and most of the other leading members of the party were also elderly.

- Many of the old Home Rule branches had faded away during the war and few people were interested in campaigning for the party. In twenty-five constituencies they did not even put up a candidate against Sinn Féin.

- By 1918 many nationalists did not think that the Home Rule Act of 1914 gave Ireland a realistic amount of independence.

- Redmond's acceptance of partition was unpopular.

A different kind of election
The 1918 election was also different in other ways. Earlier that year, parliament had passed an act that changed many of the rules about voting.

- All men over the age of twenty-one and women over thirty could now vote. This increased the number of voters by 150 per cent from *c.*700,000 to *c.*1,900,000.

- For the first time, women could be candidates for election. Sinn Féin nominated two women and one of them, Countess Markievicz, was elected. She was the first woman MP in the history of the United Kingdom, but as a Sinn Féiner, she never took her seat in Westminster.

- The borders of constituencies were re-drawn to take account of the growth of towns compared with country areas. This gave more seats to Belfast and helped the Unionist Party which had been at a disadvantage under the old system.

The election results

The results of the election were dramatic, as these figures show:

	1918	
	Before the election	After the election
Unionists	18	26
Sinn Féiners	7	73
Home Rulers	78	6*

* Four of these were the result of a pre-election pact with Sinn Féin in Ulster.

However if we look at the number of votes cast it is clear that Sinn Féin was not quite so popular as the number of seats they won suggests:

Votes cast for Sinn Féin	Votes cast for Home Rule party
485,105	237,393

That is because the British 'winner takes all' system of voting was used and not proportional representation. It is clear that many voters remained loyal to the familiar Home Rule party. Nevertheless, Sinn Féin had won a stunning victory.

The unionists and the 1918 election

While nationalists had changed dramatically since 1914, the Ulster unionists had not. They were as determined as ever to remain in the United Kingdom. Still led by Sir Edward Carson, they emerged from the 1918 election with more seats than before as a result of the re-drawing of constituency boundaries.

Countess Markievicz, first woman to be elected to Westminster Parliament, but never took her seat.

The unionists and Sinn Féin

The unionists liked Sinn Féin even less than they liked the Home Rulers:

- Sinn Féin demanded a republic which would cut **all** ties with Britain.

- it had close links with the militant Volunteers.

To Ulster unionists, Sinn Féin seemed a threat to everything they held dear. After the 1918 election they were more determined than ever to demand separation from the rest of Ireland.

Chapter 22

1919-21: The government of Dáil Éireann

January 1919: calling a Dáil

During the 1918 election campaign, the leaders of Sinn Féin had promised that its MPs would not go to Westminster. Instead they would stay at home, form an Irish government and appeal for recognition to the Peace Conference in Paris. As soon as the election was over, they set about fulfilling that promise.

It was important to act quickly. The Peace Conference was due to meet in Paris at the end of January and the appeal must be ready before then. Early in January, Sinn Féin summoned all 105 Irish MPs to meet in the Mansion House in Dublin on 21 January.

21 January: the First Dáil meets

To no one's surprise, the six Home Rule MPs and the twenty-six Unionist MPs ignored the summons and did not attend the meeting. In addition, not all Sinn Féin MPs were able to attend. Some were still in prison after the 'German plot' arrests and two, Michael Collins and Harry Boland, were in England helping de Valera to escape.

That left twenty-seven Sinn Féin members to come to the first meeting of **Dáil Éireann** on 21 January 1919. It is from that meeting that this state dates its existence.

The proceedings of the first meeting

The meeting lasted two hours and dealt with three items of business. The proceedings were conducted in Irish.

- The Dáil repeated the **Declaration of the Republic**, made in 1916.

- It issued a **'Message to the Free Nations of the World'**, calling on them to support the Irish republic's appeal for recognition at the Peace Conference. **Seán T. O'Kelly** was chosen to go to Paris and present Ireland's case for self-determination to US President, Woodrow Wilson.

- The Irish Labour party had not contested the 1918 election to let Sinn Féin have a clear run. Now its leader, **Thomas Johnson**, demanded that Sinn Féin promise social and economic reforms to improve the conditions of the poorest sections of Irish society.

Labour's demands were too socialist for Collins and other leading Sinn Féiners. They watered them down, then presented their version to the Dáil as the

Thomas Johnson, the leader of the Irish Labour Party.

Democratic Programme. It promised improved child care, a new educational system, reform of the poor law, the development of the country's natural resources and the protection and development of trade and industry.

Forming a government

The Dáil met again on the following day to set up a government. It was to be led by a **Príomh Áire** or **President** who would be elected by the Dáil. The President (who was really a Prime Minister but Sinn Féin did not want to use the British term) was then to appoint an **Executive Council** (Cabinet) of ministers with responsibility for various areas of government. Cathal Brugha was elected as temporary President.

De Valera freed

Early in February, Collins got de Valera out of Lincoln Jail. De Valera wanted to go at once to the United States to rally Irish-American opinion behind the Sinn Féin cause. Only with difficulty did Collins and others persuade him to return to Dublin to meet the Dáil.

1 April: de Valera elected President of the Dáil

Meanwhile Lloyd George had freed the other prisoners. When the Dáil met again on 1 April fifty-two Sinn Féin TDs* were present. They elected de Valera as President and he appointed his Cabinet.

---

*From now on elected representatives in Ireland were called Teachta Dála (TDs), rather than Members of Parliament (MPs).

The Sinn Féin Cabinet

Griffith became Vice-President and Minister for Home Affairs. **Brugha** was made Minister for Defence, **Collins**, Minister for Finance, **Countess Markievicz,** Minister for Labour, **Eoin MacNeill**, Minister for Industries, **William T. Cosgrave**, Minister for Local Government, **Count Plunkett**, Minister for Foreign Affairs and **Robert Barton**, Minister for Agriculture.

These people planned to take over the country. On the face of it, they seemed unlikely to succeed.

- They were young – three-quarters of the TDs were under forty-five.

- They had no experience of government. Only two had been elected to parliament before; only five had even served on a local council.

- They faced huge practical difficulties. They had no civil service to help them and they even lacked offices in which to keep files or meet people.

- Above all, they were opposing the established government of the country which could use its police and army to arrest and imprison them.

It is not surprising that at first few people took them seriously.

The appeal to the Peace Conference fails

In 1919 many people pinned their hopes for independence on the appeal to the Peace Conference. O'Kelly went to Paris but his mission was a failure. The Peace Conference was a meeting of the nations victorious in the war and Sinn Féin had allied itself to the defeated Germans. The American President, Woodrow Wilson, saw no reason to annoy his British ally by meeting the Sinn Féin representatives.

Eamon de Valera.

June 1919 – December 1920: de Valera in America

De Valera decided he must go to America and get Irish-American voters to put pressure on Wilson to change his mind. He also hoped to raise money to fund the Dáil government. He left in June 1919, intending to stay only a short time.

At first de Valera was warmly welcomed. He spoke to large and enthusiastic audiences right across the States. But Irish-Americans were divided among themselves, and de Valera, who at this stage lacked political experience, soon got caught up in their quarrels.

De Valera's quarrel with Judge Cohalan

De Valera's chief opponents were Judge Daniel Cohalan and John Devoy. They were leading members of the **Friends of Irish Freedom**. The quarrel was partly personal – de Valera and Cohalan disliked and distrusted one another. But it was also about important issues. These were:

- The funds for Ireland
  De Valera wanted to sell bonds to Irish-Americans to raise money for the Dáil. This became known as the Dáil Loan scheme. Cohalan opposed this because he did not think it was legal in the States. In fact de Valera managed to raise $6 million through this scheme.
  Devoy and Cohalan had their own separate fund. They wanted to use most of the money it raised to push the Irish cause in America, while de Valera thought all money should go back to Ireland to help the work there.

- The League of Nations
  Devoy and Cohalan were opposed to America joining the League of Nations. Members of the League were bound to recognise each others boundaries and they thought this would prevent America recognising Irish independence. De Valera, on the other hand, was in favour of the League in principle, provided Ireland was admitted as a member.

- The republic
  De Valera wanted to campaign for an Irish republic but Devoy and Cohalan thought this was too restricting. They preferred to ask for 'self-determination' for Ireland as this would gain support even from people who did not want to offend the British.

The quarrel came to a head during the 1920 American Presidential election. De Valera wanted the American Republican Party to come out in favour of an Irish republic but Cohalan pushed for a declaration in favour of Irish 'self-determination'. The result of their manoeuvring was that the Republicans avoided making any declaration on Ireland at all. The Democratic Party later did the same. After this it was unlikely that an American government would put pressure on Britain to give Ireland independence.

Throughout these quarrels, de Valera kept Griffith and the Sinn Féin Cabinet in Dublin informed of what was going on. They gave him their full support.

The results of de Valera's American mission

De Valera returned to Ireland in December 1920. He had failed in his main aim, but he did bring the Irish struggle to the attention of Americans and this put pressure on the British to open talks. He also collected money which helped to pay for the Dáil government and the war of independence. He had been away for eighteen months and he found the country greatly changed on his return.

The Dáil government

While de Valera was in the US, Arthur Griffith presided over the Dáil as 'Acting-President', until he was arrested in November 1920. Under him, the Dáil government began to function.

Michael Collins and the Department of Finance

As Minister of Finance, Collins had to raise money to pay for the activities of the Dáil. In 1919 the Dáil authorised him to sell **Dáil Bonds** to the public, both in Ireland and abroad. In Ireland, they raised £358,000. This money, together with what de Valera sent from America, not only helped to finance the Dáil, paying for salaries, office accommodation and propaganda, but also helped purchase arms for the Volunteers.

Robert Barton and the Department of Agriculture

Since 1918 small farmers in the west, angry because land purchase had halted during the war and because they were not getting more land, had been seizing large grass farms. In 1920 the Dáil's Department of Agriculture set up a land commission to try to control this development and established land courts to arbitrate in disputes about land. They also set up a Land Bank to continue the process of land purchase.

Law and order: the Sinn Féin courts

The chief mark of a successful government is its ability to maintain order in the country. This was the responsibility of the Department of Home Affairs, headed by Griffith until his arrest and then by **Austin Stack**. They were helped by a spontaneous development in parts of the west.

In 1919 people in Clare began to withdraw their cases from the British courts. They agreed to accept the arbitration of some respected local people (clergy, schoolteachers, doctors, etc) in the parish. Soon this idea spread to other areas.

The early 'Sinn Féin courts dealt with civil cases (cases where no criminal act is involved, e.g. disputes about land or debts). Since the judges in these courts were usually well off, they seldom sided with the poor.

In June 1920 Dáil Éireann issued a decree which set up a proper court system. As

Sinn Féin court in session
in Westport, 1920.

well as the parish courts, there were District Courts and Circuit Courts to try more
serious cases and a Supreme Court to which people could appeal the decisions of the
lower courts. The Department of Home Affairs sent organisers to spread this legal
system to new areas. By July 1921 there were over 900 Parish Courts and over
seventy District Courts in operation.

The Volunteers form a police force

As the power of the RIC declined (see page 258), the Volunteers began to act as a
police force. They arrested criminals, took them before the Sinn Féin courts and
inflicted punishment. This was difficult for men who were themselves on the run.
Punishments included beatings, imprisonment and in some cases the death penalty.

The dual role for the Volunteers as army and police force caused tension between
the Volunteer Headquarters and the Department of Home Affairs. As the Volunteers
were operating as a police force, the Department felt that it should have control over
them, while Army Headquarters felt that they were still soldiers and as such, were
still under its control. This tension remained until the Garda Síochána were set up
after the Treaty.

The success of the Sinn Féin justice system

Sinn Féin's success in maintaining law and order helped to bring public opinion
behind them. It even caused some Southern unionists to reconsider their opposition
to Irish independence. As this letter from a Limerick landlord shows, they had
discovered that an Irish government could protect their property as well as the
government of the United Kingdom:

> Sinn Féin rules the country – and rules it admirably. At our local races the Sinn
> Féin police controlled the traffic, the crowds etc, 'parked' the motor-cars and in

fact did all the work which has usually been done by the police and did it excellently. Petty thefts, or indeed crimes of any kind, are dealt with by the Sinn Féin courts who try the accused with perfect fairness and administer justice in a most thorough fashion .... Missing property, if the facts are reported to the Sinn Féin authorities, is inevitably found and restored to the owners. (T. J. Jones, *Whitehall Diary*, Vol 3, p. 24)

W. T. Cosgrove and the Department of Local Government

Another successful department was Local Government. In 1920 there were elections to local councils throughout the country. The British brought in voting by Proportional Representation (PR) to reduce the impact of the Sinn Féin vote. Despite this, Sinn Féin gained control of twenty-eight of the thirty-three county councils (including Tyrone and Fermanagh) and of seventy-two corporations and town councils (including Derry city).

The Dáil then called on these councils to cut their links with the British Local Government Board and to affiliate with the Dáil Department. Although this meant losing grants, all Sinn Féin-controlled local authorities had done so by October 1920.

Department of Foreign Affairs

The Dáil hoped that foreign governments would recognise Irish independence. To put its case to an international audience, it appointed representatives to Washington, Paris, Rome and other capitals. No government received these representatives officially because they did not want to offend the British.

Despite this, the Irish representatives made good use of their time. They talked to officials, politicians and the press, putting the Irish side of things and countering British propaganda. They were quite effective in this and one of the factors that convinced the British to make peace was the bad image its Irish policies had abroad.

Propaganda

Sinn Féin propaganda was not limited to foreign cities alone. In Dublin a propaganda department was run by **Desmond FitzGerald** and, after his arrest, by **Erskine Childers**.

They organised meetings between leading members of Sinn Féin and reporters and foreign visitors who had come to see the situation in Ireland for themselves. They issued a regular paper, the *Irish Bulletin*. It reported on the atrocities committed by the Black and Tans (and may even have invented a few) and was sent to sympathetic newspapers and individuals in Britain and other countries. Their work made it difficult for the British to hide what was really going on in Ireland.

The fear of arrest

All these departments worked under the greatest difficulty. Their members were 'on the run', always trying to keep one step ahead of the RIC or the Black and Tans.

Erskine Childers

Many were arrested and their offices were always in danger of being raided. Anyone associated with them or helping them was in danger of arrest and imprisonment.

Yet in spite of all these difficulties, the Dáil government managed to survive. Many of its departments had only a limited success but in the face of the difficulties, the remarkable thing is that any of them worked at all.

The failure of passive resistance

Griffith had argued that it would be possible to win independence by this kind of passive resistance alone. We can never tell if he was right because his idea was never tried. Alongside the Dáil government's attempt to rule the country peacefully was a military campaign waged by the Volunteers and the violent response to it from the British. As time passed, this war came to overshadow the attempt of Dáil Éireann to assume the government of the country.

Chapter 23

1919-21: The IRA and the War of Independence

The Volunteers and Sinn Féin

When Sinn Féin candidates asked people to vote for them in the 1918 election, they claimed they could win independence by passive resistance to the British government. But given the existence of the Volunteers in close alliance with Sinn Féin, violence was almost certain to develop.

Sinn Féin did not control the Volunteers, who had been founded separately in 1913. When the Volunteers reorganised after the rising, they elected their own **Executive Committee** and **General Headquarters (GHQ)**. Around the country they were divided into brigades and battalions, each with its own officers, elected by the men.

The Volunteers elected as their leaders men were also the leaders of Sinn Féin. De Valera was President of both organisations. Brugha was head of the Volunteer Executive, Mulcahy was Chief of Staff and Collins was Director of Organisation. This shared leadership masked the differences between the two bodies.

Richard Mulcahy, Commander-in-Chief of the IRA throughout the war of independence.

The aims of the Volunteer leaders

Unlike Sinn Féin which was a political party, the Volunteers after 1916 saw themselves as an army with a military purpose. That purpose was the defeat of British rule in Ireland. By 1918 some of the newer leaders, like Collins and Mulcahy in Dublin and some of the local commandants in the regions, were ready for another fight.

But these men knew that the romantic dream of big battles against the enemy (as in Easter Week) was unrealistic. The only hope for a small, untrained, poorly armed force was to use hit-and-run guerrilla tactics, such as Mulcahy and Ashe had used in Ashtown in 1916.

It was this view among the Volunteer leaders, rather than any decision by Sinn Féin or the Dáil, which shaped the war of independence.

The search for arms

Violence grew out of the need for arms. By the end of 1918 the Volunteers had 100,000 members on paper, but only about 15,000 of these would be willing to fight. They had few arms. Although they were able to buy some from British soldiers and smuggle more into the country, this was not enough. On several occasions in 1918, Volunteers raided private houses and gun shops to get more weapons.

21 January 1919: Soloheadbeg

As Dáil Éireann held its first meeting in the Mansion House, a group of Tipperary Volunteers led by Seán Treacy ambushed two policemen in Soloheadbeg. They shot the policemen, took their guns and the dynamite they had been escorting. These Volunteers were acting on their own. They had not got the approval of the Dáil nor of their own GHQ.

The Dáil and the Volunteers

Soloheadbeg is usually seen as the first episode in the Anglo-Irish war. That war was not declared by Dáil Éireann but developed, almost accidentally, from Volunteer actions like Soloheadbeg and from the British response to them.

At first moderate Sinn Féiners like Griffith deplored the violence of the Volunteers (or the **Irish Republican Army (IRA)** as they called themselves after the Dáil declared a republic). However as the British response grew more violent, they changed their view. In April 1921 the Dáil at last accepted responsibility for the actions of the IRA.

1919: the development of the war

In 1919 the war developed along two fronts:

- the counter-intelligence work of Collins which was mainly in Dublin.

- the arms raids, attacks on police barracks and ambushes of police patrols around the country.

These both happened together and interacted with each other, but they are easier to understand if we examine each one separately.

Counter-intelligence

Collins believed that earlier rebellions had failed because the government knew more about the rebels than the rebels did about the government. He set out to reverse this situation.

From the time he was freed in 1916, he began to build up a network of contacts around the country. They included railwaymen, hotel porters, typists, maids, civil servants working for the government, policemen and even detectives. They passed on to Collins copies of government letters, word of troop movements, rumours about raids, gossip about who was reliable and who was not.

Collins used this mass of information to outwit the government, plan ambushes on its forces, evade arrest and allow the Dáil, declared illegal in September 1919, to carry on in the face of the most determined British opposition.

The 'Squad'

Collins was also determined to stop the government getting information about the IRA and Sinn Féin.

Dublin Castle had a group of detectives known as G-men who reported on the activities of nationalist organisations. Early in 1919, Collins warned the G-men to stop their work. Some obeyed, others did not. In July 1919, he formed a hand-picked 'Squad' of twelve IRA men and told them to kill one of the detectives who had disobeyed. As a result, other detectives lost their enthusiasm for the job.

Collins ruthlessly used the Squad against anyone who seemed a threat to the movement. For example, it was they who killed an elderly accountant called Alan Bell. The government had employed Bell to trace the bank accounts where Collins was keeping money gathered through the Dáil loan scheme. One day on his way home Bell was taken from a tram and shot. His killers walked quietly away.

The cold-blooded killings shocked public opinion but Collins ignored the protests. His ruthless use of terror achieved its aims and the government's sources of information dried up.

1919-1920: the IRA campaign around the country

Collins's intelligence war was mainly confined to Dublin. Elsewhere, the fighting developed slowly and in a haphazard fashion. Each IRA commandant controlled his own area. GHQ sent him guns and information and gave him advice and encouragement, but in the end, only the local man knew how many weapons and men he had at his disposal and what the local possibilities were.

As a result, the IRA was very active in some areas such as Cork, Tipperary, Kerry, Waterford, Limerick, Clare and Longford, where local commandants like **Tom Barry,**

Liam Lynch, Michael Brennan or **Seán MacEoin** gave an active lead. Others parts of the country were much quieter, with little going on.

Attacks on the RIC

In 1919 the campaign mainly consisted of arms raids on RIC barracks in which nineteen policeman were killed. These attacks forced the RIC to close small posts and concentrate its men in heavily fortified barracks in the larger towns. At Easter 1920, in a coordinated operation, the IRA burned 400 of the small posts they had abandoned.

In 1920 the Volunteer GHQ encouraged local commandants to begin systematic attacks on the fortified barracks. Between January and June 1920, sixteen were destroyed and twenty-nine damaged. The Dáil had not approved of this campaign but in April 1919 it had called for a boycott of the RIC. Many IRA men may have regarded this as justifying their actions against the police.

The violence against the RIC removed them from many country districts in the south and west. This gave Sinn Féin a free hand to develop its own police and courts. (see page 251)

The decline of the RIC

By the end of 1919 men in the RIC faced a terrible dilemma. Most of them were ordinary Irishmen, mainly Catholic. Where, many wondered, did their loyalty now lie – with the British government, which paid their wages, or with their fellow countrymen who were shooting at them?

Some continued doggedly to serve as they had always done. Others either helped the IRA, turned a blind eye to Volunteer activity or resigned. Recruiting stopped as few young men wanted to join the police in these circumstances. By the early months of 1920 the IRA campaign had reduced the British government's main agent in Ireland to powerlessness.

1919: the lack of a British response

While this situation developed through 1919, the British government had paid little attention to Ireland. Few people in Britain took Sinn Féin's claim to be a government seriously. Also the Peace Conference in Paris occupied most of the government's attention.

By September, however, Lloyd George was forced to look again at Ireland. There were two reasons for this:

- the growing level of violence in the country.

- the 1914 Home Rule Act, which was due to come into force 'when the war was over'.

1920: Lloyd George's new Irish policy

Lloyd George decided to follow his usual tactic of combining tough action against the rebels with concessions. Early in 1920 he began a new policy. It involved:

- reorganising the government in Dublin Castle to deal with the IRA and Sinn Féin.

- restoring law and order in the country by strengthening the RIC.

- bringing in Home Rule and protecting the unionists. (This topic is dealt with in the next chapter.)

A new team in the Castle

The British administration in Dublin Castle had always been inefficient but by 1919 it was a total mess. Early in 1920 Lloyd George brought in new people to make it more effective.

- He appointed **Sir Hamar Greenwood**, who described himself as a life-long Home Ruler, as Chief Secretary and **Sir Alfred Cope**, an experienced British administrator, as Under Secretary.

- He gave command of the army to **General Macready** and put **General Tudor** in charge of the police.

- In August 1920 he got parliament to pass **the Restoration of Order in Ireland Act**. It allowed military courts to be set up in places where the civil courts could no longer be relied on.

General Macready

Relying on the police

Lloyd George was determined not to admit that Sinn Féin was a real government and the IRA a real army. He called them 'a murder gang'. The proper way to fight a murder gang was with police, not soldiers, so he refused to use the British army against them. He wanted to use the RIC instead, but Irishmen were no longer joining it. To fill the gap, he ordered that RIC men be recruited in Britain.

Recruiting policemen in Britain

Unemployment was high there in 1920. Many young men, demobilised from the army when the war ended, were happy to join the RIC, especially as the pay (50p a day) was better than average.

Those who joined were not criminals as Sinn Féin propaganda suggested. But they were tough ex-soldiers who were given the impossible task of policing a foreign and hostile country. The army commander, General Macready, wrote about them:

> as policemen they were quite useless. The value of a policeman lies in his knowledge of a locality and its inhabitants, of which these RIC recruits were necessarily ignorant. (Sir N. Macready, *Annals of an Active Life*, Vol 2, p. 482)

The 'Black and Tans' and the Auxiliaries

In March 1920 the first recruits arrived in Ireland. Because of a shortage of police uniforms, they were dressed in a mixture of army khaki and the RIC's dark-green

Units of Tans and Auxiliaries combined to hunt down the IRA. This picture captures the adventurous, devil-may-care attitude of these men who faced an unseen enemy. While admirable in its place such an attitude was disastrous when moving among a potentially hostile civilian population.

◆

uniform. They were quickly nicknamed the **'Black and Tans'**. Later, ex-army officers were recruited to form an **Auxiliary Division** of the RIC. It was led by Brigadier Crozier, formerly an officer in the Ulster Volunteers.

The 'Tans' and the 'Auxies' soon earned a reputation for ruthless and undisciplined behaviour and became the most hated of the British forces in Ireland.

Guerrilla warfare

The war got worse after the Tans arrived. They began to search for and arrest suspected Sinn Féiners and to patrol the countryside in convoys of lorries.

This forced the IRA to change its method of operating. It was no longer safe for active IRA men to live at home. Many had to go 'on the run'. They formed **flying columns** of twenty or thirty men. Paid as full-time soldiers and better trained and armed than the average Volunteer, members of the flying columns moved from place to place, living rough in the countryside or getting shelter from sympathetic families.

The columns staged ambushes, carefully planned in conjunction with the local IRA brigade. When a report was received that a convoy of Black and Tans was on its way, about a dozen men were stationed behind walls and ditches, trees were felled to halt the Tans' lorries, followed by an exchange of fire and the death or surrender of the enemy. Then the flying column could slip away and vanish among the local people.

Reprisals

The Tans, bewildered by the surprise attacks and unfamiliar with the people, could not tell who was friend and who was foe. Frustrated, they rioted, hitting back blindly at everyone, Home Ruler and unionist as well as Sinn Féiner.

- They burned houses and businesses, beat up or murdered prisoners and shot at innocent bystanders.

- Drunk with alcohol and rage, they smashed up towns like Tuam, Mallow, Balbriggan, Tubbercurry and Ennistymon in revenge for the death of their comrades.

- In the summer of 1920 Tomás MacCurtain, the Lord Mayor of Cork and head of the local IRA, was murdered in his home by policemen with their faces blackened. The government claimed he were killed by other IRA men in an internal feud but a Cork jury brought in a verdict of wilful murder against Lloyd George.

The government turned a blind eye to Black and Tan reprisals, hoping they would discourage people from supporting the IRA. In January 1921 reprisals became official policy when Macready ordered that:

> punishments including confiscations, fines, or, if necessary, the destruction of houses or property might be carried out against any person or persons, who might be considered implicated in .... outrages against the Crown forces. (Sir N. Macready, *Annals of an Active Life*, Vol 2, p. 523)

Tomás MacCurtain.

The effects of reprisals

The reprisal policy was counter-productive for the government. Many Sinn Féiners had disapproved of the actions of the IRA but now felt they had to support them against the terrorism of the Tans.

Reprisals were also good propaganda for Sinn Féin. British and other foreign journalists reported on this aspect of British rule in Ireland. Their reports outraged many people in Britain. They felt ashamed that their government, which was supposed to be upholding law and order, should engage in this kind of behaviour.

British calls for peace

The British Labour Party sent over a commission of enquiry. On its return it strongly attacked the government's policies. In parliament Asquith and the Independent Liberals demanded a change of course, and even Coalition Liberals and some Conservatives grew uneasy. A 'Peace with Ireland Council' was formed by people from all political parties to campaign for a settlement.

October-December 1920: a turning point

Any hope of peace diminished at the end of 1920 when a number of events forced the government to take a tougher line in Ireland.

25 October: the death of Terence MacSwiney

On 25 October Terence MacSwiney died in Brixton prison near London. He had succeeded the murdered MacCurtain as Lord Mayor of Cork and local IRA

American women demonstrating against British rule in Ireland.

commander, and was soon arrested. He demanded to be treated as a prisoner of war rather than a criminal. When that was refused, he went on hunger strike. He died after seventy-four days without food.

1 November: the execution of Kevin Barry
A few days later the eighteen-year-old Kevin Barry was hanged in Mountjoy jail. He was sentenced to death for his part in an ambush in Dublin when a seventeen-year-old British soldier was killed. His youth caused an outcry and various attempts were made to have the execution stopped.

21 November: Bloody Sunday
After Lloyd George's re-organisation, Dublin Castle had rebuilt its spy network. A group of agents, known as the 'Cairo gang', were brought in. Many of them lived as private citizens, apparently holding civilian jobs.

Through his sources in the Castle, Collins soon heard about them. He summoned IRA men to Dublin to supplement the Squad and on Sunday, 21 November sent them out to kill the men. Fourteen were shot, some in front of their families. Most, though not all, of those shot were agents.

Collins had chosen that Sunday because a big GAA match in Croke Park gave cover to IRA-men coming to Dublin. The authorities realised this and in the afternoon sent heavily armed Black and Tans to surround the ground and arrest suspects. Exactly who began shooting first is not clear, but the police certainly fired into the crowd, killing twelve people.

Later that night, three men, Peadar Clancy, Dick McKee and Conor Clune, who had been captured in Dublin on Saturday were shot in Dublin Castle. Two were prominent members of the IRA, the third, Clune, was an innocent civilian. According to the official report they had been trying to escape, but this was generally disbelieved.

28 November: the Kilmichael ambush

A week after Bloody Sunday, Cork IRA men ambushed an Auxiliary patrol at **Kilmichael** near Macroom. They were led by Tom Barry, a former British soldier and one of the most effective of the IRA commandants. All but one of the Auxiliaries were killed.

10 December: martial law

Bloody Sunday and Kilmichael convinced Lloyd George that he must use the British army more. Martial law was declared in Cork, Kerry, Tipperary and Limerick. It gave the army power:

- to search houses.

- to impose curfews.

- to try people in army rather than in civil courts.

- to intern suspects without trial.

11 December: the burning of Cork

The next day Auxiliaries were ambushed outside Cork. That night Black and Tans and Auxiliaries poured into the city and set fire to parts of it. This was the most spectacular of the reprisals. In the Commons, Chief Secretary Greenwood denied that the Crown forces were to blame and suggested that Cork people set fire to their own city.

January-July 1921: the IRA under pressure

Martial law and the growing involvement of the British army increased the pressure on the IRA. A wave of arrests followed it with over 500 people, including Griffith, being picked up. In January 1921 it was extended to Clare, Kilkenny, Wexford and Waterford. By July 4,500 IRA men were being held in prison camps.

Arms were now harder to get (though Collins did import a consignment of newly-invented Thompson sub-machine guns from America). It became more difficult to

The devastation caused by the Black and Tan attack on Cork city.

stage big attacks. There were only two successful attacks on police barracks in these months.

Many of Collins's spies were rooted out and he found it harder to get information on the Crown forces. The British on the other hand received more information. IRA brigades responded by shooting people they suspected of spying and dumping their bodies with the word 'spies' on signs tied around their necks. This worried the GHQ who feared it would alienate public opinion.

But martial law did not end the violence. Ambushes in Dublin streets became more common, causing the deaths of many innocent passers-by. From January to July 1921 about 300 of the Crown forces and over 700 civilians (who included IRA men) were killed.

Disputes within the leadership

At the same time dissension was growing among the leaders of the IRA. Much of it centred on the friction between Michael Collins and Cathal Brugha.

The IRA and Cathal Brugha

When the Dáil set up its government in 1919, Brugha was appointed Minister for Defence. As such, he was answerable to the Dáil (i.e. the elected representatives of the people) for the IRA's actions. As Minister for Defence, he tried to establish civilian control over the IRA. He intervened in the work of the GHQ, giving orders to Mulcahy, the Chief of Staff.

But Brugha was not directly involved in the fighting, (he continued to work in his business throughout the period) and the men who were, often found his ideas impractical. For example, he disapproved of ambushes and wanted the IRA be involved in direct battles with the Crown forces. But many IRA commandants, knowing how few men and arms they had, found this unrealistic.

Brugha also objected to the continued existence of the IRB of which Collins was President. Many IRA officers were also in the IRB. Who, Brugha wondered, would these men obey: their leaders in the secret society or in the IRA?

Part of the problem was personal. Brugha was jealous of Collins. Newspapers glorified Collins, presenting him as the glamorous hero, while they ignored Brugha, who, as minister, was Collins' boss. Collins did not help the situation, by showing contempt for Brugha, whose complaints he considered unjustified. The friction between the two affected others, with IRA men taking sides.

December 1920: de Valera returns

De Valera finally returned from America in December 1920. He found the situation in Ireland very different from when he had left. A full scale war was in progress and the country was racked by terror. Like Brugha, with whom he sided, de Valera did not approve of the nature of the IRA campaign and he too thought the press gave Collins too much credit for its successes.

In May 1921 he persuaded GHQ to launch a frontal attack on the Customs House in Dublin where the British local government records were stored. The attack was a success and the Customs House was burned. But the IRA lost over eighty men, dead or captured, and their arms. Given the pressure it was under, it could not afford victories at such a high price.

Lloyd George seeks peace

Meanwhile Lloyd George had learned that de Valera was back. He gave orders that he was not to be arrested. He thought de Valera was more moderate than Collins and he wanted one senior Sinn Féin person to be available when the time for negotiations came. That would be, as we shall see in the next chapter, when he had dealt with the unionists.

Chapter 24

1920-21: Towards partition and peace

Lloyd George and Ireland

When Lloyd George turned his attention back to Ireland in the autumn of 1919, he had two priorities. The first, with which we have dealt, was to suppress the IRA; the second was to deal with the Ulster unionists. After both of these were accomplished, he proposed to talk to Sinn Féin about a measure of independence for the rest of Ireland.

The Conservatives and Ireland

In dealing with Ireland Lloyd George was not a free agent. He was a Liberal but was also the leader of a Coalition government whose biggest party was the Conservatives. They were close allies of the Unionist Party and he had to take their views into account when dealing with Ireland.

In 1914 leading Conservatives had opposed independence for any part of Ireland but by 1920 they had changed their minds. Reluctantly, they now accepted that a limited form of independence for the nationalist areas was unavoidable. But they were determined not to force the Ulster unionists to accept the control of a Dublin parliament.

The Unionists and Sinn Féin

In the 1918 election the Unionist Party won twenty-six seats, all but four of them in Ulster. The party, still led by Sir Edward Carson and Sir James Craig, was as determined as ever to stay in the Union. They saw Sinn Féin as an even greater threat to everything they valued than the old Home Rule Party had been.

There were several reasons for this.

- The Irish-Ireland movement, of which Sinn Féin was a part, implied that the only 'real' Irish people were the native Gaelic-speaking celts. But most unionists were descended from settlers who had come from Britain in the seventeenth century. Thus unionists feared that a Sinn Féin-dominated state would discriminate against them on racial as well as on religious and economic grounds.

- As the IRA violence developed in the south in 1919, many of its victims were, inevitably, people of unionist views. This confirmed unionist fears that Irish nationalists intended to drive them out of the country by force.

- Sinn Féin wanted a republic which would cut all links with the British monarch, to whom unionists felt a strong sense of loyalty.

The strength of the Unionists

But in 1919 the Unionists were in an even stronger position to resist the nationalists than they had been in 1914:

- Their allies, the Conservatives were an important part of the Coalition government.

- With twenty-six MPs, they were the biggest Irish party in Westminster. The seventy-three Sinn Féin MPs had abstained, so that the nationalist point of view was only represented by the six remaining Home Rulers. When Lloyd George came to decide what to do about Ireland, the only Irish people he spoke to were the unionists.

September 1919 – February 1920: 'Home Rule all round'

In September 1914 the third Home Rule Bill had became law but on condition that it remain suspended until the war was over and until the unionists had been consulted. In September 1919, as the last peace treaties were being signed, Lloyd George set up a committee to decide what to do about it.

The committee came up with a new idea. It proposed that Ireland be divided into two areas, 'Northern Ireland' and 'Southern Ireland' and that **each** be given Home Rule.

Lloyd George and his Cabinet accepted this plan for 'Home Rule all round' but they wanted 'Northern Ireland' to contain all nine Ulster counties. In the nine counties, the nationalists and unionists were equally balanced and the Cabinet felt this would be fairer.

These proposals were then passed on to the Ulster unionists for their views.

- At first they were doubtful about the idea of Home Rule for 'Northern Ireland'. They had been fighting to stay in the United Kingdom, not to have Home Rule for themselves. But the more they thought about the proposal, the more attractive it seemed. With their own elected parliament they would be secure. No future British government could ever force them to accept the rule of a Dublin government.

- The unionist leaders turned down the plan for a nine-county Northern Ireland. In nine counties, the population was so evenly balanced that a small change might produce a nationalist majority and force them under a Dublin parliament.

  Instead they demanded six counties, Antrim, Down, Derry, Fermanagh and Tyrone. In that area the unionists were 65 per cent of the population and the nationalists 35 per cent. This, they felt, would give them a permanent majority and keep them safe. Unionists in Cavan, Monaghan and Donegal complained bitterly that they were being sacrificed, but the Unionist leadership ignored their protests.

- Some Liberals were uneasy at the failure to consult the nationalist population in the six counties. They wanted a referendum in each county to allow the people to choose whether their area should be in the 'north' or the 'south'. The unionists knew that this would lose them Fermanagh and Tyrone so they opposed the idea. They argued that anything less than six counties would be too small to work economically. The Conservatives backed them and the proposal was dropped.

23 December 1920: the Government of Ireland Act

The Bill with these proposals was put before parliament early in 1920. The main parts of it were as follows.

- Ireland was to be divided into two states – 'Southern Ireland', with twenty-six counties and 'Northern Ireland', with six counties.

- Each state was to have its own parliament, with two houses, a Commons and a Senate. To give minorities a fair share of seats, elections would be by Proportional Representation (PR). The unionists had opposed this but they were overruled.

- Each parliament was to elect a government, headed by a Prime Minister. The government was to be responsible for governing its area but certain powers were **reserved** for the Westminster parliament. The **reserved powers** included the monarchy, peace and war, control of the armed forces, coinage, post, income tax and excise duties.

- Each area was still to elect MPs to the Westminster parliament.

- The British wanted a united Ireland, so they included links between the two states. There would be one **Viceroy** (representing the king) and a **Council of Ireland** on which MPs from each parliament would serve. The Council would oversee areas of common interest like trade and fisheries. If both parliaments agreed, they could transfer more powers to the Council and so bring about a reunification by agreement.

The **Government of Ireland Act** finally passed through parliament on 23 December 1920 and came into effect on 3 May 1921.

Sinn Féin and the unionists

Sinn Féin played no part in these developments. Like Parnell and Redmond before them, de Valera and the other Sinn Féin leaders had never seriously considered what to do about the one million unionists who lived in the north-east and who refused to be part of an independent Ireland. They never talked to unionists, seldom visited Belfast and were unsympathetic to its industrial culture.

They tended to have two views about the unionist attitude to independence.

- The unionists were bluffing. As soon as Sinn Féin won independence, they would fall into line.

- The British were manipulating unionists' fears as a way of blocking Irish independence. Once the British gave in, they would force the unionists to make a deal with Dublin.

These views emerge clearly after a meeting between de Valera and Craig on 5 May 1921. The two men argued about the validity of the Act of Union and afterwards de Valera wrote:

> I do not see any hope of ending the struggle with England through a prior agreement with the unionist minority. At bottom the question is an Irish/English one and the solution must be sought in the larger general play of English interest. (Longford and O'Neill, *Eamon de Valera*, p. 123)

This was completely unrealistic. It did not take account of the very real fears that unionists had about being ruled by a Catholic-dominated, rurally-biased Dublin government. It also ignored the sense of obligation which British politicians, especially Conservatives, felt to the only group in Ireland who were loyal to Britain. No British government could possibly use force to push reluctant unionists **out** of the United Kingdom.

1920: violence in the north

Although the IRA was never strong in Ulster, it did manage to mount some operations in the west of the province in the early months of 1920. This provoked a response. The Ulster Volunteer Force (UVF), which had been dormant since 1914, was revived under the leadership of **Basil Brooke** and sectarian violence increased.

Basil Brooke

In June there were riots in Belfast and Derry. On 21 July a crowd of several thousand men, calling themselves 'Protestant and unionist workers' marched on Harland and Woolf shipyards. They forcibly expelled 5,000 Catholics who had worked there through the war. About the same time, there were anti-Catholic riots in Banbridge and Lisburn as a result of IRA assassinations in the south.

Over the next year, about 11,000 Catholics were driven from their jobs, many Catholic houses and shops were burned and over 500 people killed. Catholics made up 58 per cent of the casualties in these riots, although they were only one third of the population.

September 1920: the 'Special Constables'

The violence led the British to set up a government in Belfast even before the Government of Ireland Act was passed. In September it began to enrol a new force of 'Special Constables' to control the situation.

Most recruits to the 'Specials' came from the UVF and it was soon clear that they were a sectarian force. They were given a free hand to put down disorder which they did with great brutality and little impartiality. From the start they were seen by Catholics as the armed wing of the Protestant state.

The Belfast boycott

The response of the Dáil to these developments was to order a boycott of Belfast goods. By the summer of 1921 this was quite effective and harmed many northern businesses. It did nothing for northern Catholics but it confirmed unionists in their belief that southern politicians wanted to undermine their economy. Instead of encouraging unity, the Dáil's boycott seemed to reinforce the partition of the country that the London parliament was trying to introduce.

24 May 1921: the partition elections

The two Irish states set up under the Government of Ireland Act came into existence on 3 May 1921. Arrangements were made to elect the two Home Rule parliaments, one for Southern Ireland and the other for Northern Ireland on 24 May.

In Northern Ireland all fifty-two seats were contested. The Unionist Party won forty, the Nationalist Party (Home Rulers) won six, and so did Sinn Féin. The Unionist Party invited Carson to be the first Prime Minister of Northern Ireland. He refused because he was too old. The job then went to **Sir James Craig** who remained the northern Premier until his death in 1940. (see chapter 36)

In the south, Sinn Féin ignored the Act but decided to show its strength by using the elections to choose the Second Dáil. Not one seat was contested. 124 Sinn Féin candidates and four unionists (for Trinity College) were elected unopposed.

1920: Peace feelers

Once the unionists were satisfied, Lloyd George felt free to consider peace with Sinn

Féin. Anti-war feeling was building up in Britain, Europe and the US, putting the British under pressure to do something to meet the Irish demand for self-determination.

As early as November 1920 Lloyd George had tried to make contact with Sinn Féin to see what terms they wanted. Bloody Sunday and other events at that time made a settlement difficult. Lloyd George insisted that the IRA give up its arms and allow 'murderers' like Collins to be arrested. Naturally, Sinn Féin refused even to consider these conditions.

January-May 1921: drift
When de Valera came home in December 1920, Lloyd George gave orders that he was not to be arrested. He then allowed the situation to drift in the first half of 1921. There were serious economic and labour difficulties in Britain which demanded his attention and in the spring, his military advisers assured him that the IRA was nearly beaten.

May 1921: Lloyd George's need for peace
It was not until May that a number of developments made it important for him to try again.

- The establishment of a northern parliament protected the unionists. This left the Conservatives free to consider some deal with the nationalists.

- The IRA attack on the Customs House (see page 266) showed that they were not yet beaten.

- Public opinion in Britain and abroad was growing more and more uneasy at the brutality of the war and at the British refusal to grant the Irish demand for self-determination. Even members of Lloyd George's own party and some Conservatives wanted him to talk to Sinn Féin.

- The Government of Ireland Act stated that if the act was not accepted in 'Southern Ireland' the British government would take over direct control of the area. Lloyd George's military advisers warned him that to defeat the IRA they would need to impose martial law, have 100,000 troops and execute thousands of people. In the face of hostile public opinion and the need to cut government expenditure, Lloyd George could only agree to that if he could show that he had first made a real attempt to find peace.

22 June 1921: the King's plea for peace
For these reasons, Lloyd George encouraged the King, George V, to make an appeal for peace when he opened the Northern Ireland parliament in Belfast on 22 June.

The plea was welcomed in Britain. Lloyd George seized on it to issue a public invitation to de Valera 'as the chosen leader of the great majority in Southern Ireland' to 'attend a conference here in London in company with Sir James Craig, to explore

King George V opening Northern Ireland parliament in Belfast.

to the utmost the possibility of a settlement'. (D. MacArdle, *The Irish Republic*, Corgi edition, p. 431)

Sinn Féin's need for a truce
De Valera, too, was under pressure to negotiate.

- The IRA was hard pressed. The increased use of the British army against it (see page 264) had robbed it of men and arms. Collins later claimed they only had ammunition for a few more weeks.

- Irish people were growing tired of the continuing violence and might cease to back the IRA if its leaders turned down a chance of talks.

But de Valera could not accept Lloyd George's description of him as the leader of 'Southern Ireland' without seeming to accept partition. Therefore he responded by inviting Craig and Lord Midleton, the leader of the southern unionists to meet him on 4 July to discuss the terms they would put to Lloyd George.

Craig naturally refused the invitation, since to accept would have been to recognise Dublin's leadership. Midleton, however, met de Valera and brought his demand for an unconditional ceasefire to Lloyd George.

11 July 1921: the Truce
The British leader accepted. On 8 July de Valera met General Macready and they agreed that each side was to retain its arms, and that attacks and counter-attacks were to cease. The truce came into effect on 11 July.

Cartoon showing Lloyd George (alias John Bull) as an inn-keeper, offering Sinn Féin a place in his Commonwealth hotel.

Assessing the truce

The truce was a defeat for Lloyd George, forcing him to accept less favourable terms than he had intended only weeks before.

- Instead of disarming the IRA, he was forced to let it stand aside like a real army while he talked to its leaders.

- Instead of forcing the Sinn Féin TDs to return to Westminster and negotiate from inside the British system as Parnell and Redmond had done, he had to talk to them as if they were leaders of a separate government.

- Instead of forcing them to accept the Government of Ireland Act, passed by the British parliament, he had to drop it, (at least in so far as it applied to 'Southern Ireland') and start again from scratch.

But de Valera and the other Sinn Féin leaders had made concessions too. By agreeing to talk to Lloyd George at all, they had agreed to work out some compromise on the two issues that mattered most to them – the republic and the reversal of the partition. They lacked the political experience to realise the extent of this concession. Only the direct experience of negotiations would show how much they could extract from the situation.

Chapter 25

1921: Towards a Treaty

July 1921: The first phase of the negotiations

Immediately after the truce de Valera went to London. He met Lloyd George and set out Sinn Féin's demand for a republic for the whole of Ireland.

The British made it clear that they would never agree to that. Instead they offered to give 'Southern Ireland' (i.e. the twenty-six counties) the same amount of independence as dominions of the British Empire like Canada or Australia. This type of independence is usually called 'dominion status'. But the dominion status Lloyd George offered de Valera was to be limited in a number of ways.

- There was to be perpetual free trade between Ireland and Britain.

- The Irish were to contribute to the UK national debt.

- The British navy was to have free access to all Irish ports.

De Valera rejected these terms and returned to Ireland where the Cabinet and the Dáil supported him.

Eamon de Valera.

DOMINION STATUS

The dominions were the parts of the British Empire settled by white Europeans, i.e. Canada, Australia, New Zealand and South Africa, which had been given some self-government since the mid-nineteenth century. Thus 'dominion status' meant as much independence as the dominions had.

On paper, that independence seemed limited.

- The British king was the head of state in each dominion, where he was represented by a Governor-General, who was usually a British nobleman appointed by the London government.

- All their MPs had to take an oath of allegiance to him.

- He had to sign all bills passed by their parliaments and, in theory, he could veto them on the advice of the British government.

- There were also issues on which the dominion parliaments were forbidden to make laws and other issues on which the Westminster parliament could make laws which bound the dominions.

In practice, however, the position of the dominions had changed greatly by 1921.

- The dominions were emerging on the world stage as countries in their own right. In 1914 Britain took them into the war without any consultation. During the war, however, the British began to hold Imperial Conferences where dominion Prime Ministers met to discuss mutual problems. In 1919 the dominions had signed the peace treaties and joined the League of Nations as separate states.

- The British government had not tried to interfere in the dominions for many years and if it did now it would have caused great resentment.

By 1921, when the Irish delegates were in London, some lawyers believed that the dominions were independent states in all but name. If they wished, they could do anything an independent state could do, for example establish diplomatic relations with outside states, remain neutral in a war involving Britain, and even leave the Empire. This was an extreme point of view which British politicians did not accept. But Collins was aware of this thinking and was influenced by it during the treaty negotiations.

One sign of the growing independence of the dominions was that the word 'Commonwealth' began to replace the word Empire when speaking about them. It implied a group of co-operating nations rather than a single imperial government with power over all the other states. The Anglo-Irish Treaty was the first official document to contain this term.

July-October 1921: manoeuvring for position

Neither side wanted the talks to break down. Throughout August and September they exchanged letters and telegrams. Each was trying to re-open the talks without giving anything away.

Finally Lloyd George suggested a formula. An Irish delegation was to go to a conference in London

> with a view to ascertaining how the association of Ireland with the community of nations known as the British Empire may be reconciled with Irish national aspirations. (Longford, *Peace by Ordeal*, p. 88)

Picking the Irish delegation

The Dáil Cabinet, consisting of **de Valera, Griffith, Collins, Brugha, Austin Stack, William T. Cosgrave and Robert Barton** agreed to talk on these terms. Then they had to pick a negotiating team.

Everyone had assumed that the President, de Valera, would lead it as he had in July, so there was dismay when he announced that he was not going to London. He gave two reasons for his decision.

- He was needed at home to keep the more inflexible republicans in check.

- The delegates would have to refer all British proposals back to him in Dublin and this would give them an excuse for not signing anything under pressure in London.

Griffith, the Vice President, was then picked to lead the delegation. He was a dual monarchist not a republican, so his presence on the negotiating team was balanced by **Barton** who was a republican. Brugha and Stack, both hard-line republicans, refused to go. De Valera insisted that **Collins** must be on the delegation. Very reluctantly Collins agreed, primarily out of a sense of duty. **Eamonn Duggan** and **George Gavan Duffy**, both lawyers, were chosen for the team, because of their legal knowledge.

Erskine Childers, who was Barton's cousin, was appointed as the non-voting secretary to the delegation. De Valera wanted him to uphold the republican position and support Barton. But since he was not a full member, this was an impossible expectation. It also bred distrust between Childers and Griffith and Collins, who suspected him of spying on them for de Valera. Unfortunately Griffith disliked and distrusted Childers and this led to friction between them and disunity among the delegates.

Should de Valera have gone?

De Valera's decision not to lead the delegation to the Treaty negotiations has caused controversy ever since.

- His enemies claimed that after his July talks with Lloyd George he knew that the

British would never accept a republic. He therefore refused to take part in the negotiations as he did not want to be held responsible for the inevitable failure.

- His friends argued that his decision was a wise one. They blamed the delegates for failing to follow his instructions and signing the Treaty without checking it with him.

It was certainly a strange decision, as Cosgrave said, for the captain of a team not to join in its the most important match. But historians must be careful not to assume that de Valera knew in October what was going to happen in December. He could no more foretell the split over the Treaty and the civil war that followed than we can foretell what will happen to us in a year's time.

He made his decision in the light of what he knew at the time he made it. He may have been wrong, but it is unfair to blame him for what he could not know.

Would it have mattered if he went?

It is impossible to say with any certainty what would have happened had he gone to the talks but there are a number of points to note.

- The members of the Cabinet left in Dublin contained more committed republicans (Brugha, Stack and, in time, de Valera) than those who were in the delegation, where only Barton fell into this category. This led to a difference in aims between the more hard-line Dublin group and the delegates in London who were more inclined towards a compromise.

- The delegates had to refer every point back to Dublin. This caused tension. The delegates felt that the people at home did not understand how tough the going was for them. The feeling that they were not getting the backing they deserved undermined their confidence and weakened their stand against British pressure.

Perhaps if de Valera had led the delegation, some of these tensions might have been avoided.

The confusion of aims

A major weakness on the Irish side was the failure of the Cabinet to work out clearly what they wanted the delegates to achieve in the negotiations. They identified two main aims:

- to get a republic (i.e. complete separation from Britain).
- to restore the unity of Ireland as it had been before the Government of Ireland Act came into force in May.

They decided that unity mattered more to Irish people than the republic. Therefore the delegates were told that they should give up some independence in return for the restoration of unity. But this decision begged a number of questions.

- How much independence were they prepared to give up?
De Valera worked out a proposal for what he called 'external association' with the British Empire. This meant that Ireland would first leave the Empire and then sign a treaty of permanent alliance with it, recognising the King of Britain as head of that alliance. The Cabinet did not discuss what to do if, as seemed likely, the British turned this down.

- What would they offer the unionists to restore unity?
The Cabinet made no decision on this point. There was talk of giving them a parliament in Belfast which would be under the overall control of the Dáil. In one speech de Valera even suggested that unionist controlled counties should be allowed to opt out of Dublin rule and remain with Britain. But the matter was never seriously discussed and the delegates did not get instructions until several weeks after they left for London.

Sinn Féin's attitude to the unionists

The underlying Sinn Féin assumption seemed to be that the unionists did not matter. Once the British made a deal with Dublin, they would force the Ulster unionists under Dublin rule whether they liked it or not. For people who objected to being ruled by British force, this was a strange assumption. It was also unrealistic.

- The unionists already had their own parliament. It would be impossible for the British to force them to give it up.

- The Conservatives in the British Coalition government would protect the unionists if Lloyd George tried to bully them.

11 October 1921: the negotiations begin

The Irish delegates arrived in London early in October and the negotiations opened in Downing Street on 11 October.

The British delegation was led by the Prime Minister, **Lloyd George**. It included **Winston Churchill**, the Minister for War, and **Austin Chamberlain** and **Lord Birkenhead**, leaders of the Conservative Party.

Comparing the delegations

The two delegations were unevenly matched.

- The British included some of the ablest politicians of modern times, with long experience of government and international diplomacy. Lloyd George, for example, had been a government minister since 1906 and Prime Minister since 1916.

- The Irish were very inexperienced. Griffith was a journalist turned politician who had led an underground government for eighteen months. Collins was a post-office clerk turned soldier; a skilled guerrilla leader but with no experience of negotiating.

- The British had many psychological advantages. They were on their home ground. They had the power of the British Empire behind them and the skill of its civil servants to advise them. If the talks failed and war began again, it was not their country that would suffer.

- The Irish were in a hostile country. They had a small team of advisers, not much more experienced than themselves. And if they failed, their people would pay the price.

The unseen participants: Craig and the unionists

Although the unionists were not directly involved in the negotiations they were deeply concerned about them. Publicly, Craig said the talks had nothing to do with him; they were between the British and the leaders of 'Southern Ireland'. But privately he was worried that the negotiations might affect the unionist position. He relied on his friends in the Conservative Party to keep him in touch with what was going on.

The British aims

Craig had reason to worry. The British were prepared to ignore unionist protests in order to achieve a satisfactory peace with the rest of Ireland. They went into the talks with two clear aims.

- Their chief concern was the defence of Britain. A separate Ireland (i.e. a republic) might ally itself to Britain's enemy in a war and provide a backdoor for an

Collins was aware that his success as a guerrilla leader had depended on the British not knowing what he looked like. During the truce he tried to avoid being photographed and even grew a moustache.

invasion. Because of this they would not accept a republic and wanted to keep Ireland within the British Empire.

The British thought the way to ensure that was to make the Irish swear allegiance to the king. This point was more symbolic than real, but the British were as obsessed with it as many Sinn Féiners were with the republic. They believed that their own people would back them if they broke off the talks over the issue of the king and the Empire.

- The British also wanted to protect the unionists. But they considered this point less important. Therefore if they could get the Irish to agree to stay in the Empire, they were prepared to put pressure on the unionists to do a deal with the south.

They believed that many of their own people were uneasy at the way nationalists in Northern Ireland had been treated in the Government of Ireland Act and that they would accept some change in that arrangement so long as it did not involve forcing all unionists back into a united Ireland.

Lloyd George summed up the British view on these issues when he wrote:

men will die for the Throne and the Empire. I do not know who will die for Tyrone and Fermanagh. (Laffan, *The partition of Ireland*, p. 78)

The early stages of the negotiations

Between 11 and 24 October the Conference met seven times, with all the delegates present. There were too many people at these meetings for the work to progress properly, so they split into sub-committees to consider various issues.

- The less important delegates dealt with less important issues like trade, defence and the portion of the United Kingdom debt that the new Irish state would pay. Agreement on these was not too difficult.

- The leaders, Griffith and Collins on the one side and Lloyd George, Birkenhead and Chamberlain on the other, discussed the key points of independence and unity.

Ulster and the Crown

By then, the Irish had decided on their Ulster policy. They wanted a county option (each county being allowed to chose whether to go north or south), with the unionist counties retaining their own parliament but under Dublin control.

The British rejected this but offered instead that the whole six counties be put under an all-Ireland parliament provided that Ireland stayed within the Empire.

2 November: Griffith's letter

In November a pro-unionist group in the Commons put down a motion attacking the negotiations. To ensure their defeat, Lloyd George got a letter from Griffith which he

Members of the Irish delegation to the Treaty negotiations. Arthur Griffith is in the centre. On his left are Eamon Duggan, Robert Barton and George Gavan Duffy.

could show to wavering Conservative MPs. In it Griffith promised that, provided he was satisfied that the 'essential unity' of Ireland was guaranteed, he would recommend:

> a free partnership of Ireland with the other states associated within the British Commonwealth ... [and] that Ireland should consent to a recognition of the Crown as the head of the proposed association of states. (T. J. Jones, *Whitehall Diary*, Vol 3, p. 154)

In return Lloyd George promised Griffith that he would persuade Craig to agree to bring Northern Ireland under the control of an all-Ireland parliament.

8 November: the Boundary Commission idea

But the unionist leader refused even to discuss the idea. On 8 November Lloyd George's secretary, Tom Jones, told Griffith and Collins of this and made a new proposal to them.

- Northern Ireland should be left in existence but the border between it and the 'south' should be redrawn by a **Boundary Commission**. Such Commissions (i.e. small groups of men asking people which state they wanted to be in and drawing the border accordingly) were common in eastern Europe in 1919-21 where the borders of the newly emerging states like Hungary or Poland had to be decided.

Considering a Boundary Commission

Griffith and Collins were doubtful about the idea.

- Its advantage was that nationalist areas like south Down, south Armagh and Derry city would probably go to the south as well as Tyrone and Fermanagh.

- Its disadvantage was that accepting it involved admitting that the partition of Ireland was permanent.

They agreed to consider it but only as a way of bringing further pressure to bear on the unionists to come in under an all-Ireland parliament.

10 November: Lloyd George meets Craig

Craig went to London and met Lloyd George on 10 November. He refused to be intimidated by the idea of a Boundary Commission. He flatly rejected any deal with Dublin and instead demanded dominion status for Northern Ireland.

This angered Lloyd George and even some Conservative ministers but it marked a victory for the unionists. From this point on, Lloyd George gave up any idea of persuading them into a united Ireland.

Accepting the Boundary Commission

Instead he concentrated on persuading Griffith and Collins to accept a Boundary Commission. He argued that it would reduce Northern Ireland's area so much that the rest would be unworkable.

Reluctantly, the Irish delegates accepted that it was the best solution available to the question of partition and on 13 November Griffith agreed not to break off the talks on this issue. When they reported back to Dublin, the other members of the Cabinet also reluctantly accepted the idea.

The republic versus dominion status

Meanwhile discussions were also going on on the other key issue – independence. Here the British refused to budge from their demand that Ireland remain inside the Empire.

They turned down de Valera's idea of 'external association'. It involved leaving the Empire and they did not see much difference between it and a republic. British politicians were obsessed with getting the Irish to accept the king as head of the Irish state and they could not see beyond this point.

The final British proposals

In the last week of November the negotiations reached their final stage. While still rejecting external association, the British made some concessions on the oath to the king and on the exact meaning of dominion status. Then they presented the Irish with their final draft of a treaty.

Under it, the 'Irish Free State'* was to be a dominion of the Empire and to accept the king as its head of state, with TDs swearing an oath to him. A Boundary Commission was to redraw the border between north and south.

3 December: divisions in the Dáil Cabinet

The delegates carried the draft treaty back to Dublin where the Cabinet met on 3 December to consider it. The discussion was marred by deep bitterness.

- De Valera, Brugha and Stack rejected dominion status and told the delegates to go back and demand external association once more.

- Griffith replied that they had done so many times and the British had always rejected it. Almost all the discussion turned on this issue and little attention was paid to partition.

The discussion ended abruptly with the delegates having to leave to catch their boat. As they rushed away they agreed not to sign anything in London, but to bring back the terms and submit them to the Dáil for approval. There was no discussion of what to do if British threats of war made that impossible.

4 December: the negotiations break down

When the delegation arrived in London on 4 December Griffith, Collins and Duggan at first refused to go to Downing Street. They wanted the republicans, Barton and Gavan Duffy, to break off the talks. After much argument, Griffith finally agreed to go.

He again presented the case for external association to Lloyd George. The British were angry to find the Irish going back over ground they had already covered. The talks broke off in disagreement.

5 December: the final session

Next morning Lloyd George contacted Griffith and Collins. He persuaded them to return to Downing Street and resume the negotiations. The final session came that evening.

During it, Lloyd George showed his brilliance as a negotiator, mixing threats with concessions to get what he wanted. He informed the Irish that the Northern Ireland parliament was due to meet next day. He had promised to let Craig know its fate before then. Would the Irish delegates accept the Boundary Commission?

---

* Sinn Féin was using the words *Saor Stát* as the Irish for 'republic'. Lloyd George suggested that the literal translation of those words, 'Free State', be used as the English name for the new state. It would please Irish opinion, while not annoying the British as much as the use of the term 'republic' would.

They replied that they must first know Craig's attitude, but Lloyd George refused. Producing Griffith's undertaking of 13 November, he demanded to know if Griffith was about to break his promise not to repudiate the Boundary Commission? Always touchy about his honour, Griffith angrily denied the suggestion. After that, it was no longer possible to break off the talks on Ulster.

Then Lloyd George softened his line. He offered the Irish something dear to Griffith's heart – the right to protect Irish industry with tariffs on British imports. He also agreed to re-write the oath. Instead of swearing allegiance directly to the king as MPs in other dominions did, Irish TDs would first swear loyalty to the Irish constitution and only then to the king. In its new form, the oath read:

> I .... do solemnly swear true faith and allegiance to the Constitution of the Irish Free State as by law established, and that I will be faithful to His Majesty King George V, his heirs and successors by law, in virtue of the common citizenship of Ireland with Great Britain and her adherence to and membership of the group of nations forming the British Commonwealth of Nations.

This, Lloyd George said, was as far as he could go. Would the Irish accept it?

Griffith protested that they must check with Dublin before they signed anything. Lloyd George rejected this. He pointed out that their papers described them as 'plenipotentiaries' (having full power). That, he said, gave them power to sign anything and they must do so at once. If they did not, war 'immediate and terrible' would follow within three days.

6 December: signing the Treaty

Griffith said that he would accept the terms offered. The rest of the delegation insisted on withdrawing to discuss their position. Outside, Collins and Duggan said they too would sign. Barton and Gavan Duffy refused but after several hours of argument they reluctantly gave in.

At 2.10 a.m. on the morning of 6 December the delegates went back to Downing Street and signed the '**Articles of Agreement for a Treaty between Great Britain and Ireland**'.

The Treaty

The Treaty they signed contained eighteen articles in all.

- Articles 1 and 2 gave the Irish Free State the **same constitutional status as Canada and the other dominions**.

- Article 3 provided that the king's representative in Ireland would be a **Governor-General**, appointed in the same way as the Governor-General of Canada.

- Article 4 set out the **oath** to be taken by all members of the Irish parliament. (see above)

- Article 5 covered the Free State's share in the UK **war debt**.

FREE STATE OF IRELAND.

ARTICLES OF HISTORIC AGREEMENT.

A RELATIONSHIP THE SAME AS WITH CANADA.

"ULSTER" GETS A MONTH TO SAY IF SHE WILL STAY IN.

IRISH PROVISIONAL GOVERNMENT AT ONCE

Newspaper headlines of 7/8 December 1921 reporting on signing of Treaty.

- Articles 6 to 9 covered coastal defence and the provision by the Free State of **permanent port facilities at Queenstown (Cobh), Berehaven and Lough Swilly** for the British navy, with additional facilities in time of war.

- Article 10 covered the payment of pensions and compensation to former civil servants and police in the British administration.

- Articles 11 to 15 covered the position of Northern Ireland. The parliament of the Free State was to take over the functions reserved for the Westminster parliament under the Government of Ireland Act unless (and everyone knew that this would happen) the parliament of Northern Ireland petitioned to be excluded from its terms.

- In that event, Article 12 laid down that:

  a Commission consisting of three persons, one to be appointed by the Government of the Irish Free State, one to be appointed by the Government of Northern Ireland, and one, who shall be the chairman, to be appointed by the British Government, shall determine, in accordance with the wishes of the inhabitants so far as may be compatible with the economic and geographical conditions, the boundaries between Northern Ireland and the rest of Ireland.

- Article 16 forbad either government in Ireland to give special treatment to any religion.

- Articles 17 and 18 provided that the British should hand over power to a provisional government chosen by the parliament of Southern Ireland, and that both delegations should at once recommend the Articles of Agreement to their respective parliaments for ratification. (For a full text of the Treaty, see Longford, *Peace by Ordeal*, Appendix 1)

Chapter 26

1921-23: Fighting over the Treaty

Attitudes to the Treaty

News that a treaty had been signed aroused mixed feelings in Ireland. Ordinary people were probably relieved. The war would not begin again. The British army, the Black and Tans and Auxiliaries would go home and at long last Irish people could rule themselves.

Among dedicated republicans, however, there was anger and dismay. The Treaty did not bring the republic they had fought for. It was reported that some IRA men planned to arrest the returning delegates for treason.

8 December 1921: the Cabinet and the Treaty

De Valera was outraged to learn that the delegates had signed without his permission. He considered sacking Griffith, Collins and Barton from the Cabinet, but Cosgrave insisted that they be allowed to put their case.

On 8 December the Cabinet held a stormy meeting to discuss the Treaty. De Valera, Brugha and Stack wanted to reject it there and then, but the three delegates demanded that it go to the Dáil for a full debate. To de Valera's surprise, Cosgrave sided with them and by four votes to three the Cabinet sent the Treaty to the Dáil.

Taking sides on the Treaty

Before the Dáil met, each side tried to rally support.

- On 9 December de Valera issued a public statement saying:

  The terms of this agreement are in violent conflict with the wishes of the majority of this nation as expressed freely in successive elections during the past three years. I feel it my duty to inform you immediately that I cannot recommend acceptance of this Treaty either to Dáil Éireann or to the country. In this attitude I am supported by the Ministers of Home Affairs [Stack] and Defence [Brugha]. (Longford and O'Neill, *Eamon de Valera*, p. 169)

  By issuing this statement de Valera broke the tradition that discussions in the Cabinet should be confidential.

- On 10 December Collins called a meeting of the IRB Supreme Council and got its support for the Treaty. It instructed IRB men around the country to back it, although those members who were also TDs were left free to vote according to their consciences.

The Second Dáil: a very peculiar parliament

The Second Dáil met on 14 December to debate the Treaty. This Dáil was unique in Irish history. It had been chosen in May under the Government of Ireland Act. (see pages 269 and 271). Other parties had not put up candidates, thus allowing Sinn Féin to win all the seats without a single vote being cast. Whether the absence of other parties was voluntary or the result of intimidation is difficult to say.

As a result, the Second Dáil was an unelected, one party assembly, such as Lenin might have admired. This did not mean TDs did not represent Irish opinion. But since they had been hand-picked by the leaders of Sinn Féin and the IRA and not elected by the voters, there were probably more committed republicans among them than there would have been in the country as a whole.

But the Second Dáil was different from Soviet assemblies in one important way. No one told the TDs what to say or how to vote during the debate on the Treaty. It was a free debate and a free vote, probably freer than in any later Dáil when deputies were bound to speak and vote with their parties. There is plenty of evidence that individual TDs thought long and hard about the issues and in the end voted according to their consciences.

14 December: de Valera's Document No. 2

The debate began with a secret session. During it, de Valera called on TDs to reject the Treaty and replace it with an alternative treaty which he gave them.

Collins entering the Mansion House in Dublin during the Treaty Debates.

Known as **Document No. 2**, it was his external association proposal again. Under it the king would not be the head of the Irish state and there was no oath and no Governor-General but Ireland would be associated with the Empire. Otherwise it was much the same as the Treaty, even including a Boundary Commission.

De Valera wanted Document No. 2 to be given to the British as the minimum Irish demand. He hoped this would prevent the Dáil splitting but in fact it annoyed both sides. Those who supported the Treaty pointed out that the British had already rejected these demands. Republicans, on the other hand, thought Document No. 2 was little better than the Treaty. As a result de Valera withdrew the proposal.

19 December to 7 January: the public debate

On 19 December the Dáil met in public to debate the Treaty. With a short break for Christmas (22 December – 3 January) they continued until 7 January. Every deputy insisted on speaking, some at great and boring length.

The Anti-Treaty case

Among those who opposed the Treaty, there were two main points of view.

- The extreme republican arguments

The hard-line republicans rejected the Treaty completely because it did not contain the republic. They argued that the republic had been declared in 1916 and confirmed by the election of 1918 and the Dáil's declaration of 1919. It was sanctified by the blood of martyrs and they had taken an oath to uphold it.

No Treaty and no elected assembly could ever overturn the republic once it had been established. Those who voted to do so by accepting the Treaty, broke their most solemn oath and were traitors to Ireland. If the only alternative to the Treaty was to go back to war, then they urged the Dáil to choose war.

This was not an argument based on reason. For those who took this line, belief in the 'republic' was more like a religious faith than a political argument. It was the faith held by Stack and Brugha and put most forcibly by the six women deputies, including Kathleen Clarke, Mary MacSwiney and Constance Markievicz.

For them, as Mary MacSwiney argued, acceptance of the Treaty would be the 'one unforgivable crime that has ever been committed by representatives of the people of Ireland'. (*Dáil Debates on the Treaty*, p. 127)

Ominously for the future, the republican deputies made it clear from the start that if they lost, they would not accept the decision of the Dáil. As early as 17 December Liam Mellows said: 'We who stand by the republic still, will, I presume, rebel against the new government that would be set up if this Treaty is passed'. (*Dáil Debates*, p. 243)

- The moderate republican arguments

Other opponents of the Treaty were more moderate. Like de Valera, they were realistic enough to know that some kind of deal would have to be done with the

Mary MacSwiney

British but they felt that the Treaty was not good enough. They wanted to tear it up and try for better terms.

Their main objection was that the Treaty made the king the head of the Irish state, and that TDs would have to take an oath to him. This, they argued, would allow the British to go on meddling in Irish affairs. Many also felt that the oath to the king would violate the oath they had already taken to the republic. As de Valera put it:

> the Treaty makes British authority our masters in Ireland. It is said that they (TDs) had only an oath to the British king in virtue of common citizenship, but you have an oath to the Irish Constitution which will have the king of Great Britain as head of Ireland. You will swear allegiance to that Constitution and to that king. (Longford and O'Neill, *Eamon de Valera*, p. 175)

Supporters of the Treaty objected that the British did not interfere in Canada. Erskine Childers replied by pointing out that Canada and the other dominions were thousands of miles from Britain, while Ireland was on its doorstep. And in any case, Canada did not give port facilities to the British navy. While this condition lasted, Childers argued, Ireland could never follow an independent foreign policy.

The Pro-Treaty case

On the pro-Treaty side almost no one liked the Treaty. Most of the arguments put forward for accepting it were based on practical rather than idealistic grounds.

- The military argument.

Many accepted the Treaty only because they could see no alternative. If the war began again, they asked, could they win? A renewed war would bring suffering to the people, but would it bring a republic?

It was Richard Mulcahy who put this point most clearly. Ireland was still occupied by the British army and police, which the IRA had never beaten. As he said, 'we have not yet been able to drive the enemy from anything but a fairly good-sized police barracks'. (D. MacArdle, *The Irish Republic*, p. 568) It was not the IRA's military victories that made Lloyd George negotiate with Sinn Féin but the distaste of the British public for the war. If the Irish turned down the Treaty, they would lose that British sympathy.

And if they did start fighting again, as Collins and others pointed out, the IRA would be weaker than before. It had lost the advantage of surprise. Its leaders were well-known. Its opponents would be more ruthless and probably more numerous. And the Irish people whose backing had been vital, might be less supportive if the chance of peace was thrown away.

- The 'step by step' argument

Others saw the Treaty as the first step to the republic. Once the British were gone, they argued, Ireland could move on to a fuller independence. This view was put by Collins when he claimed that the Treaty 'gives us freedom, not the ultimate freedom that all nations desire and develop to, but the freedom to achieve it. (T. P. Coogan, *Michael Collins*, p. 301)

- The gains brought by the Treaty

Some pointed out that the British made great concessions in the Treaty, especially when compared with what they had offered under Home Rule. Griffith listed gains which would have seemed impossible in 1914:

> We have brought back the flag; we have brought back the evacuation of Ireland after seven hundred years by British troops and the formation of an Irish army. We have brought back to Ireland her full rights and powers of fiscal control. (D. MacArdle, *The Irish Republic*, p. 557)

- The advantages of dominion status

Finally, some even saw advantages in dominion status. They pointed out that the amount of independence enjoyed by the dominions was growing and that in time it would develop into full independence.

Kevin O'Higgins also argued that being a dominion gave Ireland greater security than a lonely independence. Other dominions like Canada would guarantee that the British did not interfere in Ireland, since to allow her to do so would diminish the freedom of all dominions.

The division grows

The debate dragged painfully along. The first speakers tried to keep to the issues, but, towards the end, personal bitterness crept in.

If the vote had been taken before Christmas, the Treaty might have been rejected. But during the week they were at home, deputies talked to their constituents. A small number became convinced that the people wanted peace. As a result, they changed their minds and backed the Treaty.

7 January 1922: the Dáil accepts the Treaty

The final vote was close. On 7 January the Dáil approved the Treaty by sixty-four votes to fifty-seven.

Griffith's new government

Even before the vote people were trying to avoid a split and keep the Sinn Féin Cabinet in place. They failed when de Valera refused to compromise.

After the vote he resigned as President and Griffith was elected in his place. He appointed a new Cabinet which included **Collins** as **Minister of Finance** and **Mulcahy** as **Minister of Defence**, **W.T. Cosgrave** as **Minister of Local Government** and **Kevin O'Higgins** as **Minister of Economic Affairs**. De Valera and his followers withdrew from the Dáil in protest.

The split in the country

Around the country, people had followed the debates closely. Like the TDs, they too were divided on the Treaty, with members of the same family sometimes taking opposite sides.

Popular support for the Treaty was greater than the narrow majority in the Dáil suggested. Twenty county councils, for example, had passed resolutions in favour of it while the Dáil debates were going on. Most people wanted peace so that they could resume their normal lives. The economy was shattered and many felt that rebuilding it was more important than abstract ideas like an oath to the king or the difference between a dominion and a republic.

Transferring power under the Treaty

Under the terms of the Treaty the Irish Free State was to come into existence on 6 December 1922, a year to the day after it was signed. During that transition year, the British would hand over power, bit by bit, to a **Provisional Government**, which was to be elected by 'the parliament of Southern Ireland' that was set up under the Government of Ireland Act.

14 January: electing the Provisional Government

This parliament was really the Second Dáil plus the four unionist TDs from Trinity who had never attended the Dáil. On 14 January it met for the only time and elected

Collins as head of the **Provisional Government**. He then appointed a Cabinet which included Cosgrave and O'Higgins.

This awkward arrangement of having two governments was another attempt to please the republicans by making it appear that the Dáil government was still in existence. Because the same men were on both Cabinets, it caused less confusion than it might have.

The tasks of the Provisional Government

The Provisional Government, working in close collaboration with Griffith's Dáil government, had a number of tasks to complete.

- It had to take over the government from the British. On 16 January Collins went to Dublin Castle, for seven hundred years the seat of British rule in Ireland, and took possession of it.

- It had to set up the administration of the new state – the army, police, civil service, court system and so on.

- It had to draw up a Constitution for the Irish Free State.

- It had to organise elections.

As head of the Provisional Government, Collins had to oversee all these developments. At the same time he was desperately trying to stop the split over the Treaty degenerating into violence.

The split in the IRA

The most urgent task was to try to control the IRA. It too was split by the Treaty. The majority of the Headquarters Staff followed Collins and Mulcahy and accepted it, but a minority, including Rory O'Connor and Liam Mellows, rejected it.

Around the country most of the local Commandants were anti-Treaty, especially in the south where **Seamus Robinson** in Tipperary and **Liam Lynch** in Cork, were among its most prominent opponents. But in Longford, **Seán MacÉoin** gave it his backing. Among the rank and file, many probably followed their local leaders, though those who were also in the IRB went with Collins. On balance, the anti-Treaty section of the IRA was probably more numerous and better armed than the government supporters.

Manoeuvring to control the army

Control of the army was vital to both sides. As soon as the Dáil had voted, Mulcahy announced that the IRA would continue to be the army of the republic. On 12 January officers asked him to call an Army Convention to discuss the Treaty. Though this was undemocratic, he agreed, despite protests from Griffith and O'Higgins. This decision held the IRA together for the time being.

Kevin O'Higgins and his wife.

Meanwhile, around the country, the British army began to withdraw from their barracks. At first they handed them over, together with supplies of arms, to the local leader, regardless of whether he was pro- or anti-Treaty. This made more arms available to the two sides but in some places, especially in Limerick and Kilkenny, clashes occurred between them during the takeover.

26 March: the Army Convention repudiates the Dáil

As it became clear that a majority in the IRA were anti-Treaty, Mulcahy cancelled the Army Convention. However 200 officers, led by **Liam Mellows** and **Rory O'Connor**, disregarded the order and met on 26 March.

They rejected the authority of the Dáil and set up their own sixteen-man **Executive**. Asked afterwards by a reporter if they acknowledged any other government in Ireland, Rory O'Connor replied, 'No'. 'Do we take it that we are going to have a military dictatorship, then?' he was asked and replied, 'You can take it that way if you like'. (Robert Kee, *The Green Flag*, p. 733)

14 April: seizure of the Four Courts

On 14 April O'Connor led his men into the Four Courts and other strong points around Dublin. Clearly this was a challenge to the authority of the Provisional Government, but Collins chose to ignore it.

He still hoped to avoid fighting with men who had so recently been his friends and comrades. But he also needed time to build up the Free State army. Recruitment and training went ahead rapidly and by June it contained 8,000 men.

Throughout the country soldiers of the newly founded Irish army took over from the British and raised the Irish tricolour in place of the Union Jack. Here we see Seán Mac Eoin raising the Irish flag over Athlone barracks.

De Valera's tactics

Meanwhile de Valera was in a difficult situation. The IRA supported him on the Treaty but the Dáil and the voters did not. He formed an anti-Treaty party, **Cumann na Poblachta**, to campaign against it. In a number of speeches he said that those who wished to finish the work of the last four years would have to wade through Irish blood to do so. And when a delegation from the Labour Party met him to beg for peace, he repeatedly stated that 'the majority have no right to do wrong'.

All this could be seen as an appeal to the extreme republicans, but at the same time de Valera annoyed them by leading his followers back into the Dáil, thereby recognising the Provisional Government.

Collins and de Valera

In February he made a deal with Collins to postpone the elections until June. Griffith was very annoyed by this. He felt that the people should be asked to vote on the Treaty as soon as possible. But Collins hoped to win de Valera and the moderate republicans over to his side by circumventing the Treaty.

The means he planned to use was the Constitution for the new Free State. He instructed the lawyers who were drawing it up to leave out all reference to the king and the oath. In this way he hoped to show de Valera that what he wanted could be achieved within the Treaty.

20 May: the Collins-de Valera 'pact'

To avoid deepening the split, the two leaders worked out a 'pact' in May, under which the pro- and anti-Treaty factions would fight the election jointly and form a coalition government afterwards.

This was an undemocratic arrangement. If carried through it would have prevented the voters from giving their opinion on the Treaty and produced an unelected Third Dáil, just like the Second. It angered Griffith and O'Higgins but Collins was desperately trying to avert the looming civil war and de Valera had more to gain from this arrangement than from a free election which he was sure to lose.

Violence in the north

Collins was also concerned with the situation in the north. The truce and Treaty had not eased the violence there as nationalists continued to reject partition and their inclusion against their will in a unionist-dominated state.

Economic depression in 1921 made the situation worse by adding competition for jobs to the usual nationalist/unionist enmity. Catholics suffered badly, especially in Belfast. They were driven from their jobs and often their homes as well.

From January to June 1922 171 Catholics and ninety-three Protestants were killed. On a population basis this was four Catholics for every Protestant and there was evidence that the police and Special Constables were either directly involved in the killings or were making no attempt to stop them.

Collins and the north

Collins wanted to protect the northern Catholics. Between January and March he met Craig three times and got promises from him that he would ensure greater protection for Catholics in return for an end to the boycott of Belfast goods. But Craig was unable to control his own extremists and the violence continued.

In April the Northern parliament passed the **Special Powers Act**. It permitted the authorities to impose curfews and made the possession of fire-arms punishable by death. The number of British troops was increased, more Special Constables (most of them former Ulster Volunteers) were enrolled and Sir Henry Wilson was engaged as military adviser, when he retired as Commander of the British army. These forces were used exclusively against the nationalist community.

Collins was extremely angry at these developments. He discouraged co-operation with the northern government and, unknown to his Cabinet colleagues, he arranged with the anti-Treaty IRA to send arms to the north. As well as helping northern Catholics, he seems to have hoped that co-operation between pro- and anti-Treaty factions on the north would prevent the split in the south.

The British response

Winston Churchill was the British minister responsible for overseeing the transfer of power to the Provisional Government. A typical British nationalist, he failed to understand the depths of the divisions in Ireland and was insensitive to the pressure the Irish leaders were under. Puzzled and angered by Collins's manoeuvres, he denounced the Collins-de Valera pact and demanded that Collins dislodge the IRA from the Four Courts.

The British and the new Constitution

In June Griffith and Collins finally brought the new Constitution to London for approval, as the Treaty demanded. Churchill and Lloyd George were horrified at what they read. There was no oath in it and no reference to the king. Conscious only of British needs, they threatened to scrap the Treaty and impose an economic blockade unless the necessary changes were made.

Collins and Griffith had no choice but to submit. The Constitution was hurriedly redrafted to include the oath and the king as head of state. Collins returned to Ireland to announce, only two days before the election, that the pact was off. Only on the morning of the election was the Constitution published, allowing de Valera to claim that the voters were unable to take it into consideration when casting their votes.

18 June 1922: the Treaty election

It is doubtful if it would have made any difference to the result. Despite the pact, other parties had contested this election, all of them supporting the Treaty. The outcome was a decisive vote for the Treaty.

Anti-Treaty Sinn Féin	Pro-Treaty Sinn Féin	Labour	Farmers	Unionists	Independents
35	58	17	7	4	7

Of the 620,283 people who voted, 239,193 gave their first preference to pro-Treaty candidates and 133,864 to anti-Treaty candidates. 247,226 supported other parties and many of these transferred their later preferences to pro-Treaty Sinn Féin.

18 to 28 June: the outbreak of Civil War

The election results gave Collins the mandate he needed to move against the Four Courts garrison. Whether he would have done so voluntarily is not clear, for two events forced his hand.

- On 22 June Sir Henry Wilson was assassinated in London by two IRA-men. Evidence has since come to light proving it was Collins, enraged by Wilson's role

299

in the north, who ordered the killing. But at the time, everyone, including the British, assumed that it was the extreme IRA in the Four Courts who were to blame.

Outraged, the British government sent orders to Macready who still commanded the British forces in Dublin, to attack the Four Courts. If he had obeyed at once the war with Britain would have begun again. Fortunately, Macready stalled until tempers cooled. Churchill withdrew the order the next day and publicly demanded that Collins take action. This made it difficult for Collins who did not want to be seen to act on the orders of a British minister.

- On 27 June the Four Court garrison seized J. J. O'Connell, Deputy Chief of Staff of the Free State Army. This gave Collins the excuse he needed. He issued an ultimatum to the garrison and early on 28 June, using fieldguns borrowed from the British army, opened fire on the Four Courts.

The point of no return
While these were not the first shots of the Civil War, they marked the point of no return. What had been merely a quarrel had become a war. Moderates had to line up with the militants. De Valera and other republican politicians joined the IRA, while the supporters of the Treaty rallied to the Free State army.

The fighting in Dublin
The fighting in Dublin lasted less than a week. The republicans, who failed to learn

The smouldering ruins in the Four Courts where the Civil War began.

the military lessons of the past three years, took up fixed positions like the rebels of 1916 and were as easily defeated.

The Four Courts fell on 30 June, but only after an explosion in the building had destroyed many of the irreplaceable records of Ireland's history. Other occupied buildings were soon taken. Hundreds of prisoners, including O'Connor and Mellows, were rounded up, and among the casualties was Cathal Brugha.

The war in Munster

Collins temporarily resigned from the government to take command of the Free State army which grew to 55,000 men by the end of the year. Munster was the republicans' stronghold. They controlled most of the area from Waterford to Limerick. Collins divided his troops, sending some to attack the republican positions from the sea and moving others south across the midlands. By the end of July he had driven the republicans from every stronghold. They then fell back on guerrilla tactics but it was only a matter of time before they would be defeated.

12 August: the death of Griffith

Arthur Griffith died suddenly on 12 August. His death changed little politically, for his failing health had already reduced his contribution to the government. Collins succeeded him. Other members of the Cabinet were worried by the power he now had, combining military and civilian leadership, and by his tendency to take decisions without consulting them.

22 August: the death of Collins

After Griffith's funeral, Collins returned to Munster. He seems to have been trying to start peace talks when he was caught in an ambush at Beál na Bláth in Co. Cork and killed. His death at the age of 32 shattered the country.

Cosgrave becomes President

The Cabinet met to pick a successor. The obvious choice was Mulcahy, who succeeded Collins as commander of the army. But the Cabinet was reluctant to give one man so much power again. Instead they chose **W.T. Cosgrave**, at forty-two the oldest man in the Cabinet and the one with the most experience of government.

Cosgrave, a quiet Dubliner, had not sought the job, but once in it he proved a steady leader who took the country through the traumatic years that were to follow.

The Third Dáil

The Third Dáil, elected in June, finally met in September. It gave the Free State government special powers, including the right to set up Army Courts and to execute people found carrying fire-arms.

De Valera and the anti-Treaty TDs refused to recognise it. They argued that because Collins had broken the pact and because the Second Dáil never met to

Michael Collins lying in state.

dissolve itself, the 1922 election was invalid. Therefore, they argued, the Second Dáil still existed and its members alone were the legitimate Dáil.

The republican leaders and the IRA

In October the anti-Treaty TDs set up a republican government with de Valera as President. In theory this was responsible for the republicans during the Civil War but in practise the IRA paid little attention to the politicians.

Atrocities

Once the Civil War moved into its guerrilla phase, it degenerated into a series of atrocities on both sides.

As part of its campaign the IRA attacked Free State supporters. People were murdered and many houses were burned. Among their victims was the elderly father of Kevin O'Higgins. In December a Free State TD, Seán Hales, was assassinated.

The Free State government retaliated with executions, some of them of doubtful legality. After Hales was killed, Rory O'Connor, Liam Mellows and two other republicans arrested in the Four Courts were shot, even though none of them could

Demonstrations were organised and funds set up by republican women. The socialist republican, Charlotte Despard, played an active part in such actions.

have been involved in his murder. It was an act of revenge, not justice. In all the Free State government executed over seventy republicans, among them Erskine Childers.

May 1923: the end of the war

By the beginning of 1923 it was clear that the republicans had no hope of winning. De Valera urged the IRA to call a halt. Liam Lynch, the IRA leader, paid no attention to him.

OFFER OF AMNESTY

(I.) Bearing in mind the acceptance by Liam De   ʳ an immediate and unconditional surrender of all arms ar.   ₁, and knowing that the reasons dictating to him that acceptance must weigh also with many leaders, and many of the rank and file, who have found themselves led step by step into a destruction that they never intended, but which has been the sequel of the line of policy adopted by those to whom they looked for leadership,

(2.) NOTICE IS HEREBY GIVEN that with a view to facilitating such a surrender the Government are prepared to offer amnesty to all persons now in arms against the Government who, on or before Sunday, 18th February, 1923, surrender with arms to any Officer of the National Forces or through any intermediary.

Risteard O Maolchatha, General,

Commander-in-Chief.

Dublin,

8th February 1923.

By the time this offer of amnesty was made many IRA soldiers, including Liam Deasy, had accepted their defeat. To encourage them, the Free State government made this offer of an amnesty in return for their giving up their arms. Considering the bitterness of the civil war, this was a generous offer but it was rejected by the hardline IRA leadership.

In April Lynch was killed. The new leader, **Frank Aiken**, was a more moderate man. He accepted de Valera's advice and, in May, called on his followers to put away their arms. For the republicans it was not a surrender but a pause; they planned to fight again another day. For the Free State it was victory and a chance at last to begin to build for the future.

Questions

ORDINARY LEVEL – A

Answer the following questions briefly. One or two sentences will be enough.

1 What part did the **IRB** play in the early years of the **GAA**?

2 Who founded the Gaelic League? Give **two** of the aims it had at that point.

3 Why did **J.M. Synge**'s play, *The Playboy of the Western World*, cause a riot in the Abbey in 1902?

4 Why were Dublin workers **locked out** in 1913?

5 Who were **Inghinidhe na hÉireann**?

6 In his book *The Resurrection of Hungary*, what action did **Arthur Griffith** propose for Irish MPs?

7 What was the **Solemn League and Covenant**? Set out **one** point that it made.

8 What did Patrick Pearse have in mind when he wrote about the **Murder Machine**?

9 What was the role of the **Aud** in the Easter Rising of 1916?

10 Who was elected leader of the **Sinn Féin** party in October 1917? Set out **three** of its aims at that point.

11 Give **two** of the decisions made by the First Dáil at its first meeting on 21 January 1919.

12 Explain the importance of the Boundary Commission idea in the negotiations for the Treaty.

13 Set out **two** of the arguments used to support the Treaty and **two** of the arguments used to oppose the Treaty during the Dáil Debates (Dec. 1921-Jan. 1922)

Questions

ORDINARY LEVEL – B

Write a short paragraph on each of the following:

1 Douglas Hyde and the Gaelic League.

2 The GAA.

3 The Abbey.

4 Carson's campaign against Home Rule, 1912-14.

5 Irishmen and World War 1.

6 Votes for Irish women.

7 Easter Week.

8 The 1918 election.

9 Collins's Squad.

10 Reasons for a civil war.

ORDINARY LEVEL – C

Write a short essay on each of the following:

1 The Home Rule party 1900 to 1918 under the headings:
   (i) Redmond's leadership.
   (ii) The Home Rule crisis, 1912-14.
   (iii) The party and the war.
   (iv) The effects of the Easter Rising.
   (v) The last year.

2 The Easter Rising under the headings:
   (i) The leaders.
   (ii) Planning the rising.
   (iii) The rising in Dublin and elsewhere.
   (iv) The effects of the rising.

3 Michael Collins under the headings:
   (i) His part in reorganising Sinn Féin.
   (ii) His part in the Dáil government and the War of Independence.
   (iii) His part in the Treaty.
   (iv) His part in events leading to the civil war.

Questions

HIGHER LEVEL

Write an essay on each of the following:

1 'The attempts to revive the Irish language and traditional games were parts of a new nationalism.'
Discuss. (80)

2 Treat of the origins and development of the labour movement in Ireland up to 1922. (80)

3 Treat of the fortunes of the Irish Parliamentary party from its reunion under Redmond in 1900 to the 1918 general election. (80)

4 Trace and evaluate the part played in Irish history by Sir Edward Carson as leader of the Unionist party between 1910 and 1921. (80)

5 Discuss the emerging role of women in Irish affairs in the first two decades of the twentieth century. (80)

6 (i) Outline the planning and organisation of the Easter Rising. (60)
(ii) Discuss critically the view of W.B. Yeats that as a result of the rising, all was 'changed, changed utterly'. (20)

7 Compare and contrast the 1916 Rising and the War of Independence (1919-21) as military enterprises. (80)

8 (i) Trace the history of Sinn Féin from the Easter Rising to its victory in the 1918 election. (60)
(ii) What were the features of that election which made it different from previous elections? (20)

9 Discuss the activities of Dáil Éireann from the first meeting of the First Dáil on 21 January 1919 to the acceptance of the Treaty by the Second Dáil on 7 January 1922. (80)

10 Compare and contrast the parts played by Michael Collins and Eamon de Valera in the independence movement between Easter 1916 and January 1922. (80)

11 (i) Treat of the circumstances leading to the passage of the Government of Ireland Act which set up Northern Ireland in 1921. (50)
(ii) Why, in your opinion, did the issue of partition attract so little attention during the Treaty debates in Dáil Éireann? (30)

SECTION FOUR

1922-1966: INDEPENDENT IRELAND

Chapter 27

The institutions of the Free State

The Free State Constitution

On 6 December 1922, one year to the day after the signing of the Anglo-Irish Treaty, the Irish Free State came into existence. Its Constitution had been passed by the Third Dáil the previous October. It contained seventy-nine articles and the Anglo-Irish Treaty, and laid down the following.

- The Free State was a **Dominion of the British Commonwealth**. The head of state was the British king. All TDs and Senators had to take an oath to him (see page 286) and he had to sign all bills passed by the **Oireachtas**.

- The king was represented in Ireland by the **Governor General**. In other Dominions the Governor General was always an English nobleman but from the start the Free State government insisted that theirs must be both an Irishman and a commoner. With reluctant British agreement, they appointed the old Home Ruler, **Tim Healy**, as the first Governor General. He was followed in the office by **James MacNeill** and **Domhnall Ó Buachalla**.

- All laws for the Free State were made by the **Oireachtas**, which consisted of two houses, the **Senate** and the **Dáil**.

James MacNeill and his wife

- The **Senate** had sixty members, elected by citizens over thirty. Every three years, fifteen Senators had to seek re-election, so that each Senator could serve a maximum of twelve years in all. The Senate could delay bills for 270 days but not stop them.

  The first Senate was set up in 1922. It was not elected. Thirty members were chosen by the Dáil and thirty by the President. As a gesture of reconciliation to unionists, Griffith nominated fifteen of their leaders to the Senate. Among them were **Sir Horace Plunkett** and **Lords Mayo** and **Dunraven** who played a prominent role in the 1902 Land Conference and the 1917-18 Irish Convention. Other Senators included the poet W.B. Yeats and Jennie Wyse-Power, a prominent Sinn Féiner and campaigner for women's rights.

- The **Dáil** had much more power than the Senate. **Teachta Dála** (TDs) were elected by all men and women over the age of twenty-one. Voting was by **proportional representation** (PR) which the British had included in the 1920 Government of Ireland Act as a way of guaranteeing representation to minorities. Each TD was to represent between 20,000 and 30,000 people. There were also TDs for each of the two Universities. The Trinity College TDs were usually ex-unionists.

- The Dáil elected the **President** (the word used instead of Prime Minister or Taoiseach from 1919 to 1937). He appointed ministers to the **Executive Council** (Cabinet). Each minister headed a government department.

- For the first eight years (later extended to sixteen) the Constitution could be changed by the Oireachtas. After that only a **referendum** could alter it. If 75,000 voters signed a petition demanding a referendum, one had to be held. This rule was removed from the Constitution in 1928 after Fianna Fáil tried to organise a referendum on the Oath and was not included in de Valera's 1937 Constitution.

- The Constitution of the Irish Free State also guaranteed freedom of speech and assembly and it forbade the government to favour one religion over any other.

Copying British models

This was a **liberal democratic constitution**, similar to the constitutions drawn up in many of the new states that appeared in Europe after the 1914-18 war. But the form of government it set up, with a prime minister elected by parliament and cabinet ministers whom he appointed, was closely modelled on that of Britain.

This was characteristic of the Irish Free State. Although the new leaders of Ireland had fought to free themselves from British control, they built the institutions of their new state along British lines, seldom asking if another model might not have suited Ireland better.

There were several reasons for this.

- Britain in the 1920s still seemed the greatest power in the world and it was the only one with which most Irish people were familiar.

- Having won independence, Irish governments were determined to disprove the British taunt that the Irish were unfit to govern themselves. What better way to do that than to model themselves on the British system and show that they could make it work?

- In 1922 and 1923, political leaders devoted their attention and energy to winning the civil war. They left the building of a new administration to British-trained civil servants and lawyers.

British-trained civil servants

The re-organisation of the civil service, which began in 1922, is the clearest example of this trend. The new political leaders lacked experience in administration. They left the organisation of a civil service to men who had learned their trade while serving in the British system. They included:

- **C.J. Gregg**, a Kilkenny man who had served in the Board of Inland Revenue in London. He was lent to the Free State from 1922 to 1924 to advise on civil service reform. As one historian has noted 'he, more than any other single man, was responsible for the organisation of ... the new civil service'. (R. Fanning, *The Irish Department of Finance*, p. 43)

- **Joseph Brennan**, from Cork, who had worked in Dublin Castle from 1912 to 1922. He had given Collins information and was rewarded by being made **Secretary of the Department of Finance**, a post he held until 1927.

- **J.J. McElligott**, a Kerryman who had served on the Local Government Board until he was sacked for his part in the Easter Rising. He earned his living as a financial journalist and was recruited into the Free State civil service in 1923 as **Assistant Secretary to the Department of Finance**. He later replaced Joseph Brennan and became the most powerful man in the Irish civil service until he retired in 1953.

Re-organising the government

These men imposed a British-style administration on the Free State. They helped to draw up the **Ministers and Secretaries Act** which was passed in 1924.

It dismantled the tangle of departments, boards etc., which had grown up in Dublin Castle since the Union (see chapter 1). They were then re-organised into eleven departments, each with its own minister who was responsible for its actions. The departments were:

- President of the Executive Council
- Finance
- Justice
- Fisheries
- Education
- Defence
- External Affairs
- Local Government and Public Health
- Industry and Commerce
- Lands and Agriculture
- Posts and Telegraphs

Existing civil servants could retire, move to Northern Ireland, or stay on in the Free State. Most opted to stay. Of the 20,000 civil servants (the majority of them postmen) who had worked under the British, 98 per cent remained. Only 200 new people, mostly Sinn Féin supporters, were recruited. These civil servants, trained in the British system, naturally went on running the Free State along the same lines as they had before independence.

The role of the Department of Finance

Within Britain, the Treasury (Finance department) controlled the money available to all other departments and took great care to limit their spending. Brennan and McElligott adopted this system, which gave great power to the Department of Finance. Backed by **Ernest Blythe**, who was **Minister for Finance** from 1923 to 1932, they cut the cost of running the civil service from £4.2 million in 1922 to £3.9 million in 1932.

The Civil Service Commission

One of their main achievements was the **Civil Service Commission**. It supervised recruitment into the civil service which was strictly by examination only. This guaranteed a high level of ability among civil servants, and it severely limited the scope for bribery or political favouritism. The result was a standard of honesty in the public service that was rare among new states.

The negative side of this was that once in the civil service, a person got promotion mainly by seniority and this discouraged new ideas or risk-taking.

Ernest Blythe

Continuity and conservatism

Thus, despite the political revolution which took place between 1918 and 1922, the methods of governing the country changed little. As a Commission reported in 1935:

'under changed masters, the same main tasks of administration continued to be performed by the same staff on the same general lines of organisation and procedure.' (B. Chubb, *The Government and Politics of Ireland*, p. 232)

This had advantages. It provided stability and a reservoir of experience and knowledge on which inexperienced politicians could draw. On the other hand, a civil service trained in old ways, contributed to the conservatism which was such a notable feature of the new state at least until a new generation emerged in the 1950s.

The legal system

The same conservatism applied in the legal system. One of the successes of the Dáil government had been the informal Sinn Féin Courts (see page 25), but in 1924 they were abolished by the **Courts of Justice Act** and replaced by an apparently new system.

Paid **District Justices** replaced the Magistrates and Justices of the Peace. **Circuit Courts**, each covering an area with a population of 400,000, replaced the Assize courts. Between them, these courts dealt with a wide range of civil and criminal cases and gave the citizen quicker and slightly cheaper access to the law.

Above them were the **Court of Criminal Appeal**, the **High Court** and the **Supreme Court**. People could appeal the decisions of lower courts to these higher courts, which could also decide whether laws passed by the Oireachtas were in line with the constitution. This last point, which was borrowed from the Americans, was the main difference between the Irish legal system after 1922 and the British system.

Within the Commonwealth, all cases could be appealed from national courts to the **Judicial Committee of the British Privy Council**. This was accepted by the Treaty but the Cosgrave government took care to prevent Irish citizens making such appeals. The right of appeal to the Privy Council was abolished by the de Valera government in the 1930s.

The lack of change

These legal changes were almost completely on the surface. New names were used but underneath little had changed. This can be seen in the way Irish lawyers and judges continued to wear the eighteenth-century wigs and gowns that had adorned their British predecessors.

The reasons for legal continuity are clear.

- The law to be administered by these courts was British law together with any additions or amendments made by the Dáil. Often the Dáil made no changes and Irish courts continued to enforce old British laws long after the British themselves had gone on to something more suited to the twentieth century.

- The judges appointed to serve in these courts and the lawyers who appeared before them were all trained under the British system. It was not till the 1960s that a new generation of Irish-trained judges and lawyers began to develop some distinctively Irish aspects in the legal system.

Local Government

Local government had been re-organised in 1898 and little changed after independence. In 1925, the rural districts, into which the 1898 Act had divided the counties, were abolished because they were too small to operate successfully. County and urban councils were retained. Until 1934 the right to vote for them was limited to ratepayers and their wives. Voting remained by PR, which the British introduced in 1920 to defeat Sinn Féin.

These councils could levy rates (a tax on property), but the income from this source was never enough to pay for all their responsibilities. Grants from the central government made up the difference. In 1923-4 these grants amounted to 22.5 per cent of local revenue, but by 1931-2 they amounted to 42 per cent.

This gave the central government control over local councils. It tried to improve their efficiency and to stamp out the corruption which had been widespread in them before 1918. During the 1920s it dissolved several local authorities and replaced them with Commissioners. This made local councils more efficient and soon local bodies began to appoint '**managers**' to work with the elected councillors. This was made compulsory in the **County Managers Act** of 1940.

The local councils were responsible for public buildings, roads, public health and sanitation within their areas. Under an Act of 1923, the Poor Law Unions were abolished and the responsibility for helping the poor was also passed to the councils.

Looking after the poor

Some workhouses were closed and others made into County Homes for the care of the old and sick. A system of home assistance for the very poor was established. This left them at the mercy of officials who still held the Victorian idea that poverty was the fault of the poor and a sign of laziness. Poor people had to undergo a humiliating means test to prove their entitlement to even the most limited help. By the 1940s about one-third of the population was receiving home assistance.

Education

Education was one area where change could have been expected. Patrick Pearse, who was a hero to so many of the leaders of the new state, had made a devastating criticism of the Irish education system, calling it a 'murder machine'. But Pearse was more honoured in words than deeds and it seems doubtful if many of those who praised him actually read what he said.

In 1924 the **Intermediate Education Act** combined the old Boards and Commissions into a single **Department of Education** under a Minister. The first Minister for

◆

Education was the scholar **Eoin MacNeill**, who might have been expected to seek improvement in the nation's schools. Yet with one notable exception, little change was made in the education system up to the 1960s.

Primary education

The Department oversaw a network of national schools which covered the country. Most of them were run by the various Churches on a parish basis, with the Department paying some of the building costs and the teachers' salaries. The Churches guarded their control of education jealously and this made it difficult for governments to interfere, even in the interests of the children of the nation.

Changes in primary education were limited to a few areas.

- The syllabus was widened to take in more subjects, and much stress was laid on encouraging nationalism, particularly in the teaching of history. Irish was made compulsory.

- Around the country there were many one-teacher schools with only a few pupils. This system was expensive to run and the Department tried to amalgamate them into bigger units. Many of the buildings were old and in a bad condition and they were slowly replaced. In the cities not enough new schools were built to take the expanding population and many classes were very overcrowded.

- In 1922 attendance at school was not compulsory and only 75 per cent of children went regularly. In 1926, compulsory attendance between the ages of six and fourteen was introduced despite the protests of farmers who wanted cheap labour during the harvest time. Nevertheless many children left before they were fourteen and only a few got a chance to go any further.

Post-primary education

Only about 10 per cent of students went beyond primary school. Secondary schools were privately owned, mostly by religious bodies. They charged fees and even though these were low, most families could not afford them. In 1921 and 1923 local authorities were allowed to levy a rate of one penny in the pound to fund scholarships to secondary schools and universities. These enabled a few clever children to get further education but the number was small.

There were some changes in the administration of post-primary education.

- The old system of 'payments by results' (see page 16) was abolished and replaced by a grant for each pupil.

- The state agreed to pay a share of teachers' salaries, provided they were properly qualified. This raised the quality of teaching.

- The old annual examinations were replaced by two new examinations, the **Intermediate**, taken after three years and the **Leaving**, taken two years later. The

Typical classroom in a country school, 1920s.

Department set the syllabus for these examinations and this gave them some control over what was taught in the schools.

Vocational education

A constant complaint at this time was the lack of any system of vocational training. In 1899 'technical schools' had been set up. By 1929 there were sixty-nine in existence, with 2,500 students. This low attendance probably reflected the low demand for technically-trained people in Ireland.

In 1930 **the Vocational Education Act** gave local councils the job of developing technical education. Thirty-eight **Vocational Education Committees** (VEC) were set up to provide free post-primary education with an emphasis on vocational skills, such as woodwork, metalwork, domestic economy and commercial subjects.

The vocational schools were badly funded and were not allowed to prepare students for the Leaving Certificate. As a result, parents did not regard them highly and they remained the poor relations of the education system until the 1960s.

Chapter 28

1922-27: The political development of the Irish Free State

The effect of the civil war

When the Free State came into existence in December 1922, the civil war still raged. The war ended in May 1923 but the divisions it caused continued to affect political life.

The origin of the main political parties

The most obvious effect of the civil war was on the political parties in the new state. Sinn Féin, the party that led the independence struggle from 1918 to 1922, was split in two by the Treaty.

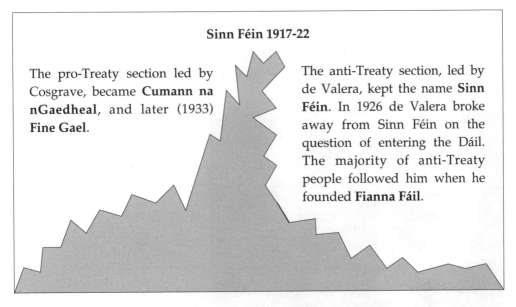

Sinn Féin 1917-22

The pro-Treaty section led by Cosgrave, became **Cumann na nGaedheal**, and later (1933) **Fine Gael**.

The anti-Treaty section, led by de Valera, kept the name **Sinn Féin**. In 1926 de Valera broke away from Sinn Féin on the question of entering the Dáil. The majority of anti-Treaty people followed him when he founded **Fianna Fáil**.

Even though the quarrel over the Treaty soon ceased to be relevant, the two parties it created have remained ever since. They dominate Irish politics, with one or other of them always in government. Other parties have been formed over the years but only one, the **Labour Party,** dating from 1912, has survived. Together, Fine Gael, Fianna Fáil and Labour form what is sometimes called the Irish 'two and a half party system'.

The Political Parties of the Free State

Cumann na nGaedheal

When Sinn Féin split on the Treaty vote in January 1922 the pro-Treaty majority, led by Griffith, formed the government of the country. In the hectic year that followed they had neither time not inclination to engage in ordinary politics. As a result, they did not build up a party organisation. In fact, they did not even have a name until early in 1923. Then they called themselves **Cumann na nGaedheal**, after one of Griffith's early movements.

W.T. Cosgrave, 1880-1965

Their leader was **William T. Cosgrave**. Born in Dublin in 1880, Cosgrave was elected to Dublin Corporation as a Sinn Féiner and in 1913 joined the Volunteers. He fought in the GPO in 1916 and was sentenced to death but his sentence was commuted to life imprisonment. After he was released, he became treasurer of Sinn Féin.

In 1918 Cosgrave was elected a TD for Carlow-Kilkenny and de Valera made him **Minister for Local Government** in the Dáil Cabinet. When the Cabinet discussed the Treaty in December 1921, he backed the Delegates and insisted that the Treaty be sent to the Dáil. In the Dáil debates, he supported the Treaty and served in Griffith's government in 1922.

After Griffith and Collins died in August 1922, other members of the Free State Cabinet picked Cosgrave as President in preference to Richard Mulcahy. Mulcahy had succeeded Collins as Commander-in-Chief of the army and some Cabinet

W. T. Cosgrave

members feared that he might use his links with the army to stage a military coup. Cosgrave was also, at forty-two, the oldest Cabinet minister and he had the widest range of experience.

Assessing Cosgrave

Cosgrave was a small, quiet man. He had not sought the leadership but once it was his he made good use of it. The circumstances in which he took over made him conservative. He concentrated more on holding things together and proving that the Irish could rule themselves than on making the changes the country needed. But he did provide stability during the difficult first decade of independence. As J.J. Lee says of him:

> His vision was limited... He had neither a capacious intellect not a commanding personality. What he did have was a basic decency, a sense of public service and a sound judgement on matters of state. (J.J. Lee, *Ireland 1912-1985*, p. 174)

Kevin O'Higgins 1892-1927

A prominent member of Cosgrave's government was **Kevin O'Higgins**. A lawyer from Laois, O'Higgins was elected a TD in 1918 and was Cosgrave's assistant in the first Dáil government from 1919 to 1922.

He vigorously supported the Treaty and became Minister for Economic Affairs in the Provisional Government. He helped to draw up the Free State Constitution and liaised with the British during the hand-over of power which finally took place in December 1922.

Cosgrave made him **Vice President** and **Minister for Home Affairs** (later called **Justice**). He carried the main responsibility for the executions that the government carried out during the civil war. O'Higgins, whose father was murdered by republicans, took a hard line on the disorder that followed the war. He was determined to enforce the law as completely as possible.

Other ministers

Other members of the Cumann na nGaedheal government included:

- **Richard Mulcahy**, Collins's successor as Commander-in-Chief of the army and leader of the IRB, who was **Minister for Defence**.
- **Ernest Blythe**, an Ulster Presbyterian, who was **Minister for Finance**.
- **Eoin MacNeill**, one of the founders of the Gaelic League, who was **Minister for Education**.
- **Desmond FitzGerald**, who was **Minister for External Affairs**.
- **Patrick Hogan**, who was **Minister for Lands**.

Desmond Fitzgerald

Cumann na nGaedheal in power

The Cumann na nGaedheal party ruled the Free State from 1922 to 1932. But during that time it never had an overall majority of Dáil seats. There were a number of reasons for this.

- From the beginning the party leaders were all busy in government and had no time to spend on political organisation.

- When the party was formed at the height of the civil war, the leaders wished to appeal to as many groups as possible. Apart from backing the Treaty, they made no attempt to develop policies. Members had different views on many issues, such as Commonwealth membership, social welfare and economic policies. Even in the Cabinet, for example, one minister favoured free trade while another wanted tariffs.

As a result, Cumann na nGaedheal never established the kind of disciplined party organisation that gave Fianna Fáil its great strength. Even in the election of August 1923, immediately after its victory in the civil war, it only won sixty-three seats. (see Table A, page 325)

Anti-Treaty Sinn Féin

When Sinn Féin split on the Treaty, the anti-Treaty section, led by de Valera, kept the name Sinn Féin*. They won thirty-five seats in the Treaty election (June 1922) but refused to enter the Dáil or recognise the Cumann na nGaedheal government as the legitimate government of the country.

---

* Historians refer to this as the 'third' Sinn Féin to distinguish it from the 'first' (1908-10) and 'second' (1917-22). It lasted from 1922 to 1925.

During the civil war, they set up their own 'republican government' with de Valera as President. This was an attempt to give legal status to their resistance to the Free State. They also hoped to imitate the First Dáil's success in resisting British rule between 1919 and 1921. But this time the public was hostile or indifferent and the republicans lost.

August 1923: the first Free State election
The civil war ended in May 1923 and preparations began for the first election under the Free State constitution. It was held in a tense atmosphere. Over 11,000 republicans, including many Sinn Féin candidates, were in prison. De Valera, who had evaded arrest during the war, was picked up while addressing an election meeting in Ennis. The country was full of troops, and meetings were marred by violence.

1923-25: Sinn Féin's abstentionist policy
Despite this, Sinn Féin got 27 per cent of the votes cast. Forty-four Sinn Féin TDs were elected but because of the oath to the king, they refused to take their seats in the Dáil. When de Valera and the other internees were freed in 1924, they set up **Comhairle na dTeachtaí** as a kind of republican parliament. De Valera was 'president of the republic' and there were 'government departments', 'republican courts' and even a 'university'.

This attempt to repeat the tactics of the First Dáil failed. The situation in 1923 was very different from 1919. An elected Irish government was in power and people looked to it to solve their problems. Sinn Féin's absence from the Dáil, where the real business of the country was carried on, left its TDs powerless to help their constituents. After de Valera was released from prison in July 1924, he realised this and began to look for a way of changing the abstentionist policy.

1912-18: the role of labour
Sinn Féin's abstention from the Dáil between 1922 and 1927, left the Labour party as the main opposition party. It had been set up by Connolly and Larkin in 1912 to fight for seats in the expected Home Rule parliament.

The failure of the 1913 strike (see pages 160-162) left the labour movement in poor shape. After Larkin's emigration in 1914 and Connolly's execution in 1916, the Irish Transport and General Workers' Union (ITGWU) fell to just 5,000 members.

It was rebuilt by **William O'Brien**. He was a trade union manager rather than a revolutionary leader like Larkin and Connolly. By 1921 the ITGWU had grown to 100,000 members. Many of these were farm labourers in Leinster and east Munster. Because of the size of his union, O'Brien also dominated the **Irish Trade Union Congress** (ITUC) where all unions met to co-ordinate labour policy.

William O'Brien

1918-22: Labour during the independence struggle

In the 1918 election, the Labour party, now led by the English-born, **Thomas Johnson**, gave way to pressure from Sinn Féin and did not put forward candidates. Their reward was Sinn Féin's acceptance of the 'Democratic Programme' which promised substantial social reform. Some historians have argued that this decision weakened the Labour party by leaving it out of the Dáil during the vital years of the independence struggle.

From 1919 and 1922, trade unionists showed their support for Sinn Féin and the IRA through strikes and other forms of direct action and they too suffered at the hands of the Black and Tans.

At the same time a radical socialism emerged. This was partly due to bad economic conditions after World War I and partly to the influence of ideas coming from the communist revolution in Russia. The latter can be seen in the formation of workers' soviets in Limerick, Mallow and other places and in attempts by small farmers and labourers to take over land in parts of the west. In 1920 James Connolly's son, Roddy, established the first Communist party in Ireland but it did not gain many members.

Labour and the Treaty

The Treaty divided the labour movement as it divided the rest of the country.

- More extreme socialists like Peadar O'Donnell sided with the republicans and wanted to continue the fight against British imperialism.

- Johnson, O'Brien and most party and ITUC leaders supported it. Johnson wanted to play a constitutional role. He insisted that the Labour party must contest elections and enter the Dáil, even if this meant taking the oath.

The Treaty election of June 1922 was the first general election that the Labour party fought. They did very well, winning seventeen seats with eighteen candidates. One of their TDs refused to take the oath but the others entered the Dáil. Johnson argued that the oath did not imply loyalty to the king. It was, he said, just:

> a formality, a condition of membership of the legislature, implying no obligation other than the ordinary obligations of every person who accepts the privileges of citizenship. (J.L. McCracken, *Representative Government in Ireland*, p. 155)

During the civil war, there was widespread industrial unrest as employers, hit by economic decline, tried to reduce wages. There were strikes among dockers, farm workers and others, sometimes accompanied by violence. In some places republicans supported the strikers. This unrest may account for the fall in support for the Labour party which won only fourteen seats in the August 1923 election. (see Table A)

1923-27: Labour in opposition

Because de Valera's Sinn Féin abstained from the Dáil, the Labour TDs were the main opposition to Cosgrave's government between 1923 and 1927. They attacked its conservative social and economic policies, especially its decision to cut old age pensions.

They constantly referred to the 1919 'Democratic Programme' and urged the government to implement it. While unemployment remained high, housing bad and social services almost non-existent, Labour argued that too much attention was paid to the frills of nation-building. **Seán O'Casey**'s ironic comment on the new school curriculum with its compulsory Irish history represents Labour thinking:

> Children who are rickety in their legs are to be told of Cuchulainn's hero's leap over walls as high as Nelson's Pillar. Children who are fed on tea and margarine are to be told of the wine and venison feasts of the Fianna. (*The Irish Statesman*, 29 November 1924, p. 362)

The weakness of Labour

However, the party won little popular support. There were many reasons for this.

- Partition had removed the country's only major industrial workforce, leaving the Free State predominantly agricultural. Up to the 1960s half the population was directly involved in farming. Farmers shared none of the aims of organised labour and distrusted many of its policies.

- The economic slump of the 1920s reduced support for trade unions. Membership of the Irish Trade Union Congress fell from 175,000 in 1924 to 92,000 in 1929.

- Farmers, the Catholic Church and other conservative groups feared 'reds' (i.e.

Seán O'Casey

communists). Although few labour politicians were in fact communist, even moderate socialists could easily be damaged by a the red smear.

- Many individuals like **Peadar O'Donnell** who would have favoured socialist economic policies were diverted into republicanism. This weakened the appeal of the Labour party, especially when Fianna Fáil began to adopt more left-wing economic policies after 1927. Discontented groups tended to vote for them rather than for Labour.

The Larkin and O'Brien split

Labour also suffered from a self-inflicted wound. This was the split which developed in the movement in the early 1920s. Although there were policies involved, it was mainly due to a quarrel between two of the dominant figures in the labour movement, James Larkin and William O'Brien.

In April 1923 Larkin returned to Ireland. He had spent almost ten years abroad, partly in the US and partly in the USSR. A convinced communist who had close ties with Moscow, he sided with the more radical groups in the labour movement.

Larkin expected to resume the leadership role he had had in 1913, but O'Brien and the conservative labour leaders resisted him. In 1924 Larkin broke away from the ITGWU and founded the **Workers' Union of Ireland**. He took a majority of Dublin-based workers with him.

This split became more and more personal as time passed, with the two men blocking any attempt to heal the breach. In the early 1940s it flared up again, splitting both the Labour party and the Irish Congress of Trade Unions. (see page 386) Only after Larkin's death in 1947 was it possible to rebuild unity.

Other parties
Other political parties appeared on the scene from time to time. In the 1920s a **Farmers' Party** represented the views of the bigger farmers. Since these were also the views of leading members of Cumann na nGaedheal they posed little threat to Cosgrave. Independents were also numerous in the early days of the state. Some of them were former unionists or former Home Rulers who were able to win seats through the PR system.

1923- 27: *Two Crises*

The Cumann na nGaedheal government
Once the civil war ended, normal political life became possible. In the 1923 election, Cumann na nGaedheal did not win an overall majority (see Table A), but the absence of the forty-four Sinn Féin TDs gave them a clear run. Through 1923 and 1924 they passed many of the laws needed to establish the new state.

Party rivalry
During this period, Cosgrave's government faced two major crises. The first was the so-called 'army mutiny'. This complicated and obscure affair seems to have been mainly an internal power struggle within the Cumann na nGaedheal party. It turned on the rivalry between the two most powerful ministers, **Richard Mulcahy**, still loyal to Collins's republican legacy, and **Kevin O'Higgins**, who feared the control Mulcahy had over the army.

The enlarged army
During the civil war the Free State army had grown to 55,000 men and 3,300 officers. Many of those who joined during the civil war were ex-British army personnel who brought useful experience and training to the new force. However, the old IRA men who had fought alongside Collins bitterly resented their presence.

Demobilising the army
This big army proved to be very costly and as soon as the war was over the government wanted to reduce it to a reasonable size. Mulcahy, as Minister for Defence and

Results of 1923 election					
Total	C. na nG.	S.F.	Lab.	Farmers	Independents
153	63	44	14	15	17

Table A ▲

Commander-in-Chief, loyally carried out this policy. By the start of 1924 only 13,000 men and 2,000 officers were left.

This caused resentment in the army. Pension and compensation payments were poor and with unemployment high, there were few jobs for those who were displaced. Old IRA-men felt that the ex-British soldiers were being kept on while they were let go. Some of them also began to complain that, now that the civil war was won, the Cosgrave government had forgotten Collins's promise that the Treaty was just a stepping stone to a full republic.

Mulcahy, who had some sympathy with these complaints, tried to defuse the unrest by reviving the IRB, to which many officers belonged. This brought him into conflict with O'Higgins who thought that the days for secret societies were past.

March 1924: the 'mutiny'

In March 1924 a further 1,000 officers were due to be laid off. The problem arose over how they were to be chosen. A peacetime army needed well-disciplined officers but some men who had worked for Collins as assassins and guerrilla fighters were not ideal for that role.

These men, who called themselves the 'Old IRA', and who were led by **Liam Tobin**, a close associate of Collins, decided to act. On 6 March they sent an ultimatum to Cosgrave demanding an end to demobilisation and the dismissal of Mulcahy and the Army Council. To cloak their self-interest, they also protested that the government was ignoring Collins's promise that the Treaty would lead to the republic.

Mulcahy, an admirer of Collins, understood their point of view. He knew it was widely shared among all sections of the army. He had been trying to use the IRB to retain the loyalty of officers and to isolate Tobin and his followers.

But O'Higgins and some other members of the Cabinet distrusted Mulcahy's tactics. When Tobin's ultimatum arrived, they saw their chance to outmanoeuvre him. They appointed the Garda Commissioner, **Eoin O'Duffy**, as Supreme Commander of the army over Mulcahy's head and made a compromise with Tobin's group.

However, a few days later, on 18 March, some of the Old IRA men met in a public house, apparently to plot some more. A senior army officer, after consulting Mulcahy but not O'Duffy, ordered their arrest.

Cosgrave, who had tried to hold the balance between Mulcahy and O'Higgins, was in hospital and O'Higgins was acting as President. He persuaded the Cabinet to demand the resignation of Mulcahy and the Army Council. But before the demand reached him, Mulcahy had already resigned.

Assessment

O'Higgins won the power struggle within Cumann na nGaedheal. He claimed that he was acting in the national interest by establishing civilian control over the army and protecting the Free State from the kind of military coup that many new states

Eoin O'Duffy

experienced. After this, the army was subjected to a rigid civilian control, often in a way which prevented it adapting to the real needs of the Irish state.

But this assessment is less than fair to Mulcahy or the officers of the Irish army. If Mulcahy had planned a coup, he would not have reduced the size of the army, and he took a tougher line with the mutineers than O'Higgins had. Mulcahy was too good a democrat to have used his control of the army to overthrow the elected government. Cosgrave showed that he appreciated this when he removed O'Duffy in 1926 and brought Mulachy back into the Cabinet in 1927.

The incident, however, highlighted the divisions in Cumann na nGaedheal. Two ministers, Mulcahy and Joe McGrath who sympathised with Tobin's group, resigned and the party was divided on the issue. Had Sinn Féin been in the Dáil, the government might have fallen. But Sinn Féin was still outside the Dáil and the small parties within were too weak to outvote the government.

The problem of the Boundary Commission

The second crisis was much more serious. It was about the vital issue of partition. Under Article XII of the Treaty, a Boundary Commission was to be set up to decide the boundary between Northern Ireland and the Free State

> in accordance with the wishes of the inhabitants, so far as may be compatible with economic and geographical conditions.

The Commission was to consist of three people, one appointed by the Northern government, one by the Free State and a neutral chairman appointed by Britain.

During the Treaty Debates, Collins and Griffith had argued that these terms would transfer large areas of Northern Ireland to the south. This was accepted without serious question by their opponents.

But this reflected wishful thinking rather than hard reality. The terms were very vague and many vital questions were not even discussed. For example:

- Who were the 'inhabitants'?

- How were they to be consulted?

- Which economic and geographical considerations had their wishes to be compatible with?

- And who decided that anyway?

Delaying the Commission

As soon as the Dáil passed the Treaty the Free State government began to prepare for the Commission but the civil war delayed further action. **Craig**, the Northern Prime Minister, who had not been consulted about the Commission, refused to have anything to do with it. These developments delayed it until 1924 and by then a great deal had changed.

- Northern Ireland, set up under the 1920 Government of Ireland Act, had become established and it would be much harder to take territory away from it then than it would have been in 1921 or 1922.

- In Britain, Lloyd George had fallen from power towards the end of 1922 and been replaced by a Conservative government. It was even less likely to side with the Free State against its unionist allies than he would have been.

Establishing the Commission

In July 1923 the Dublin government appointed its Minister for Education, **Eoin MacNeill**, a Catholic from Co. Antrim, to be its representative on the Commission. Craig refused to nominate anyone. Finally, after much discussion, the British took powers to appoint a Northern Ireland representative. They chose **J.R. Fisher**, a Belfast lawyer and a staunch unionist. They also appointed the chairman, **Justice Richard Feetham** of the South African Supreme Court.

The work of the Commission

In November 1924, the commissioners began their work. They heard legal arguments as to the interpretation of Article XII and toured the border areas to get evidence from individuals and groups. They had to decide:

- whether to redraw the 1920 border completely or merely to alter small parts of it.

- which of the two conditions, 'the wishes of the inhabitants' or 'economic and geographic conditions', should matter most.

Feetham's opinion on these points was vital. It soon became clear that he was going to give more consideration to economic and geographic conditions than to the wishes of the people and to change the 1920 border as little as possible. Two things may have influenced him.

- By 1925 there was widespread criticism of the economic damage which too much attention to 'the wishes of the people' had caused in eastern Europe after World War I.

- The border had been there since 1920; to redraw it extensively would add to the economic disruption.

MacNeill does not seem to have objected to this decision. It may be that he was overwhelmed with work because he was still an acting Minister in addition to his role in the Boundary Commission. He also failed to tell Cosgrave what was going on, though Fisher made sure that Craig was informed. Thus when the Commission's final verdict was leaked to the press, the Dublin government was taken by surprise.

Leaking the Commission report

On 7 November 1925 a Conservative newspaper, the *Morning Post*, published an article about the Boundary Commission. It forecast, with reasonable accuracy, what the Commission would say.

- The Free State was to get small parts of south Armagh and some minor areas in Fermanagh, moving about 25,000 Catholics from North to South.

- Part of east Donegal, where about 2,000 Protestants lived, was to go from the Free State to Northern Ireland. This was an unexpected blow. No one had predicted that the Free State would actually **lose** territory.

Public opinion in the South was outraged. It had not been prepared for this result, though some politicians may have feared it. A storm of angry criticism arose. On 20 November MacNeill resigned from the Cabinet.

Before the Commission began, all sides had agreed to accept its published decision. It was therefore important for Cosgrave to stop it being published. He hurried to London with some of his ministers to negotiate with the British and with Craig.

3 December 1925: the Anglo-Irish Agreement

On 3 December they signed an agreement. Under it:

- the Commission report would not be published and the border between the Six and the Twenty-six Counties, as set out in the Government of Ireland Act (1920), would remain unchanged.

- the powers reserved to the the Council of Ireland under that Act were transferred to the Northern Ireland government. This Council had been intended to maintain links between the two Irish states. By giving them up, Cosgrave acknowledged the permanence of partition.

- the Free State's commitment under Article V of the Treaty to pay part of the British national debt was cancelled.

- The Northern government no longer had to repay land annuities to the British Treasury. Cosgrave's failure to demand a similar concession for the Free State was to cost him dearly.

This agreement, as Cosgrave's opponents were quick to point out, showed that the Treaty was defective in its most important article. It made partition permanent. When he returned from London, Cosgrave was vigorously attacked in the Dáil. One prominent member of his party resigned.

Sinn Féin and the Boundary Commission

If Sinn Féin had been in the Dáil, it might have exploited the government's discomfort. But it was not in the Dáil and its absence left them secure. Once again, the futility of Sinn Féin's abstention policy was underlined.

1925: de Valera's search for a new approach

De Valera was already acutely aware of this. Even before the Boundary Commission fiasco, he had seen the need for a change of policy. The country was in recession and republicans were especially badly hit. Jobs were hard to find and Free State supporters got those that were available. In 1924-25 an estimated 100,000 persons emigrated, most of them from republican areas in the west.

Sinn Féin had nothing to offer these people. In by-elections in March 1925 and in local government elections in June, they did badly. Voters would not support abstentionists who could not help them.

But Sinn Féin was still dominated by hard line republicans and de Valera's hands were tied. To make matters worse, the IRA, at a conference in November, repudiated his 'presidency of the republic' and moved the leadership of the movement from the politicians of Sinn Féin to the IRA Army Council. When moderates like the Chief of Staff **Frank Aiken** resigned in protest, it seemed possible that the IRA might resume the civil war.

March 1926: de Valera's break with Sinn Féin

The Boundary Commission affair rescued de Valera. It allowed him make partition, which he had ignored in 1922, into the main nationalist cause. He could now claim that if Sinn Féin had been in the Dáil, they would have done something about it.

A special Ard Fheis of Sinn Féin was called for 10 March 1926. At it, de Valera proposed that if the oath were removed, Sinn Féin's entry into Dáil Éireann would be

Frank Aiken

'a question not of principle but of policy'. But the hard-liners defeated him. His proposal was turned down. Instead the party resolved:

> that it is incompatible with the fundamental principles of Sinn Féin, as it is injurious to the honour of Ireland, to send representatives into any usurping legislature set up by English law in Ireland. (P. Pyne, 'The Third Sinn Féin Party' in *Economic and Social Review*, Vol. 1, p. 45)

May 1926: the foundation of Fianna Fáil

At once, de Valera resigned as leader of Sinn Féin. Assisted by **Gerry Boland** and **Seán Lemass,** he began to plan a new party. Lemass wanted to call it the Republican Party but de Valera wanted Fianna Fáil. They finally agreed on **Fianna Fáil (the Republican party)**.

In May Fianna Fáil was formally set up and in the next few months it grew rapidly. Many Sinn Féin branches and most Sinn Féin TDs were won over to it. As Lemass, who travelled the country persuading them to switch sides, recalled later:

> Within a year of the first Fianna Fáil executive being set up, we had a nationwide organisation, the strongest in the country, fully geared for action. The speed with which the Fianna Fáil organisation came into being, from a group sitting in Dublin to a nationwide organisation extending to every parish in the country, was quite phenomenal. (B. Farrell, *Seán Lemass*, p. 18)

The new party concentrated its attack on the oath and on partition, but it also developed an economic policy designed to appeal to people suffering from unemployment and poverty.

1927: an unpopular government

An election was due in 1927 but the Cumann na nGaedheal government did little to win popular support. In the year before the election they adopted several unpopular policies.

- Their economic policy (see chapter 29) involved keeping taxes and spending low. To reduce spending, they cut the old age pension from 50p to 45p a week and tightened up other welfare benefits. Many people felt these policies were unfair to the poorest people in the community.

- In March 1926 they made the 'Ultimate Financial Agreement' with Britain, tidying up some financial issues left over from the Treaty. They committed themselves to paying certain RIC pensions and the land purchase annuities.

  The government saw the annuities as a debt of honour, but Labour and Fianna Fáil disagreed. The £3 million a year sent to Britain to pay for them should, they claimed, be spent to develop the Irish economy. In the 1925 Agreement, Northern Ireland was allowed to keep its land annuities and they argued that all obligations had thus been cancelled.

- As the IRA became more active, the government brought back detention without trial. To many people this seemed an unnecessary infringement of civil liberties.

- The loudest protests came when O'Higgins brought in the **Intoxicating Liquor Bill** in February 1927. It proposed to reduce the number of public houses and limit opening hours. Some members of Cumann na nGaedheal resigned in protest and formed the **National League**, under **William Redmond**, son of the old Home Rule leader.

June 1927: the general election

The election was called in June. Cumann na nGaedheal asked for support because it had given the country stability and good government. But this record was not enough. The party did badly and was reduced to forty-seven seats.

Fianna Fáil did well, winning forty-four seats, but it might have done better had it not still been following an abstentionist policy. As it was, many of those who opposed the government's policies turned to Labour. It won twenty-two seats. There were also many smaller parties and independents. (see Table B)

This was an inconclusive result. If the forty-four Fianna Fáil TDs took their seats, Cosgrave's government would clearly be in trouble, but would Fianna Fáil take the oath?

De Valera's campaign against the oath

On 23 June the new Dáil met. De Valera led his party to Leinster House and demanded admittance. When he was asked to sign the book containing the oath, he refused. The Fianna Fáil TDs then withdrew, declaring that:

they pledged themselves to the people that as long as they were the representatives of the people they would never take an oath of allegiance to a foreign king. (D. O'Sullivan, *The Irish Free State and its Senate*, p. 194)

De Valera then began a campaign to have the oath removed. He took advantage of a clause in the 1922 constitution which said that the government had to hold a referendum if 75,000 people signed a petition requesting one. Fianna Fáil began to collect the necessary signatures.

10 July 1927: the assassination of Kevin O'Higgins
A few days later an event occurred which totally changed the situation. On Sunday, 10 July Kevin O'Higgins was assassinated as he walked home from mass. No one was ever arrested for his murder but it was assumed to be the work of a section of the IRA.

Cosgrave reacted decisively. He got the Dáil to pass:

- a **Public Safety Act**. It gave the government power to set up a special court which could impose the death penalty for illegal possession of arms.

- a **change in the Constitution** to prevent a referendum on the oath.

- an **Electoral Amendment Act**. Under it, any candidate for election to the Dáil or Senate had to swear that, if elected, he or she would take the oath; and any elected member who refused to take the oath would lose his or her seat.

Fianna Fáil takes the oath
The Electoral Amendment Act was clearly an attempt to force Fianna Fáil to enter the Dáil. It placed de Valera in a difficult position.

- On the one hand there was pressure from within the party to enter the Dáil. Two Fianna Fáil TDs had already taken their seats, and the Labour party and the National League had approached de Valera suggesting an alliance to oust Cosgrave.

- On the other hand he had always insisted that he could never take the oath.

On 11 August the party met and issued a statement. The oath, it announced, was only 'an empty formality', so Fianna Fáil TDs were free to enter the Dáil. Again they

Results of the June 1927 election								
Total	C na nG.	F.F.	Lab	Farmers	Indep	S.F.	Nat. L.	Ind.Rep
153	47	44	22	11	14	5	8	2

Table B ▲

◆

went to Leinster House and again were presented with a book to sign. Before he did so, de Valera said:

> I want you to understand that I am not taking any oath nor giving any promise of faithfulness to the King of England or to any power outside the people of Ireland. I am putting my name here merely as a formality to get the permission necessary to enter among the other Teachtaí that were elected by the people of Ireland, and I want you to know that no other meaning is to be attached to what I am doing. (Longford and O'Neill, *Eamon de Valera*, p. 256)

Then he carried the bible to the far side of the room in case someone might think he was swearing on it. Leaving it there, he returned and signed the oath. The rest of his party followed suit. 'Thus', a modern historian has written, 'seeing no oath, hearing no oath, speaking no oath and signing no oath, the Soldiers of Destiny shuffled into Dáil Éireann.' (J.J. Lee, *Ireland 1912-85*, p. 155)

September 1927: another election

Fianna Fáil's entry into the Dáil endangered Cumann na nGaedheal. At once, they and their allies put down a motion of no confidence in the government. Everyone was sure that a combination of Fianna Fáil, Labour and the National League had one vote more than Cumann na nGaedheal, the Farmers and most of the Independents.

But when the vote was taken, **John Jinks**, a National League TD from Sligo, failed to appear. The vote was a dead heat and the **Caithearlach** (Chairman) voted with the government. Cosgrave was saved.

De Valera and other Fianna Fáil TDs approaching Leinster House in 1927.

But he could not go on like that. In September he called another election. The result showed the voters lining up in support of the two 'treaty' parties. (see Table C) Cumann na nGaedheal went up from forty-seven to sixty-two seats and Fianna Fáil from forty-four to fifty-seven. Smaller parties lost seats. Labour fell to thirteen TDs, the Farmers to six and the National League to two. Only twelve Independent TDs were elected, while Sinn Féin did not even contest a seat.

Results of the September 1927 election							
Total	C. na nG.	F.F.	Lab.	Farmers	Indep.	S.F.	Nat. L.
153	62	57	13	6	12	–	3

Table C ▲

The significance of 1927

The dramatic events of 1927 marked an important step on the road that made the Free State into a normal democracy.

- Fianna Fáil still rejected the Treaty settlement and the Free State. In the words of Seán Lemass, it was still only a 'slightly constitutional party'. But at least it now expressed its disagreement through parliamentary debate rather than armed conflict.

- Once Fianna Fáil entered the Dáil, there was a better balance between government and opposition. The large minority that had voted for it since 1922 could have its voice heard and its point of view expressed.

- Many within that minority were poor and disadvantaged. After 1927 Fianna Fáil began to develop a social and economic policy that attempted to deal with their needs.

Chapter 29

1922-32: Cumann na nGaedheal's foreign and economic policies

Introduction

After Fianna Fáil TDs entered the Dáil in 1927, they consistently attacked the policies of the Cosgrave government. Their attack focused on two main areas, the Free State's membership of the British Commonwealth and its economic policies.

Anglo-Irish Relations

Attacking Dominion Status

Even after it entered the Dáil, Fianna Fáil rejected the Free State Constitution because, in accordance with the Treaty, it included Dominion status. This, they claimed, limited Irish independence. They attacked the Cosgrave government for appearing to accept these limitations and for not fulfilling Collins's promise to use the Treaty as a stepping stone to a republic.

This was less than fair. After 1921 the British Commonwealth changed and by 1931 even the British admitted that the Dominions had full independence. The Free State government played a significant part in that development.

Ireland, the restless Dominion

From the start the Irish Free State was unlike the other Dominions. Canada, Australia, New Zealand and South Africa had been settled by people from Britain who looked back with affection to the 'mother country'. Britain had given them their independence willingly and they were content to move forward slowly within the Commonwealth.

The Irish, on the other hand, had had a long struggle for independence. In 1921 membership of the Commonwealth was a second-best solution, forced upon them under threat of war. Even those who supported the Treaty saw Dominion status as a step towards something better, not as a final solution to the old Anglo-Irish quarrel.

Dominion status in the Treaty

Though Irish people were slow to see it, the Irish Free State actually had more independence under the Treaty than any other Dominion.

- Although its Constitution accepted the king as head of state, it also made it clear that in Ireland (unlike in Britain itself) power came from the people and not from him.

- Even the hated oath of allegiance was far less royalist than the oaths taken in other Dominions or in Britain. (see page 286)

- The king's representative in each Dominion was the **Governor General**. In other Dominions, he was always an English nobleman, appointed by the British government. The Free State government from the start insisted that he must be an Irishman and a commoner. (see page 309)

The Free State seeks other contacts

Although Cosgrave's government accepted Dominion status, they did not really trust the British to respect Ireland's newly won independence. They wanted contacts with other countries to balance Commonwealth membership. A good deal of their foreign policy can be seen in this light.

- In September 1923 they joined the League of Nations despite British protests.

- They were the first Commonwealth country to have a separate (i.e. non-British) representative to Washington.

- They exchanged diplomats with several European countries.

Was it a 'treaty'?

They also tried to maximise the amount of independence they had won. The process began with the Treaty itself. The Free State came into existence because of a 'treaty', or so the Irish claimed.

But a 'treaty' is an international agreement between two independent states, so the British refused to use the word. They got Westminster to pass the terms that were agreed between the two delegations. This allowed them to claim that Irish independence was due to an act of the British parliament.

The Irish government rejected this interpretation. In 1924 they registered the Treaty at the League of Nations as an international agreement. The British protested that it was an internal affair and not the business of the League, but the Irish won their point.

Expanding dominion status at Imperial Conferences

But within a short time, Irish ministers realised that their suspicions of British intentions were unjustified. This first became clear at the Imperial Conference of 1923.

These conferences were held every few years to allow British and Dominion leaders to discuss issues of common interest. The Irish had no time to prepare for the 1923 Conference. They said little, but they were impressed by the real equality and freedom of the Dominions.

The Free State government wanted this equality to be formally stated. Over the next few years they made contact with the South Africans and Canadians who wanted the same thing. At the next Conference in 1926 their brilliant and well-prepared delegation, led by Kevin O'Higgins, worked with these two countries to get the **Balfour Declaration** issued. This stated that the Dominions were:

> autonomous (i.e. self-governing) communities within the British Empire, equal in status, in no way subordinate one to another in any aspect of their domestic or external affairs, though united by a common allegiance to the Crown and freely associated as members of the British Commonwealth of Nations. (D.W. Harkness, *The Restless Dominion*, p. 96)

The next few years were spent working out what this meant in practice. At meetings of experts in 1929 and at the 1930 Imperial Conference, the Irish delegation, now led by **Patrick McGilligan**, played a leading part.

In 1931 the British parliament passed the **Statute of Westminster** which put the decisions of these meetings into law. The Statute:

- brought an end to the British claim to make laws binding on the Dominions without their consent.

- declared that a Dominion parliament could repeal laws previously passed for them by Britain.

The implications of the Statute of Westminster
For the Free State, this was very important. Now the Dáil could alter the Treaty if it

Patrick McGilligan

wished and the British, by their own laws, could do nothing about it. Winston Churchill pointed this out during the debates on the Statute but the Prime Minister, **Ramsay MacDonald**, declared his complete faith in the good will of Mr Cosgrave and his government.

No doubt this faith was justified. Over the years the Cosgrave government had come to see advantages in being a Dominion. In 1928 Ernest Blythe told the Dáil:

> We believe that this country within the British Commonwealth of Nations can enjoy greater freedom and security than outside it. (*Annual Review*, 1928, p. 131)

But they failed to sell this idea to the public and when they stood for re-election in 1932, few people in Ireland thanked them for what was probably their major achievement. It was de Valera who reaped the benefits of the freedom that the Statute of Westminster guaranteed.

Economic Policies

Economic expectations

Throughout the nineteenth century Ireland, outside of north-east Ulster, had suffered an economic decline. Nationalists blamed the Union with Britain for this decline and believed that an independent Irish government could reverse it. Griffith and others had argued that an Irish government, by protecting Irish industries behind tariff barriers, would bring prosperity, end emigration and raise the population to eight million or more.

Economic realities

These hopes did not take account of the realities that faced the Irish state in the 1920s.

- Under the Union, the Irish economy had become closely interwoven with Britain's. Over 90 per cent of our exports went to the United Kingdom and we imported a similar percentage of our imports from there. We shared a common currency, the pound sterling. Irish banks had their headquarters in London and kept their foreign currency reserves in sterling. It would be very difficult to separate the Irish economy from the British and achieve economic independence.

- Between the wars the world economy was unfavourable to economic expansion. After a depressed period in the early 1920s there was a brief recovery before the great depression hit in 1930. The small Irish economy was affected by these developments.

- Few members of Sinn Féin had an economic policy or any experience in dealing with economic issues. By 1922 two who had, Griffith and Collins, were dead. When Cosgrave and his colleagues took over, they turned for advice to civil servants and bankers who had been trained in the British system. These men saw no reason why Ireland should look for economic independence. They encouraged Cumann na nGaedheal to follow much the same economic policies as the British had before 1914.

Cumann na nGaedheal policies

The Cosgrave government adopted a conservative economic policy.

- It decided to keep taxation as low as possible, to balance the budget (i.e. to ensure that income from taxation was equal to spending) and to avoid borrowing. This was considered good economic practice in the 1920s.

- It decided in 1926 to keep the Irish pound linked to the pound sterling. This decision left the Irish pound overvalued and made life difficult for exporters. In 1927 separate Irish notes and coins were produced but they had the same value and names as the British currency.

- It decided to concentrate on developing agricultural exports to the British market while doing little to help the industrial sector.

Agricultural problems

In 1923 farming was the country's main industry. In a total labour force of 1.3 million, 670,000 people worked in agriculture and agricultural produce made up 84 per cent of exports. But Irish farming suffered from severe structural problems.

- The majority of farms were small (see Table A) and small farmers could not afford to invest in new technology (tractors, etc) or more expensive methods of farming.

Size of farms in twenty-six Counties in 1931						
1-14 acres	15-29 acres	30-49 acres	50-99 acres	100-199 acres	Over 200 acres	Total
104,000	90,000	62,000	50,000	21,000	8,000	335,000

Table A ▲

- Farmers were always reluctant to hand over the farm to their sons who often had to wait until they were well into their thirties or forties before taking over. In the 1920s, over a quarter of them were over sixty. Old men were unlikely to try new approaches to farming.

The British market in the 1920s

There were also problems with the British market which was almost the sole outlet for Irish produce.

340

- During the 1914-18 war Irish farmers took advantage of the demand and sold substandard produce. When the war was over, British consumers turned with relief to other sources of supply.

- After the war, Britain continued its traditional cheap food policy, importing freely from around the world. Irish produce had to compete with food from other countries, including some of the new ones in eastern Europe which paid their farmers to export, a practise known as dumping. As a result, prices fell after the war and stayed low.

Agricultural policies

The Cosgrave government believed that a better performance in the farming sector would help the economy as a whole. **Patrick Hogan**, who was Minister for Agriculture and **Ernest Blythe,** who was the Minister for Finance, adopted policies which aimed at improving the competitiveness of agricultural exports.

Hogan concentrated on improving quality.

- His Department set standards for production and presentation in eggs, meat and butter. It also extended the farm advisory service and tried to improve breeding stocks and crops.

- Farmers distrusted banks and were reluctant to borrow money to make improvements. In 1927 Hogan set up the **Agricultural Credit Corporation** to make loans to farmers wanting to improve their farms. Few farmers took advantage of it and loans were small, averaging £100.

Patrick Hogan

By 1930 export performance had improved almost to 1913 levels, but this was mainly due to live cattle whose prices held up well. Other agricultural exports like butter, eggs and oats rose little. Any gains were quickly destroyed as the economic depression hit Ireland in 1931. They did not reach these levels again until 1960.

Completing land purchase

Like many at that time, Hogan believed that land purchase had been a desirable development. He wanted to complete it. His 1923 **Land Act** ordered the compulsory purchase of all land still held by landlords. By 1937 the social revolution, begun in 1870, was complete. All Irish farmers now owned their farms.

But purchase did not solve the other land problems, especially the basic ones of farms that were too small to be economically viable and farmers who were too poor to invest. The 1923 Act abolished the Congested Districts Board which had been trying to increase farm size. Its functions were taken over by the Land Commission which was much less active.

Taxation and the farmers

Ernest Blythe, the Minister for Finance, aimed to keep farmers' expenses low so that they could compete successfully on the British market. Between 1924 and 1926 he cut income tax from 25p to 15p in the pound and reduced government spending from £42 million to £24 million.

This policy helped the biggest and most productive farmers but it carried a high social cost. Cuts in government spending were achieved by cutting wages to civil servants, teachers and gardaí, and reducing old age pensions from 50p to 45p a week. Other social welfare benefits were made to depend on stringently applied means tests. The government spent little to improve housing which remained as bad as it had been in 1913.

The big farmers helped by these policies were a small minority of the farming community. (see Table A) The vast majority, small farmers and labourers, gained little. In fact, they probably lost, as many of them would have been affected by the cuts in social welfare benefits. These policies caused deep resentment and probably contributed to the success of Fianna Fáil in the 1927 and 1932 elections.

Industry

Despite the loss of the north east, industry was important in the Free State. Agriculture employed half the population but industry earned two thirds of the national income.

The debate on protection

The question of bringing in tariffs to protect industry arose at the start. Industries had varying views on the subject.

- The bigger and more important industries like Guinness and Jacobs in Dublin and Fords in Cork exported much of their produce to Britain. They wanted free trade and opposed protection which might limit their access to the British market.

- Smaller industries like footwear, furniture and textiles which supplied the home market had to face competition from British imports. They wanted the new government to follow Griffith's ideas and bring in tariffs to protect them.

Avoiding protection

In 1923 the government set up the **Fiscal Inquiry Committee** to decide what should be done. The Department of Finance, which opposed protection, filled the Committee with people who favoured free trade. They ignored the fact that most of the witnesses who appeared before them wanted protection and advised the government to avoid tariffs.

Public pressure however forced Blythe to bring in tariffs on boots, shoes, confectionery, soap, bottles, clothing and furniture. More was demanded and in 1926 the government set up the **Tariff Commission** to investigate each request on its merits. It, too, was weighted against the protectionists. By 1930 it had only reported on a small range of industries, including margarine and rosary beads.

Between 1926 and 1930 industrial employment rose by 5,000, but it is doubtful if this was due to protection. The world economy improved in these years and Ireland was part of that trend.

The Shannon scheme

One problem for Irish industry was the lack of a cheap source of power. Coal had to be imported and while there were small electricity schemes in many towns, they were all inadequate for industrial purposes.

Water power seemed the answer. In 1923 the German firm, **Siemens**, offered to develop and distribute electric power from the Shannon. The government accepted, despite the protests of the Department of Finance. It involved an investment of £5 million and it was completed by 1929.

The ESB

But Siemens were not left in control of electricity. An independent 'semi-state company', the **Electricity Supply Board**, (ESB) was established to develop and distribute electric power.

It set up one of the first national grids in Europe, carrying electricity to every town in the state by 1939 and to all rural areas by the 1950s. It became the model for later semi-state bodies by which governments developed industries that were too important, too complex or too expensive to be left to private enterprise.

The Shannon scheme was an example of foreign investment and state intervention in industry but it was exceptional. A Belgian company did start a sugar-beet

Shannon scheme.

factory in Carlow, but other attempts to develop industries with overseas investment were blocked. Cumann na nGaedheal were suspicious of foreign industrialists and they refused to give state support to industrialisation.

The impact of the depression
In 1930 the great depression hit Ireland. Exports fell by 10 per cent in 1930-31 and prices for agricultural produce declined even more rapidly. Emigration ceased and the flow of remittances from emigrants declined. The British government began to adopt protection and at home even the farmers were demanding tariffs.

These developments caused a change in policy. In 1931 the government introduced tariffs on bacon, butter and oats as well as on a range of industrial products.

Fianna Fáil's economic challenge
But these were not enough to meet the Fianna Fáil challenge. Since it was set up in

344

1926 the party had developed its own economic policy. **Seán Lemass**, who was mainly responsible, drew on Griffith's ideas to demand protection to curb imports, encourage industrial development and create jobs. Fianna Fáil TDs also attacked the government's record on social welfare and housing. The impact of the depression and the approach of the next election, due in 1932, made their criticisms even sharper.

The 1932 Election

The republicanism of Fianna Fáil

As the 1932 election approached, tension rose in the country. Some of it came from the attitudes of Fianna Fáil. Since the party had taken the oath in 1927 it had played its part as the main opposition party in Dáil Éireann. But its attitude towards the Free State and its institutions remained ambiguous. Fianna Fáil TDs refused to attend state functions and they made it clear that they had entered the Dáil only as a stage on the road to a republic.

Seán Lemass explained in 1928 that:

> Fianna Fáil is a slightly constitutional party... but before anything we are a republican party. We have adopted the method of political agitation to achieve our end, because we believe, in the present circumstances, that method is best in the interests of the nation and of the Republican movement, and for no other reason.... Our object is to establish a republican government in Ireland. If that can

Seán Lemass

be done by the present methods, we will be pleased, but if not we will not confine ourselves to them. (R. Fanning, *Independent Ireland*, p. 99)

Fianna Fáil and the IRA

This attitude affected Fianna Fáil's relationship with the IRA. Both shared the same aim of a republic. Fianna Fáil had abandoned force as a way of achieving it, but, as Lemass made clear, this was only tactical. Fianna Fáil made no secret of its ties of sympathy and understanding with those who took a different view. As de Valera put it:

> Those who continued in that organisation can claim exactly the same continuity as we claimed up to 1925. (B. Bell, *The Secret Army*, p. 97)

The IRA

Since 1925 the IRA had maintained its strength and prepared for a chance to fight a 'second round'. But as time passed, some republicans found this policy more and more futile. The IRA leaders offered nothing but violence and their occasional arms raids and attacks on Gardaí achieved little beyond public disapproval and government retaliation.

The move to the left

In 1930 and 1931, as the cold winds of the depression blew in across the seas, the time seemed ripe for a new approach. Some IRA leaders, notably **Peadar O'Donnell** and **Seán MacBride**, began to argue for a more radical socialist policy based on the ideas of James Connolly.

Peadar O'Donnell

They attacked not just the Treaty but the entire capitalist system. In Donegal, O'Donnell supported small farmers in a campaign against the payment of land annuities and in 1931 he helped set up **Saor Éire** to work for the overthrow of 'the British empire and its ally capitalism'.

This policy won some support from the left wing of the labour movement. As the depression pushed some people to the left, a number of communist groups also emerged. But it is doubtful if all these organisations together had more than a few hundred members.

The main IRA leadership rejected the move to the left and resumed their usual activities. A number of violent incidents culminated in the murder of a Garda superintendent in Tipperary in the summer of 1931.

The 'red scare'

These crimes, combined with the appearance of left-wing groups, frightened many people of property. They also gave Cumann na nGaedheal a useful weapon to use against Fianna Fáil. At a time when Stalin's collectivisation policy was emerging in the USSR, a 'red scare' might neutralise Fianna Fáil's appeal to the voters by associating it with the 'red' policies of the left.

In October 1931 the government acted. Despite violent opposition in the Dáil, it passed the **Constitution (Amendment) Act**. This inserted **Article 2A** into the Constitution. It allowed the government to declare certain organisations illegal and to set up a five-man Military Tribunal (court) to try political offenses. Twelve groups, including the IRA and Saor Éire, were immediately outlawed and many members, among them O'Donnell, were imprisoned.

At the same time Cumann na nGaedheal tried to stir up fears of a 'communist threat'. They encouraged the Catholic bishops to issue a statement, read at all masses, warning of 'evidence of a campaign of revolution and communism which, if allowed to grow unchecked, must end in the ruin of Ireland, both soul and body'. (R. Fanning, *Independent Ireland*, p. 104)

February 1932: the general election

A general election was not due till the end of 1932, but Cosgrave decide to call one in February. He faced unrest in the country and needed a mandate for an important Commonwealth meeting on tariffs due in the summer.

The Cumann na nGaedheal programme

Cumann na nGaedheal fought the election on the record of its ten years in government. It had brought stability out of the chaos of the civil war and had given the country honest government. But by 1932 this was no longer enough. Like most democratic governments across Europe, it had no solution to the collapse of trade which accompanied the depression. Cumann na nGaedheal ministers believed that the rigid government economy and balanced budgets which had worked in the '20s would see them through.

Instead of offering new policies they played the red card, emphasising the danger of electing Fianna Fáil. The Minister for Justice warned that the opposition party was associated with people whose 'aim and object is to force, by means of threats and crimes of violence, a republic of a Soviet nature in this country'. De Valera was compared to Stalin or, at best, Kerensky, and an advertisement asked: 'How will you vote tomorrow? The gunmen are voting for Fianna Fáil. The Communists are voting for Fianna Fáil'.

The Fianna Fáil programme

Fianna Fáil, on the other hand, had an elaborate programme calculated to appeal to a wide section of the electorate. In order not to alarm those who feared another civil war, it underplayed its republicanism and put most emphasis on its social and economic policies.

- The word republic was not mentioned in its manifesto. It promised to free IRA prisoners, remove the oath and reduce the power of the Governor General and of the Senate, which it attacked because of its supposed unionist sympathies.

- It promised that the £3 million paid each year to Britain in land annuities would be retained in Ireland and invested in the Irish economy.

- It argued that the country should try to be self-sufficient in food. To achieve this, it proposed to encourage farmers to switch from pasture (cattle farming) to tillage (growing crops like wheat, barley and sugar beet). Since tillage was labour intensive this would make more work for agricultural labourers.

- It promised protection and industrial development. Irish-owned factories, protected by high tariff barriers, would make goods for the Irish market and jobs for Irish workers.

- It also promised that housing and social security benefits would be improved and that the salaries of ministers and senior civil servants would be cut.

The campaign

The election campaign was reasonably peaceful but during it the government made a major blunder. It prosecuted de Valera's newly established paper, the *Irish Press*, and its editor was brought before the Military Tribunal. This looked like a serious interference with the freedom of speech and was unpopular, even among the government's own supporters.

The red scare was also resented by many people and may have backfired. As one historian has written, 'in the party politics of independent Ireland, the green suit outranked the red'. (R. Fanning, *Independent Ireland*, p. 105)

The result

When the votes were counted, Fianna Fáil's share had jumped by 9 per cent since 1927. It won seventy-two seats. Cumann na nGaedheal fell to fifty-seven seats and all other parties lost ground too. Although Fianna Fáil did not have an overall majority (see Table B) it had enough to form a government with the backing of the Labour party which shared many of its social policies.

Results of the 1932 election						
Total	C. na nG.	F. F.	Labour	Farmers	Indep.	Others
153	57	72	7	3	14	–

Table B ▲

Chapter 30

1932-39: De Valera's Ireland

9 March 1932: a peaceful transition

The test of a democracy is its ability to transfer power peacefully from one party to another. After the 1932 election, many in Ireland and outside it wondered if the Free State would pass that test.

The new Dáil assembled on 9 March. People waited tensely to see if men who had won a bitter civil war only ten years before would hand over power to their opponents. Some feared that, even if the politicians accepted the voters' decision, the army might not. A few Fianna Fáil TDs arrived at Leinster House with guns in their pockets.

Cosgrave, however, was determined to follow the democratic principles his party had preached. He took the precaution of informing the British government that they must respect the people's decision. He also called in the heads of the army, the Gardaí and civil service and told them to accept their new masters. When the Dáil met, de Valera, with Labour backing, was quietly elected President of the Executive Council.

De Valera for his part used his power responsibly. Many of his followers wanted revenge but he did not satisfy them. The men who had fought against him in the civil war were not sacked. A few civil servants in sensitive jobs were moved but they were given comparable jobs elsewhere. Everyone else remained where they were.

The Challenge to Britain

A victory for republicanism

Nevertheless, the change of government was seen as a victory for republicanism. One of the first actions of the new Minister for Defence, **Frank Aiken**, was to free republicans imprisoned under the emergency legislation of the previous year. On 18 March the Military Tribunal was suspended and the ban on the IRA and other organisations was lifted.

Abolishing the oath

De Valera, who took over the Department of External Affairs as well as the Presidency, at once began his attack on the Treaty. He adopted a step-by-step approach and kept carefully within the law. This made it difficult for the British to retaliate.

On 22 March he told the British government that he was going to abolish the oath. The Irish people, he said, had shown their desire to abandon this 'relic of medievalism'. The British Colonial Secretary, **J.H. Thomas**, angrily denied that the Treaty could be altered, except with the consent of both parties.

Ignoring his protests, de Valera introduced a bill abolishing the oath on 20 April. It quickly passed through the Dáil but was rejected by the Senate which Cumann na nGaedheal still controlled. As a result, the final abolition of the oath was postponed until May 1933.

The Governor General

De Valera would also have liked to abolish the office of Governor General. His legal advisers warned him, however, that he had to have someone to sign bills passed by the Dáil.

The Governor General in 1932 was **James MacNeill** who had succeeded T.M. Healy in 1928. Fianna Fáil ministers systematically insulted him and forced his resignation. De Valera then appointed **Domhnall Ó Buachalla**. A Fianna Fáil candidate who had failed to win a seat in the election, Ó Buachalla did not occupy the official residence in the Phoenix Park and never performed any public duties. He just put his name to anything that was placed in front of him.

Annuities and protection

Meanwhile the government was also acting on the economic front.

- De Valera announced that he would stop the payment of the land annuities to Britain. The Cosgrave government had promised to pay the annuities in

Domhnall Ó Buachalla

agreements with Britain in 1923 and 1926, but as they had not been ratified by Dáil Éireann, de Valera did not consider them binding.

- In March the Minister for Finance, **Seán MacEntee**, brought in his first budget. It contained new duties on forty-three imports. These duties were intended to protect Irish industries, but since most of the imports affected came from Britain, they looked like another part of the anti-British campaign.

The British response

De Valera hoped to keep the political and economic issues separate but for the British the two were inseparable. The Coalition government in Britain was totally ignorant of Irish politics, as they had no representative in Dublin. They were also very suspicious of de Valera. They thought he was about to take Ireland out of the Commonwealth and at the same time default on his debts.

Economic war

Talks were held in June, but de Valera had no intention of backing down. On 1 July the next instalment of the annuities was due. When it was not paid, the British retaliated. They imposed 20 per cent duties on Irish cattle and other agricultural exports.

Officially, this was to recover the annuity money. Secretly, the British hoped to cause enough economic hardship to destabilise de Valera's government and ensure the return of their friends in Cumann na nGaedheal. What they did not understand was that their action allowed Fianna Fáil ministers to do what they had intended to do anyway but to blame the consequences on Britain.

Seán MacEntee

On 23 July Fianna Fáil got the Dáil to pass the **Emergency Imposition of Duties Act**. It allowed the Irish government to impose a duty of 20 per cent on imports from Britain, including machinery, electrical goods, iron, steel and cement, as well as 25p a ton on British coal.

These duties, which were bound to hit the consumer, could now be presented as a patriotic response to the attack of the old enemy. As one historian has written:

> the 'economic war' was a godsend for Fianna Fáil as it enabled them to introduce their own protectionist programme under the guise of patriotic necessity more quickly than might otherwise have been possible. (R. Fanning, *Independent Ireland*, p. 113)

Economic and Social Policies

The episode known as the 'economic war' lasted from 1932 to 1938. It was an inextricable mixture of three separate influences:

- the pressures generated by the world depression.

- the economic war with Britain.

- Fianna Fáil's own policy of self-sufficiency.

The depression and the economic war
Even before 1932, the depression in Britain had cut the demand for Irish agricultural exports. These fell in value from £47 million in 1929 to £36 million in 1931. The economic war accelerated this trend and by 1934 they were down to £18 million.

In such a situation protection became necessary and would probably have been introduced whichever party won the 1932 election. But for Fianna Fáil in 1932, protection was not just an economic necessity, it was also a means of establishing economic independence from Britain to go with the political independence it also hoped to achieve.

Fianna Fáil's agricultural policy
In agriculture Fianna Fáil's policy was based on the idea of self-sufficiency, a concept fashionable in the 1930s. For de Valera, self-sufficiency meant growing crops like wheat and sugar-beet in Ireland to replace flour and sugar imports. The theory was that farmers would be persuaded to switch from cattle farming to producing these crops, thereby creating jobs.

De Valera appointed **James Ryan** as Minister for Agriculture and gave him the task of implementing these policies.

- Imports of wheat, sugar and other agricultural produce were restricted.

- Farmers were given a guaranteed price for wheat.

- Farmers were forced to use home-produced grain in animal feed and bakers had to include a proportion of Irish flour in their bread.

- The sugar-beet industry was expanded and new sugar factories set up. Bacon, too, was protected and subsidies were given to encourage the export of butter and bacon.

These changes did have an apparent effect. The area growing wheat rose from 24,000 acres in 1932 to 254,000 by 1936 and sugar-beet production also expanded. But this expansion was the result of farmers who had previously grown barley and other crops switching to wheat and beet because they were subsidised. Only about 10 per cent more land was being tilled in 1936 than in 1931 and even this small gain was lost in the late 1930s after the economic war with Britain ended.

The farmers who switched to growing wheat were the bigger farmers of Leinster. The small farmers of Munster and Connaught whom de Valera claimed to be helping gained nothing. Even the hoped-for increase in jobs did not materialise. Farmers who went in for tillage preferred to invest in labour-saving tractors than in labourers.

Paying for the economic war

The economic war did serious harm to the country's main export earner, the cattle trade. The government tried to compensate by giving bounties equal to the British duties. These had to be paid for by the taxpayer and government spending on agriculture rose rapidly. At the same time, the protection of bacon, flour, sugar and other food items from foreign competition caused them to go up in price. This hit the ordinary consumers, many of them poorly paid workers.

Although the Fianna Fáil agricultural policy did little for small farmers, they did gain some indirect compensation. The land annuities which were a relatively heavy burden on them were cut in half. And in 1933, Fianna Fáil extended unemployment assistance (the 'farmers' dole') to small holders. This eased the poverty of the smallest farmers in the state and made life a little better for them.

Fianna Fáil's industrial policy

But unlike Cumann na nGaedheal, Fianna Fáil regarded industry as more important than agriculture. De Valera appointed **Seán Lemass** as **Minister for Industry and Commerce** with the task of developing Irish industry behind tariff walls. With de Valera's backing, Lemass was able to overcome the reservations of the Department of Finance about state involvement in industry.

The world depression and the economic war with Britain made the task of industrialisation even harder than it might otherwise have been. Lemass had to move fast. Much of his activity was unplanned, often without adequate statistical information or any clear idea of the long-term effects of his decisions.

- Imports were limited by tariffs, quotas and import licences on over a thousand separate items.

- Behind these barriers, new companies were encouraged to set up. Those which did included factories making textiles, footwear, cutlery, ropes, cement and a wide range of other items. These were all intended to supply the home market. Few of the new industries had the capacity or the will to export their produce.

Irish ownership

Some in Fianna Fáil were worried that new companies would be foreign owned. To stop that, Lemass introduced **Control of Manufactures Acts** in 1932 and 1934. They decreed that some Irish nationals must be involved in all new firms.

This rule was often broken, in spirit at least. Foreign firms such as Ranks (flour milling) or Cadburys (chocolate) set up subsidiaries in Ireland to get round tariffs. They had a token Irishman or two on the board but control of the business remained firmly in the hands of the parent company in Britain.

Capital

Capital for new companies was always a problem. Few people in Ireland, including the banks, were willing to risk their money in starting an industry. To meet the need, Lemass set up the **Industrial Credit Company** in 1933 to provide loans.

When this proved inadequate in some high capital projects, he set up state-owned 'semi-state' companies, modelled on the ESB. These included the **Irish Sugar Company,** to develop the sugar-beet industry, **Aer Lingus** to develop air transport, the **Turf Development Board** (later **Bord na Móna**) to develop the bogs and **Irish Life** to develop an Irish-controlled insurance sector.

Banks

Irish banks were very conservative. Mostly dominated by people of a unionist outlook, they had their headquarters in London and opposed any change in the Irish currency's link with sterling. Their reserves were kept in Britain and not invested in Irish industry.

Fianna Fáil promised a commission to look into this situation but it was not set up until 1938 when the reforming urge was over. It advised against any change. A **Central Bank** was set up in 1942 but it had limited powers to control the commercial banks which continued to be centred in London.

Monopolies

The Irish market was too small and too poor to attract companies unless they could be guaranteed exclusive access to it. Lemass was quite willing to oblige and many firms, including the semi-states, were given **monopolies** on the supply of particular items in Ireland. The absence of competition allowed prices to rise even when quality fell. As usual, the cost of this policy was carried by the consumer.

Jobs and emigration

The main aim behind the Fianna Fáil industrial policy was the creation of jobs. They had some success in this area. Between 1931 and 1939 the number of people employed in industry rose from 111,000 to 166,000. This growth compensated for the loss of jobs in agriculture. For the first time since the famine, the number of people in work increased.

The rise in employment had a social value in making life better for some. But it did not end unemployment or emigration. As the world depression hit in 1932, emigration had ceased and there may even have been a net inflow of returning emigrants. But once the depression began to lift in the mid-1930s, emigration resumed, with 26,000 leaving in 1937.

Balance of payments problems

Between 1931 and 1938 gross industrial output rose from £55 million to £90 million but there was an underlying weakness. Ireland has few native raw materials, so these have to be imported. The new factories ran on imported fuel and many of them merely assembled parts brought in from abroad, mostly from Britain.

These imports had to be paid for but the depression and the economic war sharply reduced agricultural exports with which Ireland had always paid for its imports. To make matters worse, big exporters like Jacobs, Guinness and Ford responded to the depression and economic war by setting up factories in Britain.

Between 1929 and 1938 Irish export earnings fell from £47 million to £24 million. The import bill also fell (from £61 million to £41 million) but by a smaller amount. Between 1931 and 1934 the trade deficit doubled. This forced de Valera to seek an economic understanding with Britain.

1935: the Coal-Cattle Pact

By 1935 the British, too, were anxious for economic peace. The Free State was their third biggest customer and British businessmen wanted their government to heal the breach. After Fianna Fáil won the 1933 election, the British government also realised that Cosgrave would not be back for some time and that they would have to come to terms with de Valera.

In 1935 the two governments negotiated the **Coal-Cattle Pact** which eased the restrictions on these two important items of trade. The quota of Irish cattle allowed into Britain was raised by a third and the Free State took an additional 1,250,000 tons of British coal. Full settlement of the economic war had to wait, however, until the political issues were finally sorted out in 1938. (see page 368)

The Fianna Fáil social policy

Fianna Fáil accompanied its agricultural and industrial policies with a social policy that was more generous than that of Cumann na nGaedheal.

- Their **Unemployment Assistance Act** (1933) increased unemployment benefits and extended them to small farmers and farm labourers.

- The **National Health Insurance Act** (1933) improved the provision of health insurance.

- Old age and blind pensions were improved and in 1935 pensions for widows and orphans were introduced.

- Housing, which had the advantage of creating jobs, was given priority. Under the 1932 **Housing Act** the central government contributed between one- and two-thirds of the cost of local authority house-building. Almost £10 million was spent between 1932 and 1940. They built an average of 12,000 houses a year, compared with a mere 2,000 a year in the 1920s. This helped to improve the living conditions of many families, especially those in the worst city slums.

Nevertheless, poverty remained acute. Even in comparative terms Irish people got poorer. In 1931 the average Irish income was 60 per cent of the British average; by 1939 it was 49 per cent.

De Valera, the Blueshirts and the IRA

Opposition to Fianna Fáil policies
Fianna Fáil's clash with Britain over the oath and the annuities caused dismay among the opposition parties. The duties on cattle and coal damaged the larger farmers and businessmen, who were the main supporters of Cumann na nGaedheal. Many of their followers also valued their links with Britain and opposed the dismantling of the Treaty, especially as it widened the gap with Northern Ireland.

Suspicion
Some also feared that de Valera planned a dictatorship or even, given the left-wing appearance of some of the Fianna Fáil social policy, a communist take-over. The behaviour of the IRA strengthened this fear.

Once the ban on the IRA was lifted, they had mounted a campaign against Cumann na nGaedheal. At a public meeting in Dublin Peadar O'Donnell said that he was 'glad the murder-government was put out of power, but these men must be put finally out of public life'. (M. Manning, *The Blue Shirts*, pp. 32-3) His paper, *An Phoblacht*, began a campaign headed 'no free speech to traitors'.

Cumann na nGaedheal meetings were broken up by IRA men and the Gardaí seemed to be doing nothing to stop them. In December 1932 the Cumann na nGaedheal paper, *United Ireland*, wrote:

It has become all too apparent that Mr de Valera is leading the country straight into Bolshevik servitude. (M. Manning, *The Blue Shirts*, p. 44)

It was against this background of suspicion that the movement known as the **Blueshirts** emerged.

The Army Comrades Association
Shortly before the 1932 election, ex-soldiers from the Free State army had formed the **Army Comrades Association** (ACA). In August 1932 **T.F. O'Higgins**, a Cumann na nGaedheal TD and brother of Kevin O'Higgins, became its leader. He declared that the ACA would defend free speech and oppose communism. It began providing stewards at Cumann na nGaedheal meetings. This led to clashes with the IRA. Riots became common and tension rose sharply.

The National Centre party
Meanwhile in the Dáil a new party, the **National Centre Party**, emerged. It was led by **Frank MacDermot** and **James Dillon**, son of the last Home Rule leader. It drew support from the bigger farmers and was in favour of a reconciliation with Britain.

January 1933: another general election
The party grew quickly but before it became established, de Valera called a surprise election in January 1933. He hoped to secure a majority and a clear mandate for his dealings with the British. If re-elected, he promised to go on dismantling the Treaty, and to continue the programme of protection, industrialisation and social reform.

Caught off-balance, his opponents had little to offer instead. Fianna Fáil increased its share of the vote to 49 per cent and gained seventy-seven seats. Cumann na nGaedheal fell to forty-eight, while Labour won eight seats and the Centre Party eleven. (see Table A)

Results of the 1933 election						
Total 153	C. na nG. 48	F. F. 77	Lab. 8	Centre 11	Indep. 8	Ind. Lab 1

Table A ▲

Eoin O'Duffy, 1892-1944
During the election campaign there was serious rioting between the ACA and the IRA. As a result the ACA came to be seen as the militant wing of Cumann na nGaedheal. In March they adopted a uniform of blue shirts and black berets, and in July acquired a new leader.

He was **Eoin O'Duffy**, a friend of Collins, who had been Commissioner of the Garda Síochána since 1922. He had a flamboyant personality and had quarrelled with Cosgrave and O'Higgins several times in the 1920s.

O'Duffy was closely identified with the pro-Treaty side. After the election, de Valera requested his resignation as Garda Commissioner and offered him another job. O'Duffy refused and stepped down in a blaze of publicity.

The Blueshirts

O'Duffy joined the ACA and in July, replaced O'Higgins as leader. He reorganised it, made the blueshirt uniform compulsory and changed its name to the **National Guard**. Membership was limited to people who were Irish or whose parents 'profess the Christian faith' (i.e. no Jews need apply).

A few days later O'Duffy issued a programme which denounced political parties as a relic of English rule. He called for a remodelling of the Dáil, so that deputies would be elected to represent vocational groups - farmers, workers, etc - rather than territorial constituencies. This had echoes of Mussolini's corporate state in Italy.

Vocationalism

The depression of the early 1930s led many people in Europe to believe that parliamentary democracy had failed. They were looking for alternatives. Some chose communism which seemed to offer a decent life for workers. But many feared communism. To them Mussolini's fascism, not yet tainted by its alliance with the more brutal form of fascism in Germany, seemed to offer a working alternative to parliamentary democracy.

The Blueshirts.

In Ireland most people who thought like that drew their ideas for a new social order from **Pope Pius XI**'s encyclical, *Quadragessimo Anno*, which had appeared in 1931. It suggested that co-operation between vocational groups was preferable to the class war that communists preached. This idea was taken up and presented in pamphlets and articles by **James Hogan** and **Michael Tierney**, two members of Cumann na nGaedheal. O'Duffy was probably influenced by them.

The clash with de Valera

As soon as he took over the National Guard, O'Duffy announced a parade to Leinster House to commemorate the deaths of Griffith, Collins and O'Higgins. De Valera's government, remembering Mussolini's march on Rome, feared a coup d'etat, though there is no proof that O'Duffy planned anything of the kind.

De Valera took decisive action. A special police force was formed. Composed mainly of ex-IRA men, it was nicknamed the 'Broy Harriers' after O'Duffy's replacement, **Eamon Broy**. They were armed and they guarded government buildings. Guns held by politicians under licence, including O'Duffy's own and those of former Cumann na nGaedheal ministers, were called in.

At the last moment de Valera banned the march. O'Duffy obeyed the order. The government then revived the notorious Article 2A and the Military Tribunal and declared the National Guard an illegal organisation.

3 September 1933: the formation of Fine Gael

To opponents of Fianna Fáil, these actions looked like the first steps towards the dictatorship they feared. They saw themselves being deprived of their arms and of their protectors while the IRA was allowed to go armed and unmolested. Hitler had used similar tactics when he had destroyed German democracy earlier that year.

The leaders of Cumann na nGaedheal, the National Centre Party and the National Guard felt they had to make a united stand. On 3 September 1934 they joined together to form a new party, the **United Ireland Party – Fine Gael**. O'Duffy was elected leader with Cosgrave, Dillon and MacDermot as vice-presidents. The National Guard was renamed the **Young Ireland Association** and became the youth wing of the new party.

Fine Gael's programme made no reference to vocationalism or to O'Duffy's attack on political parties. Instead, it called for the reunification of Ireland within the Commonwealth, a series of social reforms and an end to the PR system of voting.

1933-34: growing violence

During the new party's first year the economic situation got worse. Cattle exports had fallen sharply and cattle were almost unsaleable. In the worst hit districts of Munster and south Leinster farmers began to refuse to pay rates and by the spring of 1934, 36 per cent of rates were in arrears.

The government used the Broy Harriers to collect the arrears. They seized animals and machines from defaulting farmers and sold them at public auctions. This led to clashes between the police and farmers, many of them wearing blue shirts. Attempts by the government to ban the movement failed, when it changed its name again, and a bill to prevent the wearing of uniforms was blocked by the Senate in May 1934.

21 September 1934: O'Duffy replaced

The violence embarrassed O'Duffy's colleagues in Fine Gael. Cosgrave, Dillon and MacDermot had always defended democracy. In July, MacDermot wrote to O'Duffy to protest at:

> the tendency of certain speakers and writers of our party to attack the parliamentary system of government and to imply that it is our official policy to replace it by a Blue Shirt ascendancy modelled on fascism. (D. Keogh, *Ireland and Europe, 1918-48*, p. 48)

O'Duffy ignored the warning. At a Blueshirt conference in August he urged farmers to withhold rates. Worse still, he began to talk wildly about invading Northern Ireland and driving the British out.

This was the last straw. At the party's first annual conference in September 1934, O'Duffy was forced to resign the leadership of Fine Gael and Cosgrave was elected in his place. O'Duffy tried to keep the Blueshirts going as a separate movement but it quickly faded into insignificance. In 1936 he made his last political gesture when he led a brigade to fight for Franco in the Spanish Civil War.

Undermining the IRA

The disappearance of the Blueshirts left the IRA in an exposed position. As a private army, it was as unacceptable to Fianna Fáil in government as it had been to Cumann na nGaedheal.

From 1932 de Valera had adopted policies which undermined support for it.

- Several hundred republicans were recruited into the Broy Harriers and many more into a Volunteer Force which was set up as a branch of the army in 1934.

- Men who had served on the anti-treaty side in the civil war were given pensions and republicans who had lost property were compensated.

All these people now had reasons to support the Free State.

At the same time, hard-line republicans who refused to be won over were growing disillusioned with de Valera. His step-by-step dismantling of the Treaty was too slow for people who had expected a republic overnight. Even the economic war with Britain seemed to the more socially conscious republicans to be just replacing foreign capitalists with native ones.

In 1934 a split developed in the IRA, when O'Donnell and other socialists tried to move the republicans to the left by forming the Marxist **Republican Congress**.

1936: de Valera acts against the IRA

Late in 1934 de Valera tried to persuade the IRA leaders to give up their arms but they refused. Still tied to them by shared memories, experiences and friendships, he hesitated about an open breach.

Their resumption of lawless violence forced his hand.

- In 1935 the IRA was responsible for a number of murders and the Military Tribunal was used against them.

- In 1936 the IRA in Cork shot the seventy-year-old Admiral Somerville for giving references to young men going to join the British navy.

- Soon after, in Waterford, they shot a young man whom they accused of spying.

These actions made toleration impossible. On 18 June 1936 de Valera banned the IRA. Its chief-of-staff, **Maurice Twomey**, was brought before the Military Tribunal and given three years hard labour. The IRA drifted, leaderless and impotent, for the next few years, seeking a new policy.

De Valera, the Treaty and the British Government

Dismantling the Treaty

Meanwhile, de Valera continued to dismantle the Treaty. His aim was to re-define the Free State's relationship with Britain so as to bring it closer to the External Association he had wanted in 1921. He kept this task to himself, acting throughout as his own Minister for External Affairs. It may be that he had learnt from the experience of the Treaty negotiations and did not want to let anyone negotiate on his behalf again.

In 1932 he had begun to remove the oath and diminish the role of the Governor General. His victory in the 1933 election convinced him that he had a clear mandate to continue this policy.

- He stripped the Governor General of power to withhold consent from bills.

- The right of an Irish citizen to appeal from Irish courts to the Judicial Committee of the Privy Council, the highest court in the Commonwealth, was abolished.

The British protested strongly. They denied that the Free State could alter the terms of the Treaty except by mutual consent. However, when they challenged de Valera before the Privy Council itself in 1935, that court decided that the Statute of Westminster had, in fact, given the Dáil complete authority to act as it wished. The British were thus deprived of any legal basis for opposing de Valera's policy.

May 1936: abolishing the Senate

In Ireland the most effective opposition to that policy was in the Senate. Fianna Fáil disliked it because they believed that it was a stronghold of unionism. In fact by 1932 most of the unionists whom Griffith had nominated to the Senate in 1922 were long gone. But because of the way it was elected, the Senate still contained a majority of Cumann na nGaedheal members.

One after another, it rejected the changes introduced by Fianna Fáil. It could only delay them but that was exasperating to a party in a hurry. In March 1934 de Valera retaliated with a bill to abolish the Senate itself. The Senate delayed this too, but it finally passed. In May 1936 the Senate ceased to exist.

Considering a new constitution

By then it was clear that the 1922 Constitution was no longer adequate. It had been much altered by both governments since 1922 and now there was no Senate and no real head of state.

It could have been re-shaped but de Valera wanted to start again. He hoped to reconcile as many republicans as possible to the state and he did not think this was possible with a Constitution written in the shadow of the Treaty and retaining elements of British rule.

In 1936 he began to work on a new one. But before the work was complete, a crisis in Britain gave him a chance to get his external association with the British crown.

December 1936: external association at last

Edward VIII, who had become king early in 1936, decided to marry an American divorcée. His ministers disapproved and he was forced to abdicate on 11 December 1936.

This gave de Valera his opening. On that day he called the Dáil and introduced two bills. The first was the **Constitution (Amendment No. 27) Bill**. It removed reference to the king and the Governor General from the Free State Constitution. The second was the **Executive Authority (External Relations) Bill**. It stated that so long as Ireland was associated with the nations of the Commonwealth and

> so long as the king, recognised by those nations as the symbol of their co-operation, continues to act on behalf of each of these nations ... for the purpose of the appointment of diplomatic and consular representatives and the conclusion of international agreements, the king ... is hereby authorised to act on behalf of Saorstát Éireann for the like purposes, as and when advised by the Executive Council to do so. (Longford and O'Neill, *Eamon de Valera*, pp. 293-4)

Since the Senate was gone, and since his party had a majority in the Dáil, de Valera was able to get these two bills through within twenty-four hours. Through them he achieved external association with the Commonwealth.

De Valera

The 1937 Constitution

In 1937 de Valera introduced the new Constitution. He was responsible for most of it, though he did consult a wide range of opinions.

- The Constitution began by declaring the right of the Irish people to decide their own form of government. The state was to be called 'Éire or in the English language, Ireland'. It was not described as a republic, though the Constitution set up a republican form of government.

- The territory of the state was to be 'the whole island of Ireland' (Article 2), but 'pending the reintegration of the national territory' its laws will only apply to the twenty-six counties (Article 3).

- The Head of State was to be a **President** elected by all voters for a seven year term. The position was largely ceremonial, but a few special powers are reserved to him/her.

The President:

(1) can refer bills to the Supreme Court to see if they conform to the Constitution before agreeing to sign them.

(2) can order a referendum on a bill if asked to do so by a majority of the Senate and one-third of the Dáil.

(3) can address a joint meeting of the Houses of the Oireachtas on matters of public importance.

(4) can refuse to allow a Taoiseach, who had lost his/her majority in the Dáil, to call a general election.

These powers were bitterly criticised at the time as opening the way for an elected dictatorship. In fact, the powers of the President have seldom been used.

- There were to be two houses of the **Oireachtas** which make the laws and agree to taxes.

  The **Dáil** was to be elected by all citizens over 21, with elections by proportional representation every five years.

  The **Senate** was to have sixty members. Forty-three were to be elected by a complicated system of vocational voting, borrowed from Mussolini's corporate state. Graduates of the two universities were to elect six more. The Senate could only delay bills passed by the Dáil, but to prevent this happening, every Taoiseach could appoint eleven Senators. This guaranteed that there would always be a government majority and turned the Senate into little more than a debating chamber.

- The head of government was to be called the **Taoiseach** and was to be elected by the majority of the Dáil. She/he then appointed other members of the Cabinet, who had to be approved by the Dáil.

- Areas relating to law and the courts were taken over from the 1922 Constitution. The five-judge Supreme Court was to have the right to interpret the Constitution and to check that Acts of the Oireachtas were within its provisions. This section, which was borrowed from the American Constitution became very important in the 1960s in expanding citizens' rights within the Constitution.

- Citizens were guaranteed the right to freedom of speech, assembly and association, but these were made 'subject to public order and morality'. This undermined the value of these rights.

- Article 41 emphasised that the place of women was 'within the home' and added that the state would try to ensure 'that mothers shall not be obliged by economic necessity to engage in labour to the neglect of their duties within the home'. This provoked protests from many women's groups which regarded it as a backwards step for women's rights but their protests were ignored.

- The Constitution protected the right to private property and education.

- It also guaranteed to uphold the integrity of the family. Divorce was made unconstitutional (Article 41). This was a denial of the civil rights of groups which accepted the legitimacy of divorce but they did not protest at the time.

- The Constitution also recognised the 'special position of the Roman Catholic Church' as the 'religion of the great majority of citizens' (Article 44), but at the same time guaranteed 'freedom of conscience and the free profession and practice of religion' to a list of other religious groups, including the Jewish community.

De Valera consulted a number of Catholic clergymen, of whom the most important was **John Charles McQuaid**, later Catholic Archbishop of Dublin, about the wording of this article. He also consulted the leaders of other denominations who were happy enough with the final version. The objections to it in 1937 came from Catholics who believed that it did not go far enough towards creating a Catholic state for a Catholic people. It is believed that among those who expressed dissatisfaction were **Pope Pius XI** and **Cardinal McRory** of Armagh. But de Valera refused to bow to their pressure.

- The Constitution could only be changed by referendum.

Assessing the Constitution
Through the Constitution de Valera tried to reconcile a number of opposing views.

- He made it fulfil nationalist aspirations by claiming to apply to the whole island but kept it realistic in limiting its practical application to the twenty-six counties.

- He made it republican in having a President as head of state but tried to avoid annoying the British or the unionists by not using that word.

- He made it liberal and democratic in protecting certain freedoms but conservatively Catholic in its treatment of divorce, women and various social issues.

July 1937: accepting the Constitution
The Constitution was submitted to the people on 1 July 1937 at the same time as a

John Charles McQuaid, Archbishop of Dublin

general election. It was passed by 685,105 votes to 527,945, with over 30 per cent of the electorate abstaining. In the election, Fianna Fáil was again returned to power, though with a reduced majority. (see Table B, page 369) Afterwards, **Douglas Hyde**, the founder of the Gaelic League, was nominated by all parties and became, unopposed, the first President.

Changing British attitudes

British leaders were unsure whether the External Relations Act and the new Constitution meant that Ireland had withdrawn from the Commonwealth. After some debate they simply issued a statement to the effect that the new Constitution did not produce 'a fundamental alteration in the position of the Irish Free State as a member of the British Commonwealth of Nations'. (N. Mansergh, 'Ireland: External Relations 1926-1939', in F.MacManus (ed), *The Year of the Great Test*, p.135)

This conciliatory response was due to **Malcolm MacDonald**, who had replaced **J.H. Thomas** as Dominions Secretary in 1935. He was a Labour member of the Coalition government which had ruled Britain since 1931. MacDonald wanted to reach an understanding with de Valera. When the Irish leader was on his way to Switzerland to consult an eye specialist, MacDonald met him secretly in London to see what could be worked out.

The inaugural procession of Douglas Hyde passing the GPO.

Neville Chamberlain

MacDonald had to move cautiously because the Conservatives in the Coalition were hostile to de Valera. He did succeed in winning over **Neville Chamberlain**, a leading Conservative, who became Prime Minister in 1937. Chamberlain was preoccupied with developments in Europe where Hitler was looking more and more dangerous. He hoped to avoid a war by appeasing German demands and he hoped that the appeasement of Ireland might keep it on Britain's side if war did come.

Talking to the British

The economic war had eased in 1935, with the Coal-Cattle Pact which was renewed and extended in 1936 and 1937. Meanwhile, secret talks took place on other issues. By 1938, with his Constitution safely in place, de Valera was content to negotiate publicly. He wanted a settlement with Britain before the war, which everyone feared was coming, broke out in Europe.

Talks opened in London on 17 January 1938. De Valera was accompanied by Lemass, MacEntee and his Minister for Agriculture, **James Ryan**.

- For de Valera the issues to be settled included the land annuities, economic relations, partition and the British occupation of the Treaty ports.

- For the British the issues were the land annuities, economic relations, defence and the Commonwealth.

April 1938: the Anglo-Irish Agreements

On 25 April, after long, complicated discussions, three Anglo-Irish Agreements were signed.

- The land annuities issue was settled when the Irish government made a single payment of £10 million.

- The economic war was ended with a three year trade agreement. Under it both Britain and Ireland would give preferential treatment to the others exports, though these were still regulated by quotas and tariffs.

- The British handed the Treaty ports to the Irish government without conditions.

In Britain, the decision to return the ports was criticised, especially by Winston Churchill. But Chamberlain was acting on the advice of the chiefs of the armed forces. The ports had been neglected since the 1920s. A big investment would have been needed to bring them into operation. The British felt this was pointless if the ports then had to be held against a hostile population.

Chamberlain hoped that this generous concession would persuade de Valera to make a defence treaty allowing Britain to use the ports in a war. But de Valera responded to this proposal by asking for a declaration against partition, which the British refused to give.

Thus for each side the agreements were only a limited success. Nevertheless, de Valera on his return home called a general election, in which the voters signified their approval by returning Fianna Fáil with a comfortable over-all majority. (see Table B)

Results of the 1937 and 1938 elections					
	Total	F. G.	F. F.	Lab.	Indep.
1937	138	48	69	13	8
1938	138	45	77	9	7

Table B ▲

Assessing the de Valera years

The 1938 Anglo-Irish Agreements mark the end both of de Valera's campaign to demolish the Treaty and the push to create economic self-sufficiency.

By 1938, the Treaty, so reluctantly accepted, was dead. The Anglo-Irish Agreements showed that even the British had acknowledged the real independence of the Irish state. Their acceptance of neutrality in the war confirmed it.

Within Ireland, the issues that had fuelled the civil war ceased to be of importance. Although bitterness between individuals remained, the political divisions the Treaty had created between politicians were no longer relevant. Apart from some intransigent republicans, all parties were now fully constitutional. Out of the turmoil of the thirties, during which the civil war had been replayed with less bloodshed but with equal bitterness, had emerged political stability.

On the economic front, too, a consensus had emerged. By 1938 a new style economy had developed. It was a mixture of that favoured by Cumann na nGaedheal in the 1920s and that supported by Fianna Fáil in the 1930s.

The attempt to get self-sufficiency in agriculture had failed. Agricultural exports to Britain were still the mainstay of the economy and in practise that meant relying on the big cattle farmers. On the other hand, industry was to go on being protected so that it could supply the home market and create protected jobs.

This policy was generally accepted by the late 1930s. But it had inherent weaknesses, especially in relation to the balance of payments. The war masked these weaknesses until the late 1940s. Even then it took a major economic crisis before people were willing to challenge the economic consensus which had become established by 1938.

Chapter 31

1939-45: Neutral Ireland

1932-39: de Valera's foreign policy

Although de Valera's main foreign policy in the 1930s concerned Britain, he did not neglect other areas. As Minister for External Affairs, he developed the diplomatic service that had been neglected during the Cosgrave period. He also increased the country's involvement in the **League of Nations** which he saw as an arena where a small country could play a part.

De Valera and the League of Nations

De Valera was undoubtedly conscious that a prominent role in the League would win good publicity at home. In 1932, just after Fianna Fáil came to power, it was Ireland's turn to hold the Presidency of the League Council. De Valera went to Geneva to speak at the meeting. He frankly criticised the extent to which the great powers followed their own interests and ignored the needs of smaller states and the ideal of collective security.

De Valera loyally supported League decisions. Although there was support in Ireland for Mussolini's invasion of Abyssinia, he backed League sanctions against Italy. Over the Spanish civil war, he followed the League line of non-intervention, in spite of great pressure from the Catholic Church and Irish public opinion which was sympathetic to Franco.

In 1938 he was elected President of the Assembly and presided over the session which followed the Munich crisis. Fearing war, he supported the appeasement of Hitler. The invasion of Czechoslovakia in March 1939 showed the failure of this policy and of collective security. War was now imminent and Ireland, like other countries, would have to look to its own interests.

Why we stayed neutral

As early as 1925 the Cumann na nGaedheal government had considered what policy this country should adopt if Britain became involved in a war. Their decision was that the Irish army must be capable of repelling any third party that tried to use us as a back-door through which to attack Britain. This would reassure the British enough to make it unnecessary for them to occupy us.

This clearly implied neutrality but it would be difficult to stay neutral so long as Britain occupied the Treaty ports. By 1939 the Treaty ports had been handed over and as war threatened, de Valera was able to opt for neutrality.

There were several reasons for taking this position.

- Irish people were divided between those who were strongly anti-British and those who were strongly pro-British, so neutrality was the least divisive policy.

- Neutrality in a war in which Britain was involved was the clearest possible statement of Irish independence.

- But the basic reason was self-protection. Some people objected that neutrality was an inadequate response to the evils of Nazism, but as the Secretary of the Department of External Affairs noted in 1941:

  small nations like Ireland do not and cannot assume a role of defenders of just causes except their own ... Existence of our own people comes before all other considerations ... no government has the right to court certain destruction for its people; they have to take the only chance of survival and stay out. (D. Keogh, *Ireland and Europe*, p.118)

Other small nations like Norway, Denmark, Switzerland, Portugal and Belgium made the same decision in 1939. We were one of the lucky few that was not invaded and that managed to remain neutral throughout the whole course of the war.

Neutrality would not be easy to sustain. Ireland was geographically close to Britain and shared a land frontier with the United Kingdom. It was also the country with which we did most of our trade. This meant that neutrality would have to be strongly biased in Britain's favour. But de Valera kept this hidden from the public. Officially, the country maintained a strict and even-handed neutrality.

Declaring neutrality

On 1 September 1939 Germany invaded Poland and the war began. On the following day, at a hastily-called meeting of the Dáil, a state of emergency was declared. The government took extensive powers to deal with any problems which might arise.

- Strict censorship was introduced to stop the expression of any opinion which might seem to favour one side over the other. At one point, even a bishop's pastoral containing anti-Nazi opinions was altered.

- Radio newscasts were confined to reading, without comment, the dispatches from each side.

- All weather forecasts were stopped in case they helped the planes or ships of either side in the war.

- Even the word 'war' was avoided. From 1939 to 1945 the situation in Europe was always referred to as 'the emergency'

The IRA campaign in Britain

One obvious danger to neutrality came from the IRA. In 1938 **Seán Russell** had become their Chief-of-Staff. He wanted to conduct a bombing campaign in England which he believed would lead the British to withdraw from Northern Ireland.

In January 1939 the IRA delivered an ultimatum to the British government demanding withdrawal from the North. When this was ignored, they launched their attack. Bombs exploded in a number of places throughout the spring and summer. In one explosion in Coventry in August five people were killed.

The result of the campaign was not British withdrawal from the North but an outburst of anti-Irish feeling. The goodwill de Valera had built up in the previous year's negotiations was undermined. Police harassed Irish communities, Irish people were expelled and controls on travel between the two countries were introduced.

IRA members, among them the sixteen-year-old **Brendan Behan**, were arrested and imprisoned. Two men were hanged for their part in the Coventry explosion. The only positive thing to emerge from the whole business was Behan's account of his prison experiences in *Borstal Boy*.

Action against the IRA

De Valera was dismayed by this development. The IRA campaign endangered his relations with Britain. In June 1939 he brought in the **Offences against the State Act**. It gave the Gardaí power to hold suspects for interrogation and allowed the government to intern suspected IRA members without trial. The **Treason Act** later authorised the death penalty for treason.

These powers were used in December when the IRA raided the Army Magazine in the Phoenix Park and stole most of the government's reserve of ammunition, though this was recovered within weeks.

Brendan Behan

The IRA and the war

Once war broke out IRA activity became a threat to neutrality. There was the possibility that the British might use their attacks as an excuse to invade us. Even more seriously, any attempt by the IRA to link up with the Germans could compromise Irish neutrality.

This was a real danger. Russell, who was in the US when the war began, went to Germany. Like the men of 1916, he was acting on the old principle of England's difficulty. He hoped to persuade the Germans to send troops and arms to Ireland. They were interested. Several German agents were parachuted into Ireland, but the Irish authorities were on the alert and most were picked up within days.

Only **Herman Goertz**, who arrived in May 1940, was able to evade capture and make contact with the IRA. He found them disorganised, quarrelling and under constant pressure from the Gardaí. Goertz himself was only able to make contact with Germany occasionally. He was finally arrested in December 1941. Russell, meanwhile, died on a submarine that was returning him to Ireland.

De Valera struck ruthlessly against this threat to the country's neutrality. Active republicans were rounded up. Many were interned without trial in the Curragh and others were given prison sentences. Six men were hanged and three who went on hunger strike were allowed to die.

By 1943 the IRA had almost ceased to exist. It got little public sympathy. Neutrality was popular and press censorship was too strict to allow much information about these events to emerge.

Diplomacy and the war

A small country with a small and inadequately armed defence force clearly had little chance of resisting invasion. Preserving neutrality would have to depend more on diplomacy and the tolerance of the big powers than on the strength of our arms.

Throughout the war, Ireland was well served by diplomats abroad, who kept Dublin informed of developments in their host countries. We were also lucky in having sympathetic German and British representatives in Dublin, though the American Minister was less so.

Edouard Hempel, the German Minister

The German Minister (until the late 1940s foreign diplomats in Ireland were called 'ministers' not 'ambassadors') in Ireland since 1938 was **Dr Edouard Hempel**. He was a career diplomat and not a Nazi. He disapproved of German contacts with the IRA and played no part in them.

Before the war began de Valera held a meeting with Hempel. He explained that Ireland's close trade links with Britain and the ease with which the British could invade us if their interests were threatened:

> rendered it inevitable for the Irish government to show a certain consideration for Britain. (M. Bromage, *Churchill and Ireland*, p. 134)

Hempel understood this position. Throughout the war his reports to Berlin urged his government to avoid any action which would justify a British invasion of Ireland.

During the Battle of Britain, the German high command did examine the possibility of an invasion. Plans seem to have been drawn up but they were not acted upon. The most likely reasons were the limited range of their planes and the difficulty of holding the country against a British counter-attack. They put more faith in IRA contacts of which Hempel, knowing how limited support for the IRA was, disapproved.

Hempel sent reports on Irish conditions and on British submarine movements back to Germany. In December 1941 de Valera demanded that he stop using the radio transmitter in his ministry. In 1943 this was taken and locked in the vault of a Dublin bank. This seriously limited his ability to communicate with Berlin and was probably helpful to the Allies in the period before the invasion of France in 1944.

Sir John Maffey, the British representative

The British did not have diplomatic representation in Dublin in the late 1930s because of their uncertainty about the country's status. Was Ireland in the Commonwealth or not?

Once war began this became less important than the need to stay in touch. They appointed a senior civil servant with considerable knowledge of Ireland, **Sir John Maffey**, as the 'United Kingdom representative for Éire'. He soon developed a good working relationship with de Valera.

David Gray, the American Minister

The United States stayed neutral until the Japanese attacked them at Pearl Harbour in December 1941. But the Roosevelt government was sympathetic to Britain and hostile to Irish neutrality.

David Gray was the American Minister in Dublin. He was a relative of President Roosevelt and not a career diplomat. He did not try to understand the Irish position, mixing mainly with a pro-British landed set. He distrusted de Valera and urged the US government to put pressure on him to force Ireland to join the allies.

British demands

As soon as the war began the Germans blockaded British shipping. The British applied to the Irish government for the use of port and harbour facilities. De Valera refused, but indicated that we would acquiesce in British planes from Northern Ireland flying over Donegal and in anti-submarine patrols off the Irish coast. This was the beginning of a pattern of co-operation with Britain, which was more friendly than strict neutrality should have allowed.

May 1940: the time of crisis

The first months of the war lulled everyone into a sense of security. It was widely expected that this war, like the last, would be fought out on the European mainland, and the Irish government made little attempt to build up stocks of food or other supplies, or to strengthen the defence forces which, after some hectic activity in September 1939, soon settled back into their well-worn routine.

The events of the early summer of 1940 shattered this complacency. In quick succession, the German army over-ran the neutral states of Denmark, Norway and Belgium. On 20 May it reached the French coast and the British army was trapped at Dunkirk.

Three days later de Valera sent representatives to London to discuss the situation with the British. They agreed that if the Germans invaded Ireland, the Irish government would invite the British army in to help to repel them. The British wanted to be able to go in as soon as the Germans landed but de Valera insisted that they must only come in response to an invitation from him.

June 1940: the offer of unity

In June France fell to Hitler. The continental mainland was now in German hands. Britain stood alone and under heavy attack from sea and air. Her only lifeline was the convoys which carried war supplies across the Atlantic through submarine-infested waters. As the Admiralty pointed out, the possession of Berehaven would have reduced the distance these convoy escort vessels had to travel by two hundred miles.

Churchill, who had become Prime Minister in May, sent Malcolm MacDonald to Dublin. He told de Valera that the Germans were planning to invade and made a dramatic offer. In return for Ireland entering the war, Britain would declare in favour of the principle of a united Ireland and set up a joint committee of representatives from the Northern and Southern governments to work out the practical details.

MacDonald urged the Irish to accept, saying:

> the present was the best opportunity that had yet offered itself for a union of the whole of Ireland being achieved ... If the North and the South could be united on the basis of their being joined together in the persecution of a war in defence of the freedom of the whole of Ireland against the Nazi attack, then the union would not be broken afterwards. (R. Fisk, *In Time of War*, p. 206)

But De Valera was not convinced and turned down the offer. He told MacDonald that:

> he could not enter into serious discussions on any basis except the immediate establishment of a united neutral Ireland ... The government would defend the country against invasion but they would not purchase unity by an act which would bring civil war and disaster to the people and would in all probability put an end to the independence we now enjoyed. (D. Keogh, *Ireland and Europe*, p. 132)

There were at least two reasons for this reaction.

- The Irish government was doubtful if the British could keep their promise to force the unionists into a united Ireland after the war.

- Some members of the government feared that Britain was losing the war. They felt that nothing was to be gained by siding with the losers.

Britain decides against invasion

The British accepted the Irish decision. The armies of the two countries co-ordinated plans to deal with a German landing. But the British also considered invading Ireland to forestall a German takeover. The plan was abandoned, partly on the advice of the generals who felt that too many of their troops would be tied down in Ireland, and partly because of the bad effect it might have on American opinion.

The fact that Northern Ireland was in the United Kingdom also removed the need to take the South. After the fall of France, most trans-Atlantic traffic was diverted north for safety and British planes and convoys could use airfields and harbours in the North. Without this, it is doubtful if British self-interest would have allowed her to respect Irish neutrality.

The army and the war

In 1940 none of this was yet clear. The British never revealed that they had decided not to invade, and de Valera was never completely sure that they would not.

After the fall of France desperate attempts were made to build up the defence forces to resist any invaders. The army was raised from 19,000 to 42,000 men. A **Local Defence Force** (LDF) was set up to supplement it and it soon had 148,000 men. An **air corps** and a **marine service** were started, and fishermen and amateur yachtsmen formed a **coastal patrol** to watch for signs of invasion.

But these men had no decent equipment. Little had been spent on defence during the 1930s and there was no native arms industry. Until the co-operation with Britain improved in 1941, they would not supply any weapons lest they fall into German hands.

Frank Aiken, appointed Minister for Co-Ordination of Defence Measures in 1939, was sent to the United States to try to buy arms. American hostility to Irish neutrality, fostered by British diplomacy ensured that he came away empty-handed.

The defence forces remained very under-equipped throughout the emergency. And once the threat from Germany receded after the invasion of the Soviet Union in 1941, government spending on them declined once more.

The economy under pressure

Churchill might have decided against invasion but there were other pressures he could apply. In December 1940 he wrote to Roosevelt:

Now that we are denied the use of Irish ports and airfields, our difficulties strain

Irish army on manoeuvres, 1942.

our flotillas to the utmost limit .... We are so hard pressed at sea that we cannot undertake any longer to carry the 400,000 tons of feeding-stuffs and fertiliser which we have hitherto convoyed to Eire through all the attacks of the enemy.

We need the tonnage for our own supply and we do not need the food which Eire has been sending us. We must now concentrate on essentials and the Cabinet proposes to let de Valera know that we cannot go on supplying him under the present conditions. He will of course have plenty of food for his people but they will not have the prosperous trading they are making now. I am sorry about this but we must think of our own self-preservation and use for our own purpose our own tonnage brought in through so many perils. (W.S. Churchill, *The Second World War, Vol. II - Their Finest Hour*, p. 535-6)

Churchill's intentions were clear. Ninety-five per cent of Irish imports were carried in British ships. In 1941 the British, already hard-pressed to supply themselves, began to limit supplies to Ireland. Soon the effects were felt throughout the Irish economy.

- The quantity of fertiliser imported fell from 89,000 tons in 1939 to 7,000 tons in 1941 and to nil in 1942. This affected the fertility of the soil and the farmers' capacity to grow food.

- The quantity of maize for animal-feed fell in the same time from 400,000 tons to 50,000 to nil. This meant that home-grown grain had to be diverted into animal feed.

- By 1943 the country was getting only 25 per cent of its requirements of petrol, 16 per cent of its gas coal and no domestic coal. These fuel shortages hit industrial and domestic users.

- Many of the new industries set up in the 1930s depended on imported raw materials and parts. Now they were unobtainable. The factories went on short-time or closed altogether.

Lemass as Minister for Supplies

The government did what it could. **Seán Lemass** had been made **Minister for Supplies** in 1939. He organised what resources were available. In 1941, as Churchill's policy began to bite, he set up the **Irish Shipping Company**. Eight ships, most of them old, were bought and five more were chartered. In these ships brave crews kept a vital trickle of supplies coming through. Most of it was grain.

Feeding the people

Self-sufficiency in food now became essential. In 1940 every farmer was ordered to till one-eighth of his land. This was raised to three-eighths in 1944. The area under wheat rose from 250,000 acres in 1939 to 660,000 in 1945. But without fertilisers the productivity of the land was reduced and the yield did not keep pace with the growth in acreage.

Strict rationing spread the available supplies with some appearance of fairness, though there was a black market for those who could afford it. Each person got a ration of 2 lb of sugar and 2 oz of tea (later reduced to 1 oz) per week. Clothes and bread were also rationed.

Despite shortages, basic foodstuffs like eggs, potatoes, meat and bacon were available. Many people added to their rations by growing vegetables and potatoes and keeping chickens in their gardens. The most often heard complaint was that brown bread had replaced the more wasteful white. At a time when many in Europe were starving, this was a small hardship to bear.

Fuel shortages

Fuel for power and heat was a major problem. Coal was very scarce, so gas and electricity were available for only a few hours each day. Turf was offered as a substitute for coal but without a great deal of success. Turf-burning trains could take up to twelve hours to travel from Dublin to Cork and many city dwellers had difficulty adapting to the use of turf.

Social effects of the war

Difficulties in industry pushed unemployment up. Many of those out of work went

The man responsible for keeping supplies at a minimum was Seán Lemass. Here he sets an example of conserving petrol.

to Britain, where the armaments industry or the armed forces absorbed an average of 18,000 Irish emigrants each year of the war.

The living standards of those who stayed at home fell. Inflation caused prices to rise by 70 per cent between 1939 and 1944 with the biggest increases in fuel and clothes. Wages were kept down by the government's **Wages Standstill Order** and rose only by 13 per cent in the same period. This caused hardship for poor wage earners. It is seen in a fall in living standards and a rise in diseases such as TB which were made worse by lack of heating and food.

Ireland and the British market

Churchill's letter illustrates a belief, widely held in Britain, that the Irish were making a fortune supplying food to the British market. This was far from the truth. The British government, remembering the profiteering which went on during World War I, strictly controlled the price paid for imported food and protected the British farmers from competition.

In 1944 food prices in Britain were lower than they had been in 1939, and lower than they were in Ireland. Irish consumers were actually subsidising the food being sold to Britain. Irish farmers, already damaged by the economic war, were further hit by an outbreak of foot-and-mouth disease in 1941. They gained little from the war and were further impoverished by their inability to buy fertilisers.

The war caused the Irish economy to stagnate. Only the fact that there was almost nothing for Ireland to buy abroad, enabled the country to maintain a favourable balance of trade.

Attitudes towards the war

Despite the economic hardships, neutrality was popular. While some approved of it because it proved Irish independence, most valued it because it saved them from the devastation of war. A few scattered bombs and one raid on Dublin, when twenty-seven people died, were the only direct effect on the country. People had only to think of the devastation of Belfast (see pages 455 & 456) and many British cities, to know the advantages of being neutral.

Neutrality was supported by all political parties. Only **James Dillon** of Fine Gael publicly attacked neutrality and demanded that Ireland join the fight against the evils of Nazism. But he won no supporters and was expelled from his party.

Even within the former unionist community there were many who supported Irish neutrality, even while they backed the British war effort. This helped to strengthen national unity but the wounds of the civil war were still too deep to allow de Valera to suggest a National Government to deal with the emergency as happened in other countries.

The 1943 election

Despite the popularity of its foreign policy, however, Fianna Fáil lost ten seats in the 1943 general election, probably because of the severe economic situation. But Fine Gael was unable to benefit from this, possibly because it was associated in people's minds with a pro-British stance. It lost fifteen seats and seemed on the way to extinction. The main beneficiaries were the Labour party and a newly established farmers' party, **Clann na Talmhan**. (see page 386)

A bomb crater at the North Strand, Dublin.

United States pressure

When the US finally entered the war in December 1941 they were more hostile to Irish neutrality than the British had been. David Gray encouraged Roosevelt to increase the pressure on the Irish economy. Churchill took the opportunity to renew his offer of unity but it was so vaguely phrased that de Valera was not tempted.

A pro-allied neutrality

The government kept up the public image of strict neutrality. Early in 1942 de Valera even protested to Roosevelt about the stationing of American troops in the North. But behind the scenes, Irish policy favoured the allies.

- Ireland was a useful source of food and manpower for Britain. About 60,000 people from the South served in the British forces and twice that number worked in British munitions factories.

- The Irish authorities turned a blind eye to allied planes overflying Irish air-space.

- Weather reports were secretly transmitted to the allies.

- Allied sailors and airmen wrecked in Ireland were allowed to slip North, while Germans were interned.

- Co-operation between the Irish and British armies increased in 1941, when there were renewed fears of a German invasion. Military supplies were sent South to help repel a German landing and plans were drawn up by senior officers from both forces for joint operations.

- The Americans were included in this co-operation after the US entered the war. In 1945 the Pentagon recommended that three senior Irish army officers be given the American Legion of Merit for 'exceptionally meritorious and outstanding services to the US' in 1943-45. (R. Fanning, *Independent Ireland*, p. 124) The proposal was dropped when it was pointed out that this would embarrass the Irish government.

All this co-operation was kept very secret. Even the British and American Ministers in Dublin and most members of the allied governments were unaware of what was going on. On the surface, Ireland was neutral to the end.

1943-45: the last years of the war

In 1943 the tide of war turned in favour of the allies. British and American pressure on Ireland to come out publicly on the allied side, increased. Popular opinion in both countries believed that Dublin, which contained German, Italian and Japanese diplomats, was a hotbed of spies.

In 1944 plans were being drawn up for the Normandy landings. The allied leadership decided to prevent a possible leak. An 'American note' was presented to de Valera, demanding that the German and Japanese legations be closed. 'Of course the

◆

answer will be no', de Valera told David Gray, who delivered the note. 'As long as I am here, it will be no'.

The refusal led to a total blackout of communications out of Ireland and a ban on travel to and from Britain until after D-Day. De Valera, however, seized the chance to call a snap election and the apparent threat to neutrality led to an increase in his support. Fianna Fáil regained nine of the ten seats lost the year before.

By then it was clear that the allies were winning. Neutrality no longer had any practical advantages. But de Valera could not have abandoned it without considerable loss of national face. This stubborn determination to retain the appearance of even-handedness to the end probably explains his actions in April 1945.

On 12 April, when the US president Franklin Roosevelt died, he called formally on the American Minister to express his regret. On 30 April, against the advice of his officials, he paid a similar call on the German Minister to express regret at the death of the German head of state, Adolf Hitler.

The effects of neutrality

The war had a profound effect on the twenty-six counties. The rationing, the economic dislocation and the suffering caused by the bombing of Dublin, small though these were compared with the ordeal of the rest of Europe, drew people together. So did their pride in maintaining neutrality to the end in the face of immense pressure.

The extent of this pressure was made clear in a public exchange between Churchill and de Valera in May 1945. Speaking in a victory broadcast, Churchill praised Britain's restraint in not laying:

> a violent hand upon Ireland, though at times it would have been quite easy and quite natural.

De Valera's reply, a few days later, was dignified and restrained. He congratulated Churchill on not adding 'another horrid chapter to the already bloodstained record' of Anglo-Irish relations and asked:

> could he not find in his heart the generosity to acknowledge that there is a small nation that stood alone, not for one year or two, but for several hundred years against aggression ... a small nation that could never be got to accept defeat and has never surrendered her soul? (Longford and O'Neill, *De Valera*, p. 414)

This speech touched a chord, even among those people who were de Valera's political enemies. At that moment he spoke for all. The war was over. The test that was neutrality had been successfully passed.

Assessing neutrality

Why was Ireland able to remain neutral when so many other countries were not?

De Valera replying to Churchill.

Irish people liked to claim that the readiness of the defence forces to fight was a factor but this is unlikely. Even well-equipped armies fell to more powerful neighbours between 1939 and 1945 and the Irish army was not well-equipped. None of the major belligerents would have had any difficulty in taking us over.

The real reason, though few Irish people were willing to admit it, was geographical. The ruthless totalitarian regimes of Hitler and Stalin were well out of reach on the other side of Britain. The Germans would have found it difficult to reach us unless Britain fell and it did not.

The two countries which could have invaded us easily were Britain and the United States. As democracies, both were restrained by their public opinion from attacking a neutral country unless the situation was desperate. Fortunately for neutral Ireland, it never was.

Chapter 32

1945-51: Post-war change

A post-war generation

In the 1940s the first post-independence generation of Irish people came to maturity. Young men and women, born since 1922, were bored by the quarrels of the civil war parties. Arguments over the Treaty had no meaning for them. Irish independence was a fact, as wartime neutrality had shown. Commonwealth membership was so curtailed by de Valera's policies in the thirties that it no longer mattered.

Among nationalist issues, only partition still seemed worth thinking about. But many believed it was important to tackle the grave social and economic ills in southern society before worrying about that.

The dominance of Fianna Fáil

But in 1945 the existing political parties offered little to these young people. Fianna Fáil which had been in office since 1932 was dominated by the charismatic figure of de Valera. All his ministers were veterans of the Anglo-Irish conflict and of the civil war. They seemed unlikely to be displaced and as long as they remained, the old issues would live on.

By 1945 Fianna Fáil seemed stronger than ever.

- Many people had an intense personal loyalty to 'Dev' which dated back to 1917.

- It was the only party with a national organisation and a secure financial basis.

- It alone drew support from a wide cross-section of society. In its early years it had drawn votes from workers in the towns and small farmers in the west. But after entering office in 1932, it adopted policies that suited businessmen and bigger farmers. After their initial hostility, many of them had switched their allegiance from Fine Gael to Fianna Fáil.

Fine Gael

Fine Gael, although the biggest opposition party, was in poor shape in 1945. It had been badly weakened by the Blueshirt episode in the thirties. In the war, some members were lukewarm about neutrality, arguing that fascism was an evil that should be fought. These were not popular policies and the party had lost seats steadily since 1932. (see Table A)

In 1944 W.T. Cosgrave resigned and Richard Mulcahy took over the leadership. Fine Gael lacked a central organisation and had no satisfactory means of raising money. Because of this its TDs tended to be wealthy business or professional men who were only part-time politicians.

The Labour party

In the early forties, it looked as if the Labour party was about to replace Fine Gael as the main opposition party. In the 1943 election Labour won 15 per cent of the vote and seventeen seats. (see Table A) This was its biggest total since 1927. The extra votes came mainly from Dublin workers who were badly hit by war-time shortages and rationing.

But Labour's old quarrel returned to haunt it. James Larkin was one of the newly-elected Labour TDs. William O'Brien, who hated Larkin, was bitterly resentful.

In 1944 he and five TDs left the party and founded the **National Labour Party**. O'Brien also withdrew the Irish Transport and General Workers Union from the Irish Trade Union Congress and set up a separate congress. To cover the personal nature of the quarrel, O'Brien accused Labour of being communist dominated. A 'red scare' followed, well supported by some Catholic newspapers.

The split damaged the Labour party. When de Valera called a snap election in 1944, it got only 8.8 per cent of the vote and eight seats. National Labour won four seats. The split in the party healed after Larkin died in 1947 but the split in the wider labour movement remained until the 1960s.

Farmer discontent and Clann na Talmhan

Although many small western farmers supported Fianna Fáil in the early 1930s, some grew disillusioned as the economic war took its toll of them. In 1938 a group of them met in Athenry, Co. Galway to found **Clann na Talmhan**.

Led by **Michael Donnellan**, the party got most support in Galway, Mayo and Roscommon. In its first election in 1943 it won fourteen seats, drawing support away equally from the two main parties. But it lacked a clear policy and a central organisation and never spread outside its main area.

Clann na Poblachta

Though Fianna Fáil won in 1944, there was still a lot of discontent with its economic

Results of elections, 1937-44							
	Total	F.F.	F.G	Lab.	Ind.	Clann na Talmhan	Nat. Lab.
1937	138	69	48	13	8	–	–
1938	138	77	45	9	7	–	–
1943	138	67	32	17	8	14	–
1944	138	76	30	8	9	11	4

Table A ▲

policies. In the June 1945 presidential election, the party's **Seán T. O'Kelly** won but by a smaller vote than expected. When the war ended a new party emerged which appealed to the disillusioned young urban voters. It was called **Clann na Poblachta**.

Seán MacBride

The founder of the new party was **Seán MacBride**, son of the executed 1916 hero John MacBride and of Maud Gonne, a prominent supporter of the republican cause. As a student, MacBride opposed the Treaty, fought in the civil war and remained in Sinn Féin after de Valera left it. He wanted it to adopt socialist policies and had supported Saor Éire.

From 1936 to 1938 he was Chief of Staff of the IRA but quarrelled with the other leaders and left in 1939 when it began a bombing campaign in England. He became a barrister and defended many republicans arrested during the war.

Like de Valera before him, MacBride now turned to constitutional politics. In 1946 he set up **Clann na Poblachta**. It drew support from republicans who had lost hope of achieving anything through violence. But the new party also attracted young people who were weary of the old nationalist policies and wanted more concern for social issues.

The desire for a new way

After the war a desire for change was widespread throughout Europe.

* People saw with horror the ruin that nationalist hatred had inflicted on Europe. They committed themselves to replacing international competition with international co-operation.

Seán MacBride

◆

- They blamed the social evils of unemployment, bad housing, poverty and disease for the rise of fascism and communism in the 1930s. They wanted to remove these evils.

People inspired by these dreams swept the British Labour party to power in 1945 and began to build the welfare state. They also started the process of international co-operation that led old enemies like France and Germany to work together in setting up the European Community in the 1950s.

This new mood influenced people in Ireland. Many of them joined Clann na Poblachta, which seemed to offer a way out of the sterile hatreds of the civil war parties. The new party grew rapidly in 1947.

Economic difficulties

In 1945 and 1946, the country faced major economic difficulties.

- Farmers had fed the country and exported to Britain, but since no fertilisers were available, the land had become exhausted. Productivity declined sharply.

- The war had starved factories of fuel, raw materials and replacements for worn-out machinery. By 1945 many had closed and the rest were barely surviving on short-time work.

- Stringent laws had kept wages low even as prices rose. This left low-paid workers in a bad way. They were often unable to afford the bare necessities. Disease rates, which had declined in the 1930s, began to rise again, a sure sign of bad living conditions.

1945-47: difficult readjustment

Once the war ended, the economy had to readjust and this caused problems.

- People rushed to buy goods as soon as they became available. This led to inflation. Since many of these goods were imported, there was also a balance of payments problem (more goods being imported than exported) .

- Workers tried to improve wages and this caused strikes. A particularly damaging one was by the **Irish National Teachers' Organisation**. Lemass set up the **Labour Court** to act as an arbitrator and it achieved some success in creating industrial peace.

- The weather added to the woes of the country. The wet summer of 1946 produced a poor harvest and forced the government to cut the bread ration. It was followed by the coldest winter of the century, when fuel for heating was almost unobtainable. Industry and transport nearly came to a standstill. People felt they were worse off than during the war, when at least there was a reason for their misery.

- In 1946 there were allegations that de Valera, Lemass and other prominent members of Fianna Fáil were involved in bribery and corruption in the sale of a distillery. A Tribunal was set up and they were completely cleared. Despite this, the case inevitably raised questions in the public's mind.

February 1948: a snap election

As a result of all these developments, discontent with Fianna Fáil grew. Clann na Poblachta benefited, winning several by-elections in 1947. De Valera, seeing this, decided to call a snap election in February 1948. He hoped to catch Clann na Poblachta off balance before it had time to develop a national organisation.

The results of the 1948 election							
Total	F.F.	F.G.	Lab.	C. na P.	C. na T.	Ind.	Nat. Lab.
147	68	31	14	10	7	12	5

Table B ▲

His tactic succeeded. Clann na Poblachta won only ten seats, far fewer than expected. And though Fianna Fáil lost eight seats, it still remained by far the biggest party in the Dáil. (see Table B)

Forming a coalition

Facing it was a motley collection of parties.

- There was the conservative Fine Gael, the party of big farmers, lucky to have thirty-one seats.

- There were two Labour parties, deeply hostile to one another, with nineteen seats between them.

- The small farmers of Clann na Talmhan had elected seven TDs.

- The republicans and socialists of Clann na Poblachta had ten.

- There were also twelve Independents.

It seemed inconceivable that they could join together to oust the mighty Fianna Fáil. And yet they did. A shared dislike of de Valera and Fianna Fáil overcame all other difficulties. After hurried negotiations, the first Coalition government in Irish history was formed.

As the biggest partner in it, Fine Gael was to provide the Taoiseach, but republicans, like MacBride, refused to serve under Richard Mulcahy because of his civil war record. As a result, **John A. Costello**, who had been Attorney General in the last Cumann na nGaedheal government, became Taoiseach. **Mulcahy** unselfishly stood aside, becoming Minister for Education.

William Norton, the Labour leader, became Tánaiste and Minister for Social Welfare. **Seán MacBride**, whose vital ten votes made the Coalition possible, became Minister for External Affairs. Clann na Poblachta was given a second ministry and MacBride appointed a young newly-elected TD, **Noel Browne**, as Minister for Health.

The new government looked weak and unlikely to last. It contained an uneasy blend of old and young, of republicans and free staters, of conservatives and socialists. In practice, however, it worked well. Costello was an excellent Taoiseach. He gave each minister a good deal of freedom to pursue his own policies. In several areas, the Coalition was very successful.

September 1948: Costello and Commonwealth membership
One issue which might have caused tensions in a Coalition composed of former free staters and ardent republicans was relations with Britain. But in fact no problems arose.

During the election campaign MacBride and Clan na Poblachta had promised to repeal the 1936 **External Relations Act** which was the last link binding Ireland to the British Commonwealth. They did not make an issue of it when joining the Coalition but both Costello and the Labour leader, Norton, shared a dislike of the Act.

In the summer of 1948 the Cabinet discussed repealing the Act but no firm decision was taken. In September Costello went on an official visit to Canada. There a reporter asked him about a report on these discussions which had appeared in the *Sunday Independent*. In reply, he publicly announced that the government intended to repeal the External Relations Act and declare a republic.

John A. Costello

1948-9: the British response

This announcement took the British Labour government by surprise. They had not been consulted about the decision, which finally took Ireland out of the Commonwealth. They were angry, but fearing they would lose the support of other Commonwealth states, they decided to make the best of things.

In 1949 the Westminster parliament passed the **Ireland Act**. Under it, Irish citizens would continue to enjoy the same rights and privileges as British citizens and could travel freely to Britain. But the Act also guaranteed that the status of Northern Ireland could not be changed except with the consent of the parliament of Northern Ireland. (see page 463) This was a fuller guarantee to Ulster unionists than any they had previously enjoyed from a British government.

1949: the Republic declared

At Easter 1949 the Republic of Ireland was formally proclaimed. Ireland at last cut the few tenuous links which had bound her to the British Commonwealth. This changed nothing of the reality of independence which had existed since 1937-38. But it did mark a final end to the old quarrel over the Treaty. The question of Irish independence was finally laid to rest. Costello expressed the hope that its removal would take the gun out of Irish politics.

Campaigning against partition

This left partition as the only outstanding national issue. The Coalition was dismayed by the Ireland Act. Like most republicans, they believed that the separate existence of Northern Ireland was based on the will of the British government rather than on the

Seán T. O'Kelly, second President of Ireland, 1945-59

will of the unionist majority. As a result, they concentrated on persuading the British to leave. This dominated their foreign policy and was actively supported from the opposition benches by de Valera.

At foreign conferences, whether it was appropriate or not, Irish delegates spoke about the 'evils of partition'. They often embarrassed and irritated other delegations who had more important things to worry about. In addition, their campaign had no effect whatsoever on the unionist government of Northern Ireland.

Neutrality

In 1948, as the Cold War intensified, the US formed the **North Atlantic Treaty Organisation** (NATO) to resist Soviet aggression. Ireland was invited to join.

MacBride, as Minister for External Affairs, refused, because it would have involved recognising Northern Ireland. But he made it clear that this did not indicate that Ireland was neutral between the United States and the Soviet Union. Catholic Ireland, he asserted, was totally hostile to atheistic communism.

In 1950 he offered to form a bi-lateral (two-sided) alliance with the United States to fight against the advance of Stalin's legions. The US refused the offer and Ireland remained outside the military alliance that drew much of Western Europe together during the Cold War.

Joining other organisations

Ireland was eager to join other international institutions which sprang up in the 1940s. In 1945 de Valera had applied to join the **United Nations** which had replaced the League. The Russians vetoed the application until a deal was worked out with the US in 1955. Ireland did, however, work with UN specialist agencies such as the **Food and Agricultural Organisation.**

From the start, Ireland was involved in the emerging European organisations. We joined the **Organisation for European Economic Co-Operation** (OEEC) and the **Council of Europe** (1949) as founder members.

American Marshall Aid to help the recovery of war-torn Europe and to build up an American sphere of influence, was channelled through the OEEC. As a firmly anti-communist country, Ireland shared in this aid, getting £36 million but as a former neutral country, most of it was in the form of a loan, not a grant. A great deal of this money was spent on land drainage in the west, and on the development of forestry, electricity and telephones.

The first moves towards European economic co-operation grew from these organisations, but Britain did not join in because of its empire and its 'special relationship' with the US. Ireland's heavy dependence on trade with Britain to which over 90 per cent of our exports went, meant that we too had to stay outside European economic co-operation in its early days.

Social policy

The development of the welfare state in Britain in the 1940s aroused admiration in Ireland and inspired some Irish politicians to expand the social services here.

Housing

House building had almost stopped during the war, and in 1946 it was estimated that 110,000 houses were needed just to meet immediate requirements. By the time the Coalition took power, cement and other necessary supplies were available.

T.J. Murphy, the Minister responsible, tackled the problem with energy, persuading the banks to make capital available. In 1951 12,000 houses were built, almost ten times the rate in 1945. At the same time, existing houses were improved, with more of them getting sewage and running water. As a result, there was a steady rise in the standard of housing around the country.

Dublin and other cities had the biggest housing problems with many city centre slums still in existence. New suburbs were built and the cities expanded in area. People also began to move in from the country and this kept the demand for new houses ahead of supply.

Rural electrification

Immediately after the war Fianna Fáil began a massive programme of rural electrification. It hoped that a supply of cheap power would make farmers more efficient. Continued by the Coalition, the programme was successful and in a little over a decade, brought electricity to the remotest parts of the country.

A modern view of corporation houses built in Dublin in the 1950s.

At first, people only used electricity for lighting. Soon, however, they came to see its value for cooking, pumping water, milking cows and a dozen other jobs which had once involved enormous manual labour. Electrification caused a quiet revolution in the lives of farming people and especially in the lives of the women on whose shoulders many of these tasks had fallen.

Health care

The provision of health care also received more attention after the war. In the early 1940s public health had become a major cause of concern.

Tuberculosis

Tuberculosis (TB) was the main killer disease and it was getting worse. Each year between 3,000 and 4,000 people, most of them in their twenties, died of TB. Poverty, malnutrition and bad housing all contributed to the disease and war-time shortages, made the situation worse. Deaths from TB rose from 109 per 100,000 in 1938 to 147 per 100,000 in 1942.

An inadequate health service

People blamed the inadequate medical services. They had hardly changed since independence. The third of the population who could not afford to pay for medical care were to be treated under the nineteenth-century Poor Law system.

- Over 600 dispensary doctors, spread all over the country, provided them with free medical care. Often the care was poor and the facilities in which it was dispensed even worse.

- Local officials decided who was entitled to this service and their probing means-test was humiliating for those seeking help.

- Local authorities provided a free hospital service, paid for by the rates. But the amount spent on hospitals and their number and quality varied enormously from place to place. Many dated back to the nineteenth century and were very grim places indeed.

Middle-income people had to pay for their own medical care. Many of them subscribed to the **National Health Insurance Society** which provided cash benefits in the case of sickness, disability or maternity. Some help was given from central funds for the treatment of TB, but most public health care was paid for by local rates or by charities. The **Hospitals Sweeps Trust**, based on a lottery, was founded to provide cash for hospital buildings, but only a proportion of its funds were allocated to this.

Fianna Fáil improvements

The Beverage Report in Britain, recommending a free health service, influenced opinion in Ireland. After the war, Fianna Fáil began to reorganise the service. In 1947 it set up a separate **Department of Health** and passed a **Health Act**. The Act proposed free medical care for all mothers and children up to the age of sixteen regardless of income.

The doctors and the Catholic bishops objected (see page 433) but Fianna Fáil fell from power before the Act came into effect. The problem then passed to the young Coalition Minister, **Noel Browne**.

Noel Browne

Browne came from a poor family, three of whom had died of TB. He qualified as a doctor and grew frustrated at the inadequacies of the health service. Joining Clann na Poblachta, he was elected a TD in 1948. MacBride appointed him Minister for Health on his first day in the Dáil. He reorganised the provision of health insurance for the middle-classes and made the benefits more generous. He used £20 million from the Hospitals Sweeps Trust and borrowed a further £10 million to speed up the building of hospitals around the country. But he is best remembered for his attack on TB.

- Free mass X-rays were used to identify TB sufferers.

- They were given free hospital treatment and their dependents were supported while they were in hospital.

- New drugs like penicillin and the BCG vaccine were used to treat them.

The results were dramatic. By 1957 the incidence of TB was down to twenty-four per 100,000 and it continued to fall until it had almost disappeared by the 1970s.

Noel Browne

The 'Mother and Child Scheme'

In 1950 Browne started to put the parts of the Fianna Fáil Health Act which related to mothers and children into effect.

Like TB, infant mortality was made worse by poverty and malnutrition. It had fallen in the 1920s and 1930s but began to rise again during the war. In 1939 sixty-six babies in every 1,000 born had died in their first year of life; by 1943 the number of deaths had increased to eighty-three per 1,000. Mothers also suffered. Almost 100 women died in childbirth each year. The worst affected were the poor who were unable to afford medical care or adequate nutrition.

Opposing the scheme

The Health Act would have given free health care to all mothers and children up to the age of sixteen regardless of income. However, it immediately ran into opposition from two sources.

- Irish doctors, like doctors in Britain, feared that free state medical care would reduce their income. They were also worried that the state would interfere between patient and doctor. They opposed the 'Mother and Child Scheme' on the grounds that it was free to all and that patients would not be allowed to choose their doctor.

- The Catholic bishops also attacked the scheme. They opposed a state maternity service. It seemed to them a dangerously communistic idea and they feared it might encourage birth control or abortion. They had made their views clear to de Valera in 1947 and in 1950-51 they repeated them to Browne. (for a fuller account see pages 433 & 434)

    Parents, they argued, had a moral duty to provide for the health of their children if they could afford to do so. But in their opinion, only 10 per cent of Irish parents were poor enough to need state help. They also worried that it was unjust to doctors to displace their private medical practice with a state system.

The defeat of Browne

Browne met the bishops and thought he had satisfied them. But he was wrong. Meanwhile he was also losing the support of his Cabinet colleagues. He had quarrelled with MacBride, and had neglected to get the Cabinet to approve of his policies. Some ministers shared the doctors' dislike of the Health Act but Browne did nothing to win them over.

In March 1951, when the bishops again stated their objections, the Cabinet would not back Browne. He refused to compromise and, on 11 April, MacBride demanded his resignation. Other Clann na Poblachta TDs followed him out of the Coalition.

Browne at once published his exchange of letters with the bishops, MacBride and Costello. This was a revolutionary act. Up to this, the bishops had communicated their wishes secretly to the government and mostly they got their way. By publishing the letters, Browne showed up the extent of their influence. The row which followed had a deep impact on relations between the Catholic Church and the Irish state. The bishops won this battle, but in future they had to be more subtle in the ways they applied pressure on the government.

The fall of the Coalition

The 'Mother and Child' affair caused a widespread debate. Some, especially in Northern Ireland concluded that the Republic was a priest-ridden society. But outside of Dublin, Browne had little public support and the affair did not destroy the Coalition.

However, it did face other problems. Prices were rising, a balance of payments crisis loomed (see page 401), and two farmer TDs withdrew support in a row over the price of milk. All of these developments led Costello to call a general election in May 1951.

The results of the 1951 election						
Total	F.F.	F.G.	Lab.	C. na P.	C. na T.	Ind.
147	69	40	16	2	6	14

Table C ▲

The results

The election result was indecisive. The Coalition parties had mixed fortunes. Clann na Poblachta was shattered. Without Browne's support, it was reduced to two seats. He and two supporters were elected as Independent TDs. The real winner was Fine Gael which went up to forty seats. This reversed the decline of the party that had lasted since 1932.

Although Fianna Fáil increased its share of the vote, it gained only one more seat. This was mainly because voters in the Coalition parties transferred their lower preference votes to their Coalition partners rather than to Fianna Fáil.

This showed that the idea of a coalition of other parties as an alternative to Fianna Fáil had taken root. From then on, coalitions of Fine Gael, Labour and perhaps other parties, alternating with Fianna Fáil, became the normal pattern of Irish politics until the late 1980s.

Fianna Fáil had not won enough seats to govern alone in 1951. But de Valera was able to form a minority government with the support of Noel Browne and two other former Clann na Poblachta TDs.

Chapter 33

1945-66: The post-war economy

A new agenda

In the 1940s Irish political debate underwent a fundamental change. Ever since Parnell's time the main issue before the voters in elections had been national independence. Up to 1918 it was Home rule versus the Union. After 1921 it was the Treaty and the amount of independence it conferred.

But in the 1930s de Valera had dismantled the Treaty and removed the remaining signs of British influence. When Ireland remained neutral during the war, it was clear that full independence had been achieved. The declaration of the republic in 1949 merely set the seal on what was already a fact. The country was completely independent of Britain.

This removed the old nationalist issues from politics. Voters were no longer interested in the old catch cries. At election time now they wanted to know:

- how the parties planned to manage the economy.

- what they proposed to do about unemployment and emigration.

- what their policies were on social issues such as health, welfare and housing.

It has been argued that the 1948 election was the first one in which economic issues took precedence over national ones. Since then they have dominated the political agenda.

The post-war economy

In the twenty years after World War II, the Irish economy had very mixed fortunes. In 1945 it was experiencing difficulties, but compared with the rest of Europe it was healthy.

- During the war, agricultural exports to Britain had been maintained though the prices farmers got were kept low by British government regulations.

- These exports earned money but there were few imports available for us to spend it on.

- As a result, the country had a healthy balance of payments surplus. In 1944 external reserves stood at £103 million compared with £65 million in 1939.

- Irish industry had suffered badly from shortages of fuel and raw materials but at least it was not bombed out of existence like the industry in many other countries.

The lessons of the war

But in spite of these relative advantages, the wartime experience had not been a happy one. Hostilities had forced Fianna Fáil ministers to adopt in deadly earnest the very policy of self-sufficiency that they had talked about in the thirties. They had discovered that self-sufficiency did not work. The country had been fed, but not from its own resources. Grain imports continued throughout the war, and the new industries suffered from severe shortages of raw materials and spare parts.

As the war drew to a close, there was another problem of which the government was very aware. Many thousands of people emigrated to Britain during the war. If World War II were followed by a depression similar to that which followed World War I and the emigrants returned home, how would the country cope?

By 1943 these problems led some civil servants and some politicians like Seán Lemass to think about the need for a new economic policy after the war.

Keynesian economics

The ideas they drew on were those of the English economist, **John Maynard Keynes**. He had proposed a number of ways of avoiding another post-war depression.

- Governments must plan the economy in a general way by setting targets for various economic sectors.

- Governments must spend money to create jobs. Those in work would then spend their wages and this would encourage further growth.

- Protection must end and free trade between nations should become the norm.

Post-war plans

Clearly, this would involve a new approach by the Irish government. Although Fianna Fáil had interfered in the economy in the 1930s, it had done so in an unsystematic and unplanned way. The wartime difficulties had given them some experience of planning, so in 1943 and 1944 they began to prepare for the post-war conditions.

Post-war development

They concentrated on government spending. Plans were drawn up for major state investment in the infrastructure. As raw materials became available after 1947 and as the money from the Marshall Aid flowed in after 1948 both Fianna Fáil and the Coalition spent heavily on housing, hospitals, roads, rural electrification and other public services. (see chapter 32)

This created a modest boom. Jobs on building sites poured money into the economy. Between 1948 and 1951 it grew by 5 per cent. Unemployment and emigration fell and in 1951 the census showed the first rise in population since the famine.

But there was an underlying problem about this government investment. It was not productive. Once a hospital or a house was built, that was the end of it. The investment ceased to earn a return for the government. The money might have been better spent on factories which would have led to continuing jobs.

The failure to plan and adapt

Government spending was the only aspect of the Keynesian programme the two governments adopted. Senior politicians and civil servants, in office since the twenties and thirties, still thought in the old ways and failed to take economic planning seriously.

This was not for want of advice. When Ireland became involved in the Organisation for European Economic Co-operation (OEEC) through which American Marshall Aid was distributed, they were required to submit a plan showing how they proposed to use the funds. The plan, published in January 1949 as the **Long Term Recovery Programme**, was totally inadequate. Most of the Marshall Aid money was also invested in long-term items like land drainage and re-afforestation.

At the same time, outside economic experts advised that the economy be re-directed away from its over-dependence on agriculture and on protection of

ESB generating station, Ferbane, Co. Offaly. Rural electrification revolutionised the Irish countryside.

industry. But this advice was not taken. Too many vested interests (those who would lose out from any change) were involved and no government had the courage to take them on.

The Coalition did set up the **Industrial Development Authority** in 1949 to encourage foreign industry to set up here and **Coras Trachtála** in 1951 to encourage exports, but they were hedged around by conditions. The IDA could only give concessions to industries setting up in remote west-coast areas. Industry starting elsewhere had to obtain a government licence if it was foreign owned. In these circumstances, American multi-national companies which were investing elsewhere in Europe, passed Ireland by.

1951: the balance of payments crisis

The consequences of this failure to adopt new policies became apparent in 1951. The prosperity of the three preceding years, with more jobs and more money in circulation, led to a consumer boom. People spent their wages on imported luxuries like cars, radios and nylon stockings. These imports had to be paid for but the country was not exporting enough to meet the bill.

Depending on agriculture

The problem lay in agriculture. Since independence, all Irish governments had assumed that agricultural exports to Britain would pay for any imports the country needed. No one thought in terms of exporting industrial goods. The factories set up in the thirties were intended to supply the home market, not to export their produce, which was often over-priced and of poor quality.

After the war these assumptions continued. In 1948 the Irish and British governments signed an agricultural agreement increasing the Irish quota of poultry and eggs going to Britain, and much of the Marshall Aid money was spent to improve agriculture.

Changing patterns of trade

But the outside world, with which Ireland had to do business, changed dramatically after 1945.

- The British government, alarmed by how near the country had been to starvation during the war, subsidised its own farmers. They began to produce poultry and pigs in great numbers. Irish pig and poultry producers could not compete with the protected British produce and the market for these items collapsed.

- Irish butter faced heavy competition from Dutch and Danish butter and only held a share in the British market because the government subsidised it heavily.

- Only exports of live cattle remained buoyant.

These developments cut the earnings from agricultural exports. They were now insufficient to pay for imports and in 1951 a balance-of-payments deficit emerged. The election was called before the situation became acute and the newly elected Fianna Fáil government was left to cope with it.

1951-54: a Fianna Fáil minority government
It was a minority government formed with the help of former Clann na Poblachta TDs. The same men who had led Fianna Fáil since it was founded returned again as ministers. De Valera was Taoiseach, Seán MacEntee, Minister for Finance and Seán Lemass, Minister for Industry and Commerce.

With the exception of Lemass, these men and the civil servants who advised them, had not grasped how much the world had changed since the war. Lemass favoured a new economic policy but he was unable to persuade his colleagues in the party to support him. In Cabinet, de Valera, whose decision was all important, sided with the more conservative ministers, especially with the Minister for Finance, Seán MacEntee.

MacEntee felt it was vital to deal with the balance of payments deficit. He brought in a harsh budget which raised income tax and tariffs on imports. The idea was to cut spending and so reduce imports. It achieved its immediate aim but at the cost of jobs. Unemployment went up sharply. MacEntee then made the situation worse by retaining the increases through 1952 and 1953.

De Valera did have one small triumph in 1951. He persuaded the Catholic bishops to accept the Mother and Child scheme by making some fairly minor alterations. Otherwise Fianna Fáil achieved little. A recent historian has commented that this 'has strong claims to be the worst de Valera government... Neither new men nor new ideas emerged'. (J.J. Lee, *Ireland, 1912-1985* p. 321)

In May 1954, as unemployment grew, the government fell. De Valera called another election. This campaign, like that of 1951, was dominated by economic issues.

1954-57: the Second Coalition
The outcome was disappointing for Fianna Fáil, which lost four seats. Fine Gael did well, winning ten extra seats. This was their best result since 1932. Costello now formed a second Coalition with Labour and the remaining Clann na Talmhan TDs. Clann na Poblachta TDs were not in the Coalition but gave it their general backing.

Costello appointed **Gerard Sweetman** as Minister for Finance. He found the balance of payments still in deficit and continued MacEntee's policies of import levies and higher taxes in 1955 and 1956.

The economic crisis of the fifties
Neither the Fianna Fáil government not the Second Coalition had tackled the basic economic problems of falling agricultural exports and industries too small and uncompetitive to export their produce. The result was that the Irish economy stagnated throughout the fifties.

Gerard Sweetman

- Jobs in industry, which had grown by 12,500 between 1946 and 1951, declined by 8,600 between 1951 and 1958.

- Wages fell and the gap between British and Irish wages widened.

- In agriculture, the small farmers who had depended on pigs, poultry and dairying, suffered because they could no longer sell these on the British market. Only big farmers producing beef cattle did well.

- Standards of living remained very much what they had been in the 1930s, at a time when people in Britain, and even more in western Europe, saw living standards rise faster than ever before in history.

Emigration

Emigration was the most obvious result all this. Everyone went - small farmers, no longer able to make a living on a few acres, young school-leavers, often barely literate and without hope of a job at home, industrial workers fed up with low wages, young people bored by the dullness and poverty of Irish life.

Most of them went to Britain, drawn by the prospect of full employment, decent wages and a better life-style. By the 1960s over one million people of Irish birth were working there in the jobs created by the post-war boom. Between 1950 and 1960 an average of 40,000 people emigrated each year and by 1961 the population of the republic was over 5 per cent lower than it had been at independence.

Those who went were young and active. More and more the Ireland that they left behind was a country of old people. So bad was it, that books and newspaper articles in the late fifties seriously discussed the possibility that the Irish were a vanishing race.

New economic ideas

The economic disaster of the fifties at last forced politicians and civil servants to re-examine the traditional policies. The change was helped by the arrival on the scene of younger men, unaffected by the policies of the thirties and more in tune with the way the world had developed since the war. Three men in particular were responsible for the change of direction.

- One was the Second Coalition's Minister for Finance, **Gerard Sweetman**. His budgets were conservative, still putting their emphasis on dealing with the balance of payments. But he also extended the role of the IDA and Coras Trachtála. The IDA could now encourage foreign investment anywhere in Ireland and could give grants and tax-concessions to industries that exported their produce. He also brought Ireland into the **International Monetary Fund**, thus ending its economic isolation.

- One of Sweetman's major contributions was to appoint **T.K. Whitaker** as Secretary of the Department of Finance. Up to this the Department had been deeply conservative and had pushed conservative policies on the ministers. Since the early 1950s Whitaker had been arguing for a change. In 1956 Sweetman gave him the chance to implement his ideas.

- But before Whitaker had his suggestions ready, the Coalition fell early in 1957. The election was held in the middle of a major economic crisis and the Coalition parties suffered. Fianna Fáil won seventy-eight seats, its first overall majority since the war, and de Valera, now seventy-five years old, became Taoiseach for the last time. This time he supported **Lemass**'s desire for a new approach.

T.K. Whitaker

While Fianna Fáil was in opposition from 1955 to 1957, Lemass had publicly urged them to adopt a new economic policy. The clear failure of MacEntee's earlier policy strengthened his hand. When the government was formed de Valera gave **Lemass** his old job as Minister for Industry and Commerce but he put **James Ryan**, a supporter of Lemass, into Finance in place of the conservative MacEntee.

1958: the first Programme for Economic Development

The first public sign of a new approach came in November 1958 when the government published the first **Programme for Economic Development**. It was based on a White Paper called *Economic Development* which Whitaker had drawn up. It was really a five-year plan, but because such an idea was associated with Stalin and communism, it could not be called that.

- The Programme was traditional in some ways. It stressed the importance of agriculture in the economy and talked about the need to expand production.

- But it also recognised that since the war the world had moved away from protection and towards free trade. In Ireland, too, as Whitaker recognised, 'sooner or later, protection will have to go and the challenge of free trade be accepted'.

   This would mean a major change of policy. The small inefficient industries the old policy had created would have to adapt to a more competitive environment or go under. The Programme suggested government training and grants to help them make the transition.

- The other important recommendation in the Programme was that foreign firms be given grants and tax breaks to set up in Ireland. They would provide industrial exports to balance the decline in agricultural and give workers and managers an opportunity to learn the skills needed for industrial development.

Implementing the Programme

The challenge of the Programme was taken up slowly but steadily over the next decade.

   The IDA encouraged foreign firms to set up in Ireland. At first they were mainly British companies, but later American, German and even Japanese firms were attracted with grants and tax-reliefs. These firms were all export-orientated, so that they helped to ease the balance-of-payments problems. They also provided training in technological and managerial skills for Irish people.

   Few moves to free trade took place under the first Programme. The government tried to prepare the older firms by giving them generous grants to modernise their factories and train managers and workers. Some of them made the necessary adaptations and survived into the new age; many failed to do so and collapsed.

Success

The First Programme aimed at a modest annual growth rate in gross national product (GNP) of 2 per cent. This was twice the rate of growth in the early 1950s. The actual growth achieved was 4 per cent a year up to 1963. Agriculture performed poorly so the growth was mainly in the industrial sector.

In 1963 a much more ambitious **Second Programme** was brought in. It had very detailed plans for industrial growth and put more stress on social development in areas like education. The Second Programme proved too ambitious and was abandoned in 1967. Nevertheless, between 1963 and 1967 annual growth averaged 5 per cent, the highest achieved since independence.

Looking outward

After the war, many countries tried to move away from the protection that had caused so much damage to the world economy in the 1930s. Ireland stood aside from these developments and failed to share in the economic growth which these countries enjoyed.

We began to become much more involved from the mid-1950s on. The Second Coalition brought us into the **General Agreement on Tariffs and Trade** (GATT) and the **World Bank**.

In 1961, when Britain, Ireland's main trading partner, applied to join the **European Economic Community** (the EEC), Denmark and Ireland, both heavily dependent on the British market, applied too. Although some commentators

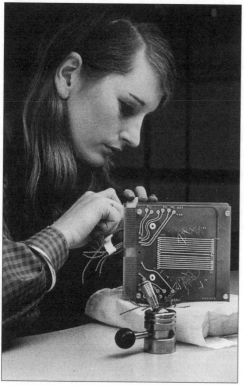

Woman working in an engineering firm in Dublin, 1960s.

wondered if the economy was yet fit for membership, Lemass was determined on full participation. The French vetoed Britain's application in 1963, and Ireland gained valuable preparation time before we were finally admitted in 1973.

Meanwhile, to reduce protection Lemass negotiated an **Anglo-Irish Free Trade Agreement** with Britain in 1965. Under this, the republic gained tariff-free access to the British market for industrial goods, while Ireland undertook to reduce tariffs on British imports by 10 per cent a year until they disappeared in 1975. Entry into the EEC in 1973 cut across this agreement.

The forces of change

The economic up-turn of the late 1950s and early 1960s came so suddenly that it seemed almost miraculous. It produced very rapid changes in Irish society as Irish people struggled to make up for lost time and catch up on the standards of living that had developed elsewhere since the war.

During the stagnant 1950s Irish society remained, on the surface at least, very much as it had been before the war. Most people still lived in rural areas or small towns and depended, directly or indirectly, on farming. Parents still exercised a good deal of control over their children and the parish priest still considered it was his duty to oversee the moral behaviour of his flock. The state itself protected society from contamination through a strict censorship of books and films. (see pages 430 & 431)

But beneath the surface, new influences were intruding. Radio and cinema let people eavesdrop on a wider world where a new popular culture challenged the old values. Young people, now beginning to think of themselves as 'teenagers', listened to the 'Top Ten' on Radio Luxemburg and rocked along with Elvis Presley. On parts of the east coast and in border areas it was possible to receive British TV stations which gave an uncensored view of another society.

A new society

These influences made many people dissatisfied with the economic and social stagnation of Irish life. They knew of the rising living standards elsewhere and wanted to share in them. In the prosperous 1960s this became possible and Irish society began to catch up on the outside world.

- Economic prosperity meant more jobs and more money to spend, but a smaller proportion of it went on food. In 1951 households spent 38 per cent of their income on food; in 1965 they spent only 32 per cent.

- People spent more on improving their houses. Carpets, fridges, electric cookers and washing machines became common. Houses were more comfortable and housework easier. More houses had running water. In 1946 only 20 per cent of houses had a bath; 57 per cent had one in 1970.

- Levels of nutrition improved and combined with better medical services to improve public health. Diseases like TB, polio and scarlet fever which had killed or maimed thousands in the forties, almost vanished due to medical advances. In 1955 seventy mothers in every 100,000 died in childbirth; by 1971 only five per 100,000 died. On the other hand, new diseases associated with affluence, such as cancer and heart attacks, were on the increase.

- The new industrial jobs were situated in towns. As a result, Irish towns began to grow for the first time since the famine, spreading new suburbs into the surrounding countryside. People continued to leave the farms but they migrated to Irish towns rather than emigrating to Britain. In some places, small farmers combined part-time farming with factory work.

- Car ownership increased as the number of cars in the country grew from 143,000 in 1958 to 330,000 in 1968. Cars often freed young people from the smothering supervision of parents and neighbours. The flocks of bicycles which were a feature of Irish cities and towns in the 1950s were replaced by traffic-jams.

Car ownership greatly increased.

Chapter 34

1959-66: The Lemass years

The old men move on

The economic and social changes of the late 1950s and early 1960s were accompanied by changes in the leadership of all the political parties. The older generation which had led the country since 1916 began to disappear and younger men began to take their place.

By 1957 several of the founders of Fianna Fáil were dead or in bad health. De Valera began to appoint newcomers, including **Jack Lynch** as Minister of Education and **Neil Blaney** as Minister for Posts and Telegraphs. In 1959 de Valera himself handed over the leadership of Fianna Fáil to Seán Lemass.

Other parties also changed their leaders about the same time. In 1959 both Richard Mulcahy and John A. Costello stepped down and **James Dillon** became leader of Fine Gael. In 1960 William Norton, who had led the Labour party since 1932, was replaced by **Brendan Corish**. Others left the scene and by 1967, only Frank Aiken, of all the early leaders of the state, still remained in office. A generation which had dominated Irish life since 1916 had moved off the stage of history.

Jack Lynch

The referendum on PR

The biggest change was undoubtedly de Valera's departure but before he resigned as Taoiseach, he wanted to do one more thing. He had become convinced that the weak governments of the 1950s were caused by the proportional representation (PR) system of election. He decided to replace it with a British style 'first past the post' voting system.

Since PR was written into the Constitution, change required a referendum, the first since the Constitution was passed. De Valera announced that it would be held on the same day as the Presidential election (17 June 1959) and that he would stand for the presidency. He hoped that by linking the immense prestige of his name to the campaign against PR he would get the voters to accept the change.

But the voters were unconvinced. After a lively debate in which the supporters of PR won most of the arguments, they decided to keep the familiar voting system. But they also elected de Valera as President by a 12 per cent margin over his opponent, another veteran of the independence struggle, Seán MacEoin.

De Valera now moved to Áras an Uachtaráin, where he served as President for a further fourteen years. There he was out of everyday politics which he had dominated for so long.

1959-66: Lemass as Taoiseach

Many in Fianna Fáil had wondered if the party could survive without de Valera, but Lemass proved an able leader. Although he was one of the founders of Fianna Fáil, he was still only fifty-nine, eighteen years younger than de Valera. His life-long interest in economics left him more in tune with the needs of the 1960s than his former leader. He devoted most of his attention to economic issues, encouraging the implementation of the Programmes for Economic Development. (see chapter 33)

Lemass continued the process of change by appointing young and able men to his government. They included **Patrick Hillery, Donogh O'Malley, Brian Lenihan** and Lemass' son-in-law, **Charles Haughey**. These men helped to implement the economic and social changes of the 1960s and were to lead Fianna Fáil over the next two decades.

One area where Lemass changed the traditional Fianna Fáil policy was in relation to Northern Ireland. Though committed to a united Ireland, he believed that unionists were more likely to be enticed into a prosperous republic than bullied into a rural Gaelic paradise.

The IRA border campaign

Up to the mid-fifties politicians had talked endlessly about the evils of partition, even if they did little about it in practice. It was a useful way of distracting the voters' attention from their economic failures. However, some people took them seriously and their rhetoric may have inspired the IRA campaign which began in 1951.

Charles Haughey

It took the form of attacks on police barracks and customs posts along the border. It was ineffectual and aroused little enthusiasm among Northern nationalists. (see page 463) On New Year's Day 1957 two young IRA men were killed attacking an RUC barracks. In the election in February Sinn Féin, the IRA's political wing, got a sympathy vote and won four seats. But the Sinn Féin TDs refused to attend the Dáil and made little impact.

Sinn Féin's electoral success did not stop de Valera from introducing internment as soon as he came to power. Over a hundred republicans were imprisoned without trial. The border campaign soon fizzled out and the IRA officially called it off in 1962. Throughout the 1960s, the IRA declined and the leadership began to move towards socialism in the hope of gaining working-class support, both North and South.

A new northern policy

After the failure of the border campaign and Lemass' accession as Taoiseach, a new Northern policy emerged. Lemass played down the old anti-partitionist line. Instead of confrontation with unionists, he proposed co-operation between the two governments on such non-political issues as tourism, hydro-electricity and fisheries.

So long as **Lord Brookeborough** was Prime Minister, he got little response. But in 1963 **Terence O'Neill**, a younger, more flexible man succeeded Brookeborough. He had met Southern ministers and officials at World Bank and IMF conferences and a friendship had developed between his secretary, **Jim Malley**, and **T.K. Whitaker**, the Secretary of the Department of Finance. As a result of these behind-the-scenes contacts, O'Neill issued an invitation to Lemass to meet him in Belfast.

411

The Lemass-O'Neill meetings

Lemass accepted and travelled to Stormont on 14 January 1965. The visit was planned in great secrecy; neither man told his Cabinet colleagues until the last minute. In the North the news had a mixed reception, but in the South the end of the cold war between the two parts of Ireland was generally welcomed.

On 9 February O'Neill paid a return visit to Lemass in Dublin. Meetings between other ministers soon followed. They discussed agricultural and trade interests. For a time it seemed as if an accommodation between the two Irish states and between the two communities within the North might be possible. Unionist resistance to change and the civil rights campaign which began in 1968 destroyed these hopes.

RTÉ

Television was one of the most important agents of change in the post-war period. Since the early fifties many Irish people on the east coast and in border areas were able to receive British programmes and this created a demand for an Irish service. In 1960 the government decided to set up **Radio Telefís Éireann** which began broadcasting on 1 January 1962.

By the mid-sixties, one in every two houses in the Republic had a TV set. Programmes, over half of which were imported from Britain or the US, opened up a whole new world to Irish people, offering them an alternative set of standards and values.

RTÉ in the 1960s.

One important result of television was to reduce the respect for authority figures. Bishops or politicians appearing on television were often subjected to questions. They had to defend their opinions in a way which would have been unthinkable for earlier generations of leaders. This change became noticeable in the 1965 election when TV first played an important part in shaping public opinion.

Changes in the Catholic Church

The Catholic Church also changed dramatically in the sixties. **Pope John XXIII** called the **Vatican Council** (1962-65) to bring the Church into the twentieth century. The Council brought about great changes in Catholic ritual and practise. But its most important effect came from its debates, which showed that bishops were far from united on many issues. The old view that the Church always spoke with a single voice was no longer sustainable.

Debates on doctrinal and social issues such as contraception, marriage and poverty became common on TV programmes like the **Late Late Show**. While the clergy debated, lay Catholics felt free to draw their own conclusions on matters which affected their lives.

This was shown clearly in the reaction to **Pope Paul VI**'s encyclical, *Humanae Vitae* (1968). It forbad Catholics to use artificial birth control. Many married Catholics, even in Ireland, decided to follow their own conscience and ignore the Pope's decision, even though the sale of contraceptives remained illegal here until the 1970s.

Ecumenical understanding

These changing attitudes affected the old divisions between Catholic and Protestant. These came to seem less important than before and the ecumenical movement made rapid strides. In 1949 at Douglas Hyde's funeral, Catholic officials stood outside St Patrick's Cathedral while the funeral service proceeded within; by 1970, joint Catholic-Protestant services were being held in parishes throughout the country.

Education

When the Programmes for Economic Development were drawn up, the need for an educated and skilled workforce was recognised. An enquiry into the education system was set up. In 1965 its report, called *Investment in Education*, was published. It painted a depressing picture of a system where almost no fundamental change had been carried out since the nineteenth century.

Primary level

- Most children, outside the towns, attended small one-or two-teacher primary schools of which 70 per cent had neither running water nor flush toilets.
- Over 60 per cent of children went no further than primary school.

- Only 26 per cent of boys and 30 per cent of girls got even the minimum qualification of a Primary Certificate (an examination taken after sixth class in primary schools).

Second level

- Most second level schools were privately owned (usually by some religious body) and fee-paying. As a result, only parents who were fairly well-off could afford to send their children to secondary schools.

- In many areas there was no day secondary school available because no one had set up a school there. This meant that only parents who could afford boarding school fees could get second level education for their children.

- Most second level education was in small, single-sex schools. Over half of them had fewer than 150 pupils and were able to offer only a very narrow range of subjects.

- While most boys and many girls studied Latin and many studied ancient Greek, only 5 per cent of boys and 12 per cent of girls learnt a modern continental language. Science was neglected with only 10 per cent of boys and very few girls studying it.

- Free second level education was available in vocational schools that were maintained by the local authorities. But these were poorly funded, offered only a limited range of subjects and were not allowed to prepare students for the Intermediate and Leaving Certificates.

The authors of *Investment in Education* argued that the education system would have to change if Ireland were to become a modern industrial society.

Educational change

Up to 1957 the job of Minister for Education was not considered very important. This changed in 1957 when de Valera appointed **Jack Lynch**. He was young, energetic and ambitious. His appointment began a trend of appointing up-and-coming young ministers to Education. Lynch was followed by Patrick Hillery and George Colley.

Under them a slow process of change began.

- Small rural primary schools were amalgamated, to improve conditions and to make better facilities available to children.

- Grants were given to build new secondary schools or expand old ones.

- In 1963 a new type of school, called a comprehensive (later community) school, was introduced to provide second-level education in new suburbs and country towns where no schools existed. Some of these schools were combinations of old secondary and vocational schools. They were usually co-educational.

• Syllabuses, which had remained unchanged since the 1920s, were revised and modernised and grants given to encourage the teaching of science.

Free education

By far the most dramatic change came in 1966. It was the personal initiative of the dynamic young Minister, **Donagh O'Malley**. Shortly after he was appointed, O'Malley announced that, from 1969, all schools up to Intermediate level would be free and that free buses would bring students from rural areas to the nearest school.

O'Malley seems to have made this decision by himself, without consulting other ministers, though he did discuss it with Lemass. Jack Lynch, who as Finance Minister had to find the money to pay for it, was dismayed. But O'Malley's announcement brought so much praise to the government that it was impossible to go back on it.

The success of the plan depended on the willingness of privately-owned schools to accept it. Over 90 per cent did, thus ensuring its success. The number of students staying on in post-primary school had doubled to 200,000 by 1970.

Access to third-level education had also been limited to those whose parents could afford the fees or who could win one of the 1,700 public scholarships. In 1949 only 6,800 students were attending university. This changed in the late sixties when the scholarship system was replaced by a system of means-tested grants which gave easier access to poor students. As a result, there were 20,500 students at university by 1972.

Foreign affairs

The fifties and sixties saw some significant developments in Irish foreign policy. In 1955 Ireland was at last admitted to the **United Nations**. When **Frank Aiken** was

Donagh O'Malley

made minister, he followed a neutral policy on Cold War issues. He backed the admission of communist China to the UN, which earned the disapproval of the United States.

One feature of this neutrality was the Irish army's participation in UN peace-keeping operations. Soldiers served in the Congo, Cyprus and the Middle East. In 1960 two battalions of 500 men were sent to avert a civil war in the Congo. In November, nine of them were killed in an ambush. No other peace-keeping mission produced so many deaths, but they gave the Irish army combat experience and foreign contacts that it might not have obtained otherwise.

Although Aiken passionately believed in Irish neutrality, Lemass was more sceptical. When he applied to join the EEC, he argued membership might involve us in a military alliance.

The closeness of Irish ties with the US was emphasised in 1960 when **John F. Kennedy** was elected as the first Irish-American Catholic to become President. Kennedy visited Ireland in 1963, amid great public celebration, and his presence

Irish UN soldiers on active duty in the Congo.

reinforced the mood of optimism which was developing. His assassination in the following year came as a severe shock to Irish opinion and President de Valera was prominent among the world leaders who attended his funeral.

Foreign travel

At a personal level, too, Irish people were getting more familiar with the outside world.

- Many went as aid workers to Third World countries.

- Far more were now enjoying continental holidays as Aer Lingus expanded its service to the continent.

- Inward tourism and foreign factories brought Irish people into more frequent contact with people from other cultures.

Political developments

The social and economic changes of the late 1950s and early 1960s had an impact on the fortunes of the political parties.

The 1961 election, the first that Fianna Fáil faced without de Valera, was fought entirely on economic issues. That party had done exceptionally well in 1957, and was bound to slip back, but Fine Gael and Labour failed to take advantage of this.

Fine Gael, now led by James Dillon, criticised the new economic policies. They argued that more attention should have been paid to farmers. But as agricultural prices were still low, this was not very convincing. Labour, under its new leader **Brendan Corish**, declared its reluctance to enter into a coalition with Fine Gael.

As a result, the voter transfers between the opposition parties which was needed to oust Fianna Fáil did not occur. Fianna Fáil lost eight seats and emerged with what Lemass called an 'overall minority of one'. With the backing of Independent TDs Lemass was again able to form a government. (see Table A)

A new look Fine Gael

In the next few years, all the parties developed new policies. Younger Fine Gael TDs urged the party to be less conservative. One of them, **Declan Costello**, son of a former Taoiseach, persuaded it to issue a policy document called *Towards a Just*

Election results 1957-65								
	Total	F.F.	F.G.	Lab.	C. na T.	C. na P.	S.F.	Ind.
1957	147	78	40	12	3	1	4	9
1961	144	70	47	16	2	1	–	8
1965	145	75	47	21	–	–	–	2

Table A ▲

Society which supported economic planning and more government intervention in the economy.

The old guard, including the party leader, James Dillon, bitterly disliked this new approach. During the 1965 general election these divisions came into the open and weakened the party. Fine Gael did poorly, gaining no seats. Dillon resigned immediately after the election and was replaced by **Liam Cosgrave**, who, though conservative on many issues, had backed the *Just Society* policy.

A new Labour

Labour, too, was changing slowly. Socialism was still a dirty word in the early sixties but their new leader, Brendan Corish, was cautiously edging the party towards it. Only in 1968 did he feel it was safe to describe the party openly as socialist.

Labour also rejected the idea of coalition with Fine Gael which had done better than it had out of the two Coalitions in the 1950s. Labour insisted that it must now follow its own independent line. In the 1965 election it won twenty-one seats, its best performance ever, but its independent line left Fianna Fáil still in power.

A new Fianna Fáil

Fianna Fáil was changing too, but the changes there were more subtle and much less openly debated than those in the other parties. Lemass continued his policy of promoting younger men, and a series of able ministers emerged. They included Jack Lynch, Patrick Hillery, George Colley and Charles Haughey. They were an energetic team who pushed through some long-delayed and much needed social and institutional reforms.

Liam Cosgrave

But these new men were very different from the traditional Fianna Fáil supporter. Dublin-based, well-educated and dedicated to the new policies of economic expansion, they seemed to many to have sold out to the international financiers and property developers who now dominated the Irish economy. Many loyal old Fianna Fáil supporters feared they had abandoned the party's original commitments to Irish nationalism, the Irish language and Irish rural values.

In 1964 **Paddy Smith**, a founder member of the party, resigned as Minister for Agriculture in protest against government concessions to industrial workers and its failure to help farmers. But with economic success everywhere evident and with the other political parties weakened by divisions, Lemass was able to ignore such criticism and win an overall majority in the 1965 election. (see Table A)

1966: the end of the Lemass era

In 1966 the Republic celebrated the fiftieth anniversary of the Easter Rising. The celebrations were exuberant and showed little thought for the sensibilities of northern unionists. This undid some of the good achieved by the O'Neill-Lemass meetings and increased communal tensions in the North.

The celebrations were a last fling for the old nationalism. In November, Seán Lemass one of the last survivors of that early nationalism, suddenly announced his retirement. He had led a change that in ten short years had transformed the social and emotional state of the nation. In the vote that followed, the Fianna Fáil party elected as its new leader Jack Lynch, the Minister for Finance. He was the most experienced of Lemass's new boys. To him fell the task of leading the country into the future that Lemass had begun.

Chapter 35

1922-66: Developments in society and culture

1966: a time to look back

In 1966 Jack Lynch replaced Seán Lemass as Taoiseach. With Lemass the generation that had led the fight for Irish independence retired from the scene. Lynch, born in 1917, was the first Irish leader to grow up in an independent Ireland. 1966 was significant in other ways. During it Irish people celebrated, with uninhibited enthusiasm, the fiftieth anniversary of the 1916 Rising.

It was a good time to look back. What had independent Ireland achieved? The founding fathers had hoped for prosperity, growth and an Irish-Ireland. How did their record stand up to examination?

Population and Emigration

Population

Nationalists had hoped that independence would bring an end to the decline in population which had lasted since the famine. But this had not been achieved.

As Table A shows, the population had actually continued to fall between 1926 and 1961. Only in the 1951 census was there a tiny increase and even this was soon reversed.

Population of the twenty-six counties	
Census year	
1926	2,973,000
1936	2,968,000
1946	2,955,000
1951	2,961,000
1956	2,898,000
1961	2,818,000
1966	2,884,000

Table A ▲

In 1966 an important item of news was that the census of that year showed the first significant growth in population since the 1840s. This was mainly due to the economic expansion of the early sixties. But the distribution of this population rise was also significant. It was almost completely confined to Leinster. The population of Dublin city had grown by 30 per cent. The west, heartland of traditional Ireland, continued to decline with all western counties, apart from Clare, losing population.

The factors that had caused the population to decline in the nineteenth century continued up to the 1960s. Poor economic performance kept Irish people from marrying as young as other Europeans and forced them to emigrate in larger numbers.

Marriage

In the 1920s the average Irish man married at the age of thirty-three and the average Irish woman at twenty-nine. This applied in both town and countryside. Late marriages reduced family size, even without the use of contraceptives. In addition, a substantial number of Irish people never married at all. In the 1950s a quarter of the population was single.

The prosperity of the 1960s altered the situation. By 1971 marriages were up 50 per cent from the 1920s' figure and the average age at marriage had dropped back to twenty-eight for men and twenty-four for women, a figure much nearer the European average. This also pushed up the birth rate. More children needed more schools and more jobs, but this did not become a problem until the 1970s and 1980s.

Irish emigrant being met by a Catholic hostel worker, London, 1950s.

Emigration

Emigration, too, continued after independence. The rate fluctuated, depending on the situation at home and in the country to which emigrants intended to move. High in the twenties, it declined at the start of the depressed thirties when high unemployment in Britain and the United States made them uninviting destinations.

When the US began to limit emigration in the 1920s, Britain became the favourite destination for Irish people. Emigration to Britain picked up in the late 1930s as the British re-armed. It became a flood during the war as the demand for labour grew in munitions factories, building sites and in the armed forces.

After the war, the brief recovery in the Irish economy slowed the rate of emigration down and the census of 1951 showed a tiny up-turn in the population. Then came the depressed 1950s when emigration became a torrent. An average of 40,000 people left each year from 1951 to 1961. Those who went were mainly young men and women and the country was left with an aging population.

This began to change in the 1960s. From 1961 to 1966 only 16,000 left each year and this decline continued into the 1970s. This also affected the population and marriage figures, as those who stayed at home married and started families of their own.

Reviving the Irish Language

The Gaelic ideal

Most of the founding fathers of the state, both those who were pro-Treaty and those who were anti-Treaty had been influenced by the Gaelic revival and the Irish-Ireland movement of the early twentieth century. One of their aims was to create an independent Ireland which would be, in the words of Patrick Pearse, 'not free merely, but Gaelic as well'. Clearly this involved halting the decline of Irish and encouraging more people to use it as their everyday language.

Reviving Irish

This was one of the first things tackled by Cosgrave's government. Under the guidance of **Eoin MacNeill,** who was the first Minister for Education, they gave the task of reviving Irish to the schools.

- An extensive and expensive programme of training primary teachers in Irish began. The Department of Education set up preparatory colleges where Irish was the school language. Students from these schools got priority in admissions to the teacher training colleges.

- All infant classes had to be taught through Irish and Irish was to be used extensively in higher classes. The teaching of other subjects like drawing, nature study, elementary science and domestic subjects had to give way to Irish.

- In secondary schools Irish became compulsory in 1928 and from 1934 students had to pass in Irish in order the pass the Certificate examinations. This was already a necessary requirement for admission to the National University.

- Extra grants were given to schools where all teaching was through Irish, and, in examinations, extra marks were given to those who answered through that language.

  These measures were continued and intensified under Fianna Fáil which, in the 1937 Constitution, made Irish the 'first official language' of the state.

The revival policy did achieve some results. By the 1940s:

- the number of primary teachers qualified to teach through Irish had risen from 10 per cent in 1922 to over 70 per cent.

- 14 per cent of primary schools used only Irish in class.

- 64 per cent of secondary students studied other subjects through Irish.

The failure of the revival campaign

But a Gaelic-speaking Ireland was no nearer to reality. Although on paper the number of people with a knowledge of Irish rose, the reality was that few of them used Irish in their everyday lives.

Even in the Gaeltacht areas, the number of Irish speakers continued to shrink in spite of government grants to each Irish-speaking household. In 1926 238,000 out of a Gaeltacht population of 427,000 were Irish speakers; by 1946 there were only 193,000 Irish speakers out of 398,000; in 1966 they numbered just 70,000.

The attempt to revive Irish through the schools alone contributed to this failure.

- The compulsory teaching of Irish destroyed much of the good-will towards the language which the early revival movement had generated.

- The use of the schools to revive Irish damaged education in general. The time spent on Irish left less time to develop basic reading and writing skills in students who, because most of them left school at fourteen or before, had only a limited period to acquire these skills. Parents resented this and transferred their resentment to Irish.

- In school most emphasis was put on written work so that children were often able to write Irish but not to speak it.

- Irish was not used in government departments, law courts, business or in the media. Therefore even those who enjoyed Irish and learnt it well had few chances to use it once they left school.

Criticism

Criticism of government policies towards Irish emerged during the war. The **Irish National Teachers' Organisation** (INTO), the primary teachers' union, published a report in 1941 which exposed the damage the policy was doing both to the education system and to the language. The government ignored them but in the 1950s the insistence on the use of Irish eased.

In the 1960s organisations like the **Language Freedom Movement** campaigned against compulsory Irish and in 1965 Fine Gael became the first party to support an easing of compulsion. When a new primary curriculum was introduced in the late 1960s, Irish took its place as one subject among others.

A new revival

In the 1940s many of those who loved the language realised that compulsion was damaging Irish. They tried to recover the enthusiasm of the early revival through a number of voluntary organisations.

- In 1943 **An Club Leabhar** was set up to publish books in Irish.

- A number of new magazines also appeared, including *Comhar*.

- In 1953 **Gael Linn** was set up. It published Irish music records and language courses and sponsored two films of Irish history, *Saoirse* and *Mise Éire*. They had musical scores by **Seán Ó Riada**, the most important Irish composer in the modern period. Gael Linn also commissioned Brendan Behan's play, *An Giall*.

- In 1951 **Comhaltas Ceoltoirí Éireann** was set up to foster a love of Irish traditional music. Together with Radio Éireann and some private individuals like **Séamus Ennis** and **Brendan Breathnach** they collected traditional music and presided over a revival of interest in Irish folk music. This found expression in

The actress Siobhán McKenna acted in many Irish language plays.

groups like the **Dubliners** and the **Chieftains** and in the annual **Fleadh Ceoil**, which in the 1960s became a mecca for young Irish people and linked Irish music into the emerging youth culture.

- A literature in modern Irish was emerging from the 1940s on. Novelists like **Mairtín Ó Cadhain** and poets like **Seán Ó Riordáin** were producing fine works that could stand comparison with any in English. One of the most popular books was *An Béal Bocht* by the satirist, **Brian O'Nolan** (alias **Myles na gCopaleen**). It was a savage attack on the stupidities of the revival movement.

These people took a more realistic approach to Irish than had been common in the 1920s and 1930s. Through them Irish and the Gaelic culture associated with it, took their place alongside other influences as part of the common inheritance of all the people of Ireland.

Irish Writers after Independence

The legacy of the Anglo-Irish movement

The new nationalism of the early twentieth century was influenced by the cultural revival, but this revival had two strands. One was the Gaelic League, the other the Anglo-Irish literary movement.

There had always been tension between the two. Some Gaelic enthusiasts found the idea of an Irish literature in English unacceptable. There was also the fact that many of those involved in the literary movement were of Protestant or landlord stock. This led the more narrow-minded Irish-Irelanders to question if they were really Irish at all.

Fortunately this view was not widespread but it did produce a sense of alienation among some of the leaders of the movement. After 1922 many of them did not feel really at home in the new Ireland.

Yeats after 1922

Yeats, the greatest figure among them, kept his links with the nationalist movement. In 1916 he had celebrated the Rising in a famous poem, but by 1922 he was questioning the cost of all the bloodshed:

> We have fed the heart on fantasies.
> The heart's grown brutal from the fare;
> More substance in our enmities
> Than in our love ...

> (W.B. Yeats, *Collected Poems*, pp. 230-1)

Yeats dominated the literary scene until his death in 1939. He produced his best poetry after 1921, some of it reflecting on the Ireland that had emerged. In 1923 he won the Nobel Prize. He was nominated to the first Senate where he fought against censorship and the ban on divorce, which he saw as sectarian. He also sat on the commission that approved the design for the new Irish coinage.

The Abbey

Yeats and Lady Gregory remained on the board of the Abbey Theatre. In 1924 they persuaded the Minister for Finance, Ernest Blythe, to give it an annual subsidy of £850. This made it the first state-subsidised theatre in the English-speaking world.

In 1941 Blythe became manager of the Abbey and he dominated it until he retired in 1967.

The Abbey had a notable success in the early 1920s when it produced three plays by **Seán O'Casey**. O'Casey was a socialist who had been closely associated with Larkin and the Irish Citizen Army. Lady Gregory encouraged him to write for the Abbey and in 1923 they put on his first play, *The Shadow of a Gunman*. It was followed by *Juno and the Paycock* in 1924 and *The Plough and the Stars* in 1926.

All three plays dealt with Dublin during the years of revolution and civil war. Like Synge's *Playboy* in 1908, they touched a raw nerve in some of their audiences and there were disturbances when the tricolour was carried into a pub during the *Plough and the Stars*.

Yeats and Lady Gregory turned down O'Casey's next play, *The Silver Tassie* because of its experimental style. O'Casey became embittered and lived in England from then on. Though he wrote more plays, none was a major success. In 1939 he

O'Casey left Ireland for good after the Abbey rejected his experimental play *The Silver Tassie*.

started to publish his autobiography which gives a fascinating account of Dublin life around the turn of the century.

After O'Casey, the Abbey opted for safe plays, mainly rural domestic dramas. In 1951 the original theatre was burned down. After a decade of exile, the Abbey finally got its own purpose-built theatre in 1966.

The Gate

In 1928 a new theatre called the **Gate** was founded by two young actors, **Hilton Edwards** and **Micheal MacLiammoir**. They wanted to put on plays from around the world and Irish plays that the Abbey would not accept. In 1930 they took over the eighteenth-century concert rooms attached to the Rotunda hospital. They got the backing of **Lord Longford** who put much of his own money into the Gate.

Over the years the Gate put on many classical and international plays. They also encouraged younger playwrights like **Denis Johnston**. A play of his which took a satirical look at Irish nationalism was turned down by the Abbey. Johnston changed the name to *The Old Lady Says No*, in honour of Lady Gregory's rejection, and it was put on in the Gate in 1929.

James Joyce (1882-1941)

The other great writer of this period, along with Yeats, was **James Joyce**. He had left Ireland in 1904 to live permanently on the continent. Despite this, all his books are set in Dublin.

In 1914 Joyce published a collection of short stories called *Dubliners*. This was followed in 1916 by a semi-autobiographical novel, *Portrait of the Artist as a Young*

James Joyce

Man. His most important work, *Ulysses* appeared in 1922. It is the story of one day, 16 June 1904, in the life of a Dublin Jew, Leopold Bloom. Joyce spent the rest of his life working on his final book, *Finnegan's Wake* which appeared in 1939.

Because of his exile and his unique style, Joyce did not belong to any particular school of writers, though he became one of the most influential novelists of the century.

The idealised Ireland

In the 1920s and 1930s there was a general assumption that writers should reflect the image of the ideal Ireland which lay behind the Irish-Ireland movement. It was a rural image, based on small but comfortable farmers who were the heirs of an ancient Gaelic world. Untouched by modern materialism, they lived contentedly on their farms, not needing the material wealth that people in industrial societies craved.

The most famous expression of this ideal came in a broadcast de Valera gave on St Patrick's Day 1943:

> The Ireland that we dreamed of would be the home of a people who ... were satisfied with frugal comfort and devoted their leisure to things of the spirit; a land whose countryside would be bright with cosy homesteads, whose fields and villages would be joyous with the sounds of industry, the romping of sturdy children, the contests of athletic youths, the laughter of comely maidens; whose firesides would be the forums of the wisdom of serene old age ... (T. Brown, *Ireland: A social and cultural history*, 1922-79, p. 146)

The new writers

But this imaginary Ireland ignored many other Irelands: the Ireland of small towns, of industrial workers, of the people of the cities. Younger writers in the 1930s began to write about these other Irelands.

- **Frank O'Connor**, a native of Cork wrote short stories about townspeople whose lives were narrowed by poverty and religion.

- **Liam O'Flaherty** from the Aran islands published novels which took a very unromantic view of the independence struggle and of Irish rural life.

- **Seán Ó Faoláin,** in his novels, journalism and historical works, rejected the Gaelic myth and stressed how much modern Ireland was a part of modern Europe.

All three men had fought in the war of independence. Through their writing they tried to understand their experiences and the new Ireland now emerging. Other writers like **Francis MacManus, Mary Lavin, Mervyn Wall, Kate O'Brien** and **Maura Laverty** were also at work, teasing out the social tensions within Irish society.

Among the younger poets, an outstanding name was **Austin Clarke**. He began, under the influence of the Gaelic revival, to use themes from ancient Irish history in his poems. Later he used the same themes to satirise the narrow and clerical-dominated Irish society of the 1940s and 1950s.

Another fine poet was **Patrick Kavanagh**. In his poem, *The Great Hunger*, published in 1942, he showed the bleak reality behind de Valera's dream. Writing of his native Monaghan with its poor small farms, Kavanagh brought out the bitter loneliness and frustration of a life of rural poverty dominated by the land and the Church.

Post-war writers

After the war, two outstanding younger writers emerged. One was **Brendan Behan**. A member of a republican family, he had joined the IRA as a teenager in the late thirties and was involved in their bombing campaign in England. Arrested, he was sent to a borstal institution, which provided the material for his novel, *Borstal Boy*, which appeared in 1958. Behan was later imprisoned in Ireland but freed in 1946. He wrote several plays, including *The Quare Fellow* (1954) and *The Hostage* (1959), and short stories.

The other writer was **Edna O'Brien**. Born on a small farm in Co. Clare, she went to Dublin where she wrote *A Country Girl* about the lives of young country girls living away from home. Its frank sexuality caused a sensation and inevitably it was banned. O'Brien left Ireland to live permanently in London where she wrote other novels.

All these writers had one thing in common. Many of their books were banned by the censor so that their ability to earn a living by their writing was seriously damaged. The leaders of the new Ireland did not want its certainties disturbed by their questioning.

Edna O'Brien

Censorship

The threat to traditional values

Even before independence, some Irish-Irelanders had worried that their idealised Ireland seemed to be threatened by a cheap English press which poured the standards and values of industrial Britain into rural Ireland. In the 1920s new threats appeared.

- Radio and moving pictures were even more powerful than the press. They seemed a threat to the traditions of story-telling and family visiting in country places.

- Public dance-halls, where new dances like the Charleston were all the rage, were replacing cross-road ceilís.

- Motor bikes and cars allowed young people to wander the countryside and freed them from the discipline of their parents and neighbours.

- Women had more economic independence and outraged the puritanical by wearing short skirts and make-up.

The demand for censorship

To conservatives, these things seemed to threaten everything they held dear. They feared that all their valued cultural traditions and moral standards would be swept aside. Most prominent among the conservatives were the Catholic clergy, many of whom were unable to separate true Christianity from the Victorian values in which they had been reared.

From the foundation of the Free State, they mounted a campaign to limit the encroachment of outside influences. Bishops' pastorals denounced dance-halls, picture houses and jazz, often in highly racist language. Zealous IRA gunmen seized and burned English papers which they considered morally doubtful or culturally dangerous.

Censorship

The rulers of the new state were sympathetic to the campaign. They felt that an independent Ireland must set a good example to an increasingly pagan and materialistic world. In 1923 they set up a system of film censorship, under which only approved films could be shown.

This was followed in 1929 by the establishment of the **Censorship Board** to censor books and periodicals. It was set up to control semi-pornographic books and magazines but its powers were loosely defined. Within a short time the censors were stopping the sale of books by such internationally famous and respected authors as **George Bernard Shaw**, **Thomas Mann** and **Ernest Hemmingway**.

The Censorship Board was especially hard on Irish writers. Many of those who attempted to give a realistic account of Irish life found their books banned. Few Irish writers of any worth escaped.

The Tailor and Ansty

A particularly bizarre example of their activities came in 1942. They banned a book called *The Tailor and Ansty*. It was a collection of stories and sayings which an English writer, **Eric Cross**, had recorded from a country tailor and his wife. They were exactly the kind of people romanticised by de Valera, but in real life their language was too broad and racy for the tender sensibilities of the censors. After the banning, their book was burned in their home village and the old couple was humiliated.

This episode provoked a heated debate in the Seanad. The critics of censorship lost, but a debate was started. It was helped along by the trenchant criticism carried in *The Bell*, a literary magazine edited by Seán O'Faoláin. In 1946 an appeal system was established but it failed to make much headway against a conservative society and conservative censors. In 1954 alone, 1,034 works were banned.

The social, religious and cultural changes of the 1960s finally caught up with censorship. Better education and a new outlook on the world made many people, including some Catholic priests, uneasy at the excesses of the Censorship Board. In 1967 the **Minister for Justice, Brian Lenihan**, liberalised the law, so that a banned book was made available again after twelve years. This move, which caused almost no controversy, unbanned 5,000 books at a single stroke.

Relations between Church and State

The religious divide

The partition of Ireland carried out in 1920, divided the island along religious lines. As a result, 92.6 per cent of the population of the South were members of the Roman Catholic Church and a mere 7.4 per cent were Protestant.

The Protestant community

While many individual Protestants from Parnell to Hyde had been active in the nationalist cause, most of the Protestant community had been unionist and opposed to independence. After the Treaty they found themselves caught in an independent Ireland to which they did not feel they belonged.

In May 1922 the Church of Ireland Synod sent a delegation to ask Collins 'if they were permitted to live in Ireland or if it was desired that they should leave the country'. (T. Brown, *Ireland: A social and cultural history, 1922-79*, p. 109) Collins assured them they were welcome and that his forces would protect them.

Despite this, 192 landlord houses were burned between December 1921 and

◆

March 1923. One of them was the home of **Sir Horace Plunkett** whose work for Ireland deserved a better reward. As a result, quite a few of the old landed gentry decided to leave.

Middle- and working-class Protestants settled in to make the best of the situation. Many of them emigrated. Partly because of this and partly because of the Catholic Church's policy on mixed marriages, the Protestant portion of the population had fallen by half by the 1960s. It was not until the ecumenical movement of the 1960s, that the Protestant community felt secure enough within the South to play a fuller part in the state.

The place of the Catholic Church

Although most would have denied it, the South became a Catholic state after 1922. This was the inevitable result of the huge Catholic majority. Most of the leaders of the new state were devout Catholics. They felt that on moral issues the Pope and the Catholic bishops were entitled to lay down the law and that it was their duty to obey.

During the civil war, the Catholic bishops had excommunicated the republicans but this had little effect on them. Cosgrave repaid this support by sending an early message of loyalty to the Pope and by establishing diplomatic relations with the Vatican.

Censorship and divorce

In the 1920s a number of issues arose where the Catholic bishops' influence was clear. The main ones were censorship of films and books and divorce.

In the United Kingdom it had been possible for a person to get a divorce by having a special bill passed through parliament. In 1922 the Free State government was asked if it planned to continue this practise. Cosgrave consulted the Catholic Archbishop of Dublin who thought it should not be allowed.

Cosgrave agreed and told the Senate that:

> the majority of people in this country regard the bond of marriage as a sacred bond which is incapable of being dissolved. I personally hold this view...
> (R. Fanning, *Independent Ireland*, p. 56)

Despite protests from Protestant Senators like W.B. Yeats that this infringed the minority's civil liberties, the decision not to allow divorce in the Irish Free State was accepted.

Celebrations

Catholics also celebrated their victory in winning independence by a number of festivals. One came in 1929 when they celebrated the centenary of the **Catholic Emancipation,** as a result of which Catholics were allowed to enter parliament. The second was in 1932 when an **International Eucharistic Congress** was held in Dublin.

De Valera and the Church

By then, de Valera was in power. He had simply ignored his excommunication and competed with Cosgrave in proving himself a good son of the Church. He took the lead in the Eucharistic Congress and his Cabinet approved the idea of not holding Dáil sessions on Church holidays.

Under Fianna Fáil, the process of including Catholic moral teachings in Irish law continued. In 1935 the importation and sale of contraceptives was outlawed and in 1937 the ban on divorce was extended by including it in the Constitution.

De Valera consulted Catholic bishops and theologians (as well as the leaders of other religious denominations) while preparing the Constitution. He included in it a guarantee of freedom of religious practise for all religions then in Ireland, as well as a special recognition of the Catholic Church as the Church of the majority of the Irish people. This was not enough for some more extreme Catholics, including the Pope himself, but de Valera resisted pressure to make it more explicit.

He was quite capable of resisting pressure in other ways, too. During the Spanish civil war he refused to support Franco in spite of massive pressure from the bishops to do so. However, he did make sure to have the backing of the bishops when he opted for neutrality in 1939.

The Mother and Child scheme

The biggest crisis between Church and state came in 1951 with the Mother and Child scheme. As stated in chapter 32, Fianna Fáil introduced a Health Act in 1947. It proposed to provide a free medical service for all mothers and for children up to the age of sixteen, regardless of their means. The Catholic bishops protested that this was contrary to Catholic social teaching.

Fianna Fáil lost power soon after and the issue passed to the first Coalition's Health Minister, Noel Browne. When he began to put this part of the Act into effect, the Catholic hierarchy wrote to the Taoiseach, John A. Costello, warning that:

> The right to provide for the health of children belongs to the parents, not to the state. The state... may help indigent or neglected parents; it may not deprive 90 per cent of parents of their rights because of 10 per cent necessitous or negligent parents... Education in regard to motherhood includes instruction in regard to sex relations, chastity and marriage. The state is not competent to give instruction in such matters. (R. Fanning, *Independent Ireland*, p. 182)

Browne tried to satisfy the bishops' objections, but failed. Costello then warned him that he and his colleagues 'would not be party to any proposals affecting moral questions which would or might come into conflict with the definite teachings of the Catholic Church'. (R. Fanning, *Independent Ireland*, p. 183) Attempts to reach a compromise failed and Browne was forced to resign.

The way the bishops were able to pressurise the government on this as on other issues might have remained hidden if Browne had not published the letters he had exchanged with the bishops, Costello and MacBride. This provoked a public debate during which Costello told the Dáil:

> I am an Irishman second and a Catholic first. If the hierarchy give me any direction with regard to Catholic social teaching or Catholic moral teaching, I accept without qualification in all respects the teaching of the hierarchy and of the Church to which I belong. (R. Fanning, *Independent Ireland*, p.185)

Browne lost and the bishops won again. It is unlikely that more than a minority of independently-minded people supported him in daring to challenge the right of the bishops to command the government on this issue.

But by bringing the matter to the public's notice he made both the Catholic bishops and the politicians a little more cautious in the future. In the 1960s a better educated Catholic public and a more open Catholic Church had to find other ways of approaching difficult social and moral issues.

Questions

ORDINARY LEVEL – A

Answer the following questions briefly. One or two sentences will be enough.

1 Mention **one** reason for the 'army mutiny' in 1924.

2 What was the **main** political result of the assassination of **Kevin O'Higgins** in 1927?

3 What was the importance of the 1931 **Statute of Westminster**?

4 What were the **two** main reasons for the economic war of the 1930s?

5 'The 1937 Constitution made the country into a republic in everything but name.' Explain how this was so.

6 Why was Ireland's admission to the the **United Nations** delayed until 1955?

7 What was the result of the repeal of the **External Relations Act** in 1949?

8 Identify **two** of the projects with which Noel Browne was involved as Minister for Health.

9 Set out **two** of the proposals in the first **Programme for Economic Development** in 1958.

10 Give **two** of the findings of the 1964 report, **Investment in Education**.

Questions

ORDINARY LEVEL – B

Write a short paragraph on each of the following:

1 The Boundary Commission.

2 The 1932 election.

3 The Blueshirts.

4 The economic war.

5 The 1937 Constitution.

6 The 1948 election.

7 Clann na Poblachta.

8 The Republic of Ireland Act 1949.

9 Donagh O'Malley.

10 Censorship in Ireland.

ORDINARY LEVEL – C

Write a short essay on each of the following:

1 The Cumann na nGaedheal government (1922-32) under the headings:
  (i)   Crises.
  (ii) Economic policies.
  (iii) Relations with Britain.
  (iv) Defeat in 1932.

2 Eamon de Valera from 1932 to 1948 under the headings:
  (i)   Relations with Britain.
  (ii) 1937 Constitution.
  (iii) Policy during the war.

3 The first Coalition (Inter-party) government (1948-51) under the headings:
  (i)   The parties involved in the Coalition.
  (ii) Economic policies.
  (iii) The Republic.
  (iv) Noel Browne and the Mother and Child Scheme.

Questions

4 Seán Lemass as Taoiseach (1959-66) under the headings:
(i) Economic policy.
(ii) Foreign policy.
(iii) Relations with Northern Ireland.

HIGHER LEVEL

1 Assess the contribution made to Irish affairs by William T. Cosgrave (1880-1965). (80)

2 (i) Trace the origin and growth of the Fianna Fáil party from 1926 to 1932. (60)
(ii) How do you account for its electoral success in 1932? (20)

3 'Anglo-Irish relations in the period 1922 to 1938 were concerned mainly with the adjustment of the Treaty settlement.' Discuss. (80)

4 Compare and contrast the economic policies followed by Cumann na nGaedheal (1922-32) with those followed by Fianna Fáil between 1932 and 1939. (80)

5 'Fianna Fail in power from 1932 to 1948 took firm action to deal with internal and external threats to the security of the state.'
Discuss. (80)

6 Outline the policies pursued by the two Inter-party (coalition) governments (1948-51 and 1954-57) and assess the extent to which these policies were successful. (80)

7 Treat of the foreign policy pursued by successive Irish governments from 1922 to 1966. (80)

8 Discuss the fortunes of the Labour party from 1912 to 1966. (80)

9 Evaluate the contribution made to Irish developments by Seán Lemass during his period as Taoiseach (1959-66). (80)

10 Discuss the fortunes of the Irish language from 1922 to 1966. (80)

11 Treat of the main developments in literature in Ireland from 1922 to 1966. (80)

SECTION FIVE

1920-1966: NORTHERN IRELAND

Chapter 36

1921-40: Sir James Craig and the early years of Northern Ireland

1919-22: A Painful Birth

The origins of Northern Ireland

Northern Ireland owed its existence to the passing of the **Government of Ireland Act** in December 1920. (see page 269) That Act grew out of Lloyd George's decision to solve the quarrel between unionists and nationalists by setting up two Home Rule parliaments in Ireland, one in Dublin and the other in Belfast. The Belfast one would rule six of the nine counties of Ulster.

The Government of Ireland Act

The Act contained the constitutional framework for Northern Ireland.

- It was to have a parliament of two houses. There was a **Commons**, with fifty-two MPs elected by proportional representation (PR), and a **Senate** containing the mayors of Belfast and Derry and twenty-four Senators elected by the Commons.

- The Commons was to elect a government. It would consist of a Prime Minister with a Cabinet containing ministers of Finance, Home Affairs, Health and Social Services, Education, Commerce and Agriculture.

- Northern Ireland was still to be part of the United Kingdom with the king as head of state. When the Act was passed in 1920, the king was to be represented in both parts of Ireland by one Viceroy.

    When Sinn Féin made the Treaty which took the South out of the United Kingdom, this part of the Act lapsed. The king's representative was then the **Governor of Northern Ireland**. He had the right to withhold assent from bills passed by the Northern Ireland parliament. This power was used only once and caused such a storm of protest that it was allowed to lapse.

Reserved powers

Under the Act, the Westminster parliament remained the supreme law-making body in the United Kingdom. The Belfast parliament was to 'make laws for the peace, order and good government' of Northern Ireland, but there were many things it was not allowed to deal with. These were **reserved** to the Westminster parliament where thirteen MPs elected in Northern Ireland were to continue to sit.

The reserved powers included the Crown, war and peace, the armed forces, foreign affairs, trade outside Northern Ireland, coinage, weights and measures and most forms of taxation. The Northern parliament could not alter its own constitution, introduce laws to support religion or confiscate property without compensation.

Sir James Craig (1871-1940)

When the Government of Ireland Act passed, Sir Edward Carson, who had led the Unionist party since 1910 announced that he was going to resign. The leadership passed to his deputy, **Sir James Craig**. A millionaire businessman, Craig had been the main organiser of the Ulster Volunteers in 1912-14. He fought on the Western Front during the war and was a minister in Lloyd George's Coalition government from 1919-21. He then became the first Prime Minister of Northern Ireland.

Fighting in the north

Under the Act, Northern Ireland was to come into existence in June 1921. But already in the summer of 1920, fighting had begun. (see pages 270 & 271) In Belfast tension was caused by growing unemployment, especially in the shipyards where Catholic workers who got jobs during the war, lost them to newly demobilised soldiers. Protestants also reacted angrily to the killing of policemen by the IRA.

These tensions interacted with the usual sectarian passions stirred up by the twelfth of July Orange processions. Violence erupted in Belfast on 21 July. It quickly spread to surrounding towns. Many died, hundreds of houses were destroyed and the traditional suspicions between the two communities deepened.

The revived Ulster Volunteers

In the border counties where the IRA was particularly active, the Ulster Volunteer Force was re-formed under the leadership of **Sir Basil Brooke**. It quickly spread and co-operated with the police, Tans and British army against the IRA.

The Special Constabulary

Macready, the British army commander, strongly disapproved of the arming of the UVF. In October the government tried to meet his objections by setting up the **Ulster Special Constabulary**. Three classes of 'Specials' were established. Class A were to serve full time, Class B were part-timers who supplemented police patrols in their own areas, and Class C acted as a reserve for emergencies. Ulster Volunteers joined the Specials in large numbers.

The 'A' and 'C' classes soon disappeared from the scene, but the **'B Specials'** were to remain a feature of Northern life for almost half a century. Because of their origins in the UVF and their use against the IRA, the 'Specials' were seen from the start as the armed militia of the Unionist party. Almost without exception they were drawn from the Protestant community.

Sir Basil Brooke

Setting up the state

Although the Northern state was not due to come into existence until June 1921, the British government decided that the violence needed a quick response. A civil servant was sent to Belfast late in 1920 to begin preparations for setting up the various government departments.

Craig was appointed as acting Prime Minister early in 1921 and elections to the Northern parliament were held on 24 May. Two nationalist parties, Sinn Féin and the old Nationalist (Home Rule) party now led by **Joseph Devlin**, contested the election, even though they refused to recognise the Northern state.

There was a large turn out and forty Unionists, six Sinn Féiners and six Nationalists were elected. King George V opened the Northern parliament on 22 June, but only Unionists attended. Nationalists still hoped that permanent partition could be avoided.

Craig and the Treaty

The Truce with Sinn Féin in July eased the situation for a time. All sides waited for the outcome of the London negotiations between the Sinn Féin delegates and Lloyd George. (see chapter 25)

Craig would not get involved. He argued that Northern Ireland was established and that the negotiations between London and Dublin did not concern him. But in fact he watched anxiously, knowing that one of the Sinn Féin aims was to end partition and that Lloyd George saw Northern Ireland as a bargaining tool.

Lloyd George, hoping to persuade the Irish delegates to accept the king, pressed Craig to agree to an all-Irish parliament. He firmly rejected the proposal and

B Specials on parade in Enniskillen.

reminded the Prime Minister that unionists had accepted the Government of Ireland Act only 'as a final settlement and supreme sacrifice in the interests of peace'. (St John Ervine, *Craigavon: Ulsterman*, p. 450) With the help of his allies in the Conservative party he was able to resist the pressure.

Nevertheless, the final version of the Treaty came as an unpleasant shock to unionists. It recognised the unity of Ireland. Unionists were allowed to opt out but only at the cost of a Boundary Commission to redraw the border between North and South, fixed by the Government of Ireland Act. Like Collins, Craig thought that Northern Ireland would lose a substantial part of its area as a result.

He hurried to London to protest. Lloyd George calmed him down, promising, in spite of his assurance to Collins and Griffith, that the Commission would do no more than tidy up the boundary line.

Violence and uncertainty

The first half of 1922 was a difficult time for the northern government. The Dáil's long debate over the Treaty left the final outcome uncertain for several weeks. Then as Sinn Féin and the IRA split over it, violence flared once more.

Collins and Craig met several times between January and March to try to make peace. Collins promised to end the boycott of northern goods which the Dáil had introduced as a protest at the violence against Catholics in 1920. Craig promised to protect northern Catholics. In the end, neither man could deliver on his promises. Attacks on Catholics continued and Collins, angered by what he considered bad faith, began to supply guns to the northern republicans.

The Special Powers Act

Meanwhile the northern government took steps to assert its authority. Craig appointed **Dawson Bates** as **Minister for Home Affairs** to deal with the problem of security.

In March 1922 Bates got parliament to pass the **Civil Authorities (Special Powers) Act**. It gave almost unlimited power to the Home Affairs Minister. He was allowed 'to take all such steps and issue all such orders as may be necessary for preserving peace'. (P. Buckland, *Irish Unionism 2: Ulster*, p.158) and could delegate these powers to any police officer. The Act laid down stiff penalties for certain offenses, (e.g. the death penalty for throwing bombs, and flogging for carrying arms) and allowed the Minister to introduce internment without trial.

At first the Special Powers Act was temporary and had to be renewed every year, but in 1933 it was made permanent. It was used almost exclusively against nationalists. It generated enormous resentment and its repeal was one of the demands of the civil rights movement of the 1960s.

The Royal Ulster Constabulary (RUC)

The police force, too, was re-organised. The RIC was disbanded and a new force, the **Royal Ulster Constabulary**, was formed in May. It was to consist of 3,000 men. Like the RIC and unlike the Gardaí, it was armed. In an attempt to win the confidence of the nationalists, one third of the places in the RUC were reserved for Catholics. Few of them joined and the RUC also came to be identified with the unionist community.

The 'Special Constables' were also re-organised and placed under the control of the Ministry of Home Affairs. The government got **Sir Henry Wilson**, recently retired as chief of the Imperial General Staff, to act as its military adviser.

As a result of these acts, the northern government had 50,000 full- and part-time policemen in its service by the summer of 1922. It could also call on thirteen battalions of British troops which were controlled from Westminster. All were deployed against the IRA.

Growing violence

The violence got steadily worse throughout the early months of 1922. The pause in the south which followed the Treaty, allowed the IRA to concentrate its energies on the north. As the split over the Treaty deepened, some in the anti-Treaty camp tried to provoke the British army along the border into retaliation. This, they hoped, would re-open the Anglo-Irish war and destroy the Treaty. The IRA attacked police and military barracks and, in places, the business premises and private homes of Protestants.

Sir Henry Wilson

This provoked retaliation from the unionist side and the death toll mounted. On 24 May the northern government declared the IRA and similar organisations illegal and that night over 500 people were rounded up. Many of them were interned on a prison ship on Belfast Lough. On 1 June a curfew was imposed and the police, 'Specials' and the British army were given wide powers of search and arrest.

These tough measures and the outbreak of civil war in the south in June, eased the situation and slowly a measure of quiet returned. But its painful birth left a deep mark on the northern state from which it has never fully recovered.

The Religious and Political Divide

Catholic attitudes to Northern Ireland

Partition had come as a nasty shock for northern Catholics. The events of 1920-22 made it worse.

The violence of these years hit Catholics disproportionately hard. In 1922, 232 people were killed and over 1,000 wounded. Two-thirds of those who died were Catholics, even though they made up only one third of the population of the six counties. At the same time, an estimated 8,750 Catholics had been driven from their jobs and 23,000 were made homeless. This convinced Catholics that the forces of the new state were directed against them.

But in 1922 Catholics could still hope that partition was only temporary. They pinned their hopes on the Boundary Commission, believing it would restore unity.

Because of this, most Catholics withheld their recognition from the new state and boycotted its institutions.

- Nationalist and Sinn Féin MPs would not take their seats in the Belfast parliament.

- County councils like Tyrone and Fermanagh, where there was a nationalist majority, stayed loyal to the Dáil.

- Catholic national teachers refused to recognise the Northern Ministry of Education. Collins supported this stand, but after his death, Cosgrave and O'Higgins ended the support.

Unionist attitudes to nationalists

Unionists bitterly resented the Catholics' attitude. They were always uncomfortably aware that there was a large Catholic majority in the whole of Ireland and they feared for the security of their new state. They saw the Catholic refusal to recognise the legally established government as proof that Catholics wanted to undermine Northern Ireland. They felt that they could not trust Catholics to be loyal citizens. The IRA campaign reinforced this feeling and added to the siege-mentality which was always a feature of unionism.

Craig had intended to treat northern Catholics fairly. He made overtures towards them, such as reserving one-third of the places in the RUC for them. But his goodwill was soon lost in the more hardline approach of some of his colleagues like Dawson Bates and in the bitterness which the fighting and the killing produced on both sides.

The unionist majority

Within Northern Ireland Protestants made up about two-thirds of the population. This gave the unionists a built-in majority. But they were never able to feel secure in this majority. They were always conscious that there was a hostile Catholic majority in the rest of the island and a large Catholic minority within their own borders. This made it difficult for them to allow normal political structures to develop.

The Unionist party

The Unionist party, which had come into existence in 1886, became the governing party in Northern Ireland. It retained its close contacts with the Orange Order. The Order bound Protestants together, giving to men of all social classes a sense of common purpose and identity which was most clearly expressed in its colourful marches on 12 July.

It has been estimated that in the 1920s two-thirds of all Protestant men were Orangemen. It was almost impossible to succeed as a Unionist politician without being a member of the Order. In 1934 Craig said in the Belfast Commons, 'I am an Orangeman first and a politician and member of parliament second'.

The Order gave the Unionist party a broad social base, but its leaders were mainly landlords and businessmen. In 1918 the **Ulster Unionist Labour Association** was set up to encourage working-class participation and the election of workers as MPs. It was never very successful because of the hostility of many party leaders. Despite this the Unionist party continued to hold the loyalty of Protestant workers, who felt that the links with the United Kingdom were vital to their own safety.

Changing the electoral system

Unionist insecurity can be clearly seen in the way they dealt with the electoral system.

The British government had been anxious to give minorities a voice in the two parts of Ireland. To achieve this they introduced voting by proportional representation (PR) for local government elections in 1919 and put it into the Government of Ireland Act for parliamentary elections. This system of voting was fairer to minorities than their own 'first past the post' system.

Ending PR in local elections

In the 1920 local elections, PR produced a nationalist majority in Fermanagh and Tyrone and in the city of Derry. These local bodies acknowledged the Dáil and refused to recognise the Belfast government.

Orangemen on parade.

In 1922 the Unionist government suspended these councils. It then abolished PR in local elections. All local government electoral boundaries were redrawn in such a way that Unionist majorities were guaranteed in Fermanagh, Tyrone and Derry city, despite the fact that Catholics formed a majority of the population in those places. (This is called gerrymandering.)

The right to vote for local councils was limited to those who held property and people with several properties had several votes. Since Protestants on the whole had more property than Catholics, this further strengthened unionist control of local government.

All this produced unvarying unionist majorities in local government. It led to widespread corruption which Craig, himself an honest man, did not try to check. These councils also discriminated seriously against Catholics in jobs, housing and other local services.

Changing PR in general elections

The unionists also disliked PR in general elections, though it had not weakened their majority in 1921. Party members wanted to change back to the 'first past the post' system but Craig resisted them. He was afraid of a hostile reaction in Britain and needed British support if the Boundary Commission came up with an unfavourable report.

By the mid-twenties, some unionists were dissatisfied with the economic situation. In the 1925 election several people stood as Independent Unionists. There were also some Labour candidates who played on the economic discontent. PR gave both groups their chance. The Unionist party lost seven seats. Four Independents and three Labour MPs were elected.

For the unionist leaders this was a warning signal. PR might fragment the unionist vote and let the nationalists in. As Craig put it, with his usual bluntness:

> At election times, people do not really understand what danger may result if they make a mistake when it comes to third, fourth, fifth or sixth preferences. By an actual mistake they might wake up to find Northern Ireland in the perilous position of being submerged in a Dublin parliament. (St John Ervine, *Craigavon: Ulsterman*, p. 516)

In 1929 Craig abolished PR and replaced it with the straight vote system. Although constituency boundaries were re-drawn, there does not seem to have been much gerrymandering and the proportion of nationalists to unionists remained much the same as before. But the change did have three effects.

- It strengthened party discipline among the Unionists and kept the party united.

- It prevented other parties such as the Labour party getting a foothold in Northern Ireland and stopped issues like the economy from being properly discussed. All elections became a straight fight between unionism and nationalism.

- Since most constituencies had a clear unionist or nationalist majority, it was often not worthwhile putting up a rival candidate. This reduced the number of contested elections in Northern Ireland. By the late 1930s there were election contests in only one-third of all seats. This produced a very stagnant political scene.

The thirteen Westminster seats were unaffected by these changes as they had always been fought on the straight vote system. Unionists never held fewer than eight of them but these members were of little importance. Under the Government of Ireland Act, the Westminster parliament was supreme over the Belfast parliament, but in practice Westminster paid almost no attention to Northern Ireland between 1922 and 1969. Unionists were able to rule their province as they wished.

Nationalist divisions

Nationalists were less united than the unionists. In 1921 six of their MPs came from Sinn Féin and six from the old Nationalist party. Both refused to take their seats but as time passed abstention became more difficult to justify. The Catholic community needed someone to speak for them on matters like education and social welfare.

In 1925 Joseph Devlin led some members of the Nationalist party into the Belfast parliament and after the failure of the Boundary Commission (see pages 327-330) made partition permanent, the rest followed. Sinn Féin, however, continued to abstain.

The Nationalists then became the main Catholic party in the North. But the division between moderate nationalists who favoured some kind of a working compromise with the unionist state and intransigent republicans who wanted nothing to do with it remained and the Catholic position was weakened by it.

Nationalist politicians were further weakened by the unreality of their position. They could not be a proper parliamentary opposition, because they could never become what all proper oppositions hope to become - the government.

When nationalists criticised the Unionist government they seemed to unionists to be denying its right to exist. Devlin tried to reassure them that 'there is not and there is not going to be any attempt of any kind, much less a conspiracy, to force the people of Northern Ireland into a Dublin or any other parliament'. (M. Wallace, *Northern Ireland: Fifty years of self-government*, p. 78), but it is doubtful if all his followers supported him or any of his opponents believed him.

Developments in education

Education was an area where the tensions between Protestant and Catholic were acute. All primary schools were divided along sectarian lines and managed by the clergymen of the various Churches. Craig was interested in improving standards and appointed Lord Londonderry as his Minister for Education.

Londonderry wanted to improve schooling for all children. In 1921 he set up a committee to enquire into the education system. Catholics boycotted it because of

A funeral passing St Comgall's primary school, Divis St, Belfast in the late 1920s.

their attitude to the northern government. The committee found that the old education system was not working. Schools were small, run down and inefficient. In Belfast, for example, 12,000 children did not have primary school places.

Acting on the committee's advice, Londonderry brought in an **Education Act** in 1923.

- It proposed to transfer control of primary schools from the clerical managers to committees consisting of four members appointed by the clergy and two by the local councils.

- These committees would appoint teachers and religion was not to count in the appointments.

- Transferred schools would teach religion outside school hours and be open to pupils of all religions.

- They would get state grants to cover the full cost of building and repairs, but schools that refused to transfer would only get a proportion of the cost of these services.

Both Catholic and Protestant clergy objected to these proposals. Catholic bishops refused to let their schools accept the committee system, so that only Protestant schools transferred. Protestant clergy, who disliked the system as much as the Catholic priests, then campaigned for more power in the transferred schools. With the help of the Unionist party, they had their way. The Education Act was amended in 1925 and 1930 to give them more control over the appointment of teachers and to permit the teaching of the Bible in school.

Londonderry resigned in 1925, his plan for non-sectarian primary schools in ruins. Protestants had captured the state school system and shaped it to their desires. Catholics were left with schools which were less well funded than those of the Protestant community and an abiding sense of grievance that soured community relations for fifty years.

There were also reforms to privately owned second-level schools. Teachers had to be properly qualified and the state began to pay their salaries. State grants were given to build more schools and a new examination system was begun. Between 1923 and 1938 government spending on second level education rose from £51,000 to £194,000, while the number of pupils between the ages of eleven and nineteen who stayed on in school went up from 6,250 to 11,500.

Social and Economic Policy

The economic link with Britain

Under the Government of Ireland Act, the northern government had little control over its own economy. It could only decide on a limited range of taxes, like stamp duties. These raised about 20 per cent of the money the government spent.

The rest of its income came from taxes that were decided by the London government and that were levied on the United Kingdom as a whole. The amount that Northern Ireland got from these taxes was to be decided by a body called the **Joint Exchequer Board**. But before that money was handed over, a sum was to be deducted to pay for the 'reserved' services – the crown, defence forces, diplomatic services and so on.

This did not work very well and in 1924 it was changed. From then on the Northern Irish contribution to the cost of the reserved services was whatever was left over after its own needs had been met.

The London Treasury feared that the unionists would use British taxpayers' money to raise the quality of services in the North. To prevent that, the 'principle of parity' was introduced. That meant that taxation and services in Northern Ireland should remain at the same level as in the rest of the United Kingdom.

This worked to the advantage of the North in the 1920s. It was a poor area and money flowed in from Britain to lift pensions and unemployment benefits there to the level of the richer parts of the United Kingdom and push them ahead of anything the South could afford. For some years during the depression of the early 1930s these payments ceased and the level of welfare fell sharply. But in 1936 the position was restored and in 1938 the British promised to make good any deficit in the Northern budget.

The parity idea reduced the economic independence of the northern government. It had little control over how it spent its money, as the main decisions were made in London. Little was left for it to spend on improving housing, health or schools. Between the wars, fewer than 8,000 houses were built by local authorities and the standard of housing remained well below that in other parts of the United Kingdom.

Agriculture

Although the north east was the most industrialised part of Ireland, agriculture was still Northern Ireland's biggest industry. In 1926 almost 150,000 people were working in it, about a quarter of the workforce and it was worth £11 million a year to the economy, far more than shipbuilding.

Most farmers had bought their farms under the land purchase acts and in 1925 a final Land Act completed purchase by making it compulsory for landlords to sell to any remaining tenants. The average size of farms was smaller than in the South.

In the 1920s the government made a determined effort to raise farming standards. Education was improved and standards of quality were established for exporters of eggs, meat, fruit and dairy produce. The **Livestock Breeding Act** set out to improve the breeding of animals and marketing boards were set up to improve the sales of farm produce.

In 1931 the United Kingdom government took steps to protect United Kingdom farmers. Northern Irish farmers benefited from state marketing and subsidies, especially when the economic war cut the South's exports to Britain. Pig numbers rose from 200,000 in 1932 to 844,000 by 1939 and sheep, poultry and cattle numbers had also increased.

Industrial depression

The key industries of Northern Ireland were shipbuilding, engineering and linen. They had all done well during the war and up to 1920, but depression set in just as the state was being set up. Shipbuilding was hit by a downturn in world trade and the linen industry which had done little to modernise itself, faced competition from new textile industries in other countries.

This depression lasted throughout the 1920s and got worse in the 1930s. It cut employment. The number of workers in the linen industry fell from 74,000 in 1924 to 55,000 in 1930. The shipyards were not so badly affected until the great depression hit them in 1930. Then demand for ships almost ceased and Belfast's second yard, **Workman and Clark** closed in 1935. Unemployment reached 28 per cent in 1931 and hardly fell below that for the rest of the 1930s.

In the 1920s the government, hampered by lack of money, did not intervene in industry. This changed in the depressed 1930s. Loans were offered to finance the purchase of ships. In 1929 the **Ulster Industrial Development Association** was set up to attract new industries. The Minister of Commerce was allowed to make grants for new factories and to offer tax remission and interest-free loans. Attempts were made to encourage linen manufacturers to switch over to new textiles, and an aircraft industry was started by **Short and Harland** in 1937.

The results of the depression

The depression hit the poor of both communities. Welfare payments were pitifully small. In Belfast a married man with one child was expected to exist on twelve shillings (60p) a week about half what was needed for bare survival. In the early 1930s 36 per cent of the population was living below the poverty line.

These conditions produced rumbles of discontent, even from unionists. In 1932 Catholic and Protestant workers demonstrated together against their conditions. This alarmed the unionists. Their leaders called on employers to give jobs to unionist workers. As one minister said:

> When will Protestant employers recognise their duty to their Protestant brothers and sisters and employ them to the exclusion of Roman Catholics... It is our duty to pass the word along and I suggest the slogan should be: Protestant employ Protestant. (P. Devlin, *Yes, we have no bananas*, p. 141)

Harland and Wolff shipyard.

To no one's surprise, this advice was taken and soon the old pattern of sectarian strife re-asserted itself.

Craig as a political leader

Craig (who was made Lord Craigavon in 1927) remained Prime Minister of Northern Ireland until his death in 1940, though his health deteriorated in his last years. He succeeded in establishing Northern Ireland after a difficult start but he did not deal with its two basic problems, the declining economic base and the sectarian divisions in society.

Craig himself was not a bigot but he was caught by those who were. He turned a blind eye to the injustices suffered by Catholics in employment, housing and other areas. Although Catholics protested to the Westminster government, Craig was able to convince the British that this was an internal matter for Northern Ireland. British politicians and civil servants, glad to have the eternal Irish question off their backs, were only too willing to be persuaded.

Craig also used the threat from the South to bolster his government and to deflect any unionist criticism of his economic policies. De Valera's victory in 1932 and his anti-partitionist rhetoric were used to ensure a comfortable win for the Unionist party in the 1933 election. Their success was helped when de Valera himself stood as a candidate in one northern constituency.

In 1938 Craig used the start of the Anglo-Irish talks, in which de Valera said partition would be an issue, to call a snap election. His aim may also have been to undermine a challenge from a group called the **Progressive Unionists** who were impatient at his inactive leadership. The ploy worked and his critics were routed.

Craig then used Chamberlain's concessions to de Valera (see page 368) to demand compensation. He got it in the form of increased agricultural subsidies and a British promise to bring social services in Northern Ireland up to British levels. This promise paid off handsomely in the welfare state after the war.

Opinions about Craig vary. For one historian he was:

A man of great physical courage [who] proved ... an exceptionally successful negotiator at an international level, an astute party leader and a successful Prime Minister by the standards of his followers. (J.J. Lee, *Ireland, 1912-1985*, p. 256)

While for another he:

was an effective organiser and administrator and he could take resolute action, but he was able to organise and to act only when he had a clearly defined and limited aim in view. What he lacked was ... the capacity to develop policies and to direct their implementation. For much of his premiership, he was content to let Northern Ireland drift with no sense of direction and to let the minority question fester. (P. Buckland, *Craig*, p. 124)

Chapter 37

1939-66: The war years and after

Northern Ireland in the War

Preparing for war

As part of the United Kingdom, Northern Ireland was directly involved in World War II. Even before it started, the London and Belfast governments had drawn up plans to deal with air raids, rationing, the requisition of supplies and the direction of factories into war production. They ordered naval ships from **Harland and Wolff**, and aircraft from **Short and Harland**. Linen mills were told to begin producing uniforms, tents and other military necessities.

The strategic importance of the North

Once war began in September 1939, the South's neutrality and its refusal to let Britain use its ports, greatly increased Northern Ireland's strategic importance to the British. After the fall of France in June 1940 Germany controlled the continental mainland. This forced much of Britain's Atlantic trade to take the northern sea routes and made Northern Ireland even more important.

From naval bases in Belfast, Derry and Larne, naval ships sailed into the Atlantic to escort convoys carrying essential supplies from the US. From airbases on the Foyle and the Erne, planes scoured the seas looking for enemy destroyers and submarines.

After America entered the war in 1941, American troops in their thousands arrived in the North. Northern Ireland was used by the allied forces as its main training ground for the Normandy invasions.

Conscription

Conscription was re-introduced in Britain in 1939, but because of nationalist objections, it was not extended to Northern Ireland. In 1940 when the fall of France put Britain in danger, the question was raised again. De Valera objected to the proposal. Although Craig protested that unionists wanted to take their full share in defending the United Kingdom, some of them were uncomfortable at the idea of arming the minority community. In the end, conscription was not imposed.

Wartime industry

The northern economy boomed during the war. The demand for shipping kept the shipyards working flat out. Between 1939 and 1945 they produced 150 warships and

123 merchant ships. Aircraft and engineering firms built 1,500 heavy bombers and over 500 tanks. New industries were developed away from Belfast. Torpedoes were built in Antrim, aircraft ballbearings in Portadown and parachutes at Carrigfergus.

Employment grew fast and the workforce in these industries rose from 32,000 in 1938 to 65,000 in 1945. The linen industry also revived, though less spectacularly. It did well until 1940 when the supply of flax from Europe stopped. An all out drive to grow flax in the North and to diversify into other fabrics, especially synthetics such as rayon, helped it to revive. Building work for the allied armies after 1942 also created many jobs.

Wartime agriculture

Agriculture was very important, with food from the North going to feed Britain. The value of agricultural production increased threefold from 1939 to 1945. Government planning and compulsory tillage orders pushed the amount of land under crops from 500,000 acres to over 800,000 acres.

Apart from flax, the most important crops were oats and potatoes. Much of this increased production was used as animal feed. Cattle numbers rose from 750,000 in 1939 to over 900,000 by 1945 and poultry from 10 million to 17.5 million.

Careful government planning lay behind these figures. It ensured that supplies of fertiliser remained available and encouraged changes in farming methods. Farmers were encouraged to mechanise with tractor numbers growing from 550 in 1938 to over 7,000 by 1945.

The British government gave a guaranteed price to farm produce. This was fixed in advance of each year's harvest and set at a level which gave farmers a reasonable profit. Since the same prices were paid in all parts of the United Kingdom, Northern Irish farmers were saved from the disadvantages which distance from their main markets had previously imposed on them.

Prosperity

The war brought prosperity. The number out of work fell from an average 25 per cent in the 1930s to 5 per cent in 1942-5. Wages rose substantially. Before the war the average wage was only 60 per cent of the average wage in Britain; by 1945 it was 75 per cent.

But the wartime expansion was marred by bad management, poor productivity rates and bad work practices. Industrial unrest flared up from time to time with several strikes, in spite of the fact that they were illegal.

Bombing Belfast

As an important industrial centre, Belfast was an obvious target for a German air attack but little was done to protect it. There were few anti-aircraft guns or search lights. Evacuation plans existed only in outline and there were almost no air-raid shelters.

On 7 April 1941 six German bombers made a small raid. They tested the city's defences and found them negligible. On the night of 15-16 April the Germans returned. A force of 150 planes flew over Belfast and dropped 203 metric tons of bombs. Most fell on the city centre, a densely populated area.

They killed over 700 people, injured 1,500 and destroyed houses, schools, churches and businesses. About 100,000 people fled in panic. De Valera sent fire brigades from Dublin, Drogheda and Dundalk to help to fight the fires and many refugees were fed and housed in the border areas.

On 5 May the Germans launched an even bigger raid with about 200 planes dropping incendiary bombs and high explosives. They hit the industrial area where fewer people lived. The Harland and Wolff shipyard was put out of action for six months and 150 people were killed. A few more bombers returned on the following night.

The raids showed up the inadequacy of the city's defences. It also revealed the lack of preparation for an evacuation. The 100,000 who fled from the city had to seek refuge with relatives, in schools, halls, barns and even ditches. Country people and local officials were deeply shocked at the extent of poverty, depravation and misery which they saw among the refugees from the city's slums. This memory remained to fuel demand for better social conditions after the war.

To avoid bombs meant for Belfast being dropped on Donegal the letters EIRE were marked on Slieve League, Co. Donegal to show German bombers they were over neutral territory.

Leadership changes

The raids brought to a head a deep-seated dissatisfaction with the government. Craig (Lord Craigavon) died suddenly in November 1940. His successor was his deputy **J.M. Andrews**. Seventy years old and deaf, Andrews had served in the Northern Ireland Cabinet since 1921. He refused to bring in younger men and his government had an air of indecision and complacency.

The bombing of Belfast showed up its incompetence. The discontent with the Unionist party grew and in 1942 they lost two normally safe seats. Early in 1943, the MPs revolted and forced Andrews to resign. The new Prime Minister was **Sir Basil Brooke**, the most able of Andrew's ministers. He got rid of some of the old guard and reorganised the government.

Attitudes to the South

The war did nothing to change unionist attitudes to the South. When Craig heard of Churchill's offer of unity to de Valera in 1940 he had protested that he was:

> profoundly shocked and disgusted by your letter making suggestions behind my back and without pre-consultation with me. To such treachery to loyal Ulster, I will never be a party. (R. Fisk, *In Time of War*, p. 207)

Fortunately for him, de Valera's refusal to consider the British proposal never forced him to choose between the needs of the British war effort and unionist opposition to a united Ireland. Instead, the North's participation in the war, while the South remained neutral, strengthened unionist ties with Britain.

Party divisions

Unlike Britain, where all parties formed a coalition to fight the Nazis, the Unionists made no overtures to the minority community. Brooke did invite one Labour MP to become a minister, but he later left the Labour party and joined the Unionists. Brooke explained his policy:

> I knew I could not invite the Nationalists to run in double harness with the Unionists. At the time they were entirely non-cooperative especially in regard to any effort during the war... (R. Fisk, *In Time of War*, p. 457)

Nationalists remained divided between republicans and constitutionalists. The IRA engaged in sporadic attacks on military targets, but without notable success. The Special Powers Act and the 'B Specials' were used against them and to harass the wider nationalist community. Internment was introduced and many people, some of them not members of the IRA, were imprisoned. By 1943 any active republican movement was almost dead.

The effect of the war

By its involvement in the war, Northern Ireland contributed to the British victory.

Almost 5,000 Northern Irish servicemen died on active service. They included two of Brooke's three sons. Ships, planes and other munitions of war were made there and food from the North helped to keep Britain fed.

But for the British, the North's main contribution was its location on the vital Atlantic shipping routes. When the war ended, Churchill and most British leaders felt they owed a debt to the unionists for their loyalty during the struggle.

1946-66: The Post-War Decades

Looking to the future

In 1945 the future was promising for unionists. The war strengthened their position, for many British politicians, Labour as well as Conservative, resented the South's neutrality and appreciated the part the North had played in defeating the Germans.

The economy too was flourishing but its future was uncertain. Could the traditional industries adapt to new conditions? If not, could new industries be found to replace them and to provide employment for those who were leaving the land?

The 1945 election

Politically the war changed little. Under Sir Basil Brooke the Unionist party lost six seats in the 1945 election but it still retained its safe majority with thirty-three of the fifty-two seats in the Stormont parliament. Nor was it likely, under Brooke's leadership, to make any concessions to the Catholic minority.

The Nationalist party had abstained from parliament during the war, but when they won ten seats in 1945 they decided to return. Labour candidates won five seats, their best ever result. This probably reflected the massive victory of the Labour party in Britain. But the labour movement was split between those who wanted a united Ireland and those who supported the Union with Britain. It was thus unable to build on this success.

The Unionists and the Labour government

In Britain, the 1945 election was won by the Labour party, led by **Clement Attlee**. For the Unionists, traditionally allies of the British Conservatives, this was alarming.

- Would they be able to work with a socialist government in London?

- Would the Labour party, which had a tradition of sympathy with the nationalist cause, continue to protect the separate existence of Northern Ireland?

In 1945 and 1946 Unionists considered leaving the United Kingdom and asking for Dominion Status within the Commonwealth to protect themselves from Labour. But Labour ministers, remembering the wartime record, had no desire to meddle in Northern Ireland. In a short time, the Unionists realised that Labour's welfare state plans would send large subsidies flowing into the North. These would be lost if they left the United Kingdom, so that debate soon died away.

Paying for the welfare state

In 1942, while the war was still in progress, plans to reform the United Kingdom education, health and social services were outlined in the **Beveredge Report**. Between 1945 and 1951, the Labour government implemented these plans and brought about the welfare state.

The reforms were extended, step by step, to Northern Ireland. But since the North could not afford them out of its own resources, the Unionist government made an agreement with London that Britain would subsidise them. In return, taxation in Northern Ireland would be kept at the same level as in Britain, and the Northern budget would be submitted to the British Treasury for approval.

This arrangement took the control of most taxation and spending away from the Northern government but the loss was worthwhile. Money from the British taxpayer flowed into the North to pay for improved services. Between 1945 and 1951 the payments grew sevenfold to £45 million a year, while tax raised in the Northern state only doubled. This subsidy allowed the Northern government to give its citizens a far higher level of health care, social service and education than they could otherwise have afforded, and of a much higher standard than was available in the South – though at a cost of higher taxes.

The welfare state

Between 1945 and 1951 social reforms were introduced in many areas.

J. M. Andrews, Craig's successor as Prime Minister of Northern Ireland.

◆

- **Social welfare**

A comprehensive system of National Insurance was introduced in 1948. Insurance contributions were collected from all employed people and generous pensions or cash payments were made to the old, the sick, the unemployed and the widowed.

- **Health**

A series of Health Acts swept away the old Poor Law health system. County and borough health authorities took charge of general health care, child and maternity services, sanitation and home help schemes. The **Northern Ireland General Health Services Board** was set up to supervise these services. Tuberculosis, as bad a scourge in the North as in the South, was tackled by the **Northern Ireland Tuberculosis Authority**. A **Hospitals' Authority** took over the supervision of hospitals.

As always, the sectarian issue caused problems. The Mater Hospital in Belfast was owned by the Mercy nuns. They feared that the Hospitals' Authority might threaten their independence. A compromise proved impossible when the Health Minister insisted that the Mater be either fully in or fully out of the scheme. The Mater refused to join which meant that it did not get building grants or state payments for its patients.

As a result, Catholics found themselves having to support their hospital by voluntary subscriptions, while paying through their taxes for the public health system. This caused considerable resentment until a compromise was finally worked out in 1972.

- **Education**

In 1947 an Education Act proposed a new system of primary, secondary and third level education.

Primary schooling was to end at twelve. The year before that, pupils were to take an examination called the **'Eleven Plus'**. The 25 per cent who passed got free places in grammar schools and could go on to third level education, for which there were generous scholarships. The pupils who failed went to secondary modern schools. They got a non-academic education and most of them left at fourteen or fifteen.

State schools, under the control of local councils, got full grants for building and maintenance and their pupils did not have to pay fees. Catholics would not send their children to these schools which as a result were almost exclusively Protestant.

Catholic-owned schools, which refused to join the state system, got 65 per cent of building grants, up from 50 per cent before the war, in spite of protests from some sections of the unionist community. Up to 80 per cent of their pupils would receive scholarships but the rest had to pay fees.

These reforms came into effect in 1948. Though the Catholic community resented the lower grants, they gained a lot from them. Many Catholics were too poor to afford much education for their children. The new system opened the chance of secondary and university education for bright boys and girls who would not otherwise have had the chance. This produced a new generation of well-educated and articulate young Catholics in the 1960s. They resented the discrimination they experienced under Unionist rule and they led the struggle to reform it.

Post-war economic problems

New economic policies were needed after the war. The traditional industries of shipbuilding and linen had done well in the war but they were old-fashioned, with major structural weaknesses. It was likely that at least parts of them would eventually close down.

This would cut jobs at a time when more people would be entering the job market from agriculture, as small, uneconomic farms were abandoned. If the disastrous levels of unemployment that had occurred during the thirties were to be avoided, government action was essential.

Industrial development

The Stormont government recognised this. In 1945 the **Industries Development Act**

'Guarding the School-children', Falls Road, Belfast in 1949.

gave factory sites as well as loans and grants to new industries. They also began a major building programme. New houses for slum dwellers and to replace those damaged by bombs, were built, as well as the schools and hospitals required by the welfare state reforms. All this created 10,000 new jobs by 1950.

But this barely kept pace with the loss of jobs in the old industries. The linen industry held up well enough in the later 1940s but declined sharply in the 1950s when 5,000 jobs were lost. Shipbuilding did well until the late 1950s, then it too declined.

As in the South, the level of government involvement in industry increased from the mid-1950s. The **Northern Ireland Development Company** was set up in 1956 to attract overseas firms. It had some success. Between 1950 and 1962 industrial production rose by 50 per cent. In that year the Wilson Report set a target of 65,000 jobs a year but the actual figure reached by 1970 was only 8,000. In spite of all the efforts, unemployment stayed between 6 per cent and 10 per cent and Northern Ireland remained the poorest part of the United Kingdom.

The job creation programme was accompanied by an attempt to improve communications. Railways were nationalised after the war and, to limit losses, about half the tracks were closed. The Dublin-Belfast route was taken over and jointly run by the two governments. The central government took over responsibility for all trunk roads from the local authorities and improved their standard greatly. In 1962 they opened Ireland's first motorway.

Agricultural policy

As in the Republic agriculture was the most important industry, with Britain as the main customer. Demand remained high in the 1940s while post-war food shortages continued. After that, cheap imports cut prices, though government subsidies cushioned UK farmers. This was especially helpful to intensive farming like pigs and poultry. Because of these policies, the 1950s and 1960s were more prosperous for northern farmers than for farmers in the South.

The campaign against partition

Nationalists both North and South had hoped that the British Labour party might be sympathetic to a united Ireland. Some Labour MPs were interested and thirty of them formed a group called '**Friends of Ireland**' to put the case for Irish unity. Partly in response to this, northern nationalists formed an **Anti-Partition League** to present the nationalist case in Britain and the United States.

Their campaign was backed by Seán MacBride, who became Minister for External Affairs in 1948. (see page 390) For the next few years nationalist politicians from the South and the North insisted on bringing up the case against partition at every international gathering they attended, often causing anger and frustration among the other participants.

The Republic and the Ireland Act

The Unionist government could afford to ignore this campaign, but it was roused to action when the Coalition in Dublin said it intended to withdraw from the Commonwealth and declare a republic. Brooke called an election, proclaiming:

> Our country is in danger... we fight to defend our very existence and the heritage of our Ulster children... Our determination to remain under the Union Jack should be immediately and overwhelmingly reaffirmed. (D. Harkness, *Northern Ireland*, p. 120)

The Anti-Partition League rallied nationalist support. A general church gate collection was held to finance its campaign and, with the £46,000 raised, it was able to nominate seventeen candidates. The unionist community, however, closed ranks to defend their state. The party regained four of the seats they had lost in 1945.

The Unionist victory was reinforced when Westminster passed the **Ireland Act**. This recognised the Republic, but also affirmed that:

> in no event will Northern Ireland or any part thereof cease to be part of His Majesty's dominions and of the United Kingdom without the consent of the parliament of Northern Ireland.

This was the firmest guarantee the unionists had ever won from the British.

The IRA's border campaign

After the war, the IRA had declined. Many of its best people were drawn off into Clann na Poblachta. But it revived in the early 1950s, perhaps encouraged by the anti-partition campaign. It attracted young people frustrated by the lack of progress towards a united Ireland. Between 1951 and 1955 the IRA attacked a number of military barracks. The most successful raid was on Gough Barracks in Armagh in June 1954.

In December 1956 the IRA announced a campaign against 'British imperialism' in Northern Ireland and called on the whole population of the North to help them. This declaration reflected IRA ignorance of the reality of Northern Ireland where the majority community cherished their union with Britain.

The campaign was fairly intensive in the first half of 1957. It consisted mainly of attacks on border posts and police barracks. Two policemen and several IRA members were killed and in the South Sinn Féin won two seats in the election.

The Stormont government used the Special Powers Act to impose internment without trial of IRA suspects. In March 1957, after Fianna Fáil won an election in the Republic, de Valera brought in internment too. This reduced the campaign to sporadic attacks on customs huts. The IRA finally called off the campaign in 1962, bitterly noting that:

> foremost among the factors responsible for the ending of the campaign has been the attitude of the general public whose minds have been deliberately distracted

Stormont castle, which was built to house the Northern Ireland parliament.

from the supreme issue facing the Irish people, the unity and freedom of Ireland. (D. Harkness, *Northern Ireland*, p. 131)

The campaign had been a spectacular failure. Confined to isolated districts near the border, it had little impact at all on the lives of most people in the North. What was most remarkable was that it got almost no support from the nationalist community. As a result, some people began to wonder if northern Catholics were at last becoming reconciled to their separation from the rest of Ireland.

Discrimination against Catholics

If the minority was at last accepting the Northern state, it was not because the majority was becoming more generous. Catholics continued to suffer discrimination.

- They were harassed by trigger-happy 'B Specials' who represented the armed might of the Protestant state.

- The **Flags and Emblems Act** (1954) banned their tricolour while protecting the unionists' Union Jack.

- Catholics got far less than their fair share of appointments in the civil service, the law, or the boards which regulated the Health Service and other bodies.

- Very few new industries were set up in the Catholic-dominated areas of the south and west, where unemployment remained well above average.

Discrimination in local government

The most blatant area of discrimination was in local government. It occurred in a number of ways.

- **Property qualification for voting**

  In local elections, only people with property were entitled to vote while a person with several properties could have up to six votes. Since Catholics were the poorest section of the population, many of them had no property and hence no vote. This system of voting was retained in Northern Ireland even though it was dropped in the rest of the United Kingdom in 1945. In 1961 a campaign to have 'one man, one vote' in local elections failed.

- **Gerrymandering**

  The boundaries of wards (constituencies) in local elections were drawn in such a way as to favour unionist candidates. In Derry, for example, wards with 8,700 Protestant voters elected twelve councillors while wards with 14,000 Catholic voters only elected eight councillors. Thus Derry with its nationalist majority was always ruled by a Unionist council.

- **Housing and jobs**

  Local councils provided jobs, housing and other benefits. Since they were Unionist-controlled, Catholics seldom got their fair share. In Fermanagh, an area with a nationalist majority, the Unionist council in the 1960s employed 338 Protestants and thirty-two Catholics.

A new approach among the minority

Discrimination did not apply everywhere. Catholics had benefited as much as Protestants from the improved education, health and social services of the welfare state. They were also aware that similar services in the South were of a lower quality and that unity with the Republic might be a mixed blessing.

In the 1960s this led to a new attitude among some younger Catholics. They began to argue that Catholics should play a greater part in the political life of the North. The policy of holding aloof, which had been followed to a greater or less degree since 1920, had done little for them. Maybe they had more to gain from participation than abstention?

Unionist dissatisfaction

This change in Catholic attitudes went unnoticed among unionists. But at the start of the 1960s many unionists were dissatisfied with Lord Brookeborough's government. (Sir Basil Brooke had been made Lord Brookeborough in 1952.)

Their main concern was with his economic policy's failure to provide employment. In 1960 alone, 10,000 people had lost their jobs in the linen, ship-building and air-craft industries. The government did not seem to be doing enough to encourage new industries to replace the old ones.

Most criticism came from middle-class unionists, many of them businessmen. They resented the landed gentry who had dominated the Unionist party since 1920.

Brookeborough, then in his seventies, was still popular with voters but his attitudes were out of tune with the times. His successor, Terence O'Neill, wrote of him that

> the tragedy of his premiership was that he did not use his tremendous charm and his deep Orange roots to try to persuade his devoted followers to accept some reforms. (T. O'Neill, *Autobiography of Terence O'Neill*, p. 47)

Terence O'Neill

Brookeborough was forced to resign in March 1963 and the Finance Minister, **Terence O'Neill,** became the new leader. At forty-eight, he was a generation younger than Brookeborough, but he came from the same landed class. He had not been elected but was chosen by an inner group in the party, while his main rival, the able middle-class Minister for Home Affairs, **Brian Faulkner**, was in America. This caused resentment among the middle-class wing of the party and meant that O'Neill could never count on their whole-hearted backing in his attempts to change Unionist policies and attitudes.

Economic development

The main task before the new Prime Minister was to encourage economic growth. After seven years as Finance Minister he knew the problems he faced. As in the Republic, the idea that governments must plan for economic growth was beginning to take hold. A number of plans were published in the early sixties. They recommended greater government spending on roads, houses and factories, incentives for overseas firms to set up in Northern Ireland, and the provision of education and training to increase the skills of the labour force.

Brian Faulkner

A controversial proposal was that the growth of Belfast be limited and that new 'growth points' be established. In line with the usual Unionist thinking, only one of these, Derry, was in the Catholic west or south. The others were all in the unionist heartland, east of the Bann. An **Economic Council** was proposed to co-ordinate these projects.

O'Neill quickly put these plans into effect. The Economic Council was set up. A sign that O'Neill might be more generous than his predecessor came when he included representatives of the Dublin-based Irish Congress of Trade Unions which Brookeborough had always refused to recognise on the Council.

Brian Faulkner was made Minister for Commerce and he produced a package of incentives (like those available in the Republic) which soon brought in big overseas companies including ICI, Du Pont, Grundig, and Courtaulds. By 1965 unemployment had fallen to its lowest level for ten years.

Reconciliation

O'Neill recognised, though to a limited extent, that reconciliation between the two communities in the North and between Northern Ireland and the Republic was necessary for progress. In this approach he had a number of advantages.

* In the Republic, de Valera retired in 1959 and was replaced by Seán Lemass (see page 409) who was much more flexible and pragmatic in his approach to the issue of partition and to relations with the North.

* The election of Pope John XXIII in 1959 and the start of the Second Vatican Council in 1962 led to a period of greater openness in the Catholic Church.

* The ecumenical movement which Pope John encouraged, led Christians to stress their common values rather than their differences. It was slower to take off in Northern Ireland than elsewhere but it did give some support to people like O'Neill and Lemass, trying to reduce the old communal hatreds.

Gestures of reconciliation

O'Neill began with small gestures. When Pope John XXIII died in 1964, he sent official condolences to the Cardinal in Armagh. He was the first northern Premier to visit a Catholic school. These small courtesies, which would have passed unnoticed elsewhere, were almost revolutionary coming from a senior Unionist politician.

The Lemass visit

O'Neill's most dramatic gesture was his invitation to Seán Lemass to visit Stormont. He had been impressed by Lemass's conciliatory references to the North and he recognised the desirability of cross-border co-operation on transport, power, agriculture and tourism. But he did not consult other ministers about the invitation and this weakened his position in the debate which followed.

The visit, on 14 January 1965, was quickly followed by an O'Neill visit to Dublin and meetings between the Ministers for Commerce and Agriculture, and their opposite numbers from the South. The meetings were well received in the Republic and among northern nationalists. Lemass encouraged the Nationalist party to become the official opposition in the Stormont parliament, a role they had refused to occupy since 1920.

Ian Paisley

The unionist response was more mixed. Many Unionist party members welcomed the new approach, but some on the conservative side objected. Outside the party, the opposition to O'Neill's policy was led by **Ian Paisley**.

He was the founder and leader of the **Free Presbyterian Church** and since the mid-fifties had been an outspoken critic of any concession to Catholics, either religious or political. His attacks on ecumenism had led to rioting in Belfast in 1964. After the Lemass visit he began to campaign against change under the slogan 'O'Neill must go'.

Limits of O'Neill's concessions

O'Neill made good-will gestures to nationalists but when power was at stake, his actions were in line with traditional unionist attitudes.

Lemass and O'Neill meet, January 1965.

- In 1965, soon after meeting Lemass, he announced the name of the new city, to be built near Lurgan. It would be called Craigavon, hardly a name likely to conciliate Catholics.

- More significant was his decision on the university question. Northern Ireland had only one university – Queen's in Belfast. As the demand for education expanded in the 1960s a new one was planned.

  A campaign began to have it located in Derry where there was already the small but well-respected **Magee College**. Derry people, both nationalist and unionist, backed the campaign. The government set up a committee, to which no Catholic was appointed, to investigate the issue. It reported that the new university should be sited in Coleraine, a solidly Protestant town. O'Neill accepted its recommendation.

The civil rights campaign

The gap between O'Neill's gestures and his performance aroused resentment in the Catholic community. But it was different from the old attitude of total hostility. For many young Catholics the idea of reunion with the South was not very attractive. They were willing to put the ideal of a united Ireland off to some distant future. What they wanted now was equal citizenship within Northern Ireland.

- In 1964 people who felt like this founded the **Campaign for Social Justice** in

A civil rights demonstration, 1968.

Dungannon. They demanded an end to discrimination in housing and jobs, especially in local government. They allied themselves to the British based **National Council for Civil Liberties**.

- In 1967 they set up the **Northern Ireland Civil Rights Association** (NICRA). Inspired by the civil rights campaign of Martin Luther King in the US, it began a peaceful campaign for 'one man, one vote' in local elections.

- In a Catholic working-class area of Belfast, a Catholic, **Gerry Fitt**, was elected to Stormont as a Labour MP in 1962. In 1966 he won a seat in Westminster, where the Labour Party had recently returned to power. He campaigned there to bring the situation of the minority in the North to a wider audience.

The new approach of Sinn Féin

Even republicans were rethinking their attitudes. The failure of the border campaign suggested to some of the leaders of Sinn Féin and the IRA that violence was futile. They began to move towards socialism, hoping to appeal to the working-class in both parts of Ireland. Although they did not completely abandon the use of force, they concentrated on political argument. In the mid-sixties they set up **Republican Clubs** where the emphasis was on spreading socialist ideas rather than on military training.

A time of hope

Despite criticisms and setbacks peaceful progress and reconciliation seemed possible in Northern Ireland in 1965 and 1966. Late in 1965, O'Neill called a snap election in which the Unionist party did well. The following year brought tensions: the

Gerry Fitt

nationalist community celebrated the fiftieth anniversary of the 1916 Rising and the unionists celebrated the Battle of the Somme in which so many of Carson's volunteers had died.

Ian Paisley sought to exploit these tensions, but was temporarily discredited when an extremist Protestant group, the **Ulster Volunteer Force**, murdered a young Catholic in Belfast. His popularity was restored when he was given a short jail sentence for his part in a riot outside the General Assembly of the Presbyterian Church which he accused of ecumenism.

Nevertheless, the year passed off quietly and to many it appeared that the fire had gone out of the old sectarian hatred. Opinion polls taken in these years suggested that a majority in each community welcomed the changes that were occurring. But there were also substantial numbers who remained unreconciled and it was their voices which were to be heard in the future.

Questions

ORDINARY LEVEL – A

Answer the following questions briefly. One or two sentences will be enough.

1. Who were the **B-Specials** and why were they set up in 1920?

2. Who represented the Northern government on the **Boundary Commission** between 1924 and 1925?

3. Why did the Unionist government end voting by **proportional representation** (PR) in 1929?

4. Why was the **geographical position** of Northern Ireland important to Britain during World War II?

5. What was the response of the Dublin government to the bombing of Belfast in 1941?

6. What guarantee did the British government give to northern unionists in the **1949 Ireland Act**? Why was this Act passed?

7. Give **two** of the problems that faced industry in the north after 1945.

8. What is meant by **gerrymandering**? Explain **one** way in which gerrymandering affected Catholics in Derry in the 1950s.

9. Give **two** reasons for the failure of the IRA border campaign of the 1950s.

10. Set out **one** of the aims of the **Northern Ireland Civil Rights Association**.

Questions
· · · · · · · · · · · · · · · · ·

ORDINARY LEVEL – B

Write a short paragraph on each of the following:

1 The Government of Ireland Act, 1920.

2 The Special Powers Act.

3 Depression in Belfast in the 1930s.

4 The Belfast bombing, 1941.

5 Health reforms in the welfare state.

6 Industrial problems in Belfast after the war.

7 Discrimination against Catholics.

8 The Lemass-O'Neill meeting.

ORDINARY LEVEL – C

Write a short essay on each of the following:

1 Sir James Craig (Lord Craigavon) as Prime Minister of Northern Ireland (1921-41) under the headings:
 (i) Setting up the new state.
 (ii) Education and social policies.
 (iii) The economy.
 (iv) The last years.

2 The Northern economy 1920-66 under the headings:
 (i) Problems in the old industries.
 (ii) The impact of the depression.
 (iii) Post-war successes and failures.

3 The position of Catholic nationalists in Northern Ireland, under the following headings:
 (i) Reaction to partition up to 1925.
 (ii) Experiences of discrimination.
 (iii) Changing attitudes in the 1950s and 1960s.

Questions

4 Terence O'Neill as Prime Minister of Northern Ireland under the following headings:
(i)   Rise to power.
(ii) New approach to nationalists.
(iii) Limitations and opposition.

HIGHER LEVEL

Write an essay on each of the following:

1 (i)   Describe the problems facing Northern Ireland when it came into existence in 1920. (30)
   (ii) To what extent had these been dealt with by 1939? (50)

2 Compare and contrast the economic problems facing the two Irish states in the 1920s and 1930s and the measures adopted to deal with them. (80)

3 Assess the administration of Sir James Craig (Lord Craigavon) as Northern Prime Minister (1921 to 1941). (80)

4 Compare and contrast the experience of war in Ireland, north and south between 1939 and 1945. (80)

5 'World War II and the welfare state legislation introduced by the British governments after 1945 had a dramatic impact on Northern Ireland.'
Discuss. (80)

6 Assess the experiences of the minority Catholic community within Northern Ireland from 1920 to 1966. (80)

7 'Terence O'Neill failed because he tried to do too little, too late.'
Discuss O'Neill's policies from 1963 to 1966 in the light of this statement. (80)

8 Compare and contrast the changes which occurred in Ireland, North and South in the period 1945 to 1966. (80)

Select Bibliography

The following books are recommended as additional reading:

J. Bower Bell — *The Secret Army* (London 1970)

Patrick Buckland — *James Craig* (Gill and Macmillan 1980)

T.P. Coogan — *Michael Collins* (Arrow 1990)

Mary E. Daly — *Social and Economic History of Ireland since 1800* (The Educational Company 1981)

Ruth D. Edwards — *Patrick Pearse: The Triumph of Failure* (Victor Gollanz Ltd 1977)

Brian Farrell — *Seán Lemass* (Gill and Macmillan 1983)

Ronan Fanning — *Independent Ireland* (Helicon 1983)

R. F. Foster — *Modern Ireland: 1600-1972* (Penguin 1986)

David Harkness — *Northern Ireland since 1920* (Helicon 1983)

J.J. Lee — *Ireland, 1912-1985* (Cambridge University Press 1989)

Michael Laffan — *The partition of Ireland, 1911-25* (Dundalk 1983)

F.S.L. Lyons — *Charles Stewart Parnell* (Collins 1977)

F.S.L. Lyons — *Ireland since the Famine* (Fontana 1972)

T.W. Moody — *Davitt and the Irish Revolution* (Oxford University Press 1981)

John A. Murphy — *Ireland in the Twentieth Century* (Gill and Macmillan 1975)

T. Ryle Dwyer — *De Valera, the man and the myth* (Poolbeg 1991)

A.T.Q. Stewart — *Edward Carson* (Gill and Macmillan 1981)

Pauric Travers — *Settlements and Divisions: Ireland 1870-1920* (Helicon 1984)

J. Whyte — *Church and State in Modern Ireland* (Gill and Macmillan 1971)